Business Transfers and Employee Rights

Business Transfers and Employee Rights

Second Edition

John McMullen

MA (Cantab), MIPM
Solicitor; Partner and Head of the Employment Unit,
Simpson Curtis; Bye Fellow and Lecturer in Law,
Girton College, Cambridge

Butterworths
London, Dublin, Edinburgh
1992

United Kingdom	Butterworth & Co (Publishers) Ltd, 88 Kingsway, LONDON WC2B 6AB and 4 Hill Street, EDINBURGH EH2 3JZ
Australia	Butterworths Pty Ltd, SYDNEY, MELBOURNE, BRISBANE, ADELAIDE, PERTH, CANBERRA and HOBART
Belgium	Butterworth & Co (Publishers) Ltd, BRUSSELS
Canada	Butterworths Canada Ltd, TORONTO and VANCOUVER
Ireland	Butterworth (Ireland) Ltd, DUBLIN
Malaysia	Malayan Law Journal Sdn Bhd, KUALA LUMPUR
New Zealand	Butterworths of New Zealand Ltd, WELLINGTON and AUCKLAND
Puerto Rico	Equity de Puerto Rico, Inc, HATO REY
Singapore	Malayan Law Journal Pte Ltd, SINGAPORE
USA	Butterworth Legal Publishers, AUSTIN, Texas; BOSTON, Massachusetts; CLEARWATER, Florida (D & S Publishers); ORFORD, New Hampshire (Equity Publishing); ST PAUL, Minnesota; and SEATTLE, Washington

A CIP Catalogue record for this book is available from the British Library.

First edition 1987

ISBN 0 406 00084 0

Typeset by Phoenix Photosetting, Chatham
Printed and bound in Great Britain by
Biddles Ltd, Guildford and King's Lynn

Preface

It is now four years since the first edition of this book. One might suppose that, in the comparatively narrow area dealt with by a monograph, the law would have been fairly static throughout this period. Not so. A major development has been the growing jurisprudence of the European Court arising out of the interpretation of the EC Council Directive 77/187 of 14 February 1977 'on the approximation of the laws of the Member States relating to the safeguarding of employees' rights in the event of transfers of undertakings, businesses or parts of businesses' (referred to in this book as 'the Acquired Rights Directive', but sometimes also known as the 'Business Transfers Directive'). It is upon this Directive that the troublesome Transfer of Undertakings (Protection of Employment) Regulations 1981 (SI 1981/1794) are based, in required implementation of the Directive. Accordingly, coverage of European Court cases on the definition and mechanics of a business transfer, such as *Foreningen af Arbejdsledere i Danmark v Daddy's Dance Hall A/s* [1988] IRLR 315, and on the mandatory effect of Article 4 (which prohibits pre-transfer dismissals connected with the transfer which are not for an economic, technical or organisational reason entailing changes in the workforce), such as *P Bork International A/s v Foreningen af Arbejdsledere i Danmark* [1989] IRLR 41, is included.

A hugely important dimension is the re-statement by the English courts of the importance of European law and its paramountcy in this area. The first edition of this book (as does this edition) had, with regret, to record significant shortcomings in the Transfer Regulations when they were compared with the Acquired Rights Directive. Now, following the momentous House of Lords decision in *Litster v Forth Dry Dock & Engineering Co Ltd (in receivership)* [1989] IRLR 161, a purposive approach to the Transfer Regulations may be taken by tribunals and the courts in order to make the Regulations conform, if possible, to the requirements of the Acquired Rights Directive. I have been able to cover this aspect fully but, like many important legal decisions, *Litster* poses as many questions for both academics and practitioners as it provides answers. I have attempted to tackle these problems as far as possible while recognising at the same time that further judicial clarification of this area is needed. Undoubtedly, the Transfer Regulations continue to remain one of the most topical and exciting areas for lawyers, be they involved in labour law or corporate law.

Not to be forgotten, however, are the provisions about continuity on change of employer contained in the Employment Protection (Consolidation) Act 1978 (the EP(C)A). These are, importantly, the business transfer provisions in Schedule 13, para 17(2), and other cases of change of employer, for example by Act of Parliament, by death of an employer and transfer to personal representatives, by change in composition of a partnership, by transfers between associated employers and by transfers to and from local education authority schools (see EP(C)A Sch 13 paras 17(3)–(5), 18 and 18A). Nor is another subject dealt with in the first edition relinquished: neither the business transfer provisions of the EP(C)A nor the Transfer Regulations apply to company take-overs by way of share sales and I continue to argue that there should be comparable protection in favour of employees in those situations (eg automatic unfairness of dismissal on transfer-connected dismissals unless for an 'economic, technical or organisational reason', and information and consultation obligations owed to recognised trade unions) that apply in the case of business transfers.

As before, practical materials are included in the appendices. These are no substitute for proper legal advice and the consideration of the facts of individual cases and should be employed accordingly; none the less I hope they may prove useful. Finally, the book confines itself, of course, as before, to employment law problems associated with business transfers. An in-depth consideration of the general law of unfair dismissal, redundancy, pensions law and corporate law is outside the remit of this book and detailed works on those subjects should be consulted when necessary. I hope the reader will find the select bibliography helpful in this regard.

I should like to thank the staff at Butterworths for their continuing advice and assistance. Last but not least I am grateful to

Janice, for her patience and understanding over the, at times, seemingly endless period I have had to devote to research and correction of drafts.

The law is stated as on 31 December 1991.

John McMullen
Leeds

31 December 1991

Contents

Table of statutes

References in this Table to *Statutes* are to Halsbury's Statutes of England (Fourth Edition) showing the volume and page at which the annotated text of the Act will be found. Page references printed in **bold** type indicate where the section of an Act is set out in part or in full.

Table of statutory instruments

Table of cases

Decisions of the European Court of Justice are listed both alphabetically and numerically. The numerical Table follows the alphabetical.

PAGE

A

C

G

H

Decisions of the European Court of Justice are listed below numerically.
These decisions are also included in the preceding alphabetical Table.

PAGE

List of abbreviations

In the book, the following abbreviations have been used:

AC	Law Reports, Appeal Cases, House of Lords and Privy Council
ACAS	Advisory, Conciliation and Arbitration Service
All ER	All England Law Reports
CA	Court of Appeal
CEA	Contracts of Employment Act 1972
ChD	Law Reports, Chancery Division
CLJ	Cambridge Law Journal
CLP	Current Legal Problems
CMLR	Common Market Law Reports
COIT	Central Office of the Industrial Tribunals
EAT	Employment Appeal Tribunal
ECJ	European Court of Justice
ELC	Employment Law Cases
EPA	Employment Protection Act 1975
EP(C)A	Employment Protection (Consolidation) Act 1978
HL	House of Lords
ICR	Industrial Cases Reports
IDS	Incomes Data Services
ILJ	Industrial Law Journal
IRA	Industrial Relations Act 1971
IRLIB	Industrial Relations Legal Information Bulletin
IRLR	Industrial Relations Law Reports
IT	Industrial Tribunal
ITR	Industrial Tribunal Reports

KIR	Knights Industrial Reports
Lloyd's Rep	Lloyd's List Reports
LS Gaz	Law Society's Gazette
MLR	Modern Law Review
NICA	Northern Ireland Court of Appeal
NIRC	National Industrial Relations Court
QB	Law Reports, Queens Bench Division
RPA	Redundancy Payments Act 1965
Transfer	Transfer of Undertakings (Protection of
Regulations	Employment) Regulations 1981
TULRA	Trade Union and Labour Relations Act 1974
VATT	Value Added Tax Tribunal
VATTR	Value Added Tax Tribunal Reports
WLR	Weekly Law Reports

Introduction

Why and when employee rights deserve protection

This book deals with the subject of employee rights on transfer of employment. One of the main areas of concern to labour lawyers is the effect on employee rights of transfers of businesses from one person (a person includes a company or other corporate or unincorporated body)[1] to another, usually by a sale by one person (or company) to another, or by other disposition. Inevitably, a substantial proportion of the text is devoted to that area. However, this study also deals, in passing, with two other cases. First, it deals with the rights of employees who transfer from one employer to another in some circumstances covered by the EP(C)A even where *no* transfer of a business has taken place between the former employer and the new employer.[2] Second, it deals, in outline, with employee rights on a transfer of share capital of an employing company where, because of the principle of corporate personality (which holds that the identity of the company is separate from its shareholders) no change in identity of employer occurs at all.[3]

---

1 Interpretation Act 1978 Sch 1 which says 'a "person" includes a body of persons corporate or unincorporate'.
2 EP(C)A Sch 13 para 17(3); EP(C)A Sch 13 para 17(4); EP(C)A Sch 13 para 17(5); EP(C)A Sch 13 para 18; EP(C)A Sch 13 para 18A.
3 *Salomon v Salomon & Co Ltd* [1897] AC 22. Despite some inroads into the principle of separate corporate personality in certain situations (see *Farrar's Company Law* (3rd edn) Ch 7) it still remains sound and is only departed from in exceptional (and unpredictable) situations. See eg *Re Securitibank Ltd (No 2)* [1978] 2 NZLR 136; *Multinational Gas and Petrochemical Co v Multinational Gas & Petrochemical Services Ltd* [1983] Ch 258, [1983] 2 All ER 563; *Lonhro Ltd v Shell Petroleum Co Ltd* [1980] QB 358, [1980] 2 WLR 367; *National Dock Labour Board v Pinn and Wheeler Ltd* [1989] BCLC 647; *Kuwait Asia Bank EC v National Mutual Life Nominees Ltd* [1990] BCC 567; *Adams v Cape Industries plc* [1990] Ch 433, [1990] BCLC 479; and, in labour law, *Dimbleby & Sons Ltd v NUJ* [1984] 1 All ER 751, [1984] ICR 386; but cf *Examite Ltd v Whittaker* [1977] IRLR 312, CA and *The Marabu Porr* [1979] 2 Lloyd's Rep 331, CA (corporate personality ignored); cf *National Dock Labour Board v Pinn and Wheeler Ltd* and see the discussion of cases where the 'veil' of incorporation was lifted in *Farrar*, op cit, Ch 7.

The British Columbia Court of Appeal, in *Sorel v Tomenson Saunders Whitehead Ltd*,[4] held that on a change of ownership of a business it was usually an implied term that an employee's previous service would be credited by the new owner. The court stated:

> 'Implication of [such a term] is reasonable. It reflects the expectation of the parties at the time of change of ownership. The purchaser in such a situation expects to retain the employees of the vendor without alteration of their terms of employment and with the benefit of their experience. The employees, for their part, expect to retain their existing employment benefits, unless expressly advised to the contrary.
>
> The implied term . . . is required to prevent employees from being faced with the unjust result that after years of employment with the new employer and after lapse of any rights to notice they might have against their former employer, they find themselves faced with the proposition that they lose the benefits arising from their years of employment prior to the take-over.'

Unfortunately (for employees) this decision is not mirrored by the English common law which steadfastly (see below) refuses to recognise the concept of transfer of employment without express agreement of the parties.

But although the common law has not accommodated their need, employees still deserve protection. On transfer of employment, and in particular where this is as a result of a business transfer, it can be of the utmost importance to employees that their acquired employment rights are preserved. Employees very often identify with the physical *indicia* of an undertaking or establishment in which they are employed rather than with the identity of the legal employer himself. So long as the working environment seems largely uninterrupted, they might quite reasonably expect their terms and conditions of employment and other acquired rights to be continuous. Sometimes they are even wholly unappreciative of the legal consequences of an actual change of ownership of the business.[5] It is a central question in this book whether labour law successfully weighs employee expectations in this area against commercial factors affecting the decision of purchasers to buy ailing businesses and whether the balance presently struck between employee and employer considerations is fair.

---

4 (1987) 39 DLR (4th) 460, cited by Tony Kerr in 'Implementation of Directive 77/187 into Irish Law and Case Law of the Court of Justice' in 'Acquired Rights of Employees', papers from the ICEL Conference, November 1988, Irish Centre for European Law, 1989.

5 A working example of such a problem can be found in *Woodhouse v Peter Brotherhood Ltd* [1972] 2 QB 520, [1972] ICR 186, CA.

1 CHANGE OF EMPLOYER AT COMMON LAW

The problem of employee rights is most acute when a transfer of employment on change of ownership of a business involves a change of identity of employer. Common law (the view of the Court of Appeal of British Columbia apart) provides no real answer when there is a change in identity of employer. Since it is a contract for personal services, the contract of employment cannot, under the common law, be unilaterally transferred from one employer to another without consent of the employee concerned.

The case most often cited in support of this principle is *Nokes v Doncaster Amalgamated Collieries Ltd*[6] where Lord Atkin stated, at page 556:

> 'My Lords, I confess it appears to me astonishing that, apart from over-riding questions of public welfare, power should be given to a court or to anyone else to transfer a man without his knowledge and possibly against his will from the service of one person to the service of another.'

He asserted that freedom of a person to contract with whomever he wished was the basic distinction between a servant and a serf. As has been pointed out elsewhere,[7] however, that philosophy comes from a different age and the case was, after all, concerned with relieving an employee from criminal liability for absenting himself without cause from work at a colliery which had just been taken over by a transferee employer. The outcome of the case was of course that, as the contract of employment was not novated, no criminal liability arose. This is hardly the same thing as tackling the issue of whether a successor to the business should be morally bound to preserve the contractual terms and acquired service of the employee who *did* join him. The supposed freedom of contract arising from *Nokes* is illusory in practice. It would boomerang to the disadvantage of an employee if a transferee employer utilised this freedom to impose upon a transferred employee entirely new and often less beneficial terms of employment than were enjoyed under the previous employer. But, notwithstanding this argument, the legal position at common law is that when a transferor employer ceases to employ an employee and transfers the business to a new proprietor, an affected employee cannot be transferred to the new proprietor with the business against his will; conversely, if he consents to move with the business to the new proprietor he cannot insist that his acquired rights be taken up by the new proprietor.

---

6 [1940] AC 1014, [1940] 3 All ER 549, HL.
7 Hepple and O'Higgins *Encyclopaedia of Labour Relations Law* para 1B 501.

Termination of employment on change of employer will amount to a dismissal by the transferor employer,[8] and whether this is lawful or unlawful will depend upon whether the contract was complied with when the contract of employment was thus terminated. If due notice of termination of the contract of employment with the transferor was given, the termination will be lawful (although it may be unfair under statute); if no notice or short notice was given, or if there was some other breach of contract in the mode of ending the first contract[9] the termination will be wrongful. Wrongful termination is a wrongful dismissal. Any claim for damages for wrongful dismissal would lie against the transferor employer. Also, under modern employment legislation, any claim for unfair dismissal[10] or redundancy[11] (if applicable) would also have to be made against the transferor employer. Similarly, any other claims (such as for arrears of wages, commission and so forth) arising from the employment relationship with the transferor would have to be made against the transferor. If, as is often the case, the employee accepted an offer of employment from the transferee employer, the transferee would, at common law, have no legal obligation to engage the employee on any particular set of terms and conditions, and, *a fortiori*, he would have no obligation to respect the terms and conditions, seniority, or continuity of employment enjoyed by the employee in the old employment. The transferee employer would even have no legal obligation to engage any of the employees employed by the transferor at all and, subject to race and sex discrimination laws and the (more recent) law on refusal of employment on grounds related to trade union membership,[12] the transferee could be entirely selective

---

8 See more recently *Lomas v Thomas Ness Ltd* 18 November 1986, EAT 529/86, (1987) IRLIB 14 April, p 4. See Ch 7 on whether, legally, the transfer, of itself, brings about termination or whether it is a repudiation which the employee is inevitably obliged to accept, thus bringing about termination. See also p 7, n 5.

9 E g non-compliance with a contractual grievance or consultation procedure see, e g *Gunton v Richmond-upon-Thames London Borough Council* [1981] Ch 448, [1980] ICR 755, CA; *Dietman v London Borough of Brent* [1988] ICR 842, [1988] IRLR 299; *Barber v Manchester Regional Hospital Board* [1958] 1 All ER 322, [1958] 1 WLR 181; *Gregory v Philip Morris Ltd* (1988) 80 ALR 455; KD Ewing 'Job Security and the Contract of Employment' (1989) ILJ 217.

10 EP(C)A Pt V.

11 EP(C)A Pt VI.

12 As to sex discrimination and race discrimination on recruitment, see, respectively, the Sex Discrimination Act 1975, Sex Discrimination Act 1986 and Race Relations Act 1976. The Employment Act 1990, s 1 makes it unlawful to refuse a person employment either because he is or is not a member of a trade union or because he is unwilling to accept a requirement either to take steps to become or cease to be, or to remain or not to become, a member of a trade union or to make payments or suffer deductions in the event of his not being a member

about who to re-engage, however arbitrary, unfair or discriminatory this might be.

2 THE NEED FOR A STATUTORY BRIDGE

Without some sort of statutory 'bridge' between the old and the new employments, the legal problems facing an employee in this sort of case would be quite serious. Upon a transfer of an employing undertaking, even if an employee is taken on by a transferee, he might be faced with unilateral revision of his terms and conditions of employment and all of his continuity of employment with the transferor would be wiped out. For a considerable qualifying period he would be at risk to unfair dismissal[13] and have no claim to various other statutory rights such as redundancy, maternity leave and written reasons for dismissal.[14] In effect, without any statutory bridge between employments, the transferee employer could, if he wished, engage employees formerly employed by the transferor and enjoy a probationary period during which he might (subject to race, sex discrimination and trade union membership victimisation laws) dismiss as he pleased.

3 PRESERVATION OF CONTINUITY OF EMPLOYMENT

Statute first made a modest inroad into the common law position to help preserve continuity of employment on transfers of businesses in the Contracts of Employment Act 1972, the relevant provisions of which are now contained in the EP(C)A 1978.

These provisions will be dealt with in some detail later in this book. But in summary, EP(C)A 1978 para 17(2), Sch 13 provides that if a 'trade, business or undertaking', is transferred from one person to another, continuity of employment of an employee

---

of a trade union. The provisions of the Employment Act 1990 mark, for the first time, a positive inroad on an employer's ability to hire labour indiscriminately (apart from sex and race discrimination laws). (The Rehabilitation of Offenders Act 1974, which provides that certain (spent) convictions need not be disclosed on job seeking, and the Disabled Persons (Employment) Acts 1944 and 1958 are of the same aim but are (certainly in the latter case) less effective.

13 The period is at present two years and became so in the case of employees commencing employment on or after 1 June 1985: EP(C)A s 64(1)(a) as amended by SI 1985/782.

14 For which the qualifying periods are, in each case, two years: EP(C)A s 81(4); EP(C)A s 33(3)(b); EP(C)A s 53(2). This is, of course, not an exhaustive statement or rights dependent on a qualifying period: see App B.

employed in that trade, business or undertaking at the time of transfer is not broken by the transfer.[15] Similar provisions preserve continuity where the employee is taken into the employment of the personal representatives of trustees of a deceased employer;[16] where there is a change in the composition of a partnership in which the employee is employed;[17] where an employee is taken into the employment of an associated employer of his former employer;[18] where another employer is substituted for the first employer by an Act of Parliament, whether public or local;[19] and, finally, when certain transfers within local authorities are made to or from local authority schools.[20]

4 REDUNDANCY LAW AND THE 'DISAPPEARING DISMISSAL'

Other provisions concerning redundancy payments, originally contained in the Redundancy Payments Act 1965 and now in EP(C)A 1978, address a similar problem. In redundancy cases, an employer may avoid a redundancy payment due under the EP(C)A if he makes either an offer of fresh employment to the employee on the same terms as before or of suitable alternative employment in each case prior to the ending of the contract which is accepted within four weeks of the ending of the old contract.[1] Subject to the enjoyment of a trial period by the employee in which he can assess the offer, in cases where the terms of the new contract differ from the old,[2] the employee will lose his right to redundancy payment if he stays on and accepts the alternative work;[3] but then, his period of continuity of employment for the purposes of acquiring seniority for a redundancy payment is preserved and he is deemed not to have been dismissed by reason of redundancy.[4]

This specialised provision concerning redundancy is applied *mutatis mutandis* by EP(C)A 1978 s 94 to a case of redundancy by change of an employer. Broadly speaking, when a business is transferred from one employer to another, as discussed above, this will, at common law, inevitably terminate the employment of the employee

---

15 EP(C)A Sch 13 para 17(2).
16 EP(C)A Sch 13 para 17(4).
17 EP(C)A Sch 13 para 17(5).
18 EP(C)A Sch 13 para 18.
19 EP(C)A Sch 13 para 17(3).
20 EP(C)A Sch 13 para 18A.
 1 EP(C)A s 82.
 2 EP(C)A s 84.
 3 EP(C)A s 84(1); he will also lose the right if he unreasonably refuses the offer of suitable alternative employment before or during the trial period allowed under s 84.
 4 EP(C)A s 84(1); EPCA Sch 13 para 11.

employed in the business transferred and this termination will amount to a dismissal as defined by the EP(C)A for these purposes.[5] This will, it is submitted, be by reason of redundancy since, borrowing statutory language, the transferor employer's requirement of work of a particular kind to be performed by the employee has certainly ceased or diminished.[6] Section 94 provides that if the new owner offers either fresh employment on the same terms as before or suitable alternative employment to the dismissed employee, on the lines already discussed that will, broadly, have the same effect as an offer of suitable alternative employment by the original owner. That is subject to the operation of a trial period where there are new terms, if the employee stays on and accepts the suitable alternative work with the new owner there is deemed to have been no dismissal by the original owner and there will be no right to claim a redundancy payment from the original owner.[7] Continuity of employment for the purposes of acquiring redundancy seniority will be preserved as against the new owner against whom a claim may be made on an appropriate occasion in the future.[8] Section 95 of the EP(C)A applies similar provisions to an employee transferred from non-Crown to Crown employment.

These provisions, because they transfer accrued redundancy liability to the new employer, have been described as allowing for a 'vanishing dismissal'.[9]

5 TRANSFERRING CONTRACTUAL RIGHTS AND PROTECTION AGAINST DISMISSAL

All this is helpful, but the only acquired right transferred by these provisions is the concept of continuity of employment[10] for the

---

5 *Nokes v Doncaster Amalgamated Collieries Ltd* [1940] AC 1014; [1940] 3 All ER 549, HL; *Brace v Calder* [1895] 2 QB 253; *Re Foster Clark Ltd's Indenture Trusts* [1966] 1 All ER 43, [1966] 1 WLR 125. See also p 4, n 8. It will take the form of either an express dismissal under s 55(2)(a) or s 83(2)(a) (respectively for unfair dismissal or redundancy purposes or a constructive dismissal under s 55(2)(c)) or s 83(2)(c) (respectively for unfair dismissal or redundancy purposes).

6 See the statutory definition of redundancy in EP(C)A s 81(2).

7 EP(C)A s 94(3); EP(C)A s 82(3)–(6). If the offer is unreasonably refused, no redundancy payment is due. It is important to note that the identity of the new employer has to be disregarded as far as assessing either whether the terms of the offer differ from the old contract or the reasonableness of the employee's refusal: EP(C)A s 94(4).

8 EP(C)A Sch 13, para 17(2) and para 11.

9 *Harvey on Industrial Relations and Employment Law* III, para 256.

10 And this is solely under Sch 13 to the EP(C)A; the redundancy provisions of the EP(C)A Pt VI, in reality, only determine who is liable, and when, for a redundancy payment.

purposes of claiming statutory rights such as unfair dismissal and redundancy in the future. These provisions afford no protection whatsoever for acquired *contractual* rights or indeed acquired non-contractual rights such as non-contractual seniority, or service-based 'entitlements' to non-contractual commissions, or bonuses. This means that even if the provisions protecting statutory continuity under the EP(C)A apply, a transferee employer has considerable scope to impose new contracts of employment on transferred employees.[11] Also, the provisions of the EP(C)A only preserve continuity if a new owner *agrees* to employ the employees employed in the business before the transfer. If he elects not to re-engage these employees, their employment ends and any claims must be against the transferor. All this does comparatively little to preserve the employee's identification with the continuum of an employing enterprise, which, with its buildings, plant and machinery, foremen, supervisors, colleagues, working conditions and trade union representation, may characterise the enterprise more than the identity of its proprietor alone.

6 TRANSFER OF EMPLOYMENT UNDER THE TRANSFER REGULATIONS

However, a stimulus to change arose from the adoption of EC Council Directive 77/187 of 14 February 1977 on the approximation of the laws of member states relating to 'the safeguarding of employees' rights in the event of transfers of undertakings, businesses or parts of businesses' (sometimes referred to as the 'Acquired Rights Directive' and sometimes as the 'Business Transfers Directive'; in the text the directive is referred to as the 'Acquired Rights Directive').[12]

First, one of the important provisions of this directive stipulates that all of a transferor's rights and obligations arising from the contract of employment or from an employment relationship should, on a transfer of an undertaking, be transferred to a transferee of that undertaking. This goes much further than the transfer simply of statutory continuity and even goes against the common

---

11 This might be constructive dismissal if in breach of contract, but will not *necessarily* be unfair dismissal: see Ch 1.

12 See B A Hepple 'Workers' Rights in Mergers and Takeovers: The EEC Proposals' (1976) ILJ 197; B A Hepple (1977) ILJ 106.

law rule that the contract of employment may not be transferred without the consent of the parties thereto.[13] Upon a transfer of an undertaking, the directive stipulates that the entire contract (and rights arising from an employment relationship) should be transferred to the transferee, providing, in effect, for an automatic novation of the contract (Art 3(1)).

Second, to prevent the transfer being used as an excuse for dismissals, as is commonly the case on business transfers, the directive provides, in Art 4, that the transfer of the undertaking, business or part thereof shall not in itself constitute grounds for dismissal save where there are 'economic, technical or organisational reasons entailing changes in the workforce'.[14] The directive goes on to provide for information to and consultation with employee representatives (Art 6) and also provides that employee representatives shall continue to enjoy the status of representation which they enjoyed with the transferor (eg trade union recognition) (Art 5), but provided the business 'preserves its autonomy'. Finally, there is provision for transfer of any collective agreement (Art 3(2)).

This directive took a long time to appear in our domestic legislation.[15] A first draft of the proposed legislation, now the Transfer of Undertakings (Protection of Employment) Regulations 1981, SI 1981/1974, languished through lack of parliamentary time during the period of office of the Labour government of 1975–1979.[16] Upon the entry into office of the Conservative government in 1979 no immediate action was taken despite the fact that the two-year period for enactment of legislation required by the directive (see Art 8) had expired. Eventually, the Transfer Regulations were

---

13 *Nokes v Doncaster Amalgamated Collieries Ltd* [1940] AC 1014, [1940] 3 All ER 549, HL.

14 The mandatory effect of Art 4 was stressed in *P Bork International A/S v Foreningen af Arbejdsledere i Danmark* [1990] 3 CMLR 701, [1989] IRLR 41. It means, importantly, that pre-transfer dismissals contrary to Art 4 (reg 8 of the Transfer Regulations) cannot negate the operation of Art 3 (reg 5 of the Transfer Regulations) concerning automatic transfer of contracts of employment of employees employed in the business at the date of transfer (see infra Chapters 7 and 8).

15 It had been suggested that the UK government would be threatened with infraction proceedings if the directive was not implemented. Mr David Waddington, Under-Secretary for Employment, when introducing the regulations, said, 'I do not believe that we could have delayed much longer in carrying out our Community obligations' (Hansard HC Deb 7 December 1981, col 677). See Ch 6.

16 (Draft) Transfer of Undertakings (Protection of Employment) Regulations 1978. See also Hansard HC Deb 7 December 1981, col 677.

introduced into the House with 'a remarkable lack of enthusiasm' (a now well-known (and ill-advised) phrase).[17]

Since then the Transfer Regulations have provided a fertile source of litigation and legal problems concerning their effect and they have been the subject of, at times, intense criticism. Initially this was on the part of labour lawyers because of perceived inadequacies in our legislative response to the requirement to comply with the Acquired Rights Directive. More recently, this has been on the part of corporate and insolvency lawyers following case law which has attempted to meet that earlier criticism by bridging the gap between any inadequate provisions in the Transfer Regulations and their more widely drawn counterparts in the Acquired Rights Directive. The consequent strengthening of the Transfer Regulations by judicial interpretation has, say the commercial lawyers, made businesses more difficult to sell.[18] Whatever their merits and demerits, however, the Transfer Regulations form an important part of the legal protection given to employees on transfers of businesses.

Upon a relevant transfer (as defined in reg 3 and reg 2(1)), reg 5 provides for automatic transfer of contracts of employment from the transferor employer to the transferee employer. This statutory protection is underpinned by reg 8 which provides that if an employee is dismissed 'in connection with' a transfer of an undertaking either before or after the transfer, either by the transferor or the transferee, that dismissal will be automatically unfair unless the dismissal was for an 'economic, technical or organisational' reason entailing changes in the workforce of either the transferor or the transferee. Other provisions in the regulations preserve, on a transfer of an undertaking, collective agreements entered into by the

---

17 Mr David Waddington, Under-Secretary for Employment, Hansard HC Deb 7 December 1981, col 680. It is suggested that this lukewarm approach to our European obligations resulted in less than full compliance with the mandatory aspects of the Acquired Rights Directive, which in turn had to be dealt with eventually by the purposive approach to construction of the Transfer Regulations that can be seen in *Litster v Forth Dry Dock & Engineering Co Ltd* [1990] 1 AC 546, [1989] IRLR 161.

18 As to criticisms of the drafting of the Transfer Regulations (particularly from the employment protection point of view) see e g P Elias 'The Transfer of Undertakings: A Reluctantly Acquired Right' (1982) Company Lawyer 147; B A Hepple 'The Transfer of Undertakings (Protection of Employment) Regulations' (1982) ILJ 29; R W Rideout 'The Great Transfer of Employee Rights Hoax' (1982) CLP 233; H Collins 'Dismissals on Transfer of a Business (1986) ILJ 244; Lord Wedderburn of Charlton 'The New Politics of Labour Law' in W E J McCarthy (ed) *Trade Unions* (2nd edn, 1985) p 502. From the employer/ insolvency practitioner's point of view, see e g M Homan *Financial Times* 22 June 1989; Floyd *Insolvency Law and Practice* (1989) p 177.

transferor and the appropriate trade union (reg 6) and also trade union recognition (reg 9) (but in the latter case only where, after the transfer, the undertaking or part transferred 'maintains an identity distinct from the remainder of the transferee's undertaking'). Information to and consultation with recognised trade unions is required in advance of a transfer, in provisions (regs 10 and 11) which mirror (although far less impressively) pre-existing consultation obligations in s 99 of the Employment Protection Act 1975 concerning redundancy dismissals.[19]

7 OVERVIEW OF STATUTORY PROTECTION

Put together, the Transfer Regulations and the provisions in EP(C)A 1978 comprise a confusing patchwork of legislative provisions. To date there has been no attempt by legislation to harmonise these various provisions into a single code of employment protection. Notwithstanding this, various tribunals and courts have striven to construe *some* aspects of the Transfer Regulations and the provisions in the EP(C)A as a harmonised whole and there is certainly some common ground. For example, a significant legal problem dealt with in this book which applies to business transfer cases is the definition of what amounts to a transfer of an 'undertaking'[20] or of a transfer of a 'trade, business or undertaking'[1] and of when there is a 'change in the ownership of a business'.[2] It has been held that there is a broad parallel between the expressions 'trade', 'business' and 'undertaking' in the EP(C)A and 'undertaking' in the Transfer Regulations (with one notable exception in that the Regulations only apply to 'commercial' ventures: see Ch 4) and they give rise to a common problem. Case law has drawn a somewhat unsatisfactory distinction between sales of assets only and a transfer of such a trade or a business or an undertaking.[3] Whether there is a transfer of a

---

19 This aspect is dealt with later in Chapter 10. It is to be noted that while minimum periods of consultation are required in the case of larger-scale redundancies under EPA, s 99, no minimum period of consultation applies under reg 10 of the Transfer Regulations. Also, an award of compensation for non-compliance under reg 11 is also limited to a maximum of two weeks' pay per employee, again far less than the maximum under EPA s 99.

20 Transfer of Undertakings (Protection of Employment) Regulations 1981.

 1 EP(C)A Sch 13 para 17(2).

 2 EP(C)A s 94.

 3 Parts of businesses or undertakings are also covered under all provisions (see EP(C)A Sch 13 para 17(2); Transfer Regulations, reg 3(1). EP(C)A s 94 does not expressly refer to 'parts' of a business but will be, it is submitted, construed accordingly.

trade or a business or undertaking has come to depend on whether there has been transferred a 'business as a going concern'. The provisions of the EP(C)A and the Transfer Regulations apply to a transfer of a trade business or undertaking as a going concern but *not* to a simple transfer of assets alone. One of the major issues in practice is determining whether there has been, in a particular case, a transfer of assets only or a transfer of a business as a going concern. This question often foxes the most experienced of lawyers and legal protection of an employee under the provisions of the EP(C)A and the Transfer Regulations may often hang on the nice distinctions involved.

A detailed discussion of the asset/business transfer dichotomy may be found in Chapter 4. Other shared features in, and, on the other hand, differences between, the statutory provisions are mentioned in this book where appropriate.[4]

---

4 See Chapters 3, 4, 5 and 7.

Chapter 1

Take-overs by acquisition of share capital

1 A CASE OUTSIDE THE RULES RELATING TO BUSINESS TRANSFERS

As will be clear from the Introduction, this book is concerned, in the main, with legal problems on *change* of employer, usually on a business transfer. As discussed, a business transfer means a transfer of a business or undertaking from one person (including a company) to another. For the sake of completeness, however, we cover, in Chapter 2, certain other types of change of employer which attract limited legal protection (ie miscellaneous cases under the EP(C)A). Here we discuss the position of employees in a company whose share capital is either taken over or which suffers a significant change in ownership where, in both cases, there is no change of employer at all. At the moment, employment protection on company take-overs by share purchase is not treated to special statutory provision. But why should it be excluded?

When a limited company, public or private, is taken over by acquisition of its share capital there is no change of employer or employees employed by the company. As such there is no need for legal protection of statutory continuity of employment for, *ex hypothesi*, there is no break in employment. Thus, neither the provisions of the EP(C)A nor the Transfer Regulations are needed to transfer either statutory continuity or the contract itself. Both are unaffected.[1]

But that is only a partial answer. When a company is taken over in this way there is *in reality* a change of identity of employer, even though, in the legal sense, there is only a change in identity of the proprietor of the share capital of the company and not the *legal* identity of the employer. This change in share ownership can be just

---

1 *Cameron v Hector Finlayson & Co Ltd* (1967) 2 KIR 182 (discussing s 13 of the Redundancy Payments Act 1965, now EP(C)A s 94, ie entitlement to redundancy on change of employer).

as important to an employee as a change in the identity of the employer following a transfer of a company's undertaking to another or the transfer of an unincorporated business from one person to another. Two aspects of the Transfer Regulations would be helpful to employees in such cases, namely automatic unfairness of dismissals in connection with the take-over and information and consultation obligations to trade unions.[2] But although the Acquired Rights Directive, which gave rise to the Transfer Regulations, originally provided, in draft form, for application of its provisions to take-overs by way of acquisition of share capital, this was eventually omitted from the final draft.[3] And, so, the Transfer Regulations do not apply to take-overs by way of acquisition of share capital.

An acquiring employer who has bought share capital certainly takes the workforce as he finds it, complete with continuity of employment and acquired contractual rights. But if he wishes expressly to dismiss by reason of reorganisation or redundancy, or if he seeks to impose a reorganisation, changing existing terms and conditions of employment without the consent of the workforce, he is governed by the ordinary principles of constructive dismissal, unfair dismissal and redundancy as apply to dismissal cases generally, and *not* by the special provisions relating to business transfers in the Transfer Regulations. These ordinary principles are not especially protective of employee rights and are not, it is argued by some, restrictive enough of managerial prerogative in business reorganisation cases.[4] Therefore, individual employment protection is far weaker in the case of take-overs of companies by acquisition of share capital than in the paradigm case of a change of employer by business transfer studied in this book. There is also no obligation on a take-over by share purchase to consult about the consequences for employees and, thus, collective protection is also much weaker for the workforce than in the case of business transfers.

2 EMPLOYMENT PROTECTION ON TAKE-OVERS OF COMPANY SHARE CAPITAL

Although this type of 'transfer' is outside the main area of scrutiny in this book, it might be useful to run through the problems and

---

2 See e g Transfer of Employment (Protection of Employment) Regulations 1981, reg 8 (automatic unfairness of dismissal) and reg 10 (information and consultation) and see Chapters 8 and 10, infra.

3 On the progress of the directive from draft to final form see Hepple (1976) ILJ 197; (1977) ILJ 106.

4 See Bowers and Clarke (1981) ILJ 34; McMullen, 'Takeovers, Transfers and Business Reorganisations' (1992) ILJ, March, forthcoming.

pitfalls that exist when a business is transferred solely by change in ownership of a company's share capital.

First, in relation to express dismissals (which should be with notice, otherwise they may be wrongful and attract a damages claim – a payment in lieu of notice may compensate for this) by the company before or after the take-over, on the ground of reorganisation or, in the case of a desire to trim back the workforce, on the ground of redundancy, the provisions of s 57 of the EP(C)A in relation to unfair dismissal must be borne in mind. All employees who have served two years' continuous employment may qualify for the right not to be unfairly dismissed under Pt V of the EP(C)A. Section 57 lays down the rules concerning unfair dismissal. The employer must establish a reason for dismissal. In practice in this sort of case, the reason will fall under s 57(2) as that of redundancy or, under s 57(1)(b), as some other 'substantial' reason.

The former is applicable to redundancy cases that fall within the statutory definition of redundancy under s 81(2) of the EP(C)A which applies when:

'. . . the dismissal is attributable wholly or mainly to –

(a) the fact that his employer has ceased, or intends to cease, to carry on the business for the purposes of which the employee was employed by him, or has ceased, or intends to cease, to carry on that business in the place where the employee was so employed, or

(b) the fact that the requirements of that business for employees to carry out work of a particular kind, or for employees to carry out work of a particular kind in the place where he was so employed, have ceased or diminished or are expected to cease or diminish.'

A redundancy payment may be due to an employee if this definition is satisfied, irrespective of liability for unfair dismissal, subject perhaps to whether the dismissal for redundancy is coupled with an offer of suitable alternative employment by the employer (or an associated employer) which is either accepted or which is unreasonably refused by the employee.

The latter, 'some other substantial reason' under s 57(1)(b), is a wide 'catch-all' category commonly applied to cases of managerial reorganisation, and organisational or technological change[5] and may apply where the definition of redundancy is not satisfied.

---

5 See *Hollister v NFU* [1979] ICR 542, [1979] IRLR 238, CA; *Bowater Containers Ltd v McCormack* [1980] IRLR 50; *Genower v Ealing Hammersmith and Hounslow Area Health Authority* [1980] IRLR 297; *Chubb Fire Security Ltd v Harper*

Once the reason for dismissal has been established, the industrial tribunal must be satisfied under s 57(3) that the employer has acted reasonably in relying upon the reason as a substantial one justifying dismissal. If there is an unfair dismissal, the compensatory award for it is set, at the time of writing, at a maximum of £10,000 (reviews are made annually) and a basic award is payable in addition thereto (but any statutory redundancy payment paid is set off against the basic award).[6] Reinstatement or re-engagement may instead be ordered, but this is not especially common. There may be higher compensation in cases where, in the alternative to compensation, reinstatement or re-engagement is ordered, and the employer refuses to comply.[7] The latest compensation levels are contained in Appendix C to this book.

Constructive dismissals[8] are subject to the same regime. A constructive dismissal might arise when, unilaterally, the new proprietors of the share capital decide to reorganise, ie change terms and conditions to harmonise perhaps with existing conditions of employees in other associated companies that they control. If such a reorganisation amounts to a serious breach of contract, the employee is entitled to accept this by terminating the contract. As well as being a wrongful dismissal at common law, this would also amount to a constructive dismissal under s 55(2)(c) of the EP(C)A (for unfair dismissal purposes) or s 83(2)(c) of the EP(C)A (for redundancy purposes). A wrongful dismissal action will be mainly

---

[1983] IRLR 311; *Richmond Precision Engineering Ltd v Pearce* [1985] IRLR 179; Bowers and Clarke (1981) ILJ 34; Davidson *The Judiciary and the Development of Employment Law* (1984). There are other reasons for dismissal under s 57(2), but they will not relate directly to a business transfer context.

6 EP(C)A s 73(9).

7 The basic award maximum (it depends on a combination of age, length of service, and the amount of a week's pay) was, for the year commencing 1 April 1991, £5,940 (s 73 and Sch 14 para 8(1)(a)); the maximum compensatory award, £10,000 (s 75); the unfair dismissal additional award (s 71 and Sch 14 para 8(1)(a)) on failure to comply with a reinstatement/re-engagement order, 13–26 weeks' pay, ie £2,574–£5,148; or (in discrimination cases) 26–52 weeks' pay, ie £5,148–£10,296. There are even higher awards in trade union membership cases (under EP(C)A ss 58 and 59(a)). All figures derive from the Employment Protection (Variation of Limits) Order 1991 (SI 1991/464) and the Unfair Dismissal (Increase of Compensation Limited) Order 1991 (SI 1991/466). In trade union membership cases, see the Unfair Dismissal (Increase of Limits of Basic and Special Awards) Order 1991 (SI 1991/467). See App C for the levels (proposed at the time of writing) for the year commencing 1 April 1992.

8 Ie employee-initiated termination in response to employer's repudiatory breach of contract; under statute, see EP(C)A s 55(2)(c) (unfair dismissal) and s 83(2)(c) (redundancy); *Western Excavating (ECC) Ltd v Sharp* [1978] QB 761, [1978] ICR 221, CA; *Harvey on Industrial Relations and Employment Law* II F.

for recovery of damages for loss of chance to earn remuneration and other benefits during a period equivalent to an employee's period of notice. If the constructive dismissal falls within the statutory definition of redundancy (above) a redundancy payment may be due. It may also be unfair under statute. For unfair dismissal purposes, once the constructive dismissal is established, the employer still has to demonstrate a reason for dismissal and to demonstrate that he acted reasonably in relying upon that reason. This can be artificial in constructive dismissal cases where the employer does not, of course, actually *intend* to dismiss at all; but it means, none the less, that any imposed change of contract must be justified as being permissible under statute, commonly in a take-over case by reason of redundancy or by reason of reorganisational change, ie for some other 'substantial' reason. It must also be reasonable in the circumstances under s 57(3).

Whether a dismissal in these circumstances, express or constructive, passes the test of reasonableness and is, therefore, fair once a reason is established, is a question of fact, and it is foolish to give illustrations or to set out rigid guidelines. Indeed, both the EAT and the Court of Appeal have eschewed the laying down of guidelines on 'reasonableness' for the benefit of industrial tribunals and any 'legalism' is deprecated.[9] None the less, relevant factors in redundancy cases at least seem to include notice, consultation (both to and with the individual and with his representative), consideration of alternative employment and application of a fair and objective selection procedure.[10]

---

9 See *Bailey v BP Oil (Kent Refinery) Ltd* [1980] ICR 642, [1980] IRLR 287; *Thomas and Betts Manufacturing Ltd v Harding* [1980] IRLR 255; *Anandarajah v Lord Chancellor's Department* [1984] IRLR 131, EAT; *O'Kelly v Trust House Forte plc* [1984] QB 90, [1983] ICR 728, CA; *Varndell v Kearney & Trecker Marwin Ltd* [1983] ICR 683, [1983] IRLR 335, CA; *UCATT v Brain* [1981] ICR 542, [1981] IRLR 224; *Gilham v Kent County Council (No 2)* [1985] ICR 233, [1985] IRLR 18, CA; *Siggs and Chapman (Contractors) Ltd v Knight* [1984] IRLR 83; *Rolls-Royce Motors Ltd v Dewhurst* [1985] ICR 869, [1985] IRLR 184.

10 See *Williams v Compair Maxam Ltd* [1982] ICR 156, [1982] IRLR 83 EAT. See also *The Industrial Relations Code of Practice* (1972), especially paras 44–46 (now repealed, see below) and the *ACAS Code of Practice 1*: 'Disciplinary Practice and Procedures in Employment' (1977) (although the latter does not relate as such to redundancy dismissals). Also of assistance is the ACAS advisory handbook 'Discipline at Work' (1988), and the ACAS advisory booklet 'Redundancy Handling' (1989). The first two documents had (in the former) and have (in the latter) the status of codes of practice issued under authority of statute (Industrial Relations Act 1971 ss 2–4; Employment Protection Act 1975 Sch 17 para 4; Employment Protection Act 1975 s 6). Codes like this are admissible in tribunals and may be taken account of (although breach of a code per se does not render a dismissal unfair (*Polkey v A E Dayton Services Ltd* [1988] AC 344, [1988] ICR 142). (The government has, however, revoked the 1972 Industrial Relations Code of Practice

The importance of the application of procedures before dismissal was stoutly emphasised by the House of Lords in the key decision of *Polkey v AE Dayton Services Ltd*.[11] This case is authority for the proposition that, while a procedural flaw, for example failure to follow a code of practice, will not automatically make a dismissal unfair, it normally will, unless there are exceptional reasons, known to the employer at the time of dismissal, why procedures should not be complied with.[12] For example, lack of consultation in redundancy cases could render a redundancy dismissal unfair because omission might cast doubt upon the objectivity of the selection process itself, which might have improved from consultation with interested parties and from employee input on his adaptability for alternative employment.[13]

In conclusion, more specific advice on the principles of contract, unfair dismissal and redundancy law may be found elsewhere.[14] But, broadly, the above principles will govern reorganisational

---

on the ground that it is obsolete (see the Employment Codes of Practice (Revocation) Order 1991 SI 1991/1264 (issued under s 12 of the Employment Act 1990). This is curious. It may be that some provisions of the 1972 codes are obsolete but not paras 44–46 on redundancy, as redundancy is *not* covered by the 1977 ACAS code.) The latter two advisory documents do not have the status of codes but their advice is sound, and probably influential.

11 [1988] ICR 142, [1987] IRLR 503.

12 Thus overturning the notorious 'no difference' rule in *British Labour Pump Co Ltd v Byrne* [1979] ICR 347, [1979] IRLR 94. On the other hand, remedy may be affected if the dismissal is only technically unfair. As far as the compensatory award (not the basic award) is concerned, this has to be what is 'just and equitable' (EP(C)A s 74(1)). If the procedural defect would have made no difference to the eventual dismissal, fairly carried out, the award could be reduced, even to nil (*Polkey v A E Dayton Services Ltd* [1988] AC 344, [1987] IRLR 503) or limited to the additional period over which the employee would have been employed had the dismissal been fair (*Mining Supplies (Longwall) Ltd v Baker* [1988] ICR 676, [1988] IRLR 417; *Abbotts and Standley v Wesson-Glynwed Steels Ltd* [1982] IRLR 51).

13 *Freud v Bentalls Ltd* [1983] ICR 77; [1982] IRLR 443, EAT; *Graham v ABF Ltd* [1986] IRLR 90, EAT; *Lafferty Construction Ltd v Duthie* [1985] IRLR 487.

14 See e g S Anderman *The Law of Unfair Dismissal* (2nd edn, 1985); C Grunfeld *The Law of Redundancy* (3rd edn, 1989); R Upex *Termination of Employment* (3rd edn, 1991); M R Freedland *The Contract of Employment; Harvey on Industrial Relations and Employment Law*. The law of unfair dismissal in particular is complex and these works should be consulted in detail on the difficult issue of whether a reorganisational dismissal falls within appropriate reasons either as 'some other substantial reason' or 'redundancy' or is fair. Also dismissals for non-reorganisational reasons must satisfy strict criteria, such as being for permissible reasons, e g for capability, conduct or statutory restriction EP(C)A s 57(2) and, of course, also satisfy the test of reasonableness under s 57(3). There are also minefields for an employer in maternity, discrimination and trade union cases, to mention a few.

dismissals on change of share capital not involving a change in the identity of the employer. As will be seen from Chapter 8, if there is a business transfer to which the Transfer Regulations apply, a dismissal 'in connection with' a transfer is *automatically* unfair. And, as will also be seen from Chapter 8, although an employer may show that the dismissal was for an economic, technical or organisational reason entailing changes in the workforce (in which case the *automatic* unfairness is removed and the matter decided on the general principles discussed above) this aspect of the Transfer Regulations can cause real problems for an employer attempting unilaterally to rationalise at the expense of employees.[15] In that respect at least, employee rights on a take-over by acquisition of share capital are less well protected than in the case of a business transfer.

3 COLLECTIVE EMPLOYMENT LAW

The situation is also less beneficial to employees in collective labour law when there is a take-over of a company by acquisition of share capital, as opposed to a transfer of a business from one person to another. Principally the provisions of regs 10 and 11 of the Transfer Regulations covering information and consultation obligations on transfer do not apply to the take-over.[16] However, if there are redundancy dismissals on the take-over, then the information and consultation provisions under s 99 of the EPA will apply requiring consultation by the dismissing employer with recognised trade unions before the first dismissal takes effect. This is covered in more detail in Chapter 10.

In summary, employment protection obviously does exist for those in a company taken over by purchase of its shares; but this is no different from the protection applicable to employees either expressly dismissed, or who are victims of breach of contract, in non-take-over situations. Both individually and collectively, employee rights are less well protected on take-overs by acquisition of share capital than on the type of business transfer discussed elsewhere in this book. Future legislators should, it is submitted,

---

15 The cases which illustrate this point are: *Wheeler v Patel* [1987] ICR 631; *Gateway Hotels Ltd v Stewart* [1988] IRLR 287 (express dismissals); *Berriman v Delabole Slate Ltd* [1985] ICR 546; *Servicepoint Ltd v Clynes* EAT 154/88 (constructive dismissals).
16 *TGWU v BICC Bryce Capacitors Ltd* COIT/33462/84, cited in *IDS Handbook* 36 p 52.

consider introducing legislation safeguarding employee rights on change of share capital of limited companies which is no less protective than on transfers of businesses. The disparity of treatment of employees' rights in these two situations seems hard to justify.[17]

---

17 This is not a new concern. The TGWU's journal came out some time ago in favour of statutory provisions of requiring consultation with the workforce of a company to be acquired by transfer of share capital and in favour of provisions requiring proposals concerning the workforce to be incorporated in a prospectus for employees (*Insolvency Law and Practice* (March/April 1986) p 49). Again, a few years ago, the Takeovers and Mergers (Employee Protection) Bill 1987 (HL) addressed some of these points. Although not a government Bill, it made interesting (and, possibly, prophetic) reading. (See also Hansard HL Deb 9 February 1987, col 427; Hansard HL Deb 25 March 1987, cols 260–282.) (It lapsed on the dissolution of Parliament before the 1987 General Election; see Appendix F.) MR Freedland's *The Contract of Employment* at pp 367–371, written in 1976, contains an interesting discussion of the issues in this area and contains many valuable references.

Chapter 2

Miscellaneous cases where continuity may be protected by the EP(C)A

Chapter 1 dealt with the case of take-overs of companies by acquisition of share capital. That situation involves no change of employer and, therefore, no break in employment. In this chapter the type of transfer of employment discussed does involve a change of employer but not necessarily because of a business transfer.

As already discussed, unless there is statutory provision allowing for the safeguard of statutory rights such as continuity or for the safeguard of other rights as provided for by the Transfer Regulations, continuity of employment will break upon any change of employer at common law. Also, upon each change of employer the contract of employment will inevitably terminate and a fresh contract of employment will form with a new employer. Following the principle in *Nokes v Doncaster Amalgamated Collieries Ltd*[1] the personal nature of a contract of employment means there cannot be automatic transfer of the contract from one employer to another (sometimes called an assignment) without consent.[2] A modern case

---

1 [1940] AC 1014, [1940] 3 All ER 549, HL.
2 *Chitty on Contracts* (26th edn) vol 1 (General Principles) para 1415: see *Nokes v Doncaster Amalgamated Collieries Ltd; Denham v Midland Employers' Mutual Assurance Ltd* [1955] 2 QB 437 at 443; *O'Brien (IT) v Bensons Hosiery (Holdings) Ltd* [1979] Ch 152 [1978] 3 All ER 1057, HL (the latter two cases are cited in *Chitty*, op cit). See also Freedland *The Contract of Employment* pp 350–354, where he states: 'The law as at present established is that there is strong positive authority against the transfer of the right to the services of the employee from one employer to another, and there is little satisfactory precedent for a transfer of the obligations of one employer to another, such as to cause the employee to acquire contractual rights against the new employer' (p 354). To be contrasted, it seems, is the position whereby wages due to an employee might be assignable by him: *Shaw & Co v Moss Empires Ltd and Bastow* (1909) 25 TLR 190 (*Chitty*, op cit, para 1416; but this is hardly an inroad into the general principle against non-assignability of obligations under a contract of employment. *Novation* of a contract of employment would be possible This, however, depends upon a tripartite agreement between the first employer, the employee and the second employer. As it depends on the agreement of the employee and all other parties concerned, it is not automatic in effect and is not, of course, in conflict with *Nokes*: see *Chitty* op cit, para 1436.

commonly quoted to support this proposition is *Lee v Barry High Ltd*.[3] There, an apprentice who contracted to serve a five-year apprenticeship suffered no fewer than three changes of employer during this period. It was held that upon each change of employer there was a break in statutory continuity of employment.[4] Similarly, in *Sir Alfred McAlpine (Northern) Ltd v Dean*[5] an employee employed by a sub-contractor was ceased to be employed when the sub-contractor ran out of funds to complete the sub-contract. As the main contractor still needed to get the work done, he took on the employees originally employed by the sub-contractor to finish the work. It was held that continuity was broken upon the transfer of the employees from the sub-contractor to the main contractor.

In these cases, had there been a transfer of a business from one person to another the answer would have been different; for, then, the provisions of EP(C)A, Sch 13, para 17(2) (and indeed the Transfer Regulations) would have applied to preserve continuity. On the other hand if the transfer is not a transfer of a business, but something less, then there will be a break in continuity[6] and neither EP(C)A, Sch 13, para 17(2) nor the Transfer Regulations apply.

There are also, however, a few miscellaneous provisions in the EP(C)A preserving continuity of employment upon change of employer and these will be briefly discussed below. Although they do not concern transfers of businesses, it is appropriate to discuss them in this book, and, on occasions, they may be of considerable importance. They each preserve statutory continuity of employment and do this irrespective of a business transfer[7] (although sometimes a business transfer may also be involved). It is important to stress that they do nothing more than preserve statutory continuity. Merely because a case of the type below occurs, it cannot be assumed

---

3　[1970] 3 All ER 1040, 6 ITR 3, CA.

4　In this case the employee was claiming a redundancy payment under the Redundancy Payments Act 1965 (now re-enacted in Part VI of the EP(C)A) against the ultimate employer.

5　EAT 2/78 (cited in *IDS Employment Law Handbook No 35: Continuity of Employment*). On sub-contractors as employers, see Ch 4.

6　*Port Talbot Engineering Co Ltd v Passmore* [1975] ICR 234, [1975] IRLR 156; *Douglas v Merchants Facilities (Glasgow) Ltd* (1966) 1 KIR 364; *Crompton v Truly Fair (International) Ltd* [1975] ICR 359, [1975] IRLR 250; *Rowlatt v Budden and Harris* (1966) 1 KIR 112; *Woodhouse v Peter Brotherhood Ltd* [1972] 2 QB 520, [1972] ICR 186, CA; *Melon v Hector Powe Ltd* [1981] 1 All ER 313, [1981] ICR 43, HL.

7　For example, it was held in *Binns v Versil Ltd* [1975] IRLR 273 that a protected move from associated employer to associated employer under (what is now) the EP(C)A Sch 13 para 18 may take place even without the consent of either employer, as long as (what is now) para 18 is satisfied.

the Transfer Regulations, with their additional safeguards (e g transfer of contractual rights, collective agreements, recognition, information and consultation etc) apply.[8] In fact, none of the cases below is covered by the Transfer Regulations (*unless*, when these situations occur, there is *also* a business transfer caught by the Transfer Regulations).

(i) Change of employer through Act of Parliament (EP(C)A Sch 13 para 17(3))

It is provided that if, under direction of Parliament (by public or local Act) a contract of employment between any body corporate and an employee is modified to substitute another body corporate as the employer the resultant change of employer will not break the continuity of employment of the employee and the period of employment with the first body corporate counts towards the period of employment with the second body corporate. This provision is probably of relatively limited importance to those involved in transfer of employment problems.

(ii) Death of an employer and transfer to personal representatives (EP(C)A Sch 13 para 17(4))

Because the contract of employment is a contract for personal services, it will terminate on the death of an individual employer.[9] The personal representatives of the deceased employer commonly retain the services of the employee but, at common law, this would be under a fresh contract of employment. It is provided, however, in para 17(4) that if, upon the death of the employer, the employee is taken into the employment of the personal representatives or trustees of the deceased employer, continuity of employment is not broken by the death of the employer and any period of employment with the deceased employer may be counted towards the period of employment with the personal representatives or trustees as the case may be.[10]

It is not clear from para 17(4) itself whether the death of the employer and re-engagement by personal representatives must be contemporaneous (although in practice it is likely to be so). But other provisions of Sch 13 will determine whether a delay between

---

8 As in *TGWU v BICC Bryce Capacitors Ltd* COIT 33462/84, cited in *IDS Handbook* 36 p 102.

9 *Farrow v Wilson* (1869) LR 4 CP 744. Termination will presumably technically be by frustration, owing to the personal nature of the relationship. Cf the policy arguments in Freedland *The Contract of Employment* pp 313–315; EP(C)A 1978, Sch 12.

10 See *Forrest v Forrest* (1966) 1 KIR 188; employment with father and thereafter the trustees of father's estate, continuous.

two employments is too long for the interim period to count towards the period of continuity of employment. Because s 151(2) of the EP(C)A states that questions of continuous employment determined under Sch 13 are looked at 'week by week' it is possible, it seems, that a short interval between employments will not necessarily break continuity, at least if a part of every week is worked with one employer or the other.[11]

However, in the context of redundancy only, a somewhat more substantial interval between death of the employer and re-engagement by the personal representatives will not be fatal (if the pun may be excused) to continuity. By virtue of Sch 12 para 14 to the EP(C)A (and Sch 13 para 11), it is provided that for the purposes of redundancy payments, if there is an offer of re-engagement by the personal representatives accepted within *eight weeks* of the death of the deceased employer, then the employee is deemed not to be dismissed and his continuity is preserved for the purposes of redundancy payments and the purposes of a future claim.

It is curious, though, that there is no parallel provision to Sch 12 para 14 in unfair dismissal law, where *semble* a different rule applies. Thus, a gap of a complete week will break continuity for the purposes of future unfair dismissal claims, but not redundancy claims, where the gap may, under Sch 12 para 14, be as much as eight weeks. This surely is a trap for the unwary employer or employee and a difference hard to justify.

The operation in practice of para 17(4) is strikingly illustrated by *Rowley Holmes & Co v Barber*.[12] Here, the employee, Barber, was employed by a solicitor as an unqualified clerk. The solicitor died, leaving the practice by will to Barber. The will also appointed Barber the solicitor's executor and trustee. Being unqualified, Barber could not run the practice and he therefore engaged Rowley to run it. In due course, the estate sold the practice to Rowley. Barber had worked continuously over these changes but was made redundant by the new owner, Rowley. It was held that upon the death of his employer Barber had been re-engaged by the personal representatives and there was, therefore, no break in continuity of employment. The fact that Barber was himself the personal representative who had effected the re-engagement was immaterial. Legally, he

---

11 See the discussion in Chapter 5 and *Teesside Times Ltd v Drury* [1980] ICR 338, [1980] IRLR 72, CA; *Macer v Abafast Ltd* [1990] ICR 234; *Gibson v Motortune Ltd* [1990] ICR 740.

12 [1977] 1 All ER 801, [1977] ICR 387 although cf an early tribunal decision, *Jones and Jones v Ministry of Labour* (1966) 1 KIR 796 (employment and trusteeship of estate incompatible, *sed quaere*).

could wear two hats, one *qua* employee and one *qua* executor. His service was unbroken for the purposes of a claim for a redundancy payment against Rowley.

(iii) Change in the composition of a partnership etc (EP(C)A Sch 13 para 17(5))

This provision applies to a change in composition of an employing partnership (ie a change of partners) and also to a change in composition of personal representatives or trustees who act as employer. But for this provision, again, because of the importance common law places on the personality of the employer, a change in the partnership (or *semble* a body of personal representatives or trustees) employing an employee will, at common law, terminate the contract.[13] Paragraph 17(5) states, overriding this rule, that where there is a change in the partners, personal representatives or trustees who employ a person, such change in partners, personal representatives or trustees will not break continuity of employment and any period of employment with the previously constituted partnership, or body of personal representatives or trustees, will count towards the employment with the newly-constituted partnership or group of individuals, as the case may be.

This provision has been discussed in several cases. One problem that has had to be addressed is that in para 17(5) *partners, personal representatives* or *trustees* appear in the *plural*. Thus, on the face of it, the provision would quite clearly cover a situation where, for example, a partner retires from a partnership of three individuals, the partnership subsequently being carried on by two or where, perhaps, an outgoing partner in a group of partners is replaced by an incoming partner. But in view of the specific use of the plural, does the provision cover a situation either where a partnership of a number of individuals ceases to be carried on and is run by only one of them in the future or, alternatively, where a business carried on by a sole trader continues to be carried on in the future by that sole trader in partnership *with others*? Some cases indicate not.[14] These authorities suggest that in the event, for example, of a cessation of a partnership, where the business is, after cessation, carried on by *one* only of the former partners, then unless there is a *transfer of a business* from the dissolving partnership to the individual former partner (in which case different rules apply under which, for

---

13 *Brace v Calder* [1895] 2 QB 253.
14 *Harold Fielding Ltd v Mansi* [1974] 1 All ER 1035, [1974] ICR 347; *Wynne v Hair Control* [1978] ICR 870, EAT.

example, continuity might be preserved by para 17(2) (and possibly also the Transfer Regulations)) there will be a break in continuity of employment. This literal construction still seems to be the law but can be criticised.

In two cases, namely *Allen & Son v Coventry*[15] and *Jeetle v Elster*[16] the EAT perceived the problems the wording of para 17(5) could cause for an employee and upheld the industrial tribunals' finding that there was a transfer of a *business* on the dissolution of a partnership and subsequent take-over of the activities by a former partner as a sole proprietor. This was even though one of these cases, *Jeetle v Elster*, concerned a doctor's partnership, and there was a prohibition on the sale of goodwill under the National Health Service Act 1977 governing doctors' partnerships.[17] In both cases, the EAT seemed thoroughly attracted to the commonsense idea of construing para 17(5) as including a change from the employing partnership to an individual former partner (and *semble* conversely from a sole trader to a partnership) but in view of its decision that there was a business transfer in both cases, its views on para 17(5) are only obiter, albeit extremely persuasive.

It can be argued that a finding by the EAT in both these cases of a transfer of a business under para 17(2) was strained. And indeed, if there is, as could follow from these cases, a transfer of a business in most cases on a change in the composition of a partnership, it would mean that para 17(5) would often be otiose, as the case would always come within para 17(2) (business transfer). Such a conclusion could not have been intended by the parliamentary draftsman. Accordingly, it is submitted that the better view (although it is not yet supported by direct judicial authority) should be that a 'change in partners' under para 17(5), as well as covering the received case of a change of individuals in a partnership of a number of people, should also include a dissolution of a partnership and a carrying on of the business by a sole trader, being a former partner, and also, *semble*, the case of a succession of a partnership of individuals to a business previously carried on by one of the partners solely.[18] (The same should also apply, *mutatis mutandis*, to changes of trustees and personal representatives.)

---

15 [1980] ICR 9, [1979] IRLR 399, EAT.
16 [1985] ICR 389, [1985] IRLR 227, EAT.
17 Such prohibition on the sale of goodwill may well, in many cases, ordinarily have led to the conclusion that there was a simple transfer of assets, if anything, to the sole practitioner in question, as opposed to a transfer of a business as a going concern. But the EAT in *Jeetle* stressed that this was essentially a question of fact for the industrial tribunal. On goodwill, see Ch 4.
18 See the view in *Harvey on Industrial Relations and Employment Law* I para 667.

The wider interpretation of para 17(5) put forward here is surely much more desirable in that it is not always possible to find a transfer of a business as a going concern (as opposed merely to assets) on a change from, say, a partnership to a sole trader and vice versa. The use here of para 17(5), which does not depend upon a transfer of a business, seems more appropriate. So it is hoped that future judicial interpretation of para 17(5) will confirm that para 17(5) should apply to transfers between a *partner* (or personal representative or trustee) or *partners* (or personal representatives and trustees) inter se and para 17(2) to transfers between a partnership (or personal representatives or trustees) and *third parties*. This, however, remains to be seen.

(iv) **Associated employers** (EP(C)A Sch 13 para 18)

This provision applies, even when there is no business transfer, to a case where an employee of an employer is taken into the employment of another employer who, at the time when the employee enters his employment, is an associated employer of the first employer. In such a case, the transfer of employment does not break continuity of employment and the period of employment with the first associated employer counts towards employment with the second associated employer.

There has been considerable litigation over the meaning of associated employer, which is defined in s 153(4) of the EP(C)A. This provides that:

'. . . any two employers are to be treated as associated if one is a company of which the other (directly or indirectly) has control, or if both are companies of which a third person (directly or indirectly) has control . . .'

It has been questioned whether control in this context includes de facto or functional control as well as simply control by a numerical majority of shares in the general meeting of a limited company. However, the balance of cases support a view that control should be determined solely by the question of whether the controller has the majority of votes in the general meeting of a company.[19]

---

19 *Secretary of State for Employment v Newbold* [1981] IRLR 305; *Washington Arts Association v Forster* [1983] ICR 346; *Hair Colour Consultants Ltd v Mena* [1984] ICR 671, [1984] IRLR 386, EAT; *Umar v Pliastar Ltd* [1981] ICR 727; *South West Launderettes Ltd v Laidler* [1986] ICR 455, [1986] IRLR 305, CA. For this purpose it would seem that shares held by nominees of a beneficial owner may not be counted towards the shares otherwise held by nominees in their own right in calculating whether the nominee has control; the nominee shareholding must be attributed to the beneficial owners: *Cann v Fairfield Rowan Ltd* (1966) 1 KIR 510.

It has also been suggested that control by a third person in this context could mean control by a common group of third persons if the group acts in concert as one.[20] This has, however, recently been qualified by the Court of Appeal in *Southwest Launderettes Ltd v Laidler*.[1] According to the Court of Appeal, even if a concept of control by a group of individuals were valid, there would have to be, at the very least, uniformity in the composition of a group of individuals whom it is alleged exercised control in relation to all allegedly associated companies.[2] Such was not the case, for example, in *Southwest Launderettes Ltd v Laidler* itself, and may often not be the case in practice.

It has been held that the definition of 'control' in s 153(4) is exhaustive and that the word 'company' means 'limited company' and does not include incorporated associations, partnerships, local authorities or the like.[3] On the other hand, two more recent cases illustrate a more robust approach to this definition. In *Pinkney v Sandpiper Drilling Ltd*[4] it was held that para 18 applied upon a transfer of an employee from a company to a partnership or joint venture of three companies of which a third person, namely a group, had control. Taking a broad view, the EAT thought it would be wrong if employee rights in this context could be defeated simply because the employer's trading form happened to be slightly unusual and comprised a joint venture or partnership as opposed to a limited company in the strict sense.[5] This seems to conflict with the Court of Appeal decision in *Merton London Borough Council v Gardiner*,[6] and for that reason should be treated with caution until further judicial comment is available; but the wide employee-oriented view in the case is commendable. In *Hancill v Marcon Engineering Ltd*[7] it was held that an overseas (American) company should be regarded as a 'company' for the purposes of s 153(4).

---

20 *Zarb and Samuels v British and Brazilian Produce Co (Sales) Ltd* [1978] IRLR 78, EAT.
1 [1986] ICR 455, [1986] IRLR 305, CA, per Mustill LJ at 307.
2 See also *Poparm Ltd v Weekes* [1984] IRLR 388; *Cann v Fairfield Rowan Ltd* (1966) 1 KIR 510; *Strudwick v IBL* [1988] ICR 796, [1988] IRLR 457; *Russell v Elmdon Freight Terminal Ltd* [1989] ICR 629. But cf the view of the EAT in *Harford v Swiftrim Ltd* [1987] ICR 439.
3 *Merton London Borough Council v Gardiner* [1981] QB 269, [1981] ICR 186, CA; *Southern Electricity Board v Collins* [1970] 1 QB 83, [1969] 2 All ER 1166; *Southwood Hostel Management Committee v Taylor* [1979] ICR 813, [1979] IRLR 397, EAT. *Hillingdon Area Health Authority v Kauders* [1979] ICR 472, [1979] IRLR 197, EAT seems no longer to be good law.
4 [1989] ICR 389, [1989] IRLR 425, EAT.
5 Cf *Wynne v Hair Control* [1978] ICR 870, EAT.
6 [1981] ICR 186, [1980] IRLR 302.
7 [1990] ICR 103, [1990] IRLR 51.

Thus, when an employee worked for an American company, Marcon Engineering Inc, and thereafter transferred to an English limited company, Marcon Engineering Limited, and both of which companies were controlled by a Dutch company, Marcon Beheermaatschappij Bv, it was held that there had been a transfer between associated employers. In this case, Wood J argued that a broad interpretation must be applied to the principle of transfer of continuity of employment on change of employer. Again this approach is welcome, albeit expressly inspired by the decision in *Litster v Forth Dry Dock & Engineering Co Ltd*,[8] a case on the Transfer Regulations and not on the provisions here under discussion.

As in all the cases discussed in this chapter, there is nothing in para 18 (or para 17 in some of the other cases in this chapter) to indicate whether an interval between employment with the first associated employer and engagement by the second, and how long an interval, is fatal. The answer to that question lies elsewhere in Sch 13 to the EP(C)A, which should always be consulted, as in other cases discussed in this chapter, to determine whether intervals between successive employments count. As discussed above, it is thought that a short interval between successive employments will not be fatal if there is employment with either employer during part of a week and no week of non-employment separates the two partly-worked weeks.[9] The size of that interval and other controversial questions concerning intervals between successive employments are discussed in Chapter 5; it is to be noted that the issue of intervals between employments for the purposes of para 17(2) has been reviewed in the light of developments in case law on the Transfer Regulations (see Chapter 5).

In para 18 it is stipulated that, at the time when the employee enters the employment of the second employer, the second employer must be 'an associated *employer* of the first . . . employer' (emphasis added). In *Charnock v Barrie Muirhead Ltd*[10] employees

---

8 [1989] ICR 341, [1989] IRLR 161. As will be seen, infra, in *Litster* a purposive interpretation was applied to the Transfer of Undertakings (Protection of Employment) Regulations 1981 to make them conform to the aims of the Acquired Rights Directive, ie to safeguard employee rights in a broad way. *Quaere* however, whether that entitles a tribunal or court to adopt such an approach under EP(C)A, Sch 13, para 18, which is not concerned with transfers of undertakings. It is at least arguable, however, that Sch 13, para 17(2) may be so interpreted (see Chs 5, 6; *Macer v Abafast Ltd* [1990] ICR 234; *Marleasing SA v La Commercial International de Alimentacion SA* (ECJ, Case C106/89)) (13 November 1990, unreported).

9 *Binns v Versil Ltd* [1975] IRLR 273; cf the result in *Logan v GUS Transport Ltd* (1969) 4 ITR 287 (employment with one employer ended on Saturday, engagement by associated employer on Monday: employment not continuous *sed quaere*).

10 [1984] ICR 641.

employed by the first employer were dismissed and a two-week interval ensued before they were re-engaged by a dormant company associated with the first employer. There were two questions. First, was the two-week interval fatal, and second, was the dominant company an associated employer, having no employees? It was held that the actual two-week interval between periods of work did not break continuity of employment by virtue of para 11 of Sch 13 to the EP(C)A (because, under EP(C)A s 55(5), the statutory minimum period of notice under s 49 not otherwise given could notionally extend the first period of employment). As to the second question, although at the time of termination of their employment the off-the-shelf company could not be said to be an employer of any employee, the EAT said that the relevant date for deciding when the second company became an employer of the employees was when the employees actually started work with the second employer. On that date the second employer became an employer because it employed the employees concerned.[11]

(v) Local education authority schools (EP(C)A Sch 13 para 18A)

Transfers between a local education authority and governors of schools and vice versa will not cause a break in continuity of employment of the employee transferred and periods of employment with one employer will count towards employment with the second employer. This prima facie catches transfers of teachers between schools within one authority, but it is also wide enough to cover and protect the transfer of non-teaching staff between authorities and governors and vice versa, again all within the same local authority area.

(vi) Other miscellaneous cases under the EP(C)A

(i) Under the maternity provisions of the EP(C)A the right of an employee to return to work after maternity leave includes a right to return to work with the successor of an employer.[12]

---

11 However, if the second employer was not *associated* with the first employer until *after* the employee joined the second employer, the provision will not apply: *Strachan v Southook Potteries Ltd* (1966) 1 ITR 336. Finally, it is important to note that EP(C)A s 55(5) (applied in *Charnock*) does not extend employment in all cases where notice has not been given. It mainly applies where a qualifying period is in issue (as in *Charnock*) or for calculating a basic award for unfair dismissal. See the possible application to intervals between employment due to a business transfer, discussed in Chs 5 and 7.

12 EP(C)A s 45(1). And an employee who returns to work in accordance with s 45(1) may treat absence through pregnancy or confinement as continuous (EP(C)A Sch 13 para 11).

(ii) Following unfair dismissal, an industrial tribunal may either order compensation or reinstatement or re-engagement. If re-engagement is ordered, it may be with the dismissing employer or his successor.[13]

(iii) In industrial tribunal complaints, ACAS has power to take action to promote settlement and this may, of course, include action which has the effect of an industrial tribunal award. If an employee is reinstated or re-engaged by an employer or the successor of an employer in consequence of action taken by an ACAS conciliation officer, or following an unfair dismissal complaint, or following a claim under a designated dismissals procedure agreement under s 65 of the EP(C)A, any break in employment does not break the employee's period of continuous employment.[14]

---

13 EP(C)A s 69(4). See Ch 7 for the importance of this remedy, post *Litster v Forth Dry Dock & Engineering Co Ltd* [1989] IRLR 161.
14 Labour Relations (Continuity of Employment) Regulations 1976, SI 1976/660.

Chapter 3

Business transfers: the scheme of statutory employment protection

1 BUSINESS TRANSFERS: AN INTRODUCTION

As discussed earlier, the major part of this work is devoted to transfers of businesses between one person and another. Most practical problems related thereto concern the application either of Sch 13 para 17(2) to the EP(C)A (on transfer of continuity on sales of businesses) or the redundancy provisions, for example in s 94, of the EP(C)A (concerning the negativing of redundancy liability on dismissals by a change of ownership (ie transfer) of a business) or, finally, and probably most importantly, the Transfer Regulations.

A transfer of a business from one person to another is a very common (although by no means universal) type of disposal of a business in this country. As 'person' here includes an individual, a company or any other body corporate or unincorporate[1] the concept of a transfer of a business from one person to another covers a great many types of transactions. It can include the transfer of the corner shop from one proprietor to another. It can also, at the other end of the scale, include the transfer of a company's undertaking or part of an undertaking to another company.

The keynote is that there must be a transfer of a business as a going concern, and this vital aspect is covered separately in Chapter 4. Broadly, it means that transfers of assets, without more, are not covered by statutory provisions saving continuity of employment and automatically transferring contracts of employment.

Although by no means all business transfers are effected formally with written agreements, legal advice and appropriate documentation is prudent. This is usually the province of the corporate, rather than employment, specialist, but helpful precedents for the sale of businesses are contained in the *Encyclopaedia of Forms and Precedents*[2] and also in *Longmans Practical Commercial*

---

1 Interpretation Act 1978 Sch 1.
2 Vol 9 (4th edn).

Precedents.[3] A perception of the aims of sellers and buyers, reflected in the structure of their legal agreements, gives us additional insight into the position of employees caught up in the mechanisms of business transfers.

Finally, although it is envisaged that this book will mostly be used by those concerned with sales of businesses and employee rights, the concept of a business transfer covers not only *sales* of businesses from one person to another but also transfers of businesses by certain *other* dispositions. The provisions of the EP(C)A and of the Transfer Regulations cover transfers otherwise than by sale, viz transfers by other types of disposition and also by operation of law. Thus, it seems, transfers by gift or exchange or surrender, transfers which are gratuitous[4] or transfers by the law of succession under a will or trust, are also covered by the statutory provisions.[5] Therefore, when the expression 'business transfer' is used, it may be considered to include both sale and these other kinds of transfer.

An added dimension has been provided by the case law of the European Court on the Acquired Rights Directive. As is discussed in more detail later, this case law confirms that the scope of the directive is not confined to change of ownership of a business. The Acquired Rights Directive applies as soon as there is a change in the

---

3 Vol 1 Precedent D5. And see also H Wine *Buying and Selling Private Companies and Businesses* (3rd edn, 1986); See also App A.

4 *Brooks v The Grays Co-operative Society Ltd* (1967) 2 ITR 345.

5 The Transfer Regulations apply 'whether the transfer is effected by sale or by some other disposition or by operation of law' (reg 3(2)). Section 94 of the EP(C)A (liability for redundancy payment on change of employer) applies whether the change in ownership is 'by virtue of a sale or other disposition or by operation of law' (sub-s (1)(a)). Paragraph 17(2) of Sch 13 to the EP(C)A is silent on the permitted modes of transfer. One view is that it only applies to sales, and events such as death of an employer, for example, could be dealt with by, say, para 17(4). But the better view is that para 17(2), as long as a business as a going concern is involved, covers disposition other than sales, along the lines of the Transfer Regulations and s 94. Case law also bears this out. In this respect all three provisions should be harmoniously construed. EP(C)A s 94 alone, however, rather unfortunately refers to a 'change in the *ownership*' of a business (and the EAT thought the concept of transfer of 'ownership' important for this provision in *SI (Systems and Instrumentation) Ltd v Grist and Riley* [1983] ICR 788, [1983] IRLR 391). As the text next states, the Transfer Regulations, it seems, do not depend on a change of absolute ownership: this follows from the case law of the European Court on the Acquired Rights Directive (see Ch 4). Nor, it seems, does Sch 13 para 17(2) necessarily require a transfer of absolute legal ownership: *Dabell v Vale Industrial Services (Nottingham) Ltd* [1988] IRLR 439, CA. The anomalous wording of s 94 is therefore unfortunate but the mind of the reader may in some part be put at rest by the practical position that, where there *is* a business transfer the provisions of s 94 are usually otiose, because of the application of the Transfer Regulations (but cf importantly transfers of non-commercial ventures: see Chs 4 and 5).

natural or legal person responsible for operating the undertaking who adopts employment obligations in respect of the business's employees (although Art 1(1) of the Directive presupposes that this comes about as a result of a legal transfer or merger).[6] It is necessary to remember that the Transfer Regulations should be construed in the light of the Acquired Rights Directive and case law thereon (see Chapters 4 and 7). This means the focus has distinctly shifted away from the traditionally perceived mode of transfer of a business involving, commonly, a sale of ownership for a consideration to the simple issue of whether the operation of the business is continued or resumed by a new employer carrying out the same or a similar business. This would support the view that the business transfer legislation covers a multitude of types of transfer, not all of which necessarily involve a change of absolute ownership. So marked is this departure from traditional norms that Hepple and O'Higgins have coined the expression the 'employment' test for the European Court's approach to the question whether the mechanics of a business transfer are satisfied, as opposed to the more orthodox and received 'conveyancing' test.[7] The received position under English law at least is that, strictly speaking, the EP(C)A may not be construed in the light of a directive it was not intended to implement (although this may now be inconsistent with the views of the European Court of Justice). But there is every merit in endeavouring to construe the EP(C)A along the same lines as the Transfer Regulations (which themselves have benefited from European law) simply in order to keep the various statutory provisions consistent.[8] A

---

6 *Foreningen af Arbejdsledere i Danmark v Daddy's Dance Hall* [1988] ECR 739, [1988] IRLR 315; *Berg and Busschers v Besselsen* [1990] ICR 396, [1989] IRLR 447; *Landsorganisationen i Danmark v Ny Molle Kro* [1989] ICR 330, [1989] IRLR 37; *P Bork International A/S v Foreningen af Arbejdsledere i Danmark* [1990] 3 CMLR 701, [1989] IRLR 41. The question whether a 'legal transfer or merger' is strictly required under the Transfer Regulations or Sch 13 para 17(2) is explored in Ch 4.

7 *Encyclopaedia of Labour Relations Law* para 1B 504.

8 The principle that regard may not be had to a later EC directive in interpreting earlier domestic legislation on the same subject matter derives from the House of Lords decision in *Duke v GEC Reliance Ltd* [1988] ICR 339, [1988] IRLR 118 (woman not entitled to rely on the Equal Treatment Directive (Council Directive 76/207 of 9 February 1976) 'on the implementation of the principle of equal treatment for men and women as regards access to employment, vocational training and promotion, and working conditions') outlawing discriminatory retirement ages, to interpret the earlier Sex Discrimination Act 1975 (which appeared to permit such discrimination between men and women). The position had to be remedied by amending legislation, in the shape of the Sex Discrimination Act 1986. However, this area may be liable to be turned on its head following comments to the contrary by the European Court (in a different, company law, context) in *Marleasing SA v La Commercial International de Alumentation* Case

number of decisions on the EP(C)A have already borne out a similarly wide interpretation anyway, seemingly ignoring any supposed requirement of a transfer involving change of absolute ownership.[9] Any trend towards harmonisation of the EP(C)A with the Transfer Regulations must be welcomed. Complete harmonisation is not made easy, however, by the existence of many statutory inconsistencies, discussed below.

2 WHY ARE THERE SEPARATE SCHEMES UNDER THE EP(C)A AND THE TRANSFER REGULATIONS?

Employee protection on business transfers is afforded by either the EP(C)A or the Transfer Regulations or both. The provisions of the EP(C)A concern continuity of employment and also the concept of deeming, under certain circumstances, a dismissal by reason of redundancy that would otherwise have occurred upon a transfer of a business from one person to another, not to have happened. The Transfer Regulations purport to transfer a contract of employment *in toto* from a transferor to a transferee. It is true that the Transfer Regulations are more ambitious and apply very specific safeguards for employees dismissed by a transferor or a

---

No 106/89 (13 November 1990, unreported) that it followed from the obligation on member states to take all measures appropriate to ensure the performance of their obligations to achieve the results provided for in directives, that in applying national law, *whether it was a case of provisions prior to or subsequent to the directive*, the national court called on to interpret it was required to do so as far as possible in the light of the wording and purpose of the directive in order to achieve the result sought by the directive. If *Marleasing* is followed and applied by English courts notwithstanding *Duke v GEC Reliance Ltd* this might allow more effective harmonisation of the Transfer Regulations and the EP(C)A by allowing the latter to be interpreted in line with the former (the former in turn interpreted in line with the Acquired Rights Directive). In fact an industrial tribunal has already followed *Marleasing* in order to interpret a case arising under the Sex Discrimination Act 1975 (or pregnancy) in line with *Dekker v Stichting Vormingscentrum voor Jonge Volwassen (VJV-Centrum) Plus* [1991] IRLR 27, a European Court case on the subsequent Equal Treatment Directive (*Cairney v Chivas Bros* (1991) COIT 3804/90, 28 April 1991). Whether this reasoning could be applied to the interpretation of the EP(C)A in the light of the Acquired Rights Directive is not at all clear. But in any event, without resorting to this jurisprudential question, Wood J has already, in *Macer v Abafast Ltd* [1990] ICR 234, [1990] IRLR 137 (see note 10), robustly interpreted EP(C)A Sch 13 para 17(2) in line with the interpretation of reg 5 of the Transfer Regulations in *Lister v Forth Dry Dock & Engineering Co Ltd* [1989] ICR 341, [1989] IRLR 161 which, in turn, relied heavily on the Acquired Rights Directive as interpreted by the European Court.

9 See eg *Dabell v Vale Industrial Services (Nottingham) Ltd* [1988] IRLR 439, CA (de facto transfer of business for the purposes of EP(C)A Sch 13 para 17(2) even though ultimate legal completion fell through).

transferee in connection with the transfer by making such dismissal automatically unfair, subject to whether the dismissal was for an economic, technical or organisational reason entailing changes in the workforce. And those affected by dismissals in connection with a transfer enjoy vicariously the right of their recognised trade union representatives to be informed and consulted about the transfer and any measures envisaged in relation to affected employees. But on the central issue of transfer of employment, the issues are similar. Nonetheless there are a number of technical differences between the provisions of the EP(C)A and the Transfer Regulations.

First, there are various situations covered by the EP(C)A in which continuity is protected which do not necessarily involve a transfer of a business or undertaking. Where these situations apply but there is no transfer of an undertaking, the provisions of the Transfer Regulations will not apply (and nor will, of course, para 17(2) of Sch 13). Thus in the following cases (see Chapter 2) continuity of employment will be preserved but the Transfer Regulations will not apply:

(a) change of employer by Act of Parliament;

(b) death of an employer and transfer to personal representatives;

(c) change in the composition of a partnership;

(d) transfers between associated employers;

(e) transfers to and from local education authority schools;

unless there is, simultaneously, a transfer of a business associated with these instances. Of course, cases like transfers between associated employers and changes in the composition of a partnership could, in theory, at the same time involve a transfer of an undertaking, but this will very often not be the case. This must have been envisaged by the draftsman of Sch 13 when he included para 17(2) concerning transfers of businesses and also, separately, the provisions of paras 17 and 18 concerning these other cases cited above. In other words, he appreciated there was a difference both in theory and, sometimes, in practice.

Second, there are aspects of the Transfer Regulations which are more restrictive than the EP(C)A in business transfer cases. For example, in relation to para 17(2) of Sch 13 to the EP(C)A and in relation to s 94 of the EP(C)A, a transfer of a business can, it is submitted, include a business which is not necessarily a commercial venture (at least in relation to Sch 13, para 17(2), when it refers to 'undertaking' and makes no express requirement that it be a *commercial* undertaking). However, non-commercial ventures are specifically excluded from the Transfer Regulations. Thus, for example, a transfer of a non-commercial venture could result in preservation of statutory continuity of employment on transfer but not attract the special protective provisions of the Transfer Regulations. This will be discussed in Chapter 4.

Finally, there is a possible, though diminishing, difference of interpretation between the Transfer Regulations and the provisions as to continuity in para 17 of Sch 13 to the EP(C)A concerning how close to the point of transfer employees have to be employed in the undertaking transferred.[10] This will be discussed in Chapter 5.

It can be seen that, in many cases, there are two separate schemes. When the Transfer Regulations apply and the continuity provisions under the EP(C)A also apply (as they more often than not will) it could be said that the two schemes overlap and are harmonious. But even then the position is not clear. Some think that the Transfer Regulations automatically transfer continuity of employment because the contract of employment itself is transferred.[11] This is very probably right.[12] But others think that, while the Transfer Regulations transfer the contract, the provisions of the EP(C)A alone must be looked at as far as statutory continuity is concerned.[13] If that is correct then, in one sense, even when they overlap, the EP(C)A provisions and the Transfer Regulations can at the same time be regarded as separate schemes. This aspect is discussed further in Chapter 5.

Now, surely, all this cannot have happened by design. Of course not. The express lack of harmony between the two schemes is accidental. The provisions of the EP(C)A go back some time in legislative

---

10 The position is somewhat improved and, to a large extent, harmonised, by the decisions of the EAT (Wood J presiding) (if they are approved on appeal) in *Macer v Abafast Ltd* [1990] ICR 234, [1990] IRLR 137 and *Gibson v Motortune Ltd* [1990] ICR 740 (see infra, Ch 5). See note 8, supra.

11 Davies and Freedland *Transfer of Employment* (1982).

12 The position probably depends on the construction of the relevant part of reg 5 of the Transfer Regulations, which refers to transfer of '. . . all of the transferor's rights, powers, duties and liabilities under or in connection with any [employment] contract. . .' To be contrasted is the wider wording in Art 3 of the Acquired Rights Directive which refers to the transfer of 'The transferor's rights and obligations arising from a contract of employment *or from an employment relationship* existing on the date of a transfer. . .' (emphasis added). If the words 'employment relationship' would broaden the scope of matters 'in connection with' a contract of employment (so as to include statutory continuity), might not the terms of reg 5 here cited be purposively construed to allow them to be read in that light after *Litster v Forth Dry Dock & Engineering Co Ltd* [1989] ICR 341, [1989] IRLR 161? (See Ch 7 on the concept of purposive construction of the Transfer Regulations.)

13 *IDS Employment Law Handbook No 36: Transfer of Undertakings.*

history and have always been concerned only with continuity of employment where as para 17(2) of Sch 13 is concerned and liability for redundancy dismissals in the case of s 94 of the EP(C)A.[14] The Transfer Regulations arose as a result of the obligation on the UK to implement the Acquired Rights Directive. As will be discussed later, this directive was unpopular with the government which enacted the Transfer Regulations.[15] The government was, apparently, threatened with infraction proceedings for not implementing the directive on time[16] and the Transfer Regulations were introduced somewhat hastily by the fairly unusual method of a statutory instrument, which led to relatively little parliamentary debate upon these provisions (the Transfer Regulations were debated in the House of Commons at 10.15 pm for one and a half hours, and in the House of Lords at 6.32 pm, ie respectively at bedtime and suppertime).[17] Because of the reluctance of the government to bring in the Transfer Regulations there was no attempt whatsoever to harmonise the Transfer Regulations with existing provisions on transfers of businesses and there has since been no indication that legislative time will be given for the purposes of harmonisation.[18] Thus there

---

14 The CEA as far as Sch 13 para 17(2) is concerned and the RPA in relation to s 94.

15 See Hansard HC Deb 7 December 1981, col 680 (Mr David Waddington).

16 Davies and Freedland *Transfer of Employment.*

17 See Hansard HC Deb 7 December 1981 col 677; Hansard HL Deb 10 December 1981, col 1482. For this point see Hepple (1982) ILJ 29 at 30.

18 The uncertainty which arose about the liability of a transferee for pre-transfer dismissals effected by a transfer in the early days of interpretation of the Transfer Regulations (see Ch 7) and other (unrelated) matters, for example the creation of the concept of Administrator under the Insolvency Act 1985 (see Ch 9), the creation of personal pension schemes (see Ch 7) and the European Court decision in *Abels v The Administrative Board of the Bedrijfsvereniging voor de Metaal Industrie en de Electrotechnische Industrie* [1927] 2 CMLR 406 (see Chs 7 and 9) led, in April 1986, to the publication of a consultative document concerning proposed changes in the Transfer Regulations (reproduced in the first edition of this book). The Court of Appeal decision in *Secretary of State for Employment v Spence* [1987] QB 179, [1986] 3 All ER 616, which held that liability only for employees employed at the point of transfer was transferred to a transferee led the Department of Employment to proceed no further on the transfer of employment point (it had recommended (see para 5) the same outcome although *Spence* has of course now been qualified by *Litster v Dry Dock & Engineering Co Ltd* [1989] ICR 341, [1989] IRLR 161 which implied additional wording into reg 5(3) to modify the *Spence* decision, giving effect to European law – see Ch 7). This has been the only indication of law reform from official sources in the UK (but see the non-government Bill on take-overs and employee rights which foundered in 1987: App F). There are no present plans to alter the regulations to take either the *Litster* or *Abels* decisions into account. In 1988 the Department of Employment decided not to amend reg 7 to exclude personal pension schemes from the Transfer Regulations. And, finally, the Department of Employment has no other

are two schemes: the reason for this is far from logical and helps us little in dealing with transfers of businesses in a simple and understandable way. Practitioners can only hope that on the point at issue with which they have to deal the EP(C)A and the Transfer Regulations will overlap. But this may not *always* happen.

---

immediate plans to make amendments to the Transfer Regulations (letter from the Department of Employment to the author, January 1991, quoted with permission). *Burdens on Business (Report of a Scrutiny of Administrative and Legislative Requirements* (1985) (at p 60) suggested a revocation(!) of the Transfer Regulations or a compensation fund for the 'unfair dismissal' element of any claims. This suggestion is in clear conflict with our European obligations and was, as a consequence, never likely to get off the ground.

Chapter 4

Defining a business transfer

1 INTRODUCTION

Neither the Transfer Regulations, nor the provisions protecting continuity of employment in para 17(2) of Sch 13 to the EP(C)A, nor the redundancy provisions in s 94 of the EP(C)A on change of ownership of a business, apply unless there is, respectively, a transfer of an *'undertaking'* (Transfer Regulations) or a transfer of a *'trade or business or an undertaking'* (para 17(2) of Sch 13 to the EP(C)A) or a change in the ownership of a *business* (s 94 of the EP(C)A). It has been held that 'trade or business or an undertaking' in Sch 13 para 17(2) to the EP(C)A should be construed in a way consistent with 'business' in s 94 of the EP(C)A.[1]

It was decided for the purposes of what are now the provisions of the EP(C)A that a prerequisite for a business transfer is whether there was a transfer of a business as a 'going concern'. The words 'going concern' do not appear in either s 94 or Sch 13, para 17(2) to the EP(C)A; this gloss on the statutory wording originates from the leading case of *Kenmir Ltd v Frizzell*[2] where Widgery J (as he then was) said:

'. . . the vital consideration is whether the effect of the transaction [is] to put the transferee in possession of a going concern the activities of which he [can] carry on without interruption'.[3]

Assets-only sales, without more, are not covered.[4]

The Transfer Regulations apply when there is simply a 'transfer of an undertaking'. When the Transfer Regulations were intro-

---

1 So it appears from the discussion (on their statutory predecessors) by the House of Lords in *Lord Advocate v De Rosa* [1974] 2 All ER 849, [1974] ICR 480, HL.
2 [1968] 1 All ER 414, 3 ITR 159. The phrase also appears in value added tax legislation (see Charlton (1986) LS Gaz 413 and cases in the Value Added Tax Tribunal Reports (VATTR)).
3 Ibid at 164.
4 See e g *Woodhouse v Peter Brotherhood Ltd* [1972] 2 QB 520, [1972] ICR 186, CA and *Melon v Hector Powe Ltd* [1981] 1 All ER 313, [1981] ICR 43, HL.

duced, their relationship and possible homogeneity with the EP(C)A was not at all clear; of course, as will be seen in this book, this still remains true in many respects. It might have been hoped that a 'transfer of an undertaking' under the Transfer Regulations would be construed more widely than the provisions of the EP(C)A, catching more sales and thus protecting more employees.[5] But it was held in *Batchelor v Premier Motors (Romford) Ltd*[6] and in *Premier Motors (Medway) Ltd v Total Oil Great Britain Ltd*[7] that the Transfer Regulations should be read together with the provisions of the EP(C)A in order to understand what a 'transfer of an undertaking' involves. So, it seems that the case law on what is a 'transfer of a trade, business or undertaking' or what constitutes a 'change in the ownership' thereof will be relevant to whether there is a transfer of an undertaking. In fact the EAT in *Michael's Travel Ltd v Giraud*[8] went further and firmly rejected any idea that 'transfer of an undertaking' under the Transfer Regulations is any wider than, for example, under Sch 13 para 17(2) to the EP(C)A (and, *semble*, s 94). However, one rider to that opinion must be added. It has been emphasised in the European Court whenever the terms of the Acquired Rights Directive (on which the Transfer Regulations are based) are in issue, that the *mechanics* of a transfer must be looked at broadly. For example, a change in absolute ownership of a business is not required. The Transfer Regulations must be construed this widely too, and in so far as the courts construe the Transfer Regulations and the EP(C)A provisions harmoniously, the EP(C)A provisions will therefore be pulled up to this European standard (to the extent this has not already been achieved by other reasoning (see below)).

What is clear, though, is that even in the light of European law, 'transfer of an undertaking' under the Transfer Regulations means transfer of an undertaking as a 'going concern' also and an asset sale alone will likewise not come under the Transfer Regulations. This was confirmed by the European Court in Case No 24/85 *Spijkers v Gebroeders Benedik Abattoir CV*[9] where, in considering the Acquired Rights Directive on which the Transfer Regulations are based, the opinion of the Advocate-General (Sir Gordon Slynn) was:

---

5 Particularly bearing in mind the aims of the Acquired Rights Directive which are to safeguard employee rights and on which the Transfer Regulations are based.
6 IT (COIT 17295/82/LN) (Chairman, Professor BA Hepple).
7 [1984] ICR 58, [1983] IRLR 471, EAT.
8 EAT 345/85 (Huchinson J presiding) LEXIS transcript. Reg 2(1) of the Transfer Regulations says 'undertaking' includes a 'trade' or 'business'.
9 [1986] 2 CMLR 296.

'The essential question is whether the transferee is put in a position, as a result of a legal transfer, whereby he can carry on the undertaking or business or part thereof.'[10]

The court further ruled in that case:

'Article 1(1) of Directive 77/187 of 14 February 1977 must be interpreted to the effect that the expression "transfer of an undertaking business or part of a business to another employer" envisages the case in which the business in question retained its identity.

In order to establish whether or not such a transfer has taken place in a case such as that before the National Court, it is necessary to consider whether, having regard to all the facts characterising the transaction, the business was disposed of as a going concern, as would be indicated *inter alia* by the fact that its operation was actually continued or resumed by the new employer with the same or similar activities.'[11]

As will be seen from the similarity of dicta on the subject of both the EP(C)A provisions and the Transfer Regulations, for most practical purposes all of the provisions are likely to be construed in the same way. It is for that reason and for ease of reference that we use the expression 'business transfer' generally throughout this book to cover cases both under the EP(C)A and under the Transfer Regulations. We must repeat our caveat on the subject of European law here, though. As already suggested in this chapter, case law emanating from the European Court on the Acquired Rights Directive is relevant in interpreting the Transfer Regulations. As is noted in more detail throughout the book the House of Lords has held in *Litster v Forth Dry Dock and Engineering Co Ltd*[12] that a purposive interpretation of the Transfer Regulations must be adopted to make them conform to the directive (as interpreted by European Court case law) on which they are based. Such case law does not, according to established wisdom (see Ch 6), strictly affect the EP(C)A provisions as they were not enacted to give effect to the Acquired Rights Directive, of course. So there could be differences of approach for this reason in looking at a business transfer for the purposes of the EP(C)A on the one hand and the Transfer Regulations on the other. As far as possible it might be supposed, however, that tribunals will try hard to apply as common an approach as possible to the various provisions. And, as suggested, if so, the EP(C)A provisions may be pulled along in the wake of this European influence. As indicated elsewhere in the book (see particularly Ch 6) the case of *Marleasing SA v La Comercial Internacional de Alimentacion SA*

10 [1986] 2 CMLR 296 at 300. See also the judgment of the court at paras 11 and 12.
11 Ibid at 304.
12 [1989] ICR 341, [1989] IRLR 161.

(European Court, Case C106/89) may also justify a unitary approach between the Acquired Rights Directive and all UK legislation.

As mentioned above, a potential difference between the Transfer Regulations and the EP(C)A and one which is at first glance less easy to elide is this. Apart from the question of what amounts to a 'business' there is also the issue of how it can be transferred, ie the *mechanics* of transfer (see above). The most common type of business transfer is of course a *sale* of a business as a going concern. But it is not only *sales* that are covered. Section 94 of the EP(C)A, for example, states that the change in ownership referred to thereunder may occur 'by virtue of a sale or other disposition or by operation of law'. It may safely be assumed that a transfer for the purposes of Sch 13 para 17(2) may occur likewise. Regulation 3(1) of the Transfer Regulations also states that a transfer may be by sale or by some other disposition or by operation of law. But it is to be noted that s 94 of the EP(C)A alone refers to a '*change in ownership*'. It has been stressed in the European Court in a number of decisions[13] that the Acquired Rights Directive applies to cases where there is simply a change of employer who has assumed employment obligations towards transferred employees and is not confined to changes of legal ownership. As Hepple and O'Higgins[14] have put it, the emphasis is not on a 'conveyancing' test but on an 'employment' test. So transfers involving a change of *less* than absolute ownership (eg surrenders, grants and assignments of leased businesses etc) are covered by the Transfer Regulations. Again there is a strong argument for the EP(C)A provisions to be construed similarly (and it seems (see later) this view had already been applied to similar cases under Sch 13 para 17(2); the exact wording of s 94 may however cause a problem).[15]

Three further points may be made. First, as mentioned in Part 5, there can be a transfer of *part* of a business or undertaking. EP(C)A Sch 13 para 17(2) makes no reference to a part of a business or undertaking, but s 94 of the EP(C)A does, and it has been held in this regard that s 94 and Sch 13 should be construed uniformly.[16]

---

13 *Foreningen af Arbejdsledere i Danmark v Daddy's Dance Hall A/S* [1988] ECR 739, [1988] IRLR 315; *Berg and Busschers v IM Besselsen* [1990] ICR 396, [1989] IRLR 447; *Landsorganisationen i Danmark v Ny Molle Kro* [1989] ICR 330, [1989] IRLR 37; *P Bork International* [1990] 3 CMLR 701, [1989] IRLR 41.

14 *Encyclopaedia of Labour Relations Law* para 1B 501–516.

15 See *SI (Systems and Instrumentation) Ltd v Grist* [1983] ICR 788, [1983] IRLR 391.

16 *Lord Advocate v De Rosa* [1974] 2 All ER 849, [1974] ICR 480, HL; cf the injustice of an early decision of an industrial tribunal, in *Meadows v J Stanbury Ltd* (1969) 5 ITR 57.

Further, it is expressly provided in the Transfer Regulations (reg 3(1)) that there may be a transfer of an undertaking if a *part* of an undertaking is transferred. The main question here seems to be whether the part of the business or undertaking transferred is, in reality, capable of standing as a separate entity,[17] even if, for the time being when run by the transferor, the part being transferred was integrated with the remaining part for the purposes of administration and efficiency.[18] Generally, it must be said that whether or not carried on separately prior to the transfer the part transferred must have been a recognisable and identifiable part of the whole business carried on by the transferor.[19]

Second, a particular feature of the Transfer Regulations is reg 3(4) which allows discrete transactions to be 'linked' and treated as one transfer, in appropriate circumstances. This is an important anti-avoidance measure, designed to prevent vendors and purchasers artificially fragmenting a business sale into diverse elements none of which, on its own, would be a business transfer. It is discussed in Chapter 6 and is mentioned throughout the book at appropriate junctures. As may be seen from the discussion in this chapter a debate ensues as to whether it covers linked transactions between the same parties or between multiple parties. Judicial opinion (see below) is moving towards the latter, thus strengthening reg 3(4). There is no express equivalent of reg 3(4) in the EP(C)A.

Third, the Transfer Regulations expressly do not apply to 'any undertaking or part of an undertaking which is not in the nature of a commercial venture'.[20] For example, in *Woodcock v Committee for the Time Being of the Friends School, Wigton and Genwise Ltd*[1] a Quaker school of charitable status was held to be an undertaking which was not in the nature of a 'commercial venture', so that the Transfer Regulations did not apply; but conversely, it has been held (obiter) that there can be a transfer of an undertaking which has been run at a loss, in *Hadden v University of Dundee Students Association*[2]. It is important to note that this limitation about the commerciality of the venture in the Transfer Regulations does not

---

17 *G D Ault (Isle of Wight) Ltd v Gregory* (1967) 2 ITR 301.
18 *McCleod v Rostron & Sons Ltd* (1972) 7 ITR 144.
19 *Green v Wavertree Heating and Plumbing Co Ltd* [1978] ICR 928; cf *Newlin Oil Co Ltd v Trafford* [1974] IRLR 205.
20 Regulation 2.
 1 [1986] IRLR 490, EAT; affd [1987] IRLR 98, CA.
 2 [1985] IRLR 449 (given the right facts: there was no business transfer in that case).

expressly apply to the provisions in the EP(C)A.[3] The ramifications of the distinction between a commercial and non-commercial venture (including the problems of privatisation of previously non-commercial activities) are discussed at the end of this chapter.

There is, however, subject to the above points, a fairly broad uniformity of treatment of the meaning of business transfer, whether for the purposes of the EP(C)A or the Transfer Regulations . For that reason it will be helpful to be aware of case law on the EP(C)A (or its predecessor) on the definition of a business transfer, even if it is only the Transfer Regulations which are under consideration. Such authorities are therefore employed as illustrations throughout this chapter.

2 IDENTIFYING BUSINESS TRANSFERS: THE VITAL DISTINCTION BETWEEN ASSET SALES AND DISPOSAL OF A BUSINESS AS A 'GOING CONCERN'

Much of this chapter will be taken up with a discussion of how to identify a business transfer. This question will be vital in practice. As a business transfer means a transfer of a business as a going concern, in the absence of a business transfer there will be an asset sale only. An asset sale, without more, breaks continuity of employment on change of employer and prevents the Transfer Regulations and the relevant provisions of the EP(C)A from applying.[4]

Perhaps a few further points ought to be made at the outset of this discussion. First, it is true that the cases since *Kenmir Ltd v Frizzell*,[5] whatever provision is in question, frequently adopt the test of whether there is a transfer of a 'going concern'. It should not, however, be forgotten that this is a gloss and is not part of any

---

3 See applications in *Ferretti v Southwark and Lambeth Archaeological Projects* COIT 1479/244 *IDS Handbook* 36 p 6; *Robinson v Bournemouth Borough Council* (1970) 5 ITR 100; *Dallow Industrial Properties v Else* and *Curd* [1967] 2 QB 449, [1967] 2 All ER 30, DC per Diplock LJ at 258 (although, on the facts, there was no business transfer, since there was only a transfer of *premises*). See infra, later in this chapter. EP(C)A, s 153(1) states that 'business', for the purposes of the EP(C)A provisions, 'includes a trade or profession and includes *any activity* carried on by a body of persons, whether corporate or unincorporate' (emphasis added). See, however, *Pittman v Davis Build plc (in liquidation)* EAT 122/90 on whether this includes non-commerical activity; see note 1, p 81.

4 See e g *Woodhouse v Peter Brotherhood Ltd* [1972] 2 QB 520, [1972] ICR 186, CA.

5 [1968] 1 All ER 414, [1968] ITR 159.

legislation; use of this phrase should not blinker an industrial tribunal's approach in looking at the situation in the round to assess whether, in all the circumstances, there has been a business transfer. For example, a slavish application of the phrase 'going concern' may not be helpful in all cases and might indeed lead to the wrong result. In *Teesside Times Ltd v Drury*[6] the employer argued that if a transferor was insolvent or about to cease business, the business carried on could not be a 'going concern'. This was rightly rejected. Any such business could be carried on as a going concern by a successor in title to the transferor. Even though the transferor had not made a success of it, it would still be a going concern for these purposes.[7]

Second, it has been decided that the question of whether there is a business transfer is a question of fact for the industrial tribunal to determine.[8] Much will therefore depend upon the evidence produced by the parties and, in cases before industrial tribunals, preparation of the case and proper presentation of the evidence will be all-important either for employers or employees. In view of pronouncements from the Court of Appeal re-asserting that appeals may only be made in this context on points of law[9] it will be difficult successfully to appeal from a finding by an industrial tribunal on the question whether there has been a business transfer. For a successful appeal, it would have to be shown that any finding of fact by the industrial tribunal had given rise to a question of law on the (fairly unusual) bases either that the industrial tribunal had taken into account an irrelevant consideration or not considered a relevant consideration[10] or, perhaps, in the alternative, had arrived at a conclusion that no reasonable tribunal could have arrived at having properly directed itself on the facts (ie that it was

---

6 [1978] ICR 822, EAT; affd [1980] ICR 338, [1980] IRLR 72, CA.

7 Otherwise there could not be a business transfer from a receiver or an ailing company. Of course these are business transfers. In fact, they comprise quite a large proportion of business transfers. See the opinion of the Advocate-General in Case 24/85 *Spijkers v Gebr Benedik Abattoir CV* [1986] 2 CMLR 296 at 298 ECJ. See also chapter 9. This is subject to the view that the Directive does not apply to insolvency by virtue of proceedings under the supervision of the competent judicial authority: *Abels v The Administrative Board of the Bedrijfsvereniging voor de Metaal Industrie en de Electrotechnische Industrie* [1987] 2 CMLR 406. See also *D'Urso v Ercole Marelli Elettromeccanica Generale SpA* [1992] IRLR 136.

8 *Melon v Hector Powe Ltd* [1981] 1 All ER 313, [1981] ICR 43, HL.

9 See e g *O'Kelly v Trusthouse Forte plc* [1984] QB 90, [1983] ICR 728, CA; *Gilham v Kent County Council* (No 2) [1985] ICR 233, [1985] IRLR 18, CA; EP(C)A s 136(1).

10 See e g *British Leyland (UK) Ltd v Swift* [1981] IRLR 91, CA.

perverse).[11] This burden is quite difficult for an appellant to discharge.[12] The Court of Appeal in *Piggott Bros and Co Ltd v Jackson*[13] has recently re-emphasised how limited are the powers of an appellate tribunal or court. Thus, to repeat, presentation of and submission on the facts is extremely important before an industrial tribunal, as a second 'bite at the cherry' may not be allowed.[14]

Finally, an industrial tribunal, it has been held, should concern itself with matters of substance, rather than form.[15] However artificially the transaction may be dressed up, the industrial tribunal may legitimately probe to the root of the matter and remove any obviously inappropriate label that the parties themselves have put on the transaction. It has become increasingly common for business transfers to be described in vending agreements as 'asset sales'. But if, in reality, they are not asset sales but transfers of business, an industrial tribunal may say so. For example, in *HA Rencoule*

---

11 See e g *Global Plant Ltd v Secretary of State for Social Services* [1972] 1 QB 139, [1971] 3 All ER 385.

12 See the strong comments from the Court of Appeal in *UCATT v Brain* [1981] ICR 542, [1981] IRLR 224, CA and *Gilham v Kent County Council (No 2)* [1985] ICR 233, [1985] IRLR 18, A; *Neale v Hereford and Worcester County Council* [1986] ICR 471; *Mannin Management Services Ltd v Ward* (1989) Times, 9 February, CA.

13 [1991] IRLR 309. May LJ, in *Neale v Hereford and Worcester County Council* [1986] ICR 471, [1986] IRLR 168, CA, used the expression 'my goodness, that was certainly wrong' as a test of perversity. This was wryly referred to by the editors of *Harvey on Industrial Relations and Employment Law* as the 'Biggles' test. In *Piggott Bros & Co Ltd v Jackson* [1991] IRLR 309, however, the Court of Appeal criticised that test as carrying a risk that the appellate tribunal might substitute its own view of the fairness of the dismissal. In the opinion of the Court of Appeal: 'A decision of an industrial tribunal can be characterised as "perverse" only if it was not a permissible option. In order to hold that a decision was not a permissible option, the EAT will almost always have to identify a finding of fact which was unsupported by *any* evidence or a clear self-misdirection in law by the industrial tribunal. If it cannot do that, the EAT should re-examine with the greatest care its preliminary conclusion that the decision under appeal was not a permissible option and was therefore perverse. Reasonableness is to be characterised as a mixed issue of fact and law but the factual element predominates.' This decision lessens the opportunity of attacking an industrial tribunal decision on grounds of perversity alone.

14 Rule 10 of the Industrial Tribunals (Rules of Procedure) Regulations 1985, SI 1985/16 allows for a review of an industrial tribunal's decision. But the grounds are extremely limited.

15 Per Widgery J in *Kenmir Ltd v Frizzell* (1968) 3 ITR 159 at 164, and per Widgery CJ in *Huggins v A and J Gordon (Aveley) Ltd* (1971) 6 ITR 164. See also the opinion of the Advocate-General in Case 24/85 *Spijkers v Gebroeders Benedik Abattoir CV* [1986] 2 CMLR 296 at 298, ECJ.

(Joiners and Shopfitters) Ltd v Hunt[16] the parties described the vending transaction as a transfer of assets, but the industrial tribunal decided, on the facts, that there was none the less a business transfer. Today, many business sales are described in legal documentation as 'asset' sales. It is important not to be hoodwinked by this.

3   DISTINGUISHING BETWEEN BUSINESS AND ASSET TRANSFERS IN PRACTICE

Two leading cases are *Woodhouse v Peter Brotherhood Ltd*[17] and *Melon v Hector Powe Ltd.*[18]

Woodhouse concerned a firm called Crossley which made diesel engines. It sold its factory to Brotherhoods who carried on the business of making turbines and spinning machines. As part of the sale arrangements Crossley asked Brotherhoods to complete five unfinished diesel engines for Crossley's customers and Brotherhoods agreed to do this. This work was completed under a contract with Crossley. The applicant employee had worked for Crossley for some considerable period of time and on the sale, went to work for Brotherhoods. For some while he also worked on exactly the same equipment and machines and in the same working environment. Quite understandably, he thought that, since his working environment was virtually uninterrupted, his continuity of employment was unbroken by the transfer. It was held, however, that there had been a simple transfer of assets and not a business transfer and, therefore, for the purposes of a subsequent redundancy claim against

---

16 (1967) 2 ITR 475. An interesting point is whether EP(C)A s 140 could apply to a statement by the parties that there was no transfer, if in reality there was. It provides that with some exceptions 'any provision in *an agreement* (*whether a contract of employment or not*) shall be void in so far as it purports: (a) to exclude or limit the operation of any provision of this Act; or (b) to preclude any person from presenting a complaint to, or bringing any proceedings under this Act before an industrial tribunal'. This is normally assumed to apply to some contract between an employer and employee. But the wording does not seem so restricted. It would be interesting if this could be applied to a false label on a transaction in a vending agreement, if its effect was to impair an employee's statutory rights. At any rate, though, the EAT in *Lumley Insurance Consultants Ltd v Pruddah* EAT 150/83, LEXIS transcript, thought s 140 would apply to a provision in a contract of employment with a transferee if that contract wrongly referred to a break in employment on transfer. See also reg 12 of the Transfer Regulations which similarly makes void any agreement to preclude the operation of regs 5, 8 or 10 '*whether [in] a contract of employment or not*'.

17 [1972] 2 QB 520, [1972] ICR 186, CA.

18 [1981] 1 All ER 313, [1981] ICR 43, HL.

Brotherhoods, he could not bring into account his previous employment with Crossley. Had he known that statutory continuity was interrupted at the time of the transfer he could have made a substantial claim against Crossley at the point of transfer. Tragically, he was totally unaware of this, and was later prevented from doing so as he was time-barred.

In *Melon*, the facts were that Hector Powe Ltd made suits at Dagenham and Blantyre. Hector Powe sold the lease of its Blantyre factory and its machinery to a company called Executex. Hector Powe also transferred some work in progress and even gave an order to Executex to help it on its way. Again the employees who worked in the factory transferred and those who were taken on by Executex continued to work and, to them, it seemed their working environment was uninterrupted. It was held, however, that there was a sale of assets only, not a business transfer.

These cases illustrate that the test applied by the courts is not employee-oriented. It matters not whether the employee himself believes that there is continuity of working environment. An industrial tribunal must look at the mechanics of the transaction and matters of fact and degree in particular cases: the continuity of an employee's working environment itself and the employee's own expectations will not decide the matter.[19]

An important consideration also is the question whether the same economic activities are carried on after, compared with before, the transfer. This test derives from the dicta of the European Court on the Acquired Rights Directive in *Spijkers v Gebr Benedik Abattoir CV*[20] extracted above. Thus, if, after the transfer, the activities are different, this may point to an asset-only sale.[1] A recent example of this approach can be found in *Cook v H Faiman Ltd*.[2] In this case the employees concerned worked in a dress shop. The owner, in financial difficulties, sold the lease to a purchaser for £40,000. There was no assignment of goodwill and the old stock was sold off and not transferred to the transferee of the lease. The new owner took on the employees and began to sell garments too. But there was new stationery, new stock and shopping bags with a new logo and the

---

19 *Woodhouse v Peter Brotherhood Ltd* [1972] 2 QB 520, [1972] ICR 186, CA; *Michael's Travel Ltd v Giraud* EAT 345/85, LEXIS transcript; *Melon v Hector Powe Ltd* [1981] 1 All ER 313, [1981] ICR 43, HL. To be noted also is the similar case of *Sura and Suckra v G Snowball (t/a STR Engineering)* EAT 373/79 (unreported) (LEXIS transcript). See also *Pittman v Davis Build plc (in liquidation)* EAT 122/90.
20 [1986] 2 CMLR 296.
 1 *Woodhouse; Applebee v Joseph Allnatt Centres* EAT 292/80; *Caterleisure Ltd v Transport and General Workers' Union* EAT 182/91.
 2 EAT 10.10.89 IDS Brief 412 January 1990, p 13.

purchaser claimed his business was different from the vendor's: it was more 'up-market'. It was held that a different business was, in reality, being carried on and there was no transfer of a business for the purposes of Sch 13 para 17(2) of the EP(C)A. Of course, the reverse assumption may apply if the activities remain unchanged.[3] Recently, in *Gibson v Motortune Ltd*[4] Wood J suggested the following test:

> 'Upon the sale or purchase of a "business concern" (I seek a neutral phrase) the purchaser will buy the physical tangible assets and premises (freehold or leasehold) but there is something more for which he may be prepared to pay an enhanced price, which is the enhanced value of the business as a whole – the intangible assets; its name; its list of customers; its business connections. The protection of these intangible assets will usually, if not always, be protected by restrictive covenants. I would also expect on the sale of a going concern for the purchaser to take over the credit and debit balances and liabilities. . .'

While this may be a very sound definition of the ideal business transfer it should not be taken as absolute. As a single test it is respectfully submitted that the passage is too demanding. Businesses can be transferred without restrictive covenants and with some of the factors enumerated by Wood J absent. It is therefore to be stressed that not all of these factors will be present in every case and as Wood J said 'no one factor is conclusive'.

The question whether a business transfer has occurred is essentially a question of fact, and so precedents can never be set. Nevertheless, the kind of factors which influence industrial tribunals in deciding between a business transfer and a simple transfer of assets can be suggested.[5] As has been discussed, these should apply for the purposes of the EP(C)A and the Transfer Regulations.

Pertinent factors in a business transfer seem to be as follows.

(a) The sale of machinery, factory premises (freehold or leasehold), stock, equipment, plant, tools and other physical artefacts will not be enough on its own.[6]

---

3 *Modiwear Ltd v Wallis Fashion Group* EAT 535/80.

4 [1990] ICR 740, EAT.

5 Although an industrial tribunal may look at the *facts* and form its *own* conclusion on them subject only to the discussion on appeals above.

6 *Woodhouse v Peter Brotherhood Ltd* [1972] 2 QB 520, [1972] ICR 186, CA; *Melon v Hector Powe Ltd* [1981] 1 All ER 313, [1981] ICR 43, HL; *Austin v AR Clemence (Lanmere Ltd)* (1966) 1 KIR 363, IT; *Dallow Industrial Properties Ltd v Else* [1967] 2 QB 449, [1967] 2 All ER 30; *McLeod v Fisher* (1966) 1 KIR 108 (director of insolvent company buying its assets: no business transfer); *Crompton*

(b) It will not *necessarily* be helpful that the transferee carries on work similar to or the same as the work which was carried on by the transferor, especially if this is done by dint only of a contract between the transferor and the transferee (whether to finish off a transferor's work in progress or for a transferee to undertake a new order at the request of the transferor). In such a case, it can hardly be said, in the light of *Kenmir*, that the transferee is put into the position of running a 'going concern the activities of which he [can] carry on without interruption'.[7] An asset sale is not a business transfer and this would probably not be altered if the transferee were only granted a contract terminable by the transferor.[8]

(c) Transfer of goodwill has traditionally been a very important factor. In many cases it has concluded the question of the difference between a transfer of assets and a transfer of a business.[9] It may be particularly important where the business may not comprise anything apart from goodwill, for example where there are very few, or no, physical assets. Such was the case concerning the transfer of an accountant's practice in Nottingham in *Ward v Haines Watts*[10] where it was held that in a professional practice the goodwill attaching to clients may indeed be the main part of the business. On the facts in that case there was, on that basis, a transfer of a business. But it needs to be stressed that the existence of goodwill on a transfer is only one factor and it would even be possible (although perhaps uncommon) for a business to be transferred even without goodwill.[11] However, in borderline cases, where other factors militate against a business transfer, the absence of goodwill has been a persuasive point against a business transfer as opposed

    v Truly Fair (International) Ltd [1975] ICR 359, [1975] IRLR 250; *Rowlatt v Budden and Harris* (1966) 1 ITR 269.

7 *Kenmir Ltd v Frizzell* [1968] 1 All ER 414, 3 ITR 159 per Widgery J at 164.

8 See again, *Woodhouse v Peter Brotherhood Ltd* [1972] 2 QB 520, [1972] ICR 186; *Melon v Hector Powe Ltd* [1981] 1 All ER 313, [1981] ICR 43, HL.

9 E g *Luckey v Hockley* (1966) 2 ITR 38; *Douglas v Merchants Facilities (Glasgow) Ltd* (1966) 1 ITR 374; *Seymour v Barber and Heron* (1970) 5 ITR 65; *Bonsor v Patara* (1967) 2 ITR 76. See also *Modiwear v Wallis Fashion Group* (1980) EAT 535/80; *Yorke Nettleson and Letheridge v Hartley* (1966) 1 KIR 797.

10 [1983] ICR 231 [1983] IRLR 285, EAT. See also *Douglas v Merchants Facilities (Glasgow) Ltd* (1966) 1 ITR 374, IT (transfer of customer accounts and transfer of business). See the opinion of the Advocate-General in Case 24/85 *Spijkers v Gebroeders Benedik Abattoir CV* [1986] 2 CMLR 296 at 298 ECJ.

11 As in *Tucker v Cox* (1967) 2 KIR 816.

to a mere assets transfer.[12] Some recent cases (particularly regarding licences and franchises (see below)[13] have suggested that it is immaterial whether a franchisor reserves ownership of goodwill on grant of a franchise: a business transfer can still take place on the grant to the franchisee (or on assignment by the franchisee). But this may just be another aspect of the European law rule that a change in absolute *ownership* is not required for a business transfer. It would be going too far to say goodwill is immaterial.[14] Finally, there does not have to be an express assignment of goodwill for there to be a business transfer (although this might be very helpful in determining its existence.)[15]

(d) The adoption by a transferee of a transferor's customers is another helpful indicator towards a business transfer but, again, this is not conclusive. The taking on of a transferor's customers especially with a transferor's assistance may thus indicate a business transfer.[16] On the other hand, a customer may, of course, go over to a transferee of his own volition without the assistance of the transferor and without an assignment of the benefit of a customer or client list from the transferor to the transferee. If this happens, it cannot of itself convert a transfer of assets into a transfer of a business.[17]

(e) Transfer of work in progress may be an indicator of a business transfer.[18] Caution has, however, to be exercised here. There can be cases where work in progress is finished off by a transferee at the request of the transferor, sometimes under a special contract with the transferor. This may not necessarily amount to an *assignment* of such work in progress as the cases of *Woodhouse v Peter Brotherhood Ltd* and *Melon v Hector Powe Ltd* illustrate.[19]

---

12 *Robert Seligman Corpn v Baker* [1983] ICR 770, EAT; *Curtis v A Collett & Sons Ltd* (1966) 1 KIR 370.
13 *LMC Drains Ltd (1) Metro-Rod Services (2) v Waugh* EAT, 5.6.91 (182/90); *Safebid Ltd v Ramiro* EAT 3.5.90 (446/89); see infra.
14 See, e g, *Stirling v Dietsmann Management Systems Ltd*, EAT, 25.6.91 (17/91).
15 *Jeetle v Elster* [1985] ICR 389, [1985] IRLR 227, EAT; *Kenmir Ltd v Frizzell* [1968] 1 All ER 414, [1968] 1 WLR 329; *Luckey v Hockley* (1966) 2 KIR 17.
16 See *Rencoule v Hunt* (1967) 2 ITR 475; *Ward v Haines Watts* [1983] ICR 231, [1983] IRLR 285, EAT; and see *MacDonald v Bull and Patterson* (1966) 1 KIR 734 where customers were sent circulars about the transfer by the vendor; cf *Curtis v A Collett & Sons Ltd* (1966) 1 KIR 370 (no list transferred).
17 *Chapman v Wilkinson* (1968) 2 ITR 39. See also *H A Rencoule (Joiners and Shopfitters) Ltd v Hunt* (1967) 2 ITR 475 (undertaking in vending agreement to introduce customers to transferee).
18 *Rencoule v Hunt* (1967) 2 ITR 475.
19 See above.

(f)   An agreement by the transferor not to compete with the trans-
      feree can mean that there has been a transfer of the transferor's
      business and not just assets.[20] In one sense, the ability to
      compete is inconsistent with an assignment of goodwill. The
      ability to compete is often cited as a factor against transfer of
      goodwill and, so, against transfer of a business.[1](Cf, however,
      the cases on franchises where legal *ownership* of goodwill was
      reserved by a franchisor without prejudice to a business transfer
      on creation or assignment of a franchise, discussed below.)

(g)   Use by a transferee of the transferor's trading name again can
      indicate that the business itself of the transferor has been trans-
      ferred, as could the transfer of trade marks.[2]

(h)   Finally, it may at first seem relevant to this question whether or
      not employees have themselves been transferred to the trans-
      feree along with any physical assets, goodwill and so forth. In
      many respects these human resources, do, in fact, form an
      integral part of a business and in reality may convert a collection
      of physical assets into an undertaking as a going concern. But
      great caution must be exercised here. In many asset sales, again
      such as in the cases of *Woodhouse v Peter Brotherhood Ltd* and
      Melon v Hector Powe Ltd, there will be in practice so tiny a gap
      between successive employments that there may be given an
      impression of a transfer of the workforce. But this impression
      would not, of itself, change the legal nature of what in reality is
      a transfer of assets only, as opposed to a transfer of a business.[3]
      None the less, the mobility of the workforce is a consideration.
      Some cases seem to suggest that if the employees have been
      expressly excluded from the sale then this goes against a busi-
      ness transfer.[4] On the other hand, simply because employees
      have been reserved from the sale of a company's undertaking,
      that will not of itself change the character of the transfer from a

---

20 *Ault v Gregory* (1967) 3 KIR 590, 2 ITR 301.
 1 *Duffen v Fuzzard* EAT 352/83. LEXIS transcript; *Frazer v Munro (Teesside) Ltd*
   IT 68095/85; *Hardy v Jirjis* IT 15260/84. In *Robert Seligman Corpn v Baker* [1983]
   ICR 770 the fact that the former employer was (in theory) able to set up in
   competition with the new concession holder was influential in the EAT's decision
   against a business transfer.
 2 *Bonsor v Patara Ltd* (1966) 2 KIR 23 (no marks transferred: no business
   transfer).
 3 *Woodhouse v Peter Brotherhood Ltd* [1972] 2 QB 520, [1972] ICR 186, CA;
   Crompton v Truly Fair (International) Ltd [1975] ICR 359, [1975] IRLR 250.
 4 Eg *Dhami v Top Spot Night Club* [1977] IRLR 231, EAT; *Angus Jowett & Co v
   NUTGW* [1985] ICR 646, [1985] IRLR 326, EAT.

transfer of a business to a transfer of assets only.[5] But, it seems doubtful whether a transfer of employees *alone* is of itself a business transfer. The transfer of a workforce without more was regarded as something of an imponderable (with some doubt as to whether there would then be a business transfer) recently by Parliament itself. In the privatisation of the dockyards, it saw prudent to provide specifically that a transfer of the services of employees alone should be treated as part of an undertaking capable of being transferred under the Transfer Regulations.[6] The implication is that a transfer of employees alone might not be a business transfer. This also seems to be confirmed by *Banking Insurance and Finance Union v Barclays Bank plc*[7] where redeployment of staff from subsidiaries of Barclays to a service company, formed to provide staff for a new investment bank set up after the 'Big Bang', involved no transfer of a business from the subsidiaries to the service company.[8]

---

5 See e g *Secretary of State for Employment v J Helliwell & Sons* EAT 186/86 (Garland J presiding) LEXIS transcript p 42. It must be remembered, too, that a purported exclusion of employees otherwise covered by reg 5 will be ignored, as it is not possible to contract out of the Transfer Regulations – see reg 12, Ch 5 and see *Foreningen v Daddy's Dance Hall A/S* [1988] ECR 739 discussed in Ch 8.

6 Dockyard Services Act 1986 s 1(4). The government was convinced that the transfer of undertakings involved in privatisation of the dockyards fell within the Transfer Regulations; none less it took on a 'fail-safe' amendment which ensured that the services of employees were, without more to be treated as part of the undertaking transferred as a business. Hansard HC Deb 8 April 1986, col 115 (Mr Norman Lamont).

7 [1987] ICR 495, EAT (although the position may not be absolute – see p 504; and consider the case of a service company – could it be in the 'business' of providing employees' services?).

8 To be contrasted is the recent industrial tribunal decision in *Adams v (1) B & H Healthcare Products Ltd (2) Tatlor Ltd* (1990) IDS Brief 429, September p 3. In this case employees were employed by B & H Healthcare. Its owner formed a new company which became Tatlor Ltd. In 1984 B & H Healthcare sold a company car to Tatlor, and later a stock of equipment. Later still a lease of the premises was assigned from B & H Healthcare to Tatlor. At this stage B & H Healthcare released the workforce which provided services to Tatlor. B & H Healthcare then went into liquidation at the behest of the DSS because it had not kept up with National Insurance payments. When the employees then transferred to Tatlor on the appointment of the liquidator the question was whether their employment was continuous. The IT held that a skilled workforce could be an asset capable of transfer under the Transfer Regulations and so employment was transferred. A number of points need to be made, however. First, this is a tribunal decision only and will therefore depend on its facts. Second, *quaere* whether, because a workforce is an 'asset', that per se amounts to a transfer of a 'business' or part. Third, a safer ground might have been to attempt to link the relevant disposals and transfers to form a linked transaction under reg 3(4) and thereby treat them as one (assuming this was the intent of the parties, of course, about which we do not know).

4 PROBLEM CASES: FARMS, LEASES, FRANCHISES, LICENCES AND CONTRACTS

In this section some of the recurrent grey areas in the distinction between business transfers and asset sales are examined in detail.

(i) Introduction

A particularly difficult problem in transfers of employment is the legal position on an assignment or surrender by an employer whose own security or interest in his business is somewhat precarious. A large number of employers are not absolute 'owners' of their 'business'. They may be tenants, contractors, concessionaires, franchisees or licensees. This occurs commonly in the brewery trade, in petrol station management, in the growing area of licensing of space within large department stores (the idea of 'shops within shops'), in the similar growing number of franchised businesses and in the general area of contracting out of the provision of ancillary services.[9] In all these cases, the ultimate owner of the site, business, space or opportunity lets or licenses it, contracts it out or, simply, delegates the management thereof to a smaller business, even as small as the one-man company or sole trader who, in turn, himself becomes an employer when he engages staff to run the contract.

Confusing problems can occur for affected employees upon the termination of their employer's franchise, tenancy, contract or licence. This might occur through contractual provision or effluxion of time in which case the franchisor, lessor or landlord may either re-assume employment obligations, or alternatively, regrant the operation of the business to a new franchisee, tenant or licensee. Or it may be that a franchise, contract or licence is assigned (if this is possible) directly from the franchisee, contractor or licensee to another franchisee, contractor or licensee without the legal intervention of the franchisor. When the employee continues with the successor or successors of the original employer, will the business transfer legislation apply to protect him?

There may, in these cases, be either a bipartite transaction or tripartite transaction. In the first, our contractor, licensee or franchisee surrenders, assigns, sells, or disposes of his interest direct to another. In the second situation there will be a surrender of an interest from the first employer to the grantor of the interest and a

---

9 See J Adams and K V Pritchard Jones *Franchising: Practice and Precedents in Business Format Franchising* (2nd edn, 1987) and the formation of the British Franchise Association (discussed in *Adams and Pritchard Jones*). See the cases at pp 66 et seq. Franchised businesses can range from national brand names such as 'Dyno-rod' and 'Wimpy' to more bespoke, and smaller, arrangements.

regrant from the grantor to a new employer. In these cases, is there a transfer of a business from the first employer to the grantor and a second transfer from the grantor to the second employer? Or alternatively, if the period of time over which this regrant takes place is very small and the involvement of the ultimate owner only technical, should there be deemed to be a direct transfer between the outgoing concessionaire and the incoming concessionaire? Diagrammatically the two situations may be seen in the figures on pp 60–61. It can be seen that bipartite cases (Figures 1 and 2) are considerably simpler than tripartite cases (Figure 3). But the problem for the lawyer is the same: has there been a transfer of a business as a going concern from one person to another and, if so, when, and to whom?

Finally it is submitted that cases in this area pose two distinct issues.

(1) Was there anything amounting to a business or part to transfer?

(2) If so, does it matter whether there was no legal change in absolute ownership, but simply, in effect, a change in management instead, and, if so, to what degree?

These should be borne in mind when examining this area. It must be recognised however that the two issues are hard to separate in practice and are often not separately examined in business transfer decisions. An attempt will be made to answer these questions in detail as they arise in this chapter.

(ii) Preliminary considerations

A reminder of the basic test in these cases of what constitutes a transfer of a business is necessary here. In *Kenmir Ltd v Frizzell*[10] the court stated that, in the end, the essential consideration is whether the effect of the transaction is to put the transferee in possession of a 'going concern', the activities of which he can carry on without interruption.[11] As has been discussed, this is a question of fact for the industrial tribunal.[12] But, as has been seen above,

---

10 [1968] 1 All ER 414, 3 ITR 159.

11 (1968) 3 ITR 159 at 164. See above.

12 See eg *Melon v Hector Powe Ltd* [1981] 1 All ER 313, [1981] ICR 43, HL. Throughout this chapter we concentrate mainly on these general principles, ie whether there has been a transfer of a business as a going concern. But a few significant problem cases are expressly highlighted. It is to be stressed, though, that these are constantly being added to. Competitive tendering in local government is one example (see below). Recent awards of the independent television franchises is another. In atypical cases not expressly covered by this book, it is appropriate to refer to the general principles here set out.

there are important factors that may be taken into account in individual cases. These include the identity of the business before and after the transaction, whether goodwill was transferred, whether there remained any contractual right for the transferor to terminate the transferee's business, whether the trading name was transferred, whether work in progress and customers were transferred and so forth.[13] In short, factors relevant to whether there has been a transfer of a business generally are equally apposite here. For example, goodwill has commonly been regarded as an important, albeit not conclusive, consideration in franchise and licence cases.[14]

One problem here, though, is that in cases of surrenders of licences and franchises to the licensor or franchisor, or even in the case of apparently direct assignments from one franchisee/licensee to another franchisee/licensee, there may be no transfer of goodwill from one employer to another. This is because, it is argued, goodwill always remains vested in the franchisor, who never parts with it. On this analysis the giving up or even transfer of the licence/franchise might involve only a giving up/transfer of assets to another and this does not amount to a transfer of a business as a going concern.[15] But on the other hand, more recently it has been held that, strictly speaking, it should not matter if absolute ownership of goodwill is reserved by the franchisor or licensor as long as other factors are consistent with a business transfer.[16] The true position is more complex than it may, at first, seem and there can, it is submitted, given appropriate facts, often be a business transfer in these atypical situations. It may be helpful to categorise some typical transactions in this area and look at how they are treated.

(iii) Farming and licensed premises

(a) Farmers

At first glance, dispositions of farms seem only to involve a transfer of land or other assets. But in spite of an early decision to this effect

---

13 See above.
14 *Robert Seligman Corpn v Baker* [1983] ICR 770, EAT; *Modiwear v Wallis Fashion Group* EAT 535/80 LEXIS transcript; *Rastill v Automatic Refreshment Services Ltd* [1978] ICR 289, EAT: and in other cases: *Kenmir Ltd v Frizzell* [1968] 1 All ER 414, 3 ITR 159; *Rencoule v Hunt* (1967) 2 ITR 475; *Ault v Gregory* (1967) 2 ITR 301; *Ward v Haines Watts* [1983] ICR 231, [1983] IRLR 285, EAT.
15 See *Woodhouse v Peter Brotherhood Ltd* [1972] 1 All ER 1047, [1972] ICR 186.
16 See e g *LMC Drains Ltd and Metro Rod Services Ltd v Waugh* [1991] 3 CMLR 172, EAT, discussed in the text, infra.

in *Bandey v Penn*[17] the courts began to be willing to find a business transfer on such a disposition. In *Lloyd v Brassey*,[18] Mr Brassey farmed a smallholding employing two workers. One of these was the appellant Mr Lloyd. Mr Brassey sold the land and buildings to a purchaser. Subsequently, the livestock and deadstock were put up for auction sale together with some of the equipment relating to the farm and a Mr Barlow purchased part of these. He then began to farm the business and kept on Mr Lloyd. Mr Lloyd claimed a redundancy payment from Mr Brassey to which, of course, he would not be entitled if there had been a transfer of a business from Mr Brassey to the purchaser, Mr Barlow. It was held there was a transfer of a business and that Mr Lloyd was not entitled to his redundancy payment. This was so despite the fact that there was no express assignment of goodwill. In the opinion of Lord Denning MR, the *business* of farming was inextricably bound up with the land and buildings on which the farm was built. Accordingly, there was a transfer of a business. Lord Denning MR said that the essence of the business of farming is the essence of cultivating land irrespective of the transfer of goodwill or the transfer of stock, for 'the livestock and deadstock are only ancillary to the business of the farm. They are not the essence of it. The essence is the land, together with the buildings.'[19]

It is, of course, important here to note that Mr Brassey *owned* the farm which was transferred to Mr Barlow. As such the case is not direct authority on whether a transfer by a tenant farmer to an assignee would be a transfer of a going concern. Indeed, in *Bandey v Penn* the court held that a transfer by one tenant farmer to another was *not* a business transfer. But Lord Denning MR in *Lloyd v Brassey* thought *Bandey v Penn* should be overruled, and seemed to consider his remark that disposal of an interest in a farm was a business transfer was applicable whether a freehold owner *or* tenant was the transferor.[20] This should be the case, *a fortiori*, nowadays, under the Transfer Regulations (see below).

17 [1968] 1 All ER 1187, 3 ITR 245.
18 [1969] 2 QB 98, 4 ITR 100. See also *Robinson v Temporal* COIT 1458/84 (repossession of a shop); *Parylak v Sutton* COIT 19836/85 (reversion of a lease).
19 [1969] 2 QB 98, 4 ITR 100 at 103.
20 Ibid (although it is true that Russell and Salmon LJJ confined their analysis to whether in this case (ie a transfer from freehold farmer) there had been a change of ownership of a business, ie a business transfer as opposed to a sale of assets: ibid at 104 and 105 respectively).

(b) Licensed premises

Employees of public house tenants or managers are sometimes employed by the tenant or manager and *not* by the brewery company concerned. What is the position of employees on change-over of employer here? In fact, the decision in *Lloyd v Brassey* was extended in a case concerning licensed public house premises in *Young v Daniel Thwaites & Co Ltd*.[1] Here Mr Young had been employed by the tenant of an hotel owned by the respondent company, Daniel Thwaites & Co Ltd, since March 1958. In January 1976 the tenant surrendered his tenancy to the respondents who from that date carried on the business themselves. Mr Young continued to be employed in the hotel by the respondents in the same capacity as previously until his dismissal by them in October 1976. Mr Young sued for unfair dismissal and for the purposes of calculating seniority for the basic award for unfair dismissal claimed that the period of employment with the tenant should be counted towards the period of employment with the respondent, in other words that there had been a transfer of a business from the tenant to the respondent in January 1976. The respondents argued that there could be no transfer here since all that had happened was that the employer's reversionary interest had fallen into possession. Mr Young's case was, however, that, because of the particular nature of the activity carried on there was a transfer of a business as a going concern. The EAT found in favour of Mr Young and in doing so applied the principle in *Lloyd v Brassey*, regarding the transfer of licensed premises as analogous to the transfer of a farming business; and so there was a transfer of a business as a going concern from one person to another.

This was applied in *Cummings v Acosta*,[2] where there was a transfer of a business as a going concern when the brewery (Whitbreads) took over management of a pub called 'The King's Arms', Cookham, from their erstwhile tenant.

Both *Young v Daniel Thwaites* and *Cummings v Acosta* represent the sequence in Figure 2 below, with a transfer from B to A and (if there is a transfer of a business as a going concern) a transfer of the rights of employees from B to A.

More difficult are the cases shown in Figures 1 and 3. In these cases, is there a transfer of a business first from B to A and then a second transfer from A to C? Or is there a direct transfer from B to C? Both are possible. To some extent it may depend on how technical or substantial the involvement of A is in the sequence of

1 [1977] ICR 877, EAT.
2 EAT 149/84 LEXIS transcript.

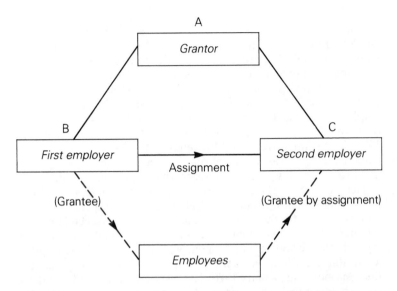

Figure 1 *Assignment by franchisee/licensee/grantee to incoming franchisee/licensee/ grantee with no (or only technical) involvement by franchisor/licensor/grantor*

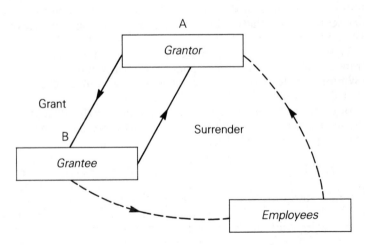

Figure 2 *Surrender by or transfer from original employer to franchisor/licensor/ grantor*

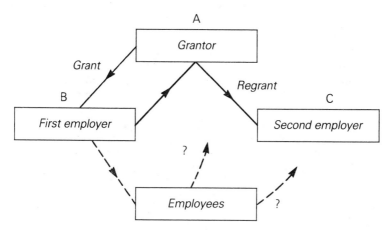

Figure 3 *Change of employer involving more than a technical intervention of the grantor in the destination of the activity from B to C. (See cases in the text on whether there will be two transfers, one from B to A and another from A to C, or whether a broad approach will allow for a direct transfer from B to C.)*

events. For example, if B runs a corner shop under his own name, as a thriving concern, and wants to sell to C, he may if he is a tenant of the premises at which the business is carried on, need to involve A to consent to the assignment of those premises to C. But that may be purely technical; for the business may be the shop, rather than the premises. In reality there should be a direct transfer from B to C. How does this work in our farm and licensed premises cases?

As to farming, in *Lloyd v Brassey* the point was not in issue. But Lord Denning MR seemed to imply, at least, that on a sale by an outgoing tenant to an incoming tenant there might be a direct transfer from tenant to tenant, when he said:

> 'When the land is occupied by a tenant farmer, who goes out, and a new tenant farmer comes in, there is a change in the ownership of the business, namely the business of farming that particular land.'[3]

The remarks are, of course, obiter.[4]

In the case of licensed premises, it will all depend on the facts. But the answer, in practice, is that the intervention of the brewery (A) *is* often purely technical and is, depending on the facts, often regarded

---

3 (1969) 4 ITR 100 at 103.
4 The other members of the court did not concern themselves with this point – see note 20 on p 59 above.

so. Very often a tenant of a public house runs not only the pub but also a catering activity and provides other amenities. If nothing else, he can transfer that aspect, and that may be *direct* without the intervention of the landlord. In *McClennan v Cody*,[5] on the change of tenancy of the 'St Nicholas Arms', Carlisle, there was held to be a transfer of a business from one outgoing tenant to another (i e from B to C in Figure 1). Of course, as stated, brewery companies these days do not operate solely under tenancy arrangements. They often, and increasingly, operate through managed houses, whereby a manager of the pub runs the public house under a contract of employment with the brewery. Often, bar staff are the brewery's responsibility, irrespective of change of manager but, sometimes, employment obligations are those of the manager. The above principles about transfer of employment were applied to the case of a change of pub manager in *Cartwright v Norton*,[6] a case under the Transfer Regulations. There the Swan Hotel, a public house, had a separate catering side to it which was run by the manager, Mr Price. The employee, Mrs Cartwright, was employed as a chef. Eventually Mr Price was replaced by the brewery's choice of another manager, Mr Norton. Mrs Cartwright remained in employment at the pub. It was held that the business had been transferred and, accordingly, any claim had to be made against Mr Norton and not Mr Price. There was still a transfer of a business from one manager to another here even though the outgoing manager, according to the facts of the case, 'left or was dismissed' and the brewery 'necessarily acquired . . . the goodwill attached to the business previously carried on by the [outgoing manager]'.[7] But the EAT ignored the intervention of the brewery, saying:

> 'When the brewery then enabled [the new manager] to carry on that business, by giving him presumably the licence to run the catering on the premises and to use the catering equipment there, they were putting [the new manager] in a position to take advantage of the business previously being conducted by [the old manager]. Therefore although there was no direct transfer from [the old manager] to [the new manager] the removal of [the old manager] and the engagement on the terms we have mentioned of [the new manager] effected of necessity a transfer of goodwill of the catering business from [the old manager] to [the new manager].'[8]

---

5 EAT 14/86 LEXIS transcript.
6 EAT 91/82 LEXIS transcript.
7 EAT 91/82 LEXIS transcript, although the finding of transfer of goodwill was doubted in *Robert Seligman Corpn v Baker* [1983] ICR 770 at 777.
8 Ibid.

Thus, depending on the facts, farming and licensed premises cases may often involve business transfers on change of employer. Where there is a change-over of tenants or managers, this (although it again must be stressed this depends on the facts) may even be a direct transfer from tenant to tenant or manager to manager if the involvement of the landlord or owner was nothing more than technical.

Finally, case law of the European Court supports the approach implicit in these decisions that a transfer of absolute ownership is not required in a business transfer (at least for the purposes of the Transfer Regulations). All that is needed under the Acquired Rights Directive (and hence the Transfer Regulations) is a change in the natural or legal person responsible for operating the undertaking and who adopts employment obligations in respect of the workforce.[9] This case law is discussed later. The broad interpretations in the decisions on tenancies and management of licensed premises and petrol stations etc seem consistent with, and are underpinned by, this European case law. A recent case has expressly dealt with transfers between incoming and outgoing licencees where the licensor retained absolute ownership. In *Safebid Ltd v Ramiro*[10] X owned premises in Regent Street, London, which were used as a discothèque and club. A lease was granted by X to Y to enable Y to carry on the business. There was an agreement whereby X expressly reserved ownership of goodwill and the trade name. That licence was terminated and a new licence granted to another company. It was held there was a transfer of a business between successive transferees notwithstanding there was a reservation of goodwill and absolute ownership.

---

9 *Foreningen af Arbejdsledere i Danmark v Daddy's Dance Hall A/S* [1988] IRLR 315; *Berg and Busschers v IM Besselsen* [1989] IRLR 447; *Landsorganisationen i Danmark v Ny Molle Kro* [1989] ICR 330, [1989] IRLR 37; *P Bork International A/S v Foreningen af Arbejdsledere i Danmark* [1990] 3 CMLR 701, [1989] IRLR 41. The Acquired Rights Directive is expressed to apply only to transfers 'as a result of a legal transfer or merger', arguably contemplating a contractual or other arrangement. Arguably cases like *Cartwright v Norton* seem to go even further than this as no legal relationship seems to have existed between transferor and transferee but none the less this was not essential for a business transfer. This was confirmed as correct recently by the EAT in *Caterleisure Ltd v TGWU* EAT 182/91 (see also *Humphreys v Co-ordinated Cleaning Ltd*, EAT 197/91). On the other hand the absence of a contractual link *might* count as a factor against a business transfer, given appropriate surrounding facts: *Caterleisure; Humphreys*.

10 EAT 3/5/90 (446/89) 105 Brief 427, August 1990, p 13. See also, in the context of franchises, *LMC Drains Ltd and Metro Rod Services Ltd v Waugh* IDS Brief 449/July 1991 EAT 5.6.91 (182/90) where formal ownership of goodwill was reserved by the franchisor but disposals by franchisees none the less amounted to business transfers.

(iv) Franchises, contracts and licences

Writing in 1980, Professor Grunfeld asserted: 'a franchise is not . . . "a business" '.[11] There are indeed a large number of cases in which the change of employer who operates a commercial franchise or contract has not involved a transfer of a business. For example in *Port Talbot Engineering Co Ltd v Passmore*[12] the appellant was an engineering company which maintained a plant belonging to the Steel company of Wales. It did so under a renewable contract. The employee was employed by the appellant and when the appellant's contract was not renewed he was taken on by the appellant's successor. It was held that there was no transfer of a business; the appellant itself had nothing to transfer. Other cases in which this view was taken include *McKinney v McCaig, Paisley & Melville*;[13] *Bumstead v John L Cars Ltd*[14] and *Olah v Trusthouses Ltd*.[15] Execution of services under a sub-contract pure and simple will, it is submitted, often fail to amount to the activity of running a business. Another good example is contract cleaning.[16]

And more recently, in *Robert Seligman Corpn v Baker*,[17] a case under the Transfer Regulations, there was also no transfer of a business in a not dissimilar situation, i e a concession. The facts were as follows. In recent years Debenhams has operated a system of 'shops within a shop'. In other words, certain concerns have been allowed to run particular services within the store as concerns in themselves, but under Debenhams' roof. This obviously has similarities with the franchise system (although it is not on all fours). In the present case, Debenhams granted a concession to Seligmans to run a ladies' hairdressing business at one of their stores in Romford. This concession was terminated and regranted to another company, Roband Investments Ltd, with effect from Monday 21 June. The applicant was employed as a manageress with Seligmans and was re-engaged by Robands when Seligmans dropped out of the picture. On 29 June the applicant was dismissed. She claimed a redundancy payment from both Seligmans and Robands, and the question concerned who was liable to pay this compensation. An industrial

---

11 *The Law of Redundancy* (2nd edn) p 323. The statement is repeated in the 3rd edn (1989) at p 219.
12 [1975] ICR 234, [1975] IRLR 156.
13 (1966) 1 ITR 240, IT.
14 (1967) 2 ITR 137, IT.
15 (1967) 2 KIR 515, IT.
16 See *Humphreys v Co-ordinated Cleaning Ltd* EAT 197/91, LEXIS transcript (change-over of contractors engaged to clean the National Westminster Bank's offices in Eastgate, City of London, did not involve a business transfer).
17 [1983] ICR 770, EAT.

tribunal found that there had been no transfer of an undertaking from Seligmans to Robands and so, if anyone was liable, Seligmans were (and the employee was still in time to claim from Seligmans). Seligmans appealed to the EAT. There, the case of *Cartwright v Norton*[18] was distinguished. In the present case there were insufficient ingredients amounting to a business to transfer. Essentially, all that had been transferred to Robands from Seligmans through Debenhams were assets. There was no relevant goodwill to transfer. The most pertinent goodwill had always belonged to Debenhams, the host store, rather than the 'store within a store'. The same result has occurred in other retail concession situations. In one industrial tribunal case,[19] the giving up of a concessionary butchery unit within a supermarket to Gateway did not amount to a business transfer. But it all, of course, depends on the facts. In the latter case relevant factors included the relative lack of individual identity of the concessionary butcher – a customer using the supermarket buying meat might have assumed the butcher belonged to Gateway. The meat was paid for at the main supermarket till and the name of the butcher was not prominently displayed. The facts of *Robert Seligman Corpn v Baker*, too, indicate that the first instance industrial tribunal considered similar factors (the customer might refer to having his or her hair styled at Debenhams).

As this is a question of fact, it need not be assumed that a case like *Robert Seligman Corpn v Baker* can *never* involve a business transfer. Industrial tribunals as arbiters of fact have, on several occasions, found business transfers on a change of employer whose only security is under a contract or a licence. The point is that in a case like *Robert Seligman Corpn v Baker*[20] it may often be extremely difficult to point to a transfer; but this does not mean to say it is impossible.

To be contrasted with *Robert Seligman*, for example, is the case of *Mannin Management Services Ltd v Ward*,[1] where a contract to manage a shopping centre was held by an industrial tribunal to have involved a transfer of a 'trade or business or undertaking' for the purposes of Sch 13 para 17(2) to the EP(C)A. The Court of Appeal declined to reverse this conclusion. (But it should be noted that the court was dealing with an industrial tribunal decision with which it was reluctant to interfere unless perverse. It should not be taken, therefore, as a decisive ruling simply because of the involvement of

---

18 EAT 91/82 LEXIS transcript.
19 *Frazer v Munro (Teesside) Ltd* IT 6809/85, cited in *IDS Handbook* 36, p 37.
20 [1983] ICR 770, EAT.
1 (1989) Times, 9 February.

the Court of Appeal. All of these cases depend on their facts.[2]) And in *Journey's Friend Ltd v Hayes*[3] an employer who ran a gift shop under a licence from an hotel was replaced by a licensee. It was held there was a business transfer; in contrast to *Robert Seligman* the licensee was ultimately responsible for profits and losses, paid nothing other than rent to the hotel, and had separate customer goodwill.

On the other hand, as already suggested, the emphasis may be shifting away from saying that transfer of absolute ownership of goodwill is necessary. In both *Safebid v Ramiro*, discussed above, and *LMC Drains Ltd and Metro Rod Services Ltd v Waugh*, discussed below, the licensor and franchisor respectively had retained formal ownership of goodwill. But this did not prevent a transfer from licensees/franchisees when they gave up their licence and franchise.

Apart from the question of transfer of ownership of goodwill (a factor now diminished by more recent cases), the fact that contracts, licences and franchises have provisions for termination by the grantor is a difficult problem especially when one remembers the words of Widgery J in *Kenmir v Frizzell* to the effect that the transferee must be able to carry on without interruption. This, of course, was why the finishing of work in progress by Executex for Hector Powe Ltd in *Melon v Hector Powe* was not as a result of a transfer from Hector Powe to Executex of a business as a going concern. It was as a result of a terminable contract to perform services. Here again, though, the mere fact that there is a power to terminate the relationship between the grantor and the grantee may not be fatal. In *Rastill v Automatic Refreshment Services Ltd*[4] a catering company took over the running of a works canteen under an exclusive licence. This was held to be a business transfer and it was not fatal that there was a power to terminate the licence. Also, in *Cartwright v Norton*, the EAT did not seem to think it material whether the outgoing tenant of a pub had 'left' or was 'dismissed', that is to say whether the contract was easily terminable by either party. And finally (although these are only industrial tribunal decisions), there have been cases where a Wimpy and a Dyno-Rod

---

2 Cf the industrial tribunal decision in *Cox v Donaldsons Property Management/ Fordgate Western Properties Ltd* COIT 2064/216, where Mannin was distinguished on the facts; see also *Millin v Elmstar Ltd* COIT 00476/90/LS/A (management agreement to manage a power house for a refinery not a business); cf however *Lumley Insurance Consultants Ltd v Pruddah* EAT 150/83: transfer of credit insurance service held to be a relevant transfer under the Transfer Regulations.

3 EAT 707/84, LEXIS transcript.

4 [1978] ICR 289, EAT.

franchise has changed hands and there has been assumed to be a business transfer.[5]

The position of employees employed by employers who hold under-concessions, licences and franchises seems, in many cases, precarious if only by reason of the atypical nature of their employer's own security of tenure. But as franchising, in particular, seems to be an increasingly popular mode of carrying on business[6] and because more and more employees will as a result be engaged by franchisees, it is to be hoped that tribunals and courts will be willing to strive to find factors tending to show a carrying on of a business by a franchisee capable of transfer as a going concern. This may also be helped by developments in European law, discussed below.

Finally, as will be seen from the detailed discussion later in this chapter, the movement away from the requirement of a change of absolute ownership on a business transfer means that as long as the activity can be characterised as a business or part of a business, it should not matter if there is no outright transfer of title to it. The surrender of a tenancy or licence is a good example of this. Also, the influence of European law and the confirmation that a change of absolute ownership is not required under the transfer of under-takings law (see below) should remove many of the doubts pre-viously expressed that franchise change-overs do not involve business transfers.

This is illustrated by probably the first franchise case to take into account some significant recent European Court cases (see below) on the subject. In *LMC Drains Ltd and Metro Rod Services Ltd v Waugh*[7] the EAT decided a case on transfer of employment between successive franchisees that may be influential in this area. Metro Rod Services Ltd had developed a system and service for drain maintenance. Metro Rod licensed this business to TR to operate in the north-east. Mr Waugh was recruited by TR as a service engineer. In June 1988 he was informed that TR's business was being transferred to another company C. He transferred his employment to C. In March 1989 Metro Rod granted a new fran-chise for the same territory to LMC. Mr Waugh duly transferred his employment to LMC. He was then dismissed. To claim unfair dismissal it was necessary for him to count service with all three franchisees in order to acquire two years' service. The EAT noted that the franchisor retained a great deal of control. For example,

---

5 *Lane v Dyno-Rod*; *Hardy v Jirjis* IT 15260/84 (Wimpy), both cited and discussed in *IDS Handbook* 36 pp 72, 37.

6 See *Adams and Pritchard Jones*.

7 *IDS Brief* 449/July 1991 p 3; EAT 5.6.91 (182/90).

franchisees were obliged to obtain a standard employment agreement from all employees and all goodwill generated in the territory during the term of the franchise agreement was to be vested exclusively in Metro Rod. It was held that on each change of franchisee, there was a transfer of an undertaking. It did not matter whether the transfer involved the intervention of the franchisor (by surrender to him and regrant to another) or whether there was a direct transfer between franchisees. It is obviously important to note that goodwill at all times expressly remained with the franchisor. Notwithstanding this, the franchisees were able to transfer 'undertakings'. This case, along with the case of *Safebid Ltd v Ramiro*[8] discussed above, casts some doubt on the decision in *Robert Seligman Corpn v Baker*[9] especially as retention of goodwill (even if not by express agreement) was thought by the EAT in *Robert Seligman* to be quite an important factor *against* a business transfer.

In summary, pure sub-contracting does not ordinarily involve a business transfer. Grant or transfer of a licence or franchise often will, depending on the facts. As to franchises in particular, to contrast with the quote from Professor Grunfeld's work on redundancy with which this section opened, Adams and Pritchard Jones in *Franchising: Practice and Precedents in Business Format Franchising* state:

> 'Clearly, whether a business exists to be transferred will be a matter for the tribunals to assess, but it is submitted that in the great majority of business format franchises a tribunal is likely to find that a business did exist to transfer.'[10]

It is respectfully suggested that this, in preference, is a correct statement of the law, in the light now of the case law of the European Court referred to above and discussed below.

(v) Petrol stations

A similar case occurs when the manager/licensee/tenant of a petrol station hands over either to the petrol company or to a new manager/licensee/tenant. This will much more commonly be a business transfer although this again depends on the facts (and on how substantial the interest of the transferring employer). This is because it is relatively common for there to be sufficient characteristics of a business to exist in relation to the management of the

---

8 *IDS Brief* 427/August 1990. p 13; EAT 3.5.90 (446/89).
9 [1983] ICR 770.
10 Para 7–047.

station by a licensee. When management changes hands, therefore, there is likely to be a business transfer (subject to the facts of each case).[11]

But it is again not clear, in a tripartite case, whether there is, upon the surrender of the contract from B (its grantee) to A (its grantor) a transfer of a business from B to A, and, if there is a regrant from A to C (a new grantee), a *second* transfer from B to C (Figure 3). In *Premier Motors (Medway) Ltd v Total Oil Great Britain Ltd*[12] the EAT thought there was a transfer from B to A, though in that case A had no real desire in practice to run a business at all and bought the business only for as long as it took to find a licensee to run it. None the less, A was a transferee of a business, however technical this was. Thus, if there was an incoming tenant there could be a second transfer from A to C (although in *Premier Motors* itself there was no 'relevant' transfer under the Transfer Regulations from A to C).

As with the case of transfers of licensed premises, such a tripartite analysis is cumbersome and sometimes over-technical. The EAT in *Robert Seligman Corpn v Baker* (obiter) was not unreceptive to the possibility that it was possible for there to be a transfer of a business from first licensee to second licensee (ie B to C in Figure 1) even when there was an indirect transfer from the first licensee to the second through a third party. In such cases, in reality, there could be a transfer from licensee to licensee, so long as the first licensee has something to transfer, ie a business and not merely assets. The EP(C)A and the Transfer Regulations are silent on this point. In the case of the Transfer Regulations, in areas of ambiguity, resort should be had to the terms of the Acquired Rights Directive (EEC Council Directive 77/187). Browne-Wilkinson J said:[13]

---

11 It might be thought that developments in this area are new. Not so: there are a number of (tribunal) decisions on the EP(C)A (or its predecessor) where transfers in such circumstances were found: see e g *Hughes v Selfridges* (1976) COIT 346/50; *Bell v Thwaites and Matthews* (1974) COIT 272/71 (cited and discussed in *IDS Brief Supplement* (17 November 1977) pp 26, 27); *Winter v Deepsawin Garages Ltd* (1969) 4 ITR 162, IT, change-over of ownership of a petrol station including transfer of the name of the service station (the 'Dorchester Service Station'). Of these earlier decisions, in *Altcorse Ltd v Orrell* (1968) 3 ITR 321 it was held that a transfer of a licence of a petrol station was a transfer of assets only. But this is too dogmatic. This particular decision was disapproved in *Lloyd v Brassey* by Lord Denning MR (1969) 4 ITR 100 at 103. All of these situations depended, of course, on their facts. Nowadays, transfers of licences of petrol stations are likely to be transfers of businesses. This is because, as a matter of fact, their activities are likely to amount to a carrying on of businesses by licensees.

12 [1984] ICR 58, [1983] IRLR 471, EAT.

13 [1983] ICR 770 at 773.

'At first sight the directive does not appear to impose any requirement as to *how* the transferor ceased to own the business or *how* the transferee became the owner: the directive seems to concentrate on the de facto change in ownership rather than the means whereby that change was brought about.'

A similar approach in the context of petrol stations was taken by *Smith v Streatley Garages Group and Sealand Petroleum Co Ltd*,[14] an industrial tribunal case. There, BP Oil were owners of a self-service filling station. Streatley were holders of a licence to run it but gave it up and BP Oil granted a new licence to Sealand. Mrs Smith, a manageress, went over to the new licensee. It was found that there was a transfer of an undertaking from Streatley to Sealand. The involvement of BP was to be ignored; there was no gap in trading.

Also in *Norris (trading as Little Brickhill Service Station) v Bedwell*[15] the EAT thought there was a business transfer between the outgoing tenant of a petrol station and the incoming petrol station tenant. Although Chevron Oil UK Ltd held the lease and there was a prohibition against assignment of the lease, oil, cutlery, crockery and equipment were sold by tenant to tenant and the EAT thought that there was a business to transfer from tenant to tenant. This contrasts with *Premier Motors* when the EAT thought there was no direct transfer from B to C (see above). But different conclusions can be arrived at by different tribunals as this is a question of fact (and, of course, there does not seem to have been contact between B and C in *Premier Motors* as there was in *Norris*). The EAT said in *Norris*, in favour of finding a basic bipartite transfer as opposed to a tripartite one:

'The reality of the position in this case is this: Mr Bedwell was carrying on a business of running a petrol station as a tenant. He wished to dispose of that business. He was not permitted by the terms of the lease to transfer the lease directly to the purchaser and so the lease had to be surrendered to the lessor . . . this is really nothing more than the transfer of a lease as machinery to get the purchaser on to the premises. This is no different from the case of a shopkeeper who wants to sell his business but cannot do so because of a covenant restricting his power to deal with the lease and transfer the lease directly to the purchaser. What he does, is to surrender the lease to the lessor and then, a lease having been transferred to the transferee, the vendor of the business simply sells it to his purchaser.'[16]

---

14 COIT 3382 4/83.
15 EAT 875/83 (President, Tudor Evans J) LEXIS transcript.
16 EAT 875/83 per Tudor Evans J.

(vi) **Bipartite and tripartite transfers: an overview**

There is no certainty, from the above discussion, about whether there can be a transfer directly from B to C in our diagrams in these cases even if there is a transfer of a business as a going concern to anyone at all. Some tribunals have been sympathetic to a view that technicalities should be avoided and the intervention of A ignored. But this depends on the facts and cannot be assumed to be the situation in every case. On the whole, the position is unsatisfactory, not least for the employees involved. Tripartite transactions of this nature cause confusion as to who the proper respondent should be. A well-advised employee will name all possible respondents. Unfortunately, not all employees are so advised. An industrial tribunal case, *Hansford v W Mumford Ltd and Graham Evans*[17] illustrates the possible injustice. On these facts the business went from B to A to C. It was found that there was no relevant transfer within the meaning of the Transfer Regulations from either B to C or A to C, only from B to A. A effected the dismissal. A was therefore liable for the compensation involved. The applicant sued B and C but not A and therefore had no claim. This is a striking example of the need for clarity in this area and it does seem that the approach of the EAT in cases like *Norris v Bedwell* is the preferable one (see also *LMC Drains Ltd and Metro Rod Services Ltd v Waugh*, discussed above).

(vii) **Linked transactions**

Finally, could reg 3(4) of the Transfer Regulations help? This states:

> 'It is hereby declared that a transfer of an undertaking or part of one may be effected by a series of two or more transactions between the same parties, but in determining whether or not such a series consti-tutes a single transfer, regard shall be had to the extent to which the undertaking or part was controlled by the transferor and transferee respectively before the last transaction, to the lapse of time between each of the transactions, to the intention of the parties and to all the other circumstances.'

An interesting point is therefore whether the various movements in tripartite cases, such as in transfers by tenants, franchisees and licensees, with the involvement sometimes technical, sometimes substantial, of the franchisor, landlord, licensor, etc are 'linked'

---

17 COIT 16015/83. Note, however, the possibility of Rule 14 of the Industrial Tribunals (Rules of Procedure) Regulations 1985 (SI 1985/16) (power of tribunal to join a relevant party to the proceedings). This was not used in *Hansford*.

transactions under reg 3(4) allowing a 'broad brush' approach to the question of whether a transfer has taken place. One problem is whether reg 3(4) has to be construed to apply to transactions between two parties only. If so, it may not help in the tripartite licence type of case.[18] Thus, the relevant part of reg 3(4) says:

'. . . a transfer of an undertaking or part of one may be effected by a series of two or more transactions between the same parties. . .'

It is submitted that the question is whether the permissiveness in the language of the regulation attaches to the multiplicity of transactions as opposed to the number of parties. And, on the wording, it is certainly arguable that the permissiveness really attaches to the number of transactions that might be involved between the parties rather than the number of parties involved. This view may also have some implicit support from the decision in *Barclays Bank v BIFU* (see above). That interpretation would mean that, although linked transactions may be caught by reg 3(4), for this to happen they must none the less be between the same parties. But this is an important issue. Multi-party transactions can be the subject of a scheme to avoid the Transfer Regulations just as much as with two-party transactions. Fortunately, there are signs that the courts are aware of just that problem.

In *Forth Estuary Engineering Ltd v Litster*[19] the EAT declined to disagree with the industrial tribunal's view that reg 3(4) was declaratory and permissive and did not make essential that all of the transactions must be between the same parties. In the EAT's view, the transactions might be between the same parties but did not *necessarily* have to be so. And more recent support for the view that reg 3(4) can be used to link multi-party transactions derives from certain remarks made by Lord Oliver in *Litster* in the House of Lords. That case involved a sale by a receiver of a company's business to a new company (see Ch 7). The consent of the Ports Authority was necessary to this transaction. It was argued that the involvement of a third party meant that reg 3(4) could not apply as the regulation contemplated only *two* parties. This was rejected by Lord Oliver who said:

'Regulation 3(4) does not purport to be any more than declaratory and cannot be properly construed as in any sense an exclusive definition of what can constitute a transfer.'

---

18 For example in *Premier Motors (Medway) Ltd v Total Oil (GB) Ltd* [1984] ICR 58.
19 [1986] IRLR 59 and 62.

It could be argued that comment on reg 3(4) was not necessary to decide the case; and the point made by counsel was conceded to be hardly 'the jewel in his crown'. But Lord Oliver's remarks do lend some support to the EAT's view that transactions between two or *more* parties may be caught.[20]

(viii) European law and the absence of a requirement of transfer of absolute ownership

In a number of European Court cases it is stressed that the directive applies as soon as there is a change in the natural or legal person responsible for operating the undertaking as a result of a legal transfer or merger, and therefore the directive has a wider scope than applying simply to business transfers which involve a change in ownership. It is submitted that these decisions support some of the cases on franchises and tenancies discussed above and since the Transfer Regulations should be construed in the light of cases in the European Court on the Acquired Rights Directive, cases such as *Norris v Bedwell* (see above) are, it is submitted, correctly decided. Additionally, it seems, a number of the domestic cases already discussed *do not* involve a 'legal transfer or merger'. However, the Transfer Regulations and EP(C)A do not expressly require this, in contrast to the directive. And there is nothing to prevent a member state improving on the floor of rights in the directive.[1]

In *Foreningen af Arbejdsledere i Danmark v Daddy's Dance Hall A/S*[2] Irma Catering had a lease with Palads Teatret which was determined on 28 January 1983 with effect from 25 February 1983. Mr Tellerup was an employee of the business operated by Irma Catering and was dismissed with notice expiring on 30 April 1983. On 25 February 1983 a new lease was granted by Palads Teatret to Daddy's Dance Hall. Mr Tellerup was re-engaged by Daddy's Dance Hall. He was, however, later dismissed by Daddy's Dance Hall on 26 April 1983. A dispute arose as to the terms of his employment that existed on the date of termination and the length of his notice to which he was entitled from Daddy's Dance Hall.

---

20 [1989] IRLR 161. See, too, the case of *Sibbald v Fraser* EAT 2987/87.

1 An interesting argument is, though, that although transfers not amounting to a 'legal transfer or merger' can be covered by domestic law (ie the EP(C)A and the Transfer Regulations), this is not required by the directive. If so it might not be possible to look to the directive to supplement other areas of eg the Transfer Regulations in such a case where the regulations in such other areas, fall short of the directive. This argument has yet to be tested. See, finally, the arguments on the requirement of a 'contractual' transfer under the directive in *Harvey on Industrial Relations and Employment Law*, III, 908.5.

2 [1988] IRLR 315.

It was held that Art 3(1) applies to a situation where after the termination of a non-transferable lease, the owner of the undertaking leases it to a new lessee who continues to run the business without any interruption with the same staff who had previously been dismissed upon the expiry of the initial lease. The European Court held:

> '. . . the directive therefore applies as soon as there is a change resulting from a conventional sale or from a merger of the natural or legal person responsible for operating the undertaking who consequently enters into obligations as an employer towards the employees working in the undertaking *and it is of no importance to know whether the ownership of the undertaking has been transferred. . .*
>
> It follows that when the lessee who has the capacity of proprietor of the undertaking at the termination of the lease loses this capacity and a third person acquires it under a new lease concluded with the owner, the resulting operation is capable of falling within the scope of application of the directive as defined in Art 1(1). The fact that in such a case the transfer takes place in two phases in the sense that as a first step the undertaking is transferred back from the original lessee to the owner who then transfers it to the new lessee, does not exclude the applicability of the directive so long as the economic unit retains its identity. This is the case in particular when, as in the instant case, the business continues to be run without interruption by the new lessee with the same staff that was employed in the undertaking before the transfer.'

In *Berg and Busschers v I M Besselsen*[3] Besselsen was the owner of a Dutch bar. Berg and Busschers were taken on as employees. In February 1983 the operation of the business was taken over by Manshanden and Tweehuizen, shareholders in a company called Summerland. They took over under a lease purchase agreement. Under a lease purchase agreement as defined by the Dutch Civil Code the parties agree that ownership does not pass on physical transfer and is retained by the vendor until the sale price is paid. Berg and Busschers then transferred to Summerland. But in November 1983 the lease purchase agreement was dissolved after breach and the business returned to Besselsen. Among the questions asked of the European Court were:

1 Can a lease purchase agreement result in the transfer of an undertaking for the purposes of Art 1(1) of the directive?

2 Can the dissolution of a lease purchase agreement result in a transfer with the legal consequence that the obligations of the

---

3 [1990] ICR 396, [1989] IRLR 447.

purchaser by lease purchase arising from the contract of employment existing at the time of the dissolution are transferred by that
transfer to the vendor by way of lease purchase?

The answer was yes on both counts. Again, it was stated:

'[The directive] applies as soon, because of a transfer as a result of a
contractual agreement or merger, as a change occurs in the natural or
legal person operating the undertaking who, in that capacity, has
obligations vis-à-vis the employees employed in the undertaking and
. . . it is of no importance whether the ownership of the undertaking
has been transferred.'

In *Landsorganisationen i Danmark v N Y Molle Kro*[4] Mrs Hannibalsen was owner of a tavern which was a seasonal business running
mainly during the summer. In 1980 she leased the tavern to a Mrs
Larsen. In January 1981 the owner rescinded the lease on grounds
of non-observance of covenants by Mrs Larsen. The business was
closed until the end of March 1981 and was thereafter run by Mrs
Hannibalsen herself. In May 1983 Mrs Larsen was taken on as an
employee (as a waitress) by Mrs Hannibalsen. Her wages were fixed
at 195 kroner per day together with a share in the turnover of the
business. She left in August 1983. When she left it was claimed that
she was underpaid for the short time she was employed, ie at less
than the collective agreement which had been operating previously
and which had bound Mrs Larsen and which, it was claimed, was
transferred to Mrs Hannibalsen when Mrs Larsen gave up the
business to Mrs Hannibalsen in 1981. There were three main questions relevant to this discussion:

1 Was there a transfer when the lease was surrendered?

2 Does the directive apply where the business was temporarily
closed at the time of the transfer so that consequently, there were
no employees?

3 Did it make any difference if the undertaking was normally closed
for part of the year through seasonal considerations?

The European Court held:

1 Article 1 must be interpreted as meaning that the directive
applies where the owner takes back the running of a leased
business following breach of the lease by a managing lessee.

---

4 [1989] ICR 330, [1989] IRLR 37.

2 Article 1 must be interpreted so that it applies whenever there is an economic entity still in existence on transfer and that is a question for the national court to decide. A temporary closure and absence of staff might mean there was no transfer, but not necessarily. And this was not necessarily fatal in the case of a seasonal business. The court said:

'It follows from the preamble and from [the provisions of the directive] that a purpose of the directive is to ensure, so far as possible, that the rights of employees are safeguarded in the event of a change of employer by enabling them to remain in employment with the new employer on the terms and conditions agreed with the transferor. The directive is therefore applicable where, following a legal transfer or merger, there is a change in the natural or legal person who is responsible for carrying on the business and who by virtue of that fact incurs the obligations of an employer vis-à-vis employees of the undertaking, regardless of whether or not ownership of the undertaking is transferred. Employees of an undertaking whose employer changes without any change in ownership are in a situation comparable to that of employees of an undertaking which is sold, and require equivalent protection . . .

Similar considerations apply where the owner of a leased undertaking takes over its operation following a breach of the lease by the lessee. Such a takeover also occurs on the basis of the lease. Consequently, in so far as its effect is that the lessee ceases to be the employer and the owner re-acquires that status, it must also be regarded as a transfer of the undertaking to another employer as a result of a legal transfer within the meaning of Article 1(1) of the Directive.'[5]

Finally, in *P Bork International A/S v Foreningen af Arbejdsledere i Danmark*[6] (including the cases of *Olsen v Junckers Industrier A/S, Hansen v Junckers Industrier A/S* and *Handels-Og Kontorfunktionaerernes Forbund i Danmark v Junckers Industrier*

---

5   There remained, of course, the employee's argument that she was brought under the terms of the collective agreement that had obtained in 1981. Article 3(2) provides 'the transferee shall continue to observe the terms and conditions agreed in any collective agreement on the same terms applicable to the transferor under that agreement'. That must be interpreted as meaning that it does not require the transferee to continue to observe the working conditions agreed under a collective agreement with regard to workers who were not employees of the undertaking at the date of transfer. So Art 3 only applies to make an employer observe a collective agreement in respect of employees employed at the time of transfer and not those recruited after that date, especially two years later, as in the case of Mrs Larsen.

  If one looks at reg 6 of the Transfer Regulations this apparently only applies to those employees caught by reg 5 and therefore reg 6 is arguably in conformity with the view of the European Court as to how Art 3 should operate. See Ch 10.

6   [1990] 3 CMLR 701, [1989] IRLR 41.

A/S) OTF leased a beechwood veneer factory in 1980 to PBI. In the autumn of 1981 PBI gave notice of termination of the lease with effect from 22 December 1981. During the month of December PBI dismissed all the workers employed in the undertaking, having given them due notice. The undertaking ceased operating on 22 December.

On 30 December JI bought the undertaking from OTF and took possession on 4 January 1982. JI took on more than half the staff previously employed by PBI. On 8 January 1982 there was an agreement between JI and PBI (in liquidation) for JI to purchase PBI's stock, spare parts, tools, auxiliary materials and furniture.

The question was, were PBI's obligations to the workers, principally wages and unpaid holiday pay, passed to JI? Did Art 1 of the directive apply to the transfer? It was held that the directive applies to a case where the owner of the undertaking, after he has given notice of termination of a lease or after forfeiture thereof, re-takes possession of the undertaking and thereafter sells it to a third party who shortly afterwards brings it back into operation. The European Court said:

'. . . the objective of Directive 77/187 is to ensure that employees' rights are safeguarded in the event of a change of employer and to allow them to remain in the employment of the new employer on the same conditions as those agreed with the transferor. The Directive therefore applies whenever within the framework of contractual relations there is any change in the natural or legal person responsible for operating the undertaking who enters into contractual obligations as an employer with the employees of the undertaking.

It follows that when the lessee in its capacity as employer loses this capacity at the end of the lease and a third party subsequently acquires this capacity under a contract of sale concluded with the owner, the resulting transaction could fall within the scope of the directive as defined in Article 1(1). The fact that in such a case the transfer takes place in two stages inasmuch as the undertaking is initially re-transferred by the lessee to the owner who then transfers it to the new owner does not preclude the application of the directive provided that the undertaking in question retains its identity which is the case where there is an economic entity still in existence, the operation of which is in fact continued or resumed by the new employer carrying on the same or a similar business.

In order to determine whether these conditions all exist, it is appropriate to take account of all the factual circumstances surrounding the transaction which may include, in particular, whether the tangible and intangible assets have been transferred as well as the major part of the staff of the undertaking, the degree of similarity between its activities before and after the transfer and the duration of any period of stoppage connected with the transfer.'

Regulation 3 will now have to be interpreted in the light of these European decisions and the focus should not necessarily be on whether there has been a change of ownership but on whether the operation of the business is continued or resumed by a new employer carrying on the same or a similar business. As mentioned earlier, Hepple and O'Higgins describe this as a shift from a 'conveyancing' test to an 'employment' test.[7]

As already stated, these European Court cases seem to contemplate some contractual nexus between transferor and transferee because of the use of the words 'as a result of a legal transfer or merger'. But, arguably, this may not be required under the Transfer Regulations and the EP(C)A. This is illustrated by many of the cases discussed above (e g *Cartwright and Norton*), and a further striking example is provided by *Dabell v Vale Industrial Services (Nottingham) Ltd*,[8] a case on the EP(C)A, discussed in Chapter 5.

Finally, in relation to tripartite transactions, we have discussed whether there should be two separate transfers, one B to A in our diagram and another B to C, or whether there was in reality only one, from B to C, thus ignoring the technical intervention of A. Two of the European cases concern tripartite (A, B and C) sequences (*Daddy's Dance Hall* and *P Bork International*) but unfortunately they are probably inconclusive on the matter. It appears from those cases, however, that the involvement of a third party was immaterial.

The recent EAT case of *LMC Drains Ltd and Metro Rod Services Ltd v Waugh*,[9] discussed above, relied upon this line of European Court authority to justify its decision that a change of franchisees involved on each occasion a transfer of an undertaking. It did not matter whether the change-over occurred by way of surrender to the franchisor and regrant to a new franchisee or whether there was a handover direct between outgoing and incoming transferees.

5 DIFFERENCES BETWEEN THE EP(C)A AND THE TRANSFER REGULATIONS; NON-COMMERCIAL VENTURES AND OTHER PROBLEMS

(i) Some basic differences between the EP(C)A and the transfer regulations

There are three main differences between the wording of the EP(C)A and of the Transfer Regulations on the issue of what is a

---

7 *Encyclopaedia of Labour Relations Law* IB 504.
8 [1988] IRLR 439.
9 [1991] 3 CMLR 172, EAT.

business as a going concern. The first two may be minor; the third is not.

(a) Transfer of a ship

It is provided by the Transfer Regulations, in reg 2(2), that:

> 'References in these regulations to the transfer of part of an undertaking are references to a transfer of a part which is being transferred as a business and accordingly do not include references to a transfer of a ship without more.'

This seems to add little to the scheme of the law as it stands under the EP(C)A. In *Watts, Watts & Co Ltd v Steeley*[10] there was a transfer of vessels belonging to one company to another. The employee was the master of one of the vessels transferred. It was held that there was a transfer of a business as a going concern. This was a question of fact for an industrial tribunal and the Divisional Court felt unable to disturb the decision of the industrial tribunal. Accordingly, the captain's employment was continuous for the purposes of what is now the EP(C)A, and he was entitled to a redundancy payment.

Regulation 2(2) of the Transfer Regulations, therefore, seems to add little to the existing law. A transfer of an asset (ie, for example, a ship) may not be a transfer of an undertaking but if there is a transfer of a ship or ships as a business as a going concern there may, it is submitted, be a transfer of an undertaking (or part thereof). This apparent difference between the EP(C)A and the Transfer Regulations is probably not, therefore, one in reality.

(b) Parts of an undertaking

Regulation 3(1) expressly includes a 'part' of an undertaking in the definition of an 'undertaking'. It states as follows:

> 'Subject to the provisions of these regulations these regulations apply to a transfer from one person to another of an undertaking situated immediately before the transfer in the United Kingdom or a part of one which is so situated.'

Although EP(C)A Sch 13 para 17(2) does not expressly include part of an undertaking, s 94 does (or, more precisely, part of a business) and the EP(C)A provisions should be construed uniformly. In cases under the EP(C)A a 'part' of an undertaking has been held to have been transferred if there is a separate and distinct activity within the transferor's undertaking that can be transferred

---

10 (1968) 3 ITR 363.

as such even if, when with the transferor, it was integrated with other parts for administration or efficiency; it is probable that this interpretation will be applied in relation to the Transfer Regulations.[11] This will be a question of fact for an industrial tribunal (see, generally, above).

(c) Commercial and non-commercial ventures

The Transfer Regulations are *narrower* than the EP(C)A in one very important respect. For it is provided in reg 2 of the Transfer Regulations that they do not apply to 'any undertaking or part of an undertaking which is not in the nature of a commercial venture'. No such express limitation appears in the EP(C)A. The restrictive provision in the Transfer Regulations was applied and interpreted recently in *Woodcock v Committee for the Time Being of the Friends' School, Wigton & Genwise Ltd*[12] where a Quaker school of charitable status was held to be an undertaking which was not in the nature of a commercial venture for the purposes of the Transfer Regulations so that the Transfer Regulations did not apply.

Recently, the EAT, in *Stirling and Baxter v Dietsmann Management Services Systems Ltd*,[13] considered that a contract to supply the crew of a motor vessel used to provide support services for Shell's activities in the North Sea was not an undertaking or part in the nature of a commercial venture. The vessel was owned by Shell and the arrangement with the independent contractor was for the management, operation and manning of the vessel for which the contractor received a fixed fee of reimbursement of costs. When the contract expired, the function reverted to Shell. The tribunal found that the contract allowed no possibility for making a profit or incurring a loss and the object of the exercise was to break even.

As discussed below, it has been decided that the word 'undertaking' can be wide enough to cover a venture run at a loss,[14] but one can envisage many cases where, because of a non-profit-making basis to the undertaking, the Transfer Regulations may not apply.

Under the EP(C)A, non-commercial ventures have been regarded as businesses or undertakings for the purposes of the EP(C)A. For example, in *Ferretti v Southwark and Lambeth*

11　*G D Ault (Isle of Wight) Ltd v Gregory* (1967) 2 ITR 301; *Green v Wavertree Heating and Plumbing Co Ltd* [1978] ICR 928; *Lumley Insurance Consultants Ltd v Pruddah* EAT 150/83. Another helpful case is *McLeod v John Rostron & Sons Ltd* (1972) 7 ITR 144.

12　[1986] IRLR 490, EAT; affd [1987] IRLR 98, CA.

13　[1991] IRLR 368, EAT.

14　*Hadden v University of Dundee Students' Association* [1985] IRLR 449, EAT.

Archaeological Projects[15] a non-profit-making archaeological dig was held to be a business which could be transferred from one person to another. And in *Robinson v Bournemouth Borough Council*[16] the transfer of a department teaching surveying from a college of technology in Bournemouth to a polytechnic in Portsmouth was held to be a transfer of a trade, business or undertaking.[17]

The question of what amounts to a commercial venture will be a question of fact for an industrial tribunal to decide. In *Woodcock v Committee for the Time Being of the Friends' School, Wigton and Genwise Ltd*[18] the EAT considered that the meaning of the words 'commercial venture' was very much a matter of first impression.[19] May LJ in the Court of Appeal agreed, saying:

'For my part, although as a general guide I think that the fact that a venture or enterprise is entered into with a view to making a profit is a consideration in deciding whether or not it is in the nature of a commercial one, that is only a general guide and I prefer the first impression approach of the Employment Appeal Tribunal to the particular question in issue.'[20]

Accordingly, the Court of Appeal was reluctant to give general guidelines as to what 'commercial' meant. The only guidance seems to be as follows:

'Without in any way seeking to give a definition but to express the sort of indication which would have its effect upon my mind, I refer to two definitions, one in the large Oxford Dictionary and one in the concise volume where in the first "commercial" is defined in one definition as "viewed as a mere matter of business, looking towards financial profit", and in the concise volume the first definition of "commercial" is "of, engaged in, bearing on commerce, interested in financial return rather than artistry". It is "rather than artistry" which I think is the pointer which has an effect on my mind in preventing me from recognising this enterprise as being in the nature of a commercial venture.'[1]

---

15 COIT 1479/244, IT, cited in *IDS Handbook* 36 p 6.

16 (1970) 5 ITR 100, IT. See also *Malik v Scunthorpe & District Community Relations Council* COIT 26176/83B; *Loughran v Coseley Community Services Ltd* COIT 19750/83; cf *Craggs v Sunderland Training and Trading Co Ltd* COIT 6209/83.

17 See also *Dallow Industrial Properties v Else and Card* [1967] 2 QB 449, 2 ITR 304. Cf, however, *Pittman v Davis Build plc (in liquidation)* EAT 122/90 n 1, p 81, below.

18 [1986] IRLR 490, EAT; affd [1987] IRLR 98, CA.

19 [1986] IRLR 490, EAT.

20 [1987] IRLR 98 at 100, CA.

1 Ibid per May LJ at 101.

If the question of whether there is a commercial venture is a matter of first impression it will be hard to predict tribunal decisions in this area and also difficult to expect consistency.

This is likely to prove a continuing problem when interpreting the Transfer Regulations and, in particular, when attempting to marry the provisions of the EP(C)A with the Transfer Regulations. Since it is, in principle, possible for a non-commercial undertaking to be transferred under the EP(C)A but not under the Transfer Regulations, statutory continuity of employment might be preserved on a transfer of a non-commercial undertaking but the Transfer Regulations would not apply, thus preventing the provisions transferring the contract of employment, collective agreements, recognition, and provisions about consultation and information from applying.[2]

A final problem is this. The Acquired Rights Directive does not expressly require that the undertaking transferred has to be in the nature of a commercial venture. The Transfer Regulations, by including this provision, therefore appear to depart from the directive and diminish the rights established by the directive. Under *Litster v Forth Dry Dock & Engineering Co Ltd* a purposive interpretation has to be applied to the Transfer Regulations so as to give effect to the terms of the Acquired Rights Directive. Is it therefore possible to use the *Litster* approach to deem the requirement of a commercial venture in the Transfer Regulations not to be included, or alternatively, to construe the requirement narrowly in order to make the Transfer Regulations conform to the directive? The former, it is suggested, may be going too far. It is one thing to read words into a provision; it is another to deem words not to be there. But the latter suggestion is certainly arguable. It is submitted that the 'commercial venture' requirement should be given as narrow a scope as possible.[3]

---

2   The 1978 Draft Regulations had a more specific definition of which types of business transfer were excluded from the proposed Transfer Regulations and did not include a wide catch-all expression such as 'not in the nature of a commercial venture'. At proof stage, the decision in *Pittman v Davis Build plc (in liquidation)* EAT 122/90 became available. In this case the EAT (Croom-Johnson J, pres) held that, contrary to the arguments here expressed, a transfer under para 17(2) of Sch 13 *also* required transfer of a commercial undertaking. Further litigation will undoubtedly follow in this controversial area.

3   But as discussed below this argument was not taken up either by the EAT in *Expro Services Ltd v Smith* or *Stirling v Dietsmann Management* and in the latter case, as explained above, the EAT was expressly of the view that the absence of mention of commercial ventures in the directive did not mean that non-commercial ventures were covered by the directive. This seems questionable and the debate is probably far from over. And see *Pittman v Davis Build plc (in liquidation)* EAT 122/90.

(ii) Issues on privatisation and hiving off of support services

Privatisation will cause continuing problems.[4] There are two types of privatisation situations relevant here.

The first is where a major corporation or undertaking is privatised as a whole and its undertaking transferred from a statutory authority or nationalised corporation to a private company. In this situation, there may or may not be a transfer of an undertaking as a going concern depending on the factors discussed earlier in this chapter. In the debates leading to the approval of the Dockyard Services Act 1986 it was thought necessary expressly to include provisions relating to transfers of undertakings and protection of employment similar to those contained in the Transfer Regulations.[5] However, this was not so much because of the fear that the transfer of aspects of the dockyards might not be a transfer of an undertaking but more that the transfer of employees from the dockyards to the privatised company without more was not a transfer of an undertaking.[6] The government was convinced that the privatisation process involved a transfer of an undertaking[7] and that each dockyard undertaking was an undertaking within the meaning of the Transfer Regulations. This also seems later to have been acknowledged by Lord Denning himself and he also quoted further examples such as the transfer of employees from the Gas Corporation to British Gas[8] where he thought the Transfer Regulations in principle would apply. The dockyards provisions, it seemed to be understood, were introduced *ex abundanti cautela*. Thus it could strongly be argued that a transfer of an undertaking from a nationalised profit- and loss-making corporation to a private corporation is a transfer of a commercial venture or, in the words of the Transfer

4 See Graham and Prosser 'Privatising Nationalised Industries: Constitutional Issues and New Legal Techniques' (1987) MLR 16.

5 Hansard DHL Deb 9 June 1986, col 54 (Lord Denning). Action was subsequently taken (unsuccessfully) by unions thereon (see *Financial Times* 28 February 1987). The action was then reported in *Institution of Professional Civil Servants v Secretary of State for Defence* [1987] 3 CMLR 35, [1987] IRLR 373.

6 Hansard HC Deb 8 April 1986, col 115 (Mr N Lamont).

7 Hansard HC Deb 8 April 1986, col 114 (Mr N Lamont).

8 Hansard HL Deb 24 July 1986, col 450. See also Graham and Prosser (1987) MLR 16, although another factor in influencing Lord Denning's well-publicised amendment to the Dockyard Services Bill was his view that recourse to the industrial tribunal alone under the Transfer Regulations in case of non-consultation would be inadequate. The amendment allowed access to the High Court: Hansard HL Deb 24 July 1986, col 449. Finally the government was of the view in the debates on the Gas Bill that the Transfer Regulations applied to the transfer from the corporation to the private sector company: Hansard HL Deb 17 July 1986 col 1057.

Regulations, a transfer of a going concern *in the nature of* a commercial venture.[9] As usual, though, this will depend on the facts (see the privatisation of the Royal Ordnance Factories, which for instance, was assumed to be a business transfer in *Royal Ordnance plc v Pilkington*[10]).

Privatisation of other entities is less clear. For example, Lord Wedderburn, in the debates on the Transfer Regulations in 1981 in the House of Lords, raised the question of the London Passenger Transport Board and the London Transport Executive and Mr Harold Walker MP raised the same issue in the House of Commons on 7 December 1981 concerning the Property Services Agency and the Ordnance Survey. Whether entities like those (which were merely examples) are commercial ventures will depend on the principles in *Woodcock v Committee of the Friends' School* discussed above. But certain governmental agencies (depending on the facts) may not be commercial ventures. For example the Gas Consumers' Council was, in the opinion of the government in 1986, not covered by the Transfer Regulations as a result of privatisation of British Gas.[11] Other examples in the light of changing circumstances will spring to mind.[12]

Another aspect of privatisation is more difficult. This involves the growing phenomenon of privatisation of local authority services by transfer to outside bodies. For example, a local authority may contract out its cleaning services, building services, repairing services, cleansing, vehicle maintenance, catering and other services to an outside body. What happens to employees who are dismissed as a result of the introduction of outside caterers or who are transferred to the outside catering body? One problem is whether this is a pure sub-contracting case outside the business transfer rules (see section (iv) above). Even if not, another is the

---

9 As seems to have been the case in *Warrington v British Transport Hotels* (1984) 25 January (IT) 1862/83/LS cited in Lightman and Moss *The Law of Receivers of Companies* (1986) p 208. See also the nature of the transfer in the Royal Bank of Scotland Act 1985 (a non-privatisation case). See also Graham and Prosser (1987) MLR 16.

10 [1989] ICR 737, [1988] IRLR 466. See also the Ordnance Factories and Military Services Act 1984.

11 Hansard HL Deb 17 July 1986 col 1057.

12 Sometimes provision is made for employees in borderline or doubtful cases by statute. We have already mentioned the Dockyard Services Act 1986. A similar problem was perceived on 'opting out' by hospitals and the formation of NHS trusts to manage them. Section 6 of the National Health Service and Community Care Act 1990 provides express protection for employees transferring employment from a Health Authority to an NHS Trust similar to that contained in reg 5 of the Transfer Regulations.

requirement under the regulations that what is transferred is a commercial venture.

In the case of *Hadden v University of Dundee Students' Association*,[13] a non-privatisation case, it was suggested that a part of an undertaking transferred need not be a part necessarily that has achieved profits. It can be a part of an undertaking that has been run at a loss. The facts of the case were that the students' association entered into a one-year agreement with ARA Services Ltd for the provision of catering services previously undertaken by themselves. Hadden, a manageress, moved from the students' asssociation to ARA and, when the contract expired, back to the association. However, her employment was not continuous as no relevant transfers had taken place. ARA were not carrying on a 'commercial venture'. On the other hand, notwithstanding the result on the facts (and it must be remembered that this was a case on appeal to the EAT which would not easily overturn a finding of fact by the industrial tribunal below) the EAT was at pains to stress that it was:

'. . . in no doubt that it is possible for an organisation such as the respondents to farm out their catering activities to contractors so as to involve the relevant transfer of a commercial undertaking. Similarly, it is possible for contractors to transfer back such undertakings to the original transferor. Normally, one would expect such contractors to employ all the staff and control the prices. On the other hand we do not doubt that it is also possible for outside contractors to be engaged to provide catering services in circumstances which do not involve the transfer of an undertaking. This could occur, in our view, where the contractor simply provides a manager and is remunerated on a fee and/or percentage basis, without having overall control.'

The EAT thought that the case before it was somewhere between the two situations posed above, but thought it material that the provision of premises, equipment, staff and pricing control were retained by the association throughout. As a general principle (see above) the EAT quite clearly thought it was possible for a contracting-out exercise in the private sector similar to the above to be covered by the Transfer Regulations.

In *Rastill v Automatic Refreshment Services Ltd*[14] (again a non-privatisation case) a catering company took over the running of a company's works canteen. It was held that the operation of the canteen had been part of the company's business and was an independent commercial venture and there had been a transfer of

---

13 [1985] IRLR 449.
14 [1978] ICR 289, EAT (approved in *Humphreys v Co-ordinated Cleaning Ltd* EAT 197/91 LEXIS transcript).

goodwill. The transfer had been of an entity which enabled the transferee to undertake to make a profit and there was a change in ownership of a business for the purposes of what is now EP(C)A, s 94.[15] *Rastill* was in the private sector, but why should it not apply in the public sector? But there is a body of opinion that privatisation of local authority services may in many cases not involve a transfer of part of the local authority's undertaking amounting to a commercial venture. And in at least two cases, privatisations of maintenance of public lavatories and of hostel cleaning have been held not to be business transfers under the Transfer Regulations.[16]

As mentioned (see above) the use of private contractors by local authorities has been growing over the years. Another dimension is that this has become more formalised with the introduction of compulsory competitive tendering, initially by Part III of the Local Government, Planning and Land Act 1980, which introduced the competitive tendering process to the categories of construction, building maintenance and highways work. This was continued by the Local Government Act 1988 which, by Part I, extended competitive tendering to other services, namely refuse collection, building cleaning, street cleaning, schools and welfare catering, other catering, ground maintenance and repair and maintenance of vehicles.

The legislation itself is silent on whether contracting out under these provisions involves a business transfer. Official guidance was offered by the Audit Commission not on competitive tendering, but on management buy-outs in its report, 'Management Buy-outs: Public Interest or Private Gain' Paper No 6 of January 1990. The view of the Audit Commission in that paper was that 'the Transfer

---

15 As will be seen the line between the actual results in *Hadden and Rastill* is quite fine. It has been suggested (in *IDS Employment Law Handbook No 36: Transfer of Undertakings*) that where the local authority (or other former employer as in *Hadden* or *Rastill*) retains a measure of control over these services contracted out, say a local authority (or other former employer) reserves the right to monitor and supervise the contractor's performance, then that might be an additional factor against a transfer of a commercial venture. This is illustrated outside the privatisation context in *Hadden* where the association continued to be responsible for employing non-supervisory staff as well as other matters. The private contractors were remunerated on the basis of a percentage commission and fee. When the association took its catering operation back there was no business transfer because the contractor had, previously, simply undertaken management of the catering operation without having overall control. (See the discussion in *IDS Employment Law Handbook No 36*.)

16 See *Hawkins v Automatic Cleaning Services Ltd* COIT 1729/57; *Johnstone v Sketchley Contract Cleaning Services Ltd* COIT 1674/151 (both in *IDS Employment Law Handbook No 36: Transfer of Undertakings* p 12). See also *Dawkins v Initial Service Cleaners Ltd* COIT 1709/245 (although, here, EP(C)A Sch 13 para 17(2) was held to apply instead).

of Undertakings Regulations of 1981 do not apply to buy-out companies'. It is submitted, however, that the view that management buy-outs in the public sector do not involve a business transfer is questionable. And this may also be questionable advice if given in relation to competitive tendering.[17]

After all, the Transfer Regulations say that a transfer of an undertaking does not include an undertaking or part of an undertaking 'which is *not in the nature* of a commercial venture'. If it is not a commercial venture before privatisation but capable of being such thereafter, why should it not be covered? It seems ridiculous that part of a local authority's activities which prior to privatisation are not actually separate and 'commercial' but which after privatisation are run privately in the manner of a business for profit, cannot involve a transfer of (part of) an undertaking in the nature 'of a commercial venture'. If they were not so, there would be absolutely no incentive for the private contractor to take them on. And there can be few cases of more commercial activity than competitive tendering! It is submitted too that the possibility of a commercial venture increases in tendering cases after 1980. Since the Local Government, Planning and Land Act 1980 every local authority, whether entrusting the execution of the relevant services to private contractors or not, still has to prepare a balance sheet or revenue account and make a statement of rate of return. Thus, with this requirement to, in effect, form a separate accounting unit and create a client/contractor split, the activity concerned would already have the appearance of a separate accounting unit and therefore something in the nature of a commercial venture before any contracting out (relevant also is the requirement under the 1988 Act that a return on capital is made (s 10) and that contracts should exclude non-commercial considerations (s 17)). Finally, as a pointer to the future, similar issues will also inevitably arise in connection with the EC public procurement regime. Further case law or (more likely) amendment of the Transfer Regulations is necessary to clarify the position. As indicated, tribunals have not, unfortunately, been ready to find business transfers in cases of privatisation of local authority services so far.

A further, more recent, blow to workers' rights are the two cases of *Expro Services Ltd v Smith*[18] and *Stirling v Dietsmann Manage-*

---

17 See Cirell and Bennett (1990) Solicitors' Journal Vol 134 No 17, 27 April 1990, p 469. I am grateful to John Bennett for helpful remarks on this part of the text. See also S Fredman and G S Morris, *The State as Employer: Labour Law in the Public Services* (1989), p 11.

18 [1991] ICR 577, [1991] IRLR 156.

ment Systems Ltd.[19] In the first case Mrs Smith was employed by the Minister of Defence in April 1987 as a steward at the Officers' Mess, Bassingbourne Barracks, Royston. In 1987 the Minister of Defence put the provision of catering support services out to tender to Expro. Mrs Smith transferred to Expro in 1988. In May 1989, she was dismissed. She wanted to claim unfair dismissal. But, of course, she needed a qualifying period of two years with her employer. Only if there was a transfer of an undertaking could she satisfy this requirement because only if she could count her employment with the Ministry of Defence towards her service with Expro could she manage to attain the two years.

An industrial tribunal held there had been a transfer of undertaking and they were satisfied that what had been transferred amounted to a commercial venture. The industrial tribunal looked at the dictionary definition of commercial and found that it meant 'interested in financial return, rather than artistry'. It held that the contractor was certainly interested in financial return.

Not so, held the EAT, albeit in a brief judgment. The EAT held there was no commercial venture involved. In its opinion it did not follow that because the catering and cleaning business was a commercial venture as carried on by Expro, it amounted to a commercial venture for the purposes of the Transfer Regulations. In the opinion of the EAT, for a commercial venture to exist there must already have been a commercial venture in existence before the transfer. This was not the case while the MoD retained the catering and cleaning services. This decision will therefore be of considerable interest to private contractors and will be of some dismay to employees who have no alternative but to join private contractors when their former employer no longer wishes to employ them to carry out ancillary and support services.

But, for reasons already argued, a major criticism can be made of the EAT's approach. The Acquired Rights Directive, as discussed, on which the Transfer Regulations are based, contains no requirement that what is being transferred has to be a commercial venture. As such, the Transfer Regulations depart from the terms of the directive and contain provisions less favourable towards employees. This conflicts with the aims of the directive and, as stated, under *Litster*, a purposive construction has to be applied to the Transfer Regulations to make them conform to the terms of the Acquired Rights Directive. That issue was not properly canvassed before the EAT in the present case. It would therefore be open, as already suggested, for a future tribunal or court to apply *Litster* at

---

19 [1991] IRLR 368.

the very least to say that the requirement of a commercial venture must be given a very narrow interpretation.

The other reason why Mrs Smith might feel hard done by is that the EAT did not hear argument on the terms of para 17(2) of Sch 13 to the 1978 Act. All that she wanted in this case was for her continuity of employment to be preserved. Again, as discussed, para 17(2) of Sch 13 which deals with continuity (see Ch 5) also contains no express requirement that the business or undertaking to be transferred has to be in the nature of a commercial venture. As has been seen, there is case law on transfers of parts of non-profit-making organisations which have been held to amount to a transfer of a trade or business or undertaking for the purposes of para 17(2) of Sch 13.[20]

Alas, these arguments did not avail the employees in *Stirling v Dietsmann Management Systems Ltd*. In this case, as discussed above, there was a diving support vessel owned by Shell (UK). Shell entered into a contract with Seaforth Maritime for its management and operation. Shell then put the contract out to tender. Another company got the tender. The question was whether a transfer of undertaking had occurred on the change of contractors. The EAT held that the venture was not in the nature of a commercial venture. There was a fixed fee for the operation and there was no prospect of further exploitation of the situation by making profits over and above the fixed fee or indeed of making losses. This case differs from *Expro* in that the EAT did specifically consider whether the directive was wider than the Transfer Regulations but ruled that the directive was not wider than the Transfer Regulations, and merely because the directive did not expressly mention commercial ventures, that did not mean that non-commercial ventures were covered by the directive.

Such a conclusion is controversial among labour and indeed commercial lawyers who have experience of the word 'undertaking' in a legislative context, and there seems no general principle why undertaking should mean commercial undertaking (see Rubenstein, [1991] IRLR 365–6). Obviously there will be further litigation over the expression.

---

20 However, as already mentioned at fn 1, p 81, in *Pittman v Davis Build plc (in liquidation)* EAT 122/90, it was held that para 17(2) of Sch 13 should be construed in the same way as the Transfer Regulations on this point.

6 WHEN DOES A TRANSFER TAKE PLACE?

Another problem is that those involved in business transfers will want to know when the transfer is to take place. This is important, inter alia, for the question of whether employees are still employed 'immediately before' the transfer for the purposes of reg 5, and for the obligation under reg 10, under which certain information must be given to unions 'long enough before' the transfer for consultation to take place. Usually the point of transfer is pinpointed in sale documentation. If so, does it take place at exchange of contracts or on completion of a transfer?

In *Kestongate Ltd v Miller*[1] the EAT thought the transfer could take place on exchange of contracts. This is also supported by *Kennedy Brookes Hotel Catering Ltd v Reilly and Cook*[2] and *Wright v A W Smith (Gosport) Ltd.*[3]

However, the majority of opinion seems to favour the view that transfer takes place on completion.[4] Also recently, in *Wheeler v Patel*,[5] some doubt was cast on whether *Kestongate* was correct especially as it was decided before *Spence* and the EAT came down firmly on the side of the view that the transfer takes place on completion. In *Secretary of State for Employment v Galbraith*[6] the EAT gave leave to appeal but expressed its preference for the view that a transfer took place on completion. *Brook Lane Finance Co Ltd v Bradley*[7] also lends support to the fact that transfer takes place at the date of completion. Finally, the idea that reg 3(4) (see above) can be used to link exchange of contracts and completion so that the transfer starts on exchange was firmly rejected when argued in the EAT in *Wheeler v Patel.*[8]

It follows that the moment of transfer should ideally be managed by the parties in accordance with their intentions. If not, problems could arise. For the question when it took place will be one of fact for the tribunal (see *Mohammed v Delaney*[9] and also *Dabell*'s case, discussed in Ch 5) and a tribunal might determine a transfer to have taken place before the parties supposed it to have taken place.

---

1 [1986] ICR 672.
2 EAT 53/82.
3 COIT 17923/86.
4 *Bachelor v Premier Motors Ltd* COIT 17295/82; *Dickinson v Bryant* EAT 73/84; *Field v Barnett* EAT 761/84; *Secretary of State for Employment v Spence* [1987] QB 179, [1986] 3 All ER 616.
5 [1987] ICR 631, [1987] IRLR 211.
6 EAT 107/87 (82/87).
7 [1988] ICR 423, [1988] IRLR 283.
8 [1987] ICR 631, [1987] IRLR 211.
9 EAT 606/86.

Another very important point is that the European Court has favoured a test for the determination of whether a transfer has occurred which shifts the emphasis away from the concept of change in ownership to a change of management. This is, as already stated, according to Hepple and O'Higgins (op cit) an 'employment' rather than 'conveyancing' test. It should mean that if there is de facto change-over before a formal legal transfer or completion the transfer may occur at the earlier point (e g if a proposed purchaser were to be let into possession early).

And perhaps a good example of this is the case of *Brook Lane Finance Co Ltd v Bradley*,[10] where the decision was that the completion date was the point of transfer and for that reason an employee who had left to join the transferee three weeks earlier could not claim the protection of reg 5 (as he was not employed 'immediately before' the transfer). But Hepple and O'Higgins[11] warn that the finding in the case may now be considered dubious on the facts; when the employee left to join the transferee, the transferee was also let into possession. With hindsight, under the 'employment' test it is suggested that the transfer might have occurred then.

---

10 [1988] ICR 423, [1988] IRLR 283.
11 Op cit, IB 504.

Chapter 5

The EP(C)A and business transfers

1 INTRODUCTION

This chapter explains when and how the EP(C)A applies to transfers of businesses. It may be thought, at first glance, that if the Transfer Regulations (which are discussed in more detail in the succeeding chapters) apply to a particular transaction, the provisions of the EP(C)A herein discussed are no longer needed. In the main this may be true; but not always. For:

(i) although if the Transfer Regulations apply there is no dismissal by virtue of the transfer and, therefore, no need for a redundancy dismissal to 'disappear' on re-engagement by a transferee as envisaged by s 94 of the EP(C)A for redundancy purposes, statutory continuity is still calculated (and preserved) *stricto sensu* under the EP(C)A;

(ii) there are differences between the EP(C)A and the Transfer Regulations such that the Transfer Regulations may not apply to all business transfers arguably caught none the less by the EP(C)A (principally, transfers of non-commercial ventures (see Ch 4)). The EP(C)A rules relating to both continuity and redundancy (ie the pre-existing law before the Transfer Regulations) would then apply.

It will be remembered that there are, in the main, two relevant areas under the EP(C)A. First, Sch 13 to the EP(C)A makes specific provision to deal with continuity of employment upon change of employer. It is stated, in para 17(2), that:

'If a trade or business or an undertaking (whether or not it be an undertaking established by or under an Act of Parliament) is transferred from one person to another the period of employment of an employee in the trade or business or undertaking at the time of the transfer shall count as a period of employment with the transferee and the transfer shall not break the continuity of the period of employment.'

Second, the redundancy payments provisions of the EP(C)A make provision for settling liability for a redundancy payment. It is provided, in s 94 of the EP(C)A, that a transferee may make an offer of continued employment to an employee which, under certain conditions (one of which being that the transferee must have made the offer to take the employee before the ending of the old employment) if accepted, may mean that any dismissal by a transferor on account of redundancy 'disappears', and the employees concerned are deemed not to have been dismissed. Section 94(1) has effect where:

'(a) a change occurs (whether by virtue of a sale or other disposition or by operation of law) in the ownership of a business for the purposes of which a person is employed, or a part of such business; and

(b) in connection with that change the person by whom the employee is employed immediately before the change occurs (in this section referred to as "the previous owner") terminates the employee's contract of employment whether by notice or without notice.'

It is important to note that these two provisions deal with quite separate matters. Schedule 13 is concerned solely with continuity of employment. Section 94 provides a transferor who has dismissed an employee employed in the business before the transfer on account of redundancy with a defence to a claim for a redundancy payment on the basis that a new offer of employment has been made to the employee, not by him, but by the transferee, with the result that the redundancy dismissal is deemed not to have taken place. Outside the context of transfers of businesses, if an employer, having dismissed an employee, makes him an offer of a new contract which is suitable alternative employment, the redundancy dismissal is negatived if the offer is accepted.[1] Section 94 achieves broadly the same sort of result in the context of change of employer, by providing that the offer of suitable alternative employment can be made by the re-engaging transferee instead.

None the less, despite their different functions, the two provisions employ similar concepts, ie bridging or blurring the gap between successive employments that occurs on change of employer through business transfer. It has also been held that these

---

1 EP(C)A ss 82 and 84.

provisions should be construed similarly. Thus, s 94 is to be read as if it referred to a 'trade, business or undertaking', not simply a business and, conversely, para 17(2) is to be construed as if 'transfer' included a 'change in the ownership of a business'. Authority for this can be found in a number of cases.[2] On the other hand, it can also be argued that the wording of s 94 may be more restrictive than Sch 13 para 17(2) because it refers to a change in *ownership*. Not all transfers, of course, involve a change of absolute ownership. As will be seen from Chapter 4, change-overs of employer occur in surrenders of tenancies, assignment of tenancies, replacement of managers and creation and termination of licences.[3] Schedule 13 para 17(2) does not expressly refer to changes of ownership. An example of the potential width, therefore, of Sch 13 para 17(2) is *Dabell v Vale Industrial Services (Nottingham) Limited.*[4] There the Court of Appeal held that there can be a transfer of a business notwithstanding that a proposed merger is subsequently called off. Whether or not there has been a transfer of business must, according to the court, be judged as at the date when the act of which the employee complains occurred, not as at the date of formal transfer of ownership (which never occurred in that case). In this case Mr Dabell was employed by Vale Industrial Services. Vale became technically insolvent. It received an offer for the purchase of its business from Nofotec. An agreement in principle was reached and orders, machines and other items and materials transferred together with a list of Vale's debtors. Three employees of Vale, including Mr Dabell, were sent to the site under the control of Nofotec where they started work. Shortly thereafter Mr Dabell claimed constructive dismissal and also unfair dismissal. Sometime afterwards negotiations between Vale and Nofotec foundered and the merger did not actually take place. It was held that at the time of the resignation Vale had closed its premises and everything had been handed over to Nofotec, including machines, customer connections, goodwill, existing contracts and employees. Thus, there was a transfer of an undertaking. Such an interpretation may be supported by cases in the European Court on the Acquired Rights Directive and which are directly relevant to the interpretation of the Transfer Regulations. These cases stress there can be a transfer for

---

2 E g *Lloyd v Brassey* [1969] 2 QB 98, (1969) 4 ITR 100, CA; *Lord Advocate v De Rosa* [1974] 2 All ER 849, [1974] ICR 480, HL; *Newlin Oil Co Ltd v Trafford* [1974] IRLR 205, (1974) 9 ITR 324; *G D Ault (Isle of Wight) Ltd v Gregory* (1967) 2 ITR 301; *Kenmir Ltd v Frizzell* [1968] 1 All ER 414, 3 ITR 159; *Woodhouse v Peter Brotherhood Ltd* [1972] 2 QB 520, [1972] ICR 186, CA.

3 See, in detail, Ch 4, pp 54 et seq.

4 [1988] IRLR 439.

the purposes of the directive whether or not a change of absolute ownership occurs.[5] *Quaere*, however, whether the terms of s 94 of the EP(C)A with its express words 'change of ownership' would be capable of the same construction,[6] even though a consistent approach would be desirable.

The case of *Lord Advocate v De Rosa*[7] illustrates how these two provisions (EP(C)A Sch 13 para 17(2) and s 94), which apart from the above discussion are similarly construed, none the less have different functions. It is important to note that the following discussion presupposes non-application of the Transfer Regulations which would, in most cases, now apply (see below). To illustrate the distinction between Sch 13 para 17(2) and s 94 though, s 94 may for example have determined which employer, transferee or transferor *should* have been liable for a redundancy payment. But suppose, for example, a transferee was *not* liable for a redundancy payment under s 94 (because, perhaps, no offer was made by the transferee *prior* to the ending of the old employment). In that case, the transferor would be liable for the payment. If the payment is made by him, continuity is broken for redundancy purposes even if the employee goes over to work for the new employer more or less immediately. What would happen if the redundancy payment was not actually claimed from the transferor and the employee simply went over to work for the new employer?

In *De Rosa* there was a transfer of a business in 1967. The

---

5 See *Foreniengen af Arbejdsledere i Danmark v Daddy's Dance Hall A/S* [1988] IRLR 315; *Berg and Busschers v IM Besselsen* [1989] IRLR 447; *Landsorganisationen i Danmark v Ny Molle Kro* [1989] IRLR 37; *P Bork International A/S v Foreningen af Arbejdsledere i Danmark* [1989] IRLR 41. It is to be noted, however, that Art 1 of the Acquired Rights Directive only applies to a transfer 'as a result of a legal transfer or merger'. See the discussion in Ch 4.

6 See *SI (Systems and Instrumentation) Ltd v Grist* [1983] ICR 788. This case concerned a situation where the proposed purchaser moved into occupation without completion of a legal transaction. On the other hand the Court of Appeal in *Dabell* (see text) found no difficulty in finding a transfer for the purposes of Sch 13 para 17(2) when no legal transfer occurred. The position, even under s 94, might be consistent with para 17(2) of Sch 13 where *some* disposition takes place however, even though disposition of absolute ownership does not occur. It has been argued (editorial note to *IDS Employment Law Cases* on *Landsorganisation i Danmark v Ny Molle Kro* ELC 9.2.31) that 'ownership' under domestic law has already been given a wide interpretation consistent with European law so that transfer of 'ownership' also means transfers of leases and licences. Hopefully s 94 would be construed, notwithstanding its wording, consistently with para 17(2) of Sch 13 in those cases. This argument may be strengthened by the case of *Marleasing SA v La Comercial Internacional de Alimentacion SA* (Case C 106/89, European Court), discussed in Ch 6.

7 [1974] 2 All ER 849, [1974] ICR 480, HL.

applicant, a transport manager, was offered a new job in the transferee's company as a docks manager. This he accepted. Subsequently, he was made redundant by the transferee. It was held that he was entitled to count his service with the transferor and the transferee in calculating the redundancy payment due from the transferee. It was established that because the offer of fresh employment had not been made *in writing* prior to the ending of the old employment (as then required),[8] s 94 (or rather its statutory predecessor[9]) would have made the transferor liable. But since no redundancy payment had been made and since any gap in employment had not been so great as to break continuity under the provisions of Sch 13 (because there was a transfer of a business with the meaning of Sch 13 and immediate engagement of the employees by the transferee) continuity was preserved.

As has been mentioned, if a redundancy payment is actually made by the transferor then, however contemporaneous the old employment and the new, there will be a break in continuity of employment for the purpose of redundancy at least.[10] Despite this, continuity of employment might be *unbroken* for the purposes of unfair dismissal and other claims as long as the conditions of para 17(2) of Sch 13 and other provisions of Sch 13 are satisfied. Thus the two provisions are complementary, yet independent.

2 DO THE TRANSFER REGULATIONS MAKE THE EP(C)A PROVISIONS OTIOSE?

If there is a transfer of a trade, business or undertaking, are either of these provisions in the EP(C)A (para 17(2) of Sch 13 and s 94) now relevant at all if, as it would seem at first glance, the Transfer Regulations apply and there is a relevant transfer under the Transfer Regulations?

As to redundancy payments liability the EP(C)A does indeed seem to be otiose. If the Transfer Regulations apply it must be clear that there would, of course, be no need to consider provisions concerning redundancy and change of ownership in the EP(C)A (such as s 94) in relation to dismissals that might otherwise arise out of the transfer itself. Liability for a redundancy payment only arises when there is a dismissal. Although, but for the Transfer Regula-

---

8　Section 82(3) of the EP(C)A now says that the offer may be made in writing or not.
9　Redundancy Payments Act 1965 s 13.
10　EP(C)A Sch 13 para 12.

tions, there would be a dismissal by a transferor or a transferee by refusing to employ the employee any longer in the old business (and this should be by reason of redundancy) it is provided by the Transfer Regulations that the transfer itself does *not* amount to a termination of contract. If there is no dismissal, s 94 does not arise.

As to statutory continuity of employment, it has in fact been argued[11] that reg 5 of the Transfer Regulations is sufficiently widely drafted so as to effect a transfer of continuity as well as to transfer the pure contractual and other incidents of the individual employment relation. Regulation 5(2) states that upon the completion of the transfer of the undertaking and upon the transfer of the contract of employment:

> '(a) All the transferor's rights, powers, duties and liabilities, under or in connection with any such contract, shall be transferred by virtue of this regulation to the transferee; and
>
> (b) Anything done before the transfer is completed by or in relation to the transferor in respect of that contract or a person employed in that undertaking or part shall be deemed to have been done by or in relation to the transferee.'

Davies and Freedland[12] are of the view that these words are wide enough to carry over the obligation to honour statutory continuity of employment from a transferor to a transferee on a transfer of a business. If right, this would mean that it might seem there is no need to consider the provisions of Sch 13 at all in a case where there is a transfer of an undertaking. This interpretation is compelling.

But there are three points here. First, there is an alternative view that reg 5 is *not* of itself widely enough drafted to cover transfer of statutory continuity of employment even when there is a relevant transfer under the Transfer Regulations.[13] In that event, the pro-

---

11 Davies and Freedland *Transfer of Employment* (1982).

12 In *Transfer of Employment* ibid. See also Lord Lyell, 425 Hansard HL Deb 10 December 1981, cols 1499–1500. Article 3(1) of the Acquired Rights Directive (EC Directive 77/187) would also be consistent with this since it provides, as set out in n 13 below, for the transfer of rights and obligations arising not only from a contract of employment but also from an 'employment relationship'.

13 This view was originally held by the learned editors of *Harvey on Industrial Relations and Employment Law* and also by the authors of *IDS Employment Law Handbook No 35: Continuity of Employment*. The issue may turn on the words of the Transfer Regulations, reg 5(2) which refers to the transfer of the '. . . transferor's rights, powers, duties and liabilities under or in connection with [an employment] contract'. To be contrasted are the wider words of the Acquired Rights Directive, Art 3(1) which refers to the transfer of '. . . the transferor's rights and obligations arising from a contract of employment *or from an employment relationship*' (emphasis added). See later in this book on suggestions

visions of the EP(C)A would still have to be considered for that purpose. Naturally, if the Davies and Freedland interpretation is correct, much of the following discussion will be academic because, save in cases where the Transfer Regulations are narrower than the EP(C)A (such as the case of a non-commercial venture: see below) reg 5 will have transferred employment from the transferor to the transferee and this should include both contractual aspects *and* statutory continuity.

Second, even assuming that reg 5 is wide enough not only to transfer the contract but also *continuity*, the provisions of the EP(C)A are still in existence. They were not repealed by the Transfer Regulations. It is true that if reg 5 has applied to transfer the contract, it may be (see above) that the EP(C)A is academic on continuity because continuity has already been transferred. In other words, there will be a 'belt and braces' effect. If reg 5 applies, so will para 17(2) of Sch 13. However, is the converse true? That is, if reg 5 does not apply because of, for example, *Secretary of State for Employment v Spence*[14] (see below) (in a case presumably where *Litster v Forth Dry Dock & Engineering Co Ltd*[15] (see below) does not apply) will statutory continuity be broken if the employee goes to work for the transferee?

As is discussed later in this chapter, the position under the Transfer Regulations is that, ordinarily, employment must be continued up to the actual point of transfer for reg 5, and transfer of employment thereunder to be triggered.[16] This is subject to the principle in *Litster v Forth Dry Dock & Engineering Co Ltd*[17] that where employment has not continued to the point of transfer and this is because of a pre-transfer dismissal which is automatically unfair under reg 8 of the Transfer Regulations, employment may be deemed statutorily to be construed to the point of transfer notwithstanding an actual interval in employment. However, it is arguable, at least, that *Litster* may only apply to those enjoying a qualifying period for unfair dismissal (see Ch 7). If so, how do such short-serving employees who are re-engaged protect their continuity if dismissed prior to the transfer? Only Sch 13 para 17(2) can do this. The application of Sch 13 para 17(2) in such situations and indeed generally, and a comparison of the relevance of intervals between successive employments for the purposes of the Transfer Regula-

whether these wider words could be used to interpret the Transfer Regulations and thus cover continuity of employment.

14 [1987] QB 179, [1986] 3 All ER 616.
15 [1989] ICR 341, [1989] IRLR 161.
16 *Secretary of State for Employment v Spence* [1986] ICR 651, [1986] IRLR 248.
17 [1989] IRLR 161.

tions on the one hand and Sch 13 para 17(2) on the other, is discussed in more detail later in this chapter.

Third, there *could* be situations where the EP(C)A might apply and the Transfer Regulations do not, even though, at first glance, there is a transfer of an undertaking attracting both sets of provisions. It can be argued that, in some respects, the definition of a transfer of an undertaking in the Transfer Regulations is narrower than that which applies under the EP(C)A. For example, it is provided in the Transfer Regulations that the regulations do not apply to 'any undertaking or part of an undertaking which is not in the nature of a *commercial venture*'.[18] No such express limitation appears in the EP(C)A. As discussed, this restrictive provision was applied recently in *Woodcock v Committee for the Time Being of the Friends' School, Wigton and Genwise Ltd*,[19] where a Quaker school of charitable status was held to be an undertaking which was not in the nature of a commercial venture for the purposes of the Transfer Regulations so that the Transfer Regulations did not apply. One can think of many other employers who might have charitable or non-profit-making purposes and in such cases, as discussed, the Transfer Regulations may similarly not apply.[20] In cases under the EP(C)A many non-commercial ventures *were* regarded as undertakings for the purposes of the EP(C)A. The reader is referred to Chapter 4 where this issue is discussed in detail.[1]

If the Transfer Regulations do not apply, because there is a transfer of a non-commercial venture, but the EP(C)A does, then an imposed transfer of employment will amount to a dismissal and liability for a redundancy payment will be determined under the provisions of s 94 and the question of continuity of employment upon the transfer of employment will be determined by Sch 13.

---

18 Reg 2(1).
19 [1987] IRLR 98, CA.
20 Although it has been decided that the word 'undertaking' could be wide enough to cover a venture run at a loss (*Hadden v University of Dundee Students' Association* [1985] IRLR 449, EAT).
 1 See *Ferretti v Southwark and Lambeth Archaeological Projects* COIT 1479/244, IT, *IDS Handbook* 36 p 6 and *Robinson v Bournemouth Borough Council* (1970) 5 ITR 100, IT (non-profit-making archaeological dig and surveying department in a college transferred to another college held in both cases to be a business transfer). See also *Dallow Industrial Properties v Else and Curd* [1976] 2 QB 449, 2 ITR 304. See, now, however, *Pittman v Davis Build plc (in liquidation)* (EAT 122/90) which suggests that para 17(2) of Sch 13 to the EP(C)A is confined also to commercial undertaking (see also Ch 4).

3 CONTINUITY OF EMPLOYMENT UNDER THE EP(C)A

It must be stressed again here that, under the EP(C)A, statutory continuity of employment, where more than one employer is involved, will only be preserved by virtue of Sch 13 para 17 or 18. Miscellaneous cases under para 18 where there has been a change in employment from one employer to another and where, none the less, continuity may be preserved, have been dealt with earlier in this book.[2] The relevant provision for transfers of businesses is para 17(2). A number of issues may have to be considered before para 17(2) is applied.

(i) Proving continuity on change of employment

Frequently, there may be a dispute as to whether para 17(2) applies to an employee's period of employment with successive employers and whether the employee may count together periods of employment with such successive employers. In Sch 13, it is provided that there is a presumption of continuity until the contrary is shown. In other words, it is for the employer to disprove this.[3] However, does that presumption apply to the provisions of Sch 13 generally, which apply to continuity of employment with the one employer only, or does it also apply to the provisions of para 17 which apply to employment with more than one employer? The point is a difficult one, although one would have thought that the better view on policy grounds should be that the presumption of continuity still applies where there are successive employments. That is, in a case where the ultimate employer disputes the length of continuous employment because there has been a change in employer at some previous stage, it should be for that employer to establish that there was a break in continuity, in other words that the case is not covered by para 17. However, the case law does not support this view. The question bears detailed examination generally, and it is also an issue raised in Chapter 11.

It is well established that the presumption of continuity of employment applies to cases where employment is with one employer throughout.[4] Paragraph 17(1) of Sch 13 says that:

---

2 See Ch 2.
3 Sch 13 para 1(3).
4 See Sch 13 para 1(3) and *Nicoll v Nocorrode Ltd* [1981] ICR 348, [1981] IRLR 163, EAT (although there, the EAT suggested that the onus may be on the *employee* to establish at least that he was employed during the *first* week of his employment with the employer: *sed quaere*.)

'Subject to this paragraph and paragraphs 18 and 18A the foregoing provisions of this Schedule relate to employment with the one employer.'

In *Evenden v Guildford City Association Football Club*[5] the Court of Appeal (Lord Denning MR, Browne LJ and Brightman J) thought that the presumption of continuity *did* apply even in a case where there was more than one employer. But in other (earlier) cases, this had been doubted.[6] In *Secretary of State for Employment v Globe Elastic Thread Co Ltd*[7] Lord Wilberforce considered that the presumption of continuity could not apply in a case of successive employments.[8] In *Umar v Pliastar Ltd*[9] the result on the facts was that it could not be established whether a transferred employee's case fell under para 17 or para 18. Because this could not be proved it was held his claim to continuity with more than one employer should fail. This case might indirectly lend support to the view that the onus rested on the employee, who could not discharge it in that case (the situation might have been otherwise if the presumption of continuity had been applied in his favour). However, the point was not directly dealt with in the case. Finally however, in *Secretary of State for Employment v Cohen and Beaupress Ltd*[10] Scott J emphatically ruled that the presumption does not apply to a transfer of employment case and that it is for the employee to satisfy the industrial tribunal on the balance of probabilities that there was a transfer. Since this is the most recent authority, it is, in the absence of a pronouncement by the Court of Appeal, likely to be of some weight. It also has the advantage, albeit an EAT decision, of being relatively unequivocal about the issue and, taken with doubts in earlier decisions and the view of Lord Wilberforce in *Globe Elastic*, probably extinguishes any argument that the statutory presumption of continuity applies where there is employment with more than one employer (see also Ch 11).

---

5 [1975] QB 917, [1975] ICR 367, CA, overruled by *Secretary of State for Employment v Globe Elastic Thread Co Ltd* [1980] AC 506, [1979] 2 All ER 1077 (note 7, below) on a different point.
6 *Newsham v Dunlop Textiles Ltd (No 2)* (1969) ITR 268; *Spencer v Miller Bros & Buckley Ltd* (1968) 3 ITR 371; *Chapman v Wilkinson* (1967) 2 ITR 39 (per Lord Parker CJ; although Salmon LJ and Widgery J expressed no opinion).
7 [1980] AC 506, [1979] ICR 706.
8 [1979] ICR 706 at 711. Although this was obiter, the view is obviously persuasive.
9 [1981] ICR 727 (relied on in part in *Secretary of State v Cohen*, n 10, below).
10 [1987] ICR 570, [1987] IRLR 169, EAT.

(ii) Employment 'at the time of the transfer'

On a transfer of a business, para 17(2) of Sch 13 to the EP(C)A only applies to an employee employed by the transferor in the 'trade, business or undertaking *at the time of the transfer*'. Only if the employee is so employed will the transfer fail to break continuity of employment.[11] The question of the potentially destructive effect on continuous employment of intervals between successive employments is of considerable practical significance. This is especially so given occasional attempts by vendors and purchasers to effect breaks in actual employment of employees employed in the transferor's business before the transfer in order that they might be re-engaged by a transferee thereafter with a break in continuous employment.

Similar questions arise, of course, in relation to transfer of contracts under reg 5 of the Transfer Regulations.[12] Regulation 5 of the Transfer Regulations applies only when employees are employed in the undertaking 'immediately before the transfer'. As will be seen from the extended discussion in Chapter 7, in *Secretary of State for Employment v Spence*[13] the Court of Appeal, recognising that employment contracts were not automatically transferred to a transferee of a business under reg 5 unless employees were employed in that business 'immediately before' the transfer, held that this meant that employees had to be employed actually at the *point* or *moment* of transfer in order to be protected by the regulation. This meant that employees effectively dismissed by the transferor prior to the transfer (whether or not this was a blatant attempt to get round the Transfer Regulations; see *Forth Estuary Engineering Co Ltd v Litster*)[14] were not, *ex hypothesi*, employed in the business immediately before the transfer and, thus, not transferred to the transferee. Instead, their employment claims, including those arising out of the termination of their employment, had to be made against the transferor and the transferee was free to engage the employees concerned if he wanted to be free of their existing contracts of employment.

The decision in *Spence*, however, had been made without the

---

11 Sch 13 para 17(2) to the EP(C)A. EP(C)A s 94 (settlement of redundancy liability on business transfer) also applies only when the employee is employed 'immediately before' a change in ownership of the business occurs. This is similar wording to Sch 13 para 17(2) and almost exactly similar to that employed in reg 5 of the Transfer Regulations. But Sch 13 para 17(2) (here under discussion) seems to have been more frequently litigated.
12 Discussed in more detail in Ch 7.
13 [1985] ICR 646.
14 [1988] IRLR 289 (Court of Session).

benefit of discussion of certain European Court cases which had dealt with the mandatory effect of Art 4(1) of the Acquired Rights Directive, which states that dismissals in connection with a transfer should not take place save where they are for an 'economic, technical or organisational reason entailing changes in the workforce'.[15]

Regulation 8(1) of the Transfer Regulations provides that dismissals in connection with a transfer are automatically unfair unless for an 'economic, technical or organisational reason'. However, it is not at first glance easy to see how this affects the interpretation in *Spence* of reg 5. But to meet the problem, the House of Lords held in *Litster v Forth Dry Dock & Engineering Co Ltd*[16] that the Transfer Regulations had to be construed to give effect to our obligations under the directive as interpreted by the European Court and therefore had to be read to the effect that an employee who is dismissed in connection with an impending transfer where there is no economic, technical or organisational reason for dismissal is automatically transferred to the transferee whether or not there was an interval between dismissal and transfer. The way the House of Lords achieved this objective was to construe reg 5(1), which refers to a person being employed 'immediately before' the transfer, as reading, additionally, as if there were inserted immediately after those words further words to the effect 'or would have been so employed if he had not been unfairly dismissed in the circumstances described in reg 8(1)'.[17]

It would be a happy state of affairs if this also governed the position under Sch 13 para 17(2). However, as discussed above, the question of statutory continuity of employment is a separate issue from reg 5. As discussed above, some argue that statutory continuity of employment falls solely to be decided under EP(C)A para 17(2) Sch 13 *even where* reg 5 applies (although some, to be fair, argue that if employment under reg 5 is transferred, statutory continuity will also, inevitably, follow – see the arguments above). Imagine, then, the application of the facts in *Spence* to para 17(2). Is the appropriate construction of Sch 13 para 17(2) and case law under it the same? Is any interval between successive employments fatal (as is the case under reg 5 when *Spence* applies) for an employee? The interpretation of reg 5 in *Litster* has been influenced by the case law of the European Court. But the Transfer Regulations were enacted to give effect to European law and are therefore, it seems, subject to interpretation accordingly. On an orthodox

---

15 *P Bork International v Foreningen af Arbejdsledere i Danmark* [1989] IRLR 41.
16 [1989] ICR 341, [1989] IRLR 161.
17 See Ch 7.

view, this does not apply to the EP(C)A (see Ch 6).[18] However, as will be seen below, the European Court's decision in *Marleasing SA v La Comercial Internacional de Alimentacion SA* (Case C 106/89) may now encourage harmonious interpretation.

The question of any difference of approach between the Transfer Regulations and para 17(2) can be important. We have already mentioned non-commercial ventures (see Ch 4). Another problem briefly mentioned earlier is this. Suppose *Litster* were applied to the case of a number of employees apparently automatically unfairly dismissed before a transfer. This would ordinarily have the result of transfer of their employment to a transferee notwithstanding an interval between successive employments. The question arises whether *all* would be able to claim the benefit of *Litster*. The issue is whether *Litster* only applies in favour of those who have a qualifying period of employment for unfair dismissal purposes (ie two years). This problem seems inherent from the use of the automatically unfair dismissal provisions of reg 8 (see below) to cause deemed continuation of contract. Of course this would be unfair, especially as many rights an employee might seek to have honoured by a transferee employer (eg notice monies, arrears of wages, etc) might have nothing to do with unfair dismissal. Case law does not cover this proposition although there is a strong argument in all equity for all employees to be covered irrespective of a qualifying period. On the other hand, Art 4(1) of the directive stipulates that:

> 'member states may provide that [the prohibition against transfer connected dismissals] shall not apply to certain specific categories of employees who are not covered by the laws or practice of the member states in respect of protection against dismissal.'

It could therefore be argued that this legitimises exclusion from *Litster* of those with short service.[19] If this is correct, as discussed, only para 17(2) of Sch 13 can provide a statutory umbrella for employees.

Until recently, the leading case on Sch 13 para 17(2) concerning proximity of successive employments in the context of statutory continuity was the Court of Appeal decision in *Teesside Times Ltd v Drury*.[20] In this case the employee worked for Champion Publications Limited. A liquidator was appointed to that company who agreed the sale of the company's business to Teesside Times. Employees were dismissed by the liquidator on behalf of Champion

---

18 And see the discussion in Ch 7, below.
19 And see the comments of Wood J in *Macer v Abafast Ltd* [1990] IRLR 137 at 141.
20 [1980] ICR 338.

during the day of the transfer which was a Friday and re-engaged by
Teesside later, after the transfer, on the same Friday evening.

It will be seen that the wording of para 17(2) of Sch 13 contemplates that employees are employed in the business 'at the time of
the transfer'. The case was decided on now repealed provisions then
contained in Sch 1 to the Contracts of Employment Act 1972 (now
see EP(C)A Sch 13) but which have now been overtaken by the
Employment Act 1982 (see below). However, in the alternative,
the court expressed some view on the meaning of 'at the time of the
transfer'. Goff LJ thought that an employee had to be employed
actually at the point of transfer to be covered by para 17(2) holding
that employment 'at the time of transfer' referred to employment
continuing 'to the moment when the transaction of transferring the
business from one owner to another is effected, or such short period
as is necessary to enable that to be carried out'.[1] However, he
thought in the face of the facts in *Teesside Times Ltd* that the
particular interval in question between dismissal and transfer could,
in effect, be ignored, stating 'had it been necessary, I would have
felt very strongly inclined to conclude on the facts found by the
tribunal that the time of the transfer was *eo instanti* with the
dismissal. . .'. On the other hand, Stephenson LJ thought that 'time
of transfer' meant 'period' of transfer. He stated:

'. . . "the time" and "the transfer" cannot and should not be considered separately; "the time" of something must take its meaning
from what that thing is, and if the transfer – of a trade or business or
undertaking – is something which takes time, I would infer that "the
time of a transfer" more naturally means a period of time than a
moment of time. A transfer of a business is as [Counsel] said "a
complex of operations which are part of a continuous process through
different stages, including dismissal and re-engagement of staff".'

On the other hand, it is arguably implicit from his judgment that
he thought that the interval must none the less come under and be
saved by the various provisions of Sch 13 stating:

'I accept that apart from the computing provisions of [Sch 13] the gap
between dismissal and anything which can reasonably be called
"transfer" will defeat the application of [para 17(2)] and break the
continuity of employment.'

The third judge, Eveleigh LJ, went further and thought that the
length of the break between employments was not material. He
considered that the period of employment of an employee in the
trade or business at the time of transfer means the period which is

---

1 At p 355.

vested in him at the time of transfer. It should be added to that which begins on the date of re-engagement. He considered that in effect, the length of the interval between successive employments could be unlimited so long as it was caught up in the mechanics of transfer and, as he stated, if 'the dismissal was a step towards the re-engagement'.

The wide view of Eveleigh LJ did not find favour with his colleagues in the Court of Appeal. But, if Stephenson LJ's 'middle ground' view is adopted, it can be argued that even if the general provisions of Sch 13 are to be taken into account, this none the less allows for a potentially lengthy interval between dismissal and transfer to be ignored for the purposes of calculating whether the employee is employed in the business at the time of transfer. Thus, the general provisions of Sch 13 seem to count weeks towards continuity of employment where there is employment during all or any part of a week where relations are governed by a contract normally involving 16 hours or more work per week. Any employment during part of that week counts towards continuity. So, if an employee is dismissed by a transferor say on Monday of week 1 and he is engaged by the transferee on Friday of week 2, his employment on this argument could be continuous. This is because there is employment during parts of two continuous weeks. *A fortiori* it could be argued that if an employee is dismissed on Monday of a week and re-engaged by a transferee on Thursday or Friday of that week, his employment will be continuous because there is one week during which he is employed by both employers and, *a fortiori*, if he is dismissed early one day by the transferor and re-engaged later in the same day by the transferee. It should be remembered that the Employment Act 1982 altered the rules about starting and finishing employment, thereby putting a stop to the argument that if employment actually ended during part of a week, the whole of the week could count towards the length of continuous employment. But it did not alter the rules, it can be argued, about counting weeks in the *middle* of employment. There are certainly a number of cases outside the context of para 17(2) where the mid-employment counting weeks rule has meant that a significant interval between employments has not been fatal as long as there are successive counting weeks under the above analysis.[2] However, these cases

---

2 Cases confirming that Sch 13 para 4 (or its predecessor) allows part weeks *during* employment to count (notwithstanding employment in only part) include *Loggie v Alexander Hall & Son (Builders) Ltd* (1969) 4 ITR 390 and *Jennings v Salford Community Service Agency* [1981] ICR 399; [1981] IRLR 76. Although these are cases decided before the Employment Act 1982 there is no reason to suppose they are no longer valid on this point: see, for example, recently, *Leitch v Currie* EAT

have related to employment with the *one* employer and it is possible that the mid-employment counting weeks rule may not apply where there are successive employments with different employers as opposed to with one employer alone. Such a doubt has indeed been expressed by Hepple and O'Higgins.[3]

However, once *Spence* was decided in the context of the Transfer Regulations, it was always possible that an appellate court would try to harmonise the approach to the Transfer Regulations and para 17(2) by applying to para 17(2) the interpretation seen in *Spence*. This can be seen in *Brook Lane Finance Co Ltd v Bradley*.[4] In this case Mr Bradley was employed as the company secretary of Hunt Finance. In February 1976 sale of that business was agreed. On 28 February 1986 a Deed of Assignment of Loans and Debts to the transferee was concluded which, it was held, effectively put the transferee in possession. However, it was not until 26 March that a formal agreement for the sale and purchase of the company's office fixtures and fittings, loans and debts which were the subject of the deed of assignment and of the goodwill of the business, was completed. Bradley ceased to work for Hunt Finance on 28 February and on 1 March he began to work solely for the transferee. The Employment Appeal Tribunal found that the date of completion of the transaction was 26 March and this was the date of transfer. As a result, Mr Bradley was not employed in the business at the time of a transfer, having gone earlier than the date of transfer to work for the transferee.

Inter alia it was argued for the employee that 'time of transfer' for the purposes of para 17(2) of Sch 13 meant 'a period of time'. Popplewell J thought, however, that the obiter remarks in *Teesside Times Ltd v Drury* to the effect that time of transfer could be over a period of time, conflicted with the Court of Appeal decision in

---

27.1.87 – resignation and re-engagement – interval between employments not fatal as there was employment throughout some part of successive counting weeks. In *Roach v CBS (Moulds) Ltd* [1991] ICR 349, [1991] IRLR 200 the EAT declined to apply Sch 13 para 4 where an employee left his employer and joined another employer before returning to the first employer, holding that para 4 was confined to a situation where there is one contract of employment where the employee is employed at the same job. It is submitted, however, that this is wrong: as long as the counting weeks argument is satisfied it should be immaterial what the employee does during the protected interval.

3 *Encyclopaedia of Labour Relations Law* op cit. An equally fascinating argument concerns the possible use here of para 9(1)(b) (absence from work on account of temporary cessation of work) or para 9(1)(c) (absence by arrangement or custom) of Sch 13 to bridge an interval between successive employments (see *Robert Edgar Ltd v Elliott*, EAT 581/85).

4 [1988] ICR 423, [1988] IRLR 283.

Secretary of State for Employment v Spence about reg 5 of the Transfer Regulations. He held that the time of transfer must be construed in the same way, i e to mean a moment in time, under the EP(C)A as under the Transfer Regulations and considered the EAT bound by the decision in *Spence*. Leave to appeal was given to enable the Court of Appeal to decide whether *Spence* was *per incuriam* in the light of the *Teesside Times* decision or whether the *Teesside Times* decision was to be treated as overruled by *Spence*. At the end of the day an appeal was not, however, pursued and the question left unresolved. Although there are differences in the statutory wording, the logic of the EAT that there ought to be a harmonious approach between that of *Spence* under the Transfer Regulations and for the purposes of para 17(2) of Sch 13 has its attractions. If adopted it would mean that for the purposes of both provisions, any interval between successive employments would be fatal, on the one hand under *Spence* to transfer of contracts of employment and, on the other, under para 17(2) of Sch 13, to preservation of continuity of employment.

On the other hand, of course, this logic would equally say now that *Spence* has been qualified by *Litster*, thus allowing for some intervals between successive employments to be, in the context of reg 5, effectively ignored, a re-appraisal ought to take place of the position about statutory continuity. As *Brook Lane Finance Co Ltd v Bradley* was decided before *Litster* what effect would *Litster* (if any) have (and indeed could it have) on the judicial approach to para 17(2)?

The answer has recently been provided by the EAT in *Macer v Abafast Ltd*.[5] In this case Mr Macer, a director, was employed for four-and-a-half years by CTR Limited. Talks started with Abafast for the take-over of the firm. It was the intention that the business of CTR would be transferred to a subsidiary of Abafast, to be called CTR (Recruitment) Limited. On 31 December 1986 the employees of CTR, including Mr Macer, were told their employments were at an end with CTR but that there would be jobs with Recruitment. These employees (but not Mr Macer) were offered employment with Recruitment to start on 1 January 1987. The transfer took place in stages, exchange being on 19 February 1987 and completion not until 12 February 1988. On 21 January 1987 Abafast wrote to Mr Macer offering him employment (apparently retrospectively) with effect from 12 January 1987, 12 days after the others had started. It was admitted in proceedings that Abafast was attempting to create a 12-day interval in successive employments to break continuity of

5 [1990] ICR 234, [1990] IRLR 137.

employment. In the end, Mr Macer was dismissed on 23 September 1987 and claimed unfair dismissal. To do so, of course, he had to show his employment was continuous from some time before the transfer. The industrial tribunal held that the transfer took place either over a series of transactions caught by reg 3(4), the first of which was on 18 January 1987 when the liquidator of CTR accepted Abafast's offer of sale *or* on exchange, on 19 February 1987. But in either case, according to the tribunal, which followed *Spence*, Mr Macer was not employed by the transferor 'immediately before' the transfer (or, alternatively, the first transaction therein) (for the purposes of the Transfer Regulations) or, alternatively, at the time of the transfer (for the purposes of para 17(2)). Therefore his employment was not transferred and the tribunal had no jurisdiction. As can be seen, Mr Macer fell into the same trap as Mr Bradley, in that by leaving his old employer early (in Mr Bradley's case to assist the transferee) prior to the transfer, he was not in employment in the business of the transferor at the time of transfer.[6]

But what could be done for Mr Macer? Wood J was clearly influenced by *Litster*, stating:

'. . . in approaching the proper construction to be given to the words of the Act of 1978, a court should lean in favour of that interpretation which best gives effect to the preservation of continuity of service and hence to the preservation of rights of the employee and to obviate and discourage a tactical manoeuvre which seeks to avoid the clear intention of Parliament.'

The time therefore had come, in his view, for a re-consideration of the Transfer Regulations and the EP(C)A provisions in the light of *Litster*. Accordingly, the EAT was reluctant to hold that the words 'at the time of the transfer' in para 17(2) meant 'at the moment of transfer' as interpreted by *Spence* in the context of the

6 Although (see Ch 4) it has been suggested by Hepple and O'Higgins (*Encyclopaedia of Labour Relations Law*) that on the facts of *Brook Lane Finance v Bradley* Mr Bradley might well have been employed at the point of transfer as recent European cases on the Transfer Regulations at least emphasise that the point of transfer is not to be judged solely from the perspective of an absolute change of ownership but, rather, when there is a change of employer who adopts employment obligations towards employees. In the view of Hepple and O'Higgins, the transfer could well have taken place upon the entering into possession by the transferee on the deed of assignment of loans and debts on 28 February at which time Mr Bradley was, of course, still employed in the business: *Foreningen af Arbejdsledere i Danmark v Daddy's Dance Hall A/S* [1988] ECR 739, [1988] IRLR 315; *Berg and Busschers v IM Besselsen* [1989] 3 CMLR 817, [1989] IRLR 447; *Landsorganisationen i Danmark v Ny Molle Kro* [1989] ICR 330, [1989] IRLR 37; *P Bork International A/S v Foreningen af Arbejdsledere i Danmark* [1989] IRLR 41.

Transfer Regulations. Wood J adopted the suggestion of Eveleigh LJ in *Teesside Times Ltd v Drury* that the period of employment of an employee in the business at the time of transfer meant that period which is vested in him at the time of transfer. It was of course acknowledged that some commentators argue that any gap between successive employment by transferor and transferee could be no more than one counting week as contemplated by para 1(1) of Sch 13 (see above). Wood J, however, rejected this argument. The gap, in order for it to be ignored, must be a gap which is related to the machinery of transfer and if it was too long it might not be viewed in that way. However, to make an arbitrary rule that a gap of more than one week breaks continuity of employment but that a gap of less than one week does not, allowed manipulation of the situation and was contrary to the intention of the legislation and the guidance in *Litster*. The decision of the EAT in *Brook Lane Finance Co Ltd v Bradley* would therefore not be followed as it was given before the guidance in *Litster*.

Welcome though the decision is, it does warrant some further examination. First, Sch 13 para 1, for example, states clearly that a week which does not count breaks continuity. This, it would seem, is certainly an argument against the view that the length of the interval between employments is immaterial as long as it is connected with the machinery of transfer. Wood J answered this criticism, however, by saying:

'. . . it has been suggested that if the gap between the period of employment by the transferor and the period of employment by the transferee is allowed to exceed the statutory week referred to in the earlier paragraphs of Schedule 13 then at any time in the future the employee may be able to add together two periods of continuous employment. We do not feel that this criticism is well founded for three reasons. The first is that the gap must be a gap which is related to the machinery of transfer and if the gap was too long it might not be viewed in that way. Secondly, it seems to us unlikely that the transfer period would be very long in the normal event as the transferees will be losing money if the business is not operating. Thirdly, however, it is said that the wording of para 17(1) applies the provisions of the earlier to the gap during the transfer process. With respect to that view, we do not share it. It seems to us that the earlier provisions of the Schedule relate "only to employment by the one employer". They thus apply to the period of employment with the transferor and to the period of employment with the transferee. It is to provide for the period between those two employments and to provide continuity of employment despite that gap that para 17(2) is drafted. Once again it seems to us that to make an arbitrary rule that a gap of more than one week, e g that 10 days, breaks the continuity of employment, but that gap if less than one week does not, allows manipulation of the situation and is contrary to the intentions of the legislation and the guidance in *Litster*'s case.'

Second, in reaching a view that the length of the interval is immaterial, Wood J was influenced by the guidance in *Litster*. However, some would say that the broad view of the Transfer Regulations in *Litster* does not necessarily permit so broad an interpretation of para 17(2) of Sch 13 but that would make it conflict with para 1 of Sch 13, particularly as neither Sch 13 nor any part of the EP(C)A was enacted to comply with the Acquired Rights Directive: this has traditionally made it more difficult to apply broad purposive approaches in conflict with clear drafting.[7] However, the European Court in *Marleasing SA v La Commercial Internacional de Alimentacion SA*, Case 106/89, has recently held that national law must be applied in the light of a directive if it pre-dates *or* post-dates the directive; whether this could be applied to Sch 13 para 17(2) is not yet decided, but its possibilities are exciting (see Ch 6).

Third, Wood J's desire to marry up the interpretation of reg 5 of the Transfer Regulations in the light of *Litster* with the position under para 17(2) of Sch 13 is commendable. But if one thinks about it, the exact parallel interpretation of the two provisions may not have been achieved. *Litster*, as will be remembered, states that if there is a pre-transfer dismissal contrary to reg 8(1) an employee dismissed prior to the transfer may be deemed to have statutorily continued his employment to the point of transfer and thus the interval between his dismissal and the transfer may be ignored. *Semble* there can be no limit to the length of the interval which can thus be ignored (although if the interval is too long, it is doubtful whether the dismissal will have been considered to be transfer-connected in the first place). Otherwise, if the pre-transfer dismissal does not fall under *Litster* the employee's claim to transfer of his contract will fail as he will not have been employed in the business at the moment of transfer. The law on the Transfer Regulations therefore draws a distinction between transfer-connected dismissals contrary to reg 8(1), where the length of any interval between successive employments is immaterial and a *Spence* case, where any interval is fatal. It can be argued that the approach in *Macer v Abafast* which holds that, on a business transfer, a re-engaged employee may count towards future employment any period of

---

7 The received position in English law is that domestic legislation cannot be construed to give effect to European law if the domestic legislation pre-dates European legislation: *Duke v GEC Reliance Ltd* [1988] ICR 339.

112 *The EP(C)A and business transfers*

employment with the transferor which is vested in him at the time of
transfer, poses no such distinction. However, it could be argued
that as the gap, in order for it to be ignored, must be one which is
'*related to the machinery of transfer*', this is saying that the transfer
must in effect be transfer-connected for the gap to be bridged, a
result similar to that in *Litster*. A pre-transfer dismissal unconnected with the transfer could be argued to give rise to a gap between
successive employments which is unrelated to the machinery of
transfer.

The issue arose again before the EAT and before Wood J, in
Gibson v Motortune Ltd.[8] In this case Gibson had been employed as
an operative in a car body repair shop since April 1984. The business was owned by Charles Ivey Limited (CIL). An informal on-
going relationship was struck with a company called Motortune
Limited (M). Pursuant to this, in March 1987, the lease held by CIL
to carry on its business was assigned to Motortune which also
purchased equipment and materials used in the shop. Mr Gibson's
employment with CIL ended on 27 February 1987 and he began
fresh employment with Motortune on 2 March 1987. He was dismissed in February 1988 and complained of unfair dismissal, maintaining that his employment with CIL could be added to his
employment with Motortune for the purposes of establishing a
qualifying period for unfair dismissal. The majority of the EAT
supported the industrial tribunal's finding that there had been a
transfer of an undertaking. The industrial tribunal found that the
transfer took place on Monday 2 March 1987. The question arose of
whether Mr Gibson had continuous employment as he was not, on
the face of it, employed in the business precisely at the time of
transfer, having left the transferor a couple of days earlier on 28
February.

However, the applicant had finished work with the transferor on
Friday 27 February and joined the transferee on the immediately
following Monday 2 March 1987. These were adjacent weeks and in
both the appellant had worked during all or part of a week during
which his relations with an employer were governed by a contract of
employment ordinarily requiring sixteen or more hours per week. It
was argued for the appellant that because of the provisions of the
EP(C)A calculation of continuity is by reference to weeks as
defined by Sch 13 and therefore, if a person works for only one day
during two adjacent relevant weeks, then continuity is preserved. In
other words, the counting weeks argument discussed earlier in this
text should apply.

8 [1990] ICR 740, 21 August 1990, p 13.

Without commenting on such an argument, however, the EAT decided that because of its own decision in *Macer v Abafast Ltd* there can be bridging of continuity of employment notwithstanding an interval between successive employments as long as the interval is connected with the machinery of transfer, and irrespective of the adjacent weeks argument. *Macer v Abafast* was therefore applied and upheld, albeit by the very same division of the EAT which had decided it. There the position rests for the moment.

In conclusion, the House of Lords in *Litster* intended to give effect to the aims of the Acquired Rights Directive upon which the Transfer Regulations were based, namely to safeguard 'employees' rights in the event of transfers of undertakings, businesses or parts of businesses'. Its effect was to stop the device commonly implemented by the transferor and transferee to effect pre-transfer dismissal prior to a transfer and thus cause an interval between successive employments in order to outflank the provisions of reg 5 and the automatic transfer of contracts of employment. In *Macer v Abafast* the EAT took an equally bold step in widely interpreting the provisions of para 17(2) of Sch 13 to the EP(C)A to provide that continuity of employment was not prejudiced in similar circumstances. It may be that to construe the EP(C)A provisions so widely (particularly in stating that the length of the interval between successive employments may be ignored even if longer than one counting week under the provisions of Sch 13 is immaterial) is not at first glance supported by the express wording of the EP(C)A; but in the context of present judicial views on the legislation protecting employees on business transfers it would be unfortunate if an appellate court decided to retrace the steps made by the EAT in *Macer v Abafast Ltd*. And, to repeat, it is at least arguable that the *Marleasing* case (see above and Ch 6) allows para 17(2) of Sch 13 to be interpreted in a manner broadly consistent with *Litster*.

4 REDUNDANCY PAYMENTS AND CHANGE OF OWNERSHIP UNDER THE EP(C)A

Generally, if the Transfer Regulations and, in particular, reg 5, apply, the EP(C)A provisions about redundancy on a change in the ownership of a business are not relevant. If the Transfer Regulations apply, and the employment contract is transferred, there will be no dismissal at all by reason of the transfer itself. If, thereafter, the transferee dismisses the employee by reason of redundancy, the general law of redundancy is applicable, in that subject to the statutory definition of redundancy being satisfied, a redundancy payment will be payable by the dismissing employer; but that has nothing to do with the provisions concerning redundancy liability on change of employer.

It could, therefore, be argued that a detailed examination of s 94 of the EP(C)A is now academic. In many, if not most, situations of business transfer this will, indeed, be the case. But there may be an area of residual applicability of s 94.

First, as discussed above in relation to continuity of employment, certain business transfers may not be covered by the Transfer Regulations which are none the less covered by the EP(C)A. For example, as above, a transfer of a non-commercial venture might not be a transfer caught by the Transfer Regulations, but might still be a transfer caught by Sch 13 *and* by s 94 of the EP(C)A in relation to the provisions concerning a change of ownership in the business. Second, again as above, it is not yet entirely clear whether the law governing the status of an interval between employments is the same under the provisions concerning redundancy payments under s 94 and that governing intervals between employment under the Transfer Regulations (although this point concerns continuity of employment under Sch 13 as applicable in redundancy cases rather than s 94 itself; see above and the discussion on *Macer v Abafast*, a case which, as discussed, now appears to bridge the gap).

Thus, for example, in the case of a transfer which is apparently a business transfer under the EP(C)A but not a transfer of an undertaking for the purposes of the Transfer Regulations (for example, the transfer of a non-commercial venture), reg 5 will *not* automatically transfer contracts of employment of employees transferred. The provisions of s 94 of the EP(C)A would then have to be considered in relation to redundancy payments liability.

In such a case, if the employee is dismissed by the transferor (and, in cases outside the Transfer Regulations, the sale of the business will inevitably result in a dismissal as the transferor can no longer employ), he is prima facie entitled to a redundancy payment from the transferor.[9] However, this may be negatived if there is reinstatement by the transferee within four weeks of the ending of the old employment or if there is re-engagement under a different job within four weeks of the ending of the employment provided that, in the latter case, an offer (whether in writing or not) in respect of the new job has been made to the employee before the ending of the old contract and, in both cases, that there is a trial period – unless the

---

9 The cessation of employment will usually meet the definition of redundancy in s 81(2) of the EP(C)A.

job offered is identical.[10] If either of these situations occurs and, subject to the trial period, the offer of fresh employment is unreasonably refused, the employee will not be entitled to a redundancy payment from the transferor even though he ceases employment altogether.[11] If it is reasonably refused he gets his redundancy payment from the transferor. The change of identity of employer has to be ignored in deciding whether it was reasonable to refuse the offer by the transferor.[12] If the offer of new employment with the transferee under the above conditions is accepted, there is no entitlement to a redundancy payment from either the transferor or transferee, but continuity of employment is preserved for the purposes of any future redundancy claim against the transferee.[13]

Bridging of *continuity* when the new offer is accepted is brought about by the provisions of para 11(2) of Sch 13 to the EP(C)A. Interestingly, under these provisions, a gap of up to four weeks is contemplated by Sch 13 as not breaking continuity of employment for the purposes of redundancy claims in the future against the transferee when s 94 applies.[14]

We have already discussed the rules about intervals between employment for the purposes of Sch 13, para 17(2) and we have noted how the decision in *Macer v Abafast* may have simplified them. It remains to be seen whether *Macer* also applies to s 94 cases. But there seems no reason why not. If that is wrong the statutory provisions are arguably more generous here than under para 17(2). It is, therefore, possible, that, say in a non-commercial venture case, where the Transfer Regulations do not apply but the EP(C)A does, the EP(C)A will allow an interval of up to four weeks[15] to count towards continuous employment for the purposes of a redundancy claim against a successor employer. It should be noted though (again in a case not covered by the Transfer Regulations but none the less by the EP(C)A) that while an interval as long as four weeks may not break continuity for *redundancy payments* purposes the rules about whether an interval is fatal for *unfair dismissal* continuity purposes (and indeed for any other statutory

---

10 EP(C)A s 94 and s 82(3)–(6). The identity of the new employer is to be ignored in considering whether or not the new job is identical to the old.
11 EP(C)A s 94 and s 82.
12 EP(C)A s 94(4).
13 EP(C)A Sch 13 para 11(2); para 17(2).
14 It will be remembered that if there is a change of employer by death of employer and re-engagement by personal representatives, the allowable interval may be *eight* weeks (EP(C)A Sch 13 para 15); see Ch 2.
15 Or, exceptionally, eight weeks (see note 14 above).

claims depending on continuous service) depend on the discussion earlier, about *Teesside Times* and *Macer v Abafast*.

5 CONCLUSION ON THE EP(C)A PROVISIONS

The various rules are over-complicated and confusing. This is perhaps best illustrated by the position on intervals between successive employments. At first glance, since in the context of a business transfer, employment has to subsist 'at the time of transfer' for continuity to be preserved under Sch 13 para 17(2), it could be thought any interval is fatal. But it is submitted that an interval of a week or less might still preserve continuity for unfair dismissal purposes if there is re-engagement by a transferee. This follows, it is submitted, from Sch 13 itself. The EAT in *Macer v Abafast Ltd* would go further and held an interval between employments could be disregarded if to do with the mechanics of transfer. And, depending on the circumstances, a gap of up to four weeks[16] could expressly preserve continuity for redundancy payments purposes if there is a re-engagement by a transferee. If this interpretation is correct, then to avoid continuous employment for unfair dismissal purposes the transferee must allow a full working week's gap to elapse between successive employments, ie from Sunday through to Saturday, and, in relation to redundancy payments, perhaps even considerably longer depending on the facts and the type of transfer of employment. But if the interval is to do with the mechanics of transfer the interval might be entirely disregarded by a tribunal, according to the EAT in *Macer v Abafast*, irrespective of its length.

All this illustrates that in this complex area, problems and pitfalls continue to remain. However, since the first edition of this book the House of Lords in *Litster v Forth Dry Dock & Engineering Co Ltd* has strengthened Reg 5 of the Transfer Regulations by allowing intervals between dismissal and transfer to be ignored if they result from an automatically unfair dismissal. The adoption by the EAT in *Macer v Abafast* of the minority view in *Teesside Times Ltd v Drury* that an interval can be ignored if, connected with the 'mechanics of transfer', is a long overdue attempt to marry up the EP(C)A rules with Transfer Regulations in this area.

---

16 And, in exceptional circumstances, eight weeks, (see note 14 above).

6 THE EP(C)A AND ASSET SALES – A REMINDER

Despite some possible areas where the EP(C)A may apply but where the Transfer Regulations do not, it must be remembered that an asset-only sale will not attract the protection of the EP(C)A *nor* of the Transfer Regulations and should result in no liability for a transferee. The transferor will have to meet all employer obligations to the employees on transfer including redundancy payments and unfair dismissal compensation, if appropriate. The transferee, meanwhile, can selectively re-engage the workforce as he wishes. Against this he has, in theory, acquired only assets and no goodwill, nor any other characteristics of a going concern. But this will, however, presumably have been reflected in the price he has paid for the assets and both parties should be satisfied with this arrangement, if that is what they have genuinely agreed.

There are two major pitfalls for employees here. These have been touched on already in Chapter 4, but their importance bears repetition. First, in relation to those re-engaged after a transfer outside the EP(C)A and the Transfer Regulations there might at first sight seem to be no injustice at all to the employees re-engaged by a transferee of assets, for they may, on occasions, get the best of both worlds. In other words, their rights are met up to date by the transferor, including accrued holiday remuneration, notice payments and a redundancy payment. But if the transferor has unfairly dismissed the workforce, their claims for unfair dismissal, too, will lie against the transferor. However, it must be remembered that in many cases the transferor will be insolvent. The transferor will therefore be unable to meet these claims. It is true that the majority of claims will be met by the Secretary of State under the reimbursement provisions of s 122 of the EP(C)A. But, significantly, the Secretary of State has no power to reimburse the compensatory award for unfair dismissal which might be, in many cases, the most substantial payment concerned.

Second, it may not always be clear to those affected by a transfer of assets whether there has in fact been an asset sale or a transfer of a business, particularly in a case where employees are re-engaged by the transferee within a very short space of time, perhaps even on the next day following the transfer (especially when one of the assets transferred is the workplace itself). In some cases, continuity of working environment may be very similar to that enjoyed by the employee prior to the transfer. An employee may, for example, be working in the same place, on the same machine. But it can be the case that although the continuity of working environment is there, there is no transfer of a business. The facts of *Woodhouse v Peter*

Brotherhood Ltd[17] and *Melon v Hector Powe Ltd*[18] illustrate this well. If the fact that there is only an asset sale goes unappreciated by the employee concerned he may sit on his rights and fail to claim a redundancy payment and/or unfair dismissal from the transferor, as he should. The limitation period for unfair dismissal is three months with a discretion (sparingly exercised) by the industrial tribunal to admit late claims,[19] and in the case of redundancy payments six months,[20] again with a wider discretion to admit late claims for a further six months.[1]

Suppose on a sale of major assets it goes unappreciated that there is in law a simple asset sale only, and not a transfer of a business. The 'transferred' employee is dismissed by the transferee 18 months after the transfer. Or suppose another transferred employee had 18 years' service with the transferor and two years after the transfer is made redundant by the transferee. Will these employees respectively have appreciated that they were at risk to unfair dismissal for two years following the transfer or that a claim for redundancy based on 18 years' service should have been made against the transferor and in relation to the transferee the claim will be worth really nothing but a sum based only on two years' service?

A legal position where the question of entitlement to accrued rights is so complex that its niceties will go unappreciated by

---

17 [1972] 2 QB 520, [1972] ICR 186, CA.

18 [1981] 1 All ER 313, [1981] ICR 43, HL.

19 EP(C)A s 67(2). The test is quite a strict one. See e g *Dedman v British Building and Engineering Appliances Ltd* [1974] 1 All ER 520, [1974] ICR 53, CA; *Wall's Meat Co Ltd v Khan* [1979] ICR 52 [1978] IRLR 499, CA; *Riley v Tesco Stores Ltd* [1980] ICR 323, [1980] IRLR 103, CA.

20 EP(C)A s 101(1).

1 EP(C)A s 101(2). Although at least in relation to redundancy payments, some practical advice can be offered. In the context of unfair dismissal, a claim has to be submitted to an industrial tribunal within the limitation period (three months). The position is more flexible with redundancy payments. Under EP(C)A s 101 within the six-month limitation period the following must occur:

'(a) the payment has been agreed and paid, or
 (b) the employee has made a claim for the payment by notice in writing given to the employer, or
 (c) a question as to the right of the employee to the payment, or as to the amount of the payment, has been referred to an industrial tribunal, or
 (d) a complaint relating to his dismissal has been presented by the employee under section 67 [unfair dismissal].'

The practical advice for employees uncertain about their rights is to give notice in writing to all prospective employers who might, it is envisaged, be joined into tribunal proceedings. As long as this is done within six months, no tribunal claim need be filed and when an issue as to entitlement arises even if this is many years hence, a tribunal will have jurisdiction.

employees is hardly just. It has been argued elsewhere[2] that there is now a very strong case indeed for employers to be required (whether they be transferors or transferees) to give the employee a statement upon a transfer of either assets or business indicating that there is a transaction on which at least they should seek advice on how best to protect their position.[3]

---

2 See McMullen (1985) LS Gaz 1950.
3 EP(C)A s 53(2) provides that a statement of written reasons for dismissal must be provided by an employer on dismissal. It is not beyond the wit of man to draw on this provision to devise a written statement provision in the context discussed in the text. In an entirely different context, the House of Lords, in *Scally v Southern Health and Social Services Board* [1991] ICR 771, [1991] IRLR 522 has held that it is necessary (subject to certain conditions) to imply an obligation on an employer to take reasonable steps to bring a term of a contract of employment to an employee's attention, so that he may be in a position to enjoy its benefit. It is not suggested that this case would impose any common law duty on an employer to draw an employee's attention to possible transfer-related problems in the manner discussed here. But its philosophy arguably lends weight to any view that there ought to be more statutory compulsion to provide information generally.

Chapter 6

The Transfer of Undertakings (Protection of Employment) Regulations 1981

1 BACKGROUND

The Transfer of Undertakings (Protection of Employment) Regulations 1981[1] were introduced, 'with a remarkable lack of enthusiasm'
(the words of Mr David Waddington, the then Under-Secretary of
State for Employment[2]), in order to implement the EC Acquired
Rights Directive.[3] Draft regulations were first issued in 1978 which
were intended to come into force in 1979. But they were not,
ultimately, introduced. The matter drifted on until 1981 after the
change of government from Labour to Conservative in 1979. Meanwhile, the European Commission had threatened to commence
infraction proceedings unless the directive was implemented and, as
a result, the present Transfer Regulations were introduced. Mr
David Waddington, in so introducing them, reported to the House
of Commons that, 'I do not believe that we could have delayed
much longer in carrying out our Community obligations.'[4]

In the end, the drafting of the Transfer Regulations can be seen to
reflect that government's expressed lack of enthusiasm. There are,
for example, several important areas where the terms of the Transfer Regulations are narrower than the provisions of the directive
and, therefore, fall short of meeting our European obligations. The
legal problems that arise from this are a constant theme throughout
this book although they have been mitigated, since the first edition,
by the landmark decision of the House of Lords in *Litster v Forth
Dry Dock & Engineering Co Ltd*[5] which states, inter alia, that the

---

1 SI 81/1794.
2 991 Hansard HC Deb col 680.
3 EC Council Directive 77/187 of 14 February 1977.
4 991 Hansard HC Deb col 677. The parliamentary debates on the content of the
  Transfer Regulations upon their introduction in the House of Commons and in
  the House of Lords may be found in 991 Hansard HC Deb cols 677–698 and 435
  Hansard HL Deb cols 1482–1501.
5 [1989] ICR 341, [1989] IRLR 161.

Transfer Regulations must be given a purposive interpretation to make them conform to the Acquired Rights Directive (see below). Finally, the failure to integrate the Transfer Regulations with the already existing provisions of the EP(C)A concerned with business transfers causes obvious problems unless courts are willing to take a broad view and ignore the differences (see below).

The Acquired Rights Directive itself underwent some change during its gestation period. An earlier draft of the directive applied not only to business transfers but also to take-overs of companies. The final version of the directive excludes take-overs of companies by way of acquisition of share capital, an omission with serious consequences in this country, where a very large number of take-overs are *not* by simple transfer of undertakings from one person to another, but by sale of share capital.[6] The Transfer Regulations follow the narrower final version and do not apply to take-overs by way of acquisition of share capital.[7]

2 METHOD OF IMPLEMENTATION OF THE TRANSFER REGULATIONS

The Transfer Regulations were brought into force by statutory instrument, as the European Communities Act 1972 allows subordinate legislation to be made 'for the purpose of implementing any Community obligations of the United Kingdom'.[8] Although the

---

6 The progress of the directive and earlier drafts is well noted by Hepple (1976) ILJ 197 and (1977) ILJ 106.

7 An interesting perspective on the question of the directive and its interaction with the economic and social policy behind it may be found in P L Davies, 'Acquired Rights, Creditors' Rights, Freedom of Contract, and Industrial Democracy' in 9 (1989) *Year-Book of European Law* p 21.

8 European Communities Act 1972 s 2(2)(a). Another criticism is that introduction of the Transfer Regulations by statutory instrument left less scope for debate and amendment; also, surely, they were too important to be left to the simpler procedure applicable to statutory instruments as opposed to passage of a Bill through Parliament leading to an Act: see Mr T Taylor, 991 Hansard HC Deb col 679. The Acquired Rights Directive has been implemented in other EC states, in Belgium by the *Collective Agreement* No 32 dated 28.2.78 and later by *Collective Agreement* No 32(b) dated 7.6.85 and by *Collective Agreement* No 32 dated 2.12.86; in Denmark by the *Act on the Legal Position of Employees in connection with Transfers of Undertakings* (Act No 111 dated 21.3.79); in the Republic of Ireland by the *European Communities (Safeguarding of Employees' Rights on Transfer of Undertakings) Regulations 1980* (see Ch 7); in France by Article L122–12 of the *French Labour Code*; in Italy by Article 2112 of the *Italian Civil Code*; in the Netherlands by the Act of 15.5.81; in Spain by Article 44 of the *Workers' Statute*; in West Germany by, inter alia, Section 613(a) of the *German Civil Code*; and in Greece by the *Presidential Decree* No 572/1 of December 1988

Acquired Rights Directive provides that member states *may*, in domestic legislation, make more favourable provision than is stipulated by the directive, the view was taken by the Department of Employment that because of the use of subordinate legislation, to *exceed* the provisions of the directive would be ultra vires the European Community Act 1972 (the parent legislation). This continues to be the main argument both against using the Transfer Regulations as a vehicle for reform and harmonisation of the law relating to continuity and transfer of employment,[9] and against the Transfer Regulations containing more general protection for employees than laid down in the directive, because it was thought important that the directive was not departed from in any way.[10]

3 MEETING EUROPEAN STANDARDS AND THE USE OF EUROPEAN LAW

As has been discussed, far from exceeding Community obligations, the Transfer Regulations provide a *lower* threshold of protection for employees than envisaged by the directive in certain areas. For example, it is probable that the provisions relating to hiving down under reg 4 (which restricts the operation of transfer of contracts of employment upon the creation of a wholly-owned subsidiary of the insolvent parent company) are not permitted by the directive; the requirement of a 'commercial venture' (reg 2(1)) on a transfer is not

---

(source: *Croner's Europe*, which also contains a valuable survey of the content of such laws of different member states and an overview of the Transfer of Undertakings and other labour legislation across the EC).

9 See the letter from the Secretary of State for Employment quoted by Mr Harold Walker MP: 991 Hansard HC Deb col 686; Lord Lyell 435 Hansard HL Deb col 1497.

10 In spite of this caution, one commentator (P Elias (1982) Company Lawyer 147) has suggested that some of the Transfer Regulations might still, none the less, have fallen outside the enabling powers of the parent Act, because they fall short of (and, therefore, depart from) the terms of the directive (Elias cites three examples: the hiving down provisions of reg 4; the modified and less generous consultation provisions (in particular the inclusion of the 'special circumstances' defence); and the compulsory nature of automatic transfer of employment of individuals). If this commentator's argument were correct, the consequences are not at all clear. For example, would it have been possible for a party to raise the ultra vires point in proceedings before a domestic court or tribunal against the application of one or more of the Transfer Regulations to the sale of an undertaking? As far as is known this point has not been taken. Anyway, it is surely overtaken now by the clear recognition that domestic legislation must be construed in the light of the relevant EC directive (see below).

contained in the directive; consultation with trade union representatives under the directive should be 'with a view to seeking agreement',[11] whereas the consultation provisions of the Transfer Regulations contain no such exhortation;[12] and also in relation to the information/consultation obligations, the Transfer Regulations, in breach of the directive, include a 'special circumstances' defence, and the poor financial remedy for breach of reg 10 arguably breaches the principle in *Von Colson and Kamann v Land Nordrhein–Westfalen*[13] that:

> 'the transposition of [a] directive must . . . produce effective results . . . [Although a directive], for the purpose of imposing a sanction for the breach of the [obligation imposed by a directive], leaves the member states free to choose between the different solutions suitable for achieving its objective, it nevertheless requires that if a member state chooses to penalise breaches of that prohibition by the award of compensation, then in order to ensure that it is effective and that it has a deterrent effect, that compensation must in any event be adequate in relation to the damage sustained and must therefore amount to more than purely nominal compensation . . .'

There are three consequences of such failure to meet European obligations.

First, it would be open for the European Commission to threaten or commence proceedings against the UK for failing properly to implement Community legislation.[14] It was stated by the European Court in *Re Collective Redundancies: EC Commission v Belgium* (Case 215/83)[15] that:

> 'The Court has consistently held that the member states must fulfil their obligations under Community directives in every respect and may not plead provisions, practices or circumstances existing in their internal legal system in order to justify a failure to comply with those obligations.'

---

11 Art 6(2). As stated in Chapter 10, this almost amounts to a duty to bargain in good faith. Davies, op cit, points out that the obligation to negotiate is found in German legislation, in Article 112 of the German *Betriebsverfassungsgesetz* of 1972. The same problem applies to the provisions of s 99 of the Employment Protection Act 1975 concerning implementation of the Collective Redundancies Directive (see Ch 10) where again, the directive states that consultation shall be with a view to reaching an agreement whereas the EPA provisions impose no such obligation. It can be seen that imposing an obligation to negotiate would make an enormous difference to industrial relations practice on business transfers and redundancies.

12 Reg 10.

13 Reg 2(1).

14 Under the Treaty of Rome Art 169.

15 [1985] 3 CMLR 624.

Infringement action has, of course, been brought in the areas of sex discrimination and equal pay[16] and, on such occasions, has resulted in a finding by the European Court against the UK and the introduction then of amending UK legislation to put the omission right.[17] This is, of course, in theory, of little use to an individual affected by the breach of European obligations, until such action is taken and amending legislation passed. There is, at present, by all accounts, a proposal for action against the UK by the European Commission in respect of the shortcomings between the Transfer Regulations and the directive suggested in this book.[18] At the time of writing it is believed that this is at a very early stage following preparation of a report for the Commission.

Until such action is taken, might an individual in a case on the Transfer Regulations in this country seek to rely directly upon the more favourable terms of EC legislation itself? First, it is thought possible that a claim can directly be sustained upon the words of *some* EC legislation, independent of, and additional to, a domestic statute[19] or statutory instrument. If so, a claim on such European law might be justiciable in a domestic court, and, even, in industrial tribunals.[20] So far, this has been held to be possible in the case of some rights arising from the EC Treaty: in labour law Article 119 (equal pay) is the best example.[1] But it has always been arguable

---

16 EC Case 61/82 *EC Commission v United Kingdom* [1982] ICR 578, [1982] IRLR 333, ECJ (on equal pay for work of equal value) and Case 165/82 *EC Commission v United Kingdom* [1984] 1 All ER 353, [1984] ICR 192, ECJ (on the Equal Treatment Directive).

17 Eg the Equal Pay (Amendment) Regulations 1983 and the Sex Discrimination Act 1986.

18 In *Re Business Transfer Legislation: EC Commission v Italy (Case No 235/84)* [1987] 3 CMLR 115 the Commission brought proceedings under Art 169 of the Treaty and succeeded in obtaining a declaration that the Italian Government had failed satisfactorily to implement Art 6 of the Acquired Rights Directive. Another interesting development is the ruling of the European Court in *Francovich v Italian Republic* [1992] IRLR 84, that, under certain conditions, an *individual* may sue a member state for damages directly under Community law for failure to take all necessary steps to implement a directive.

19 See Hepple and Fredman *Labour Law and Industrial Relations in Great Britain* p 25.

20 See Lord Denning MR in *McCarthy's Ltd v Smith (No 2)* [1980] IRLR 209, CA. An industrial tribunal has even broken new ground by referring a case to the European Court of Justice for a preliminary ruling under Art 177. See *Neath v Hugh Steeper Ltd* (1991) IRLIB 16.

1 *Defrenne v SA Belge de Navigation Aérienne (Sabena)* [1976] ECR 455, [1976] ICR 547, ECJ; *McCarthy's Ltd v Smith (No 2)* [1980] IRLR 209, CA (on Art 119 of the Treaty of Rome). And see also *Barber v Guardian Royal Exchange Assurance Group* [1991] 1 QB 344, [1990] 2 All ER 660.

whether this could occur in the case of an EC directive[2] such as, in our case, the Acquired Rights Directive. The received viewpoint seems to be that the terms of a directive are *not* enforceable by an individual but are enforceable only as between the EC and the member state by way of infraction proceedings leading to amendment of the offending domestic provisions by the member state in the manner described above.[3] In other words, directives generally have 'vertical' effect and not 'horizontal' effect (in contrast, say, to Article 119).

But it has been suggested that while individuals may not as against other private individuals rely on the directive *direct*, a person might rely upon the directive's terms, so long as the directive were unconditional and sufficiently precise, as against the government of the UK itself or, at least, an agency of the state.[4] In other words subject to the above conditions, a directive might, it was agreed, have horizontal effect against the state or its equivalent. This point has now been resolved in the leading case of *Marshall v Southampton and South West Hampshire Area Health Authority (Teaching)*.[5] There it was confirmed that the terms of a directive cannot be directly relied upon between private individuals (including companies) inter se but that it might, none the less, be possible for an individual to rely upon the terms of the directive in a case against the state or an 'emanation' of the state, ie a state or quasi-state employer. 'Emanation of the state' has, not surprisingly, given rise to some litigation. The *Marshall* case itself of course decided that a local area health authority was an 'emanation of the state'.[6] The question then arose whether a nationalised corporation could also be an emanation of the state. The point came up in proceedings against British Gas (before privatisation) and the position was eventually clarified by a ruling of the European Court in

---

2 Case 152/84 *Marshall v Southampton and South West Hampshire Area Health Authority (Teaching)* [1986] IRLR 140 at 145, ECJ.
3 Case 8/82 *Becker v Finanzamt Münster-Innenstadt* [1982] ECR 53, [1982] 1 CMLR 499. See also Warner 'The Relationship between European Community Law and the National Laws of Member States' (1977) 93 LQR 349; *Hugh-Jones v St John's College, Cambridge* [1979] ICR 848, EAT; *ASTMS v Beaufort Air Sea Equipment Ltd* IDS Brief 153 (March 1979) p 11, IT; Hepple (1982) ILJ 30.
4 See eg *Van Duyn v Home Office (No 2)* [1975] Ch 358, [1974] ECR 1337. The principles of direct effect are discussed in Steiner *Textbook on EEC Law*, 2nd edn, Ch 2.
5 [1986] QB 401, [1986] ICR 335, ECJ.
6 Case 152/84 *Marshall v Southampton and South West Hampshire Area Health Authority (Teaching)* [1986] QB 401, [1986] ICR 335, EAT; and see also *Parsons v East Surrey Health Authority* [1986] ICR 837.

Foster v British Gas plc.[7] In that case the court ruled that the status of British Gas *was* such that the Equal Treatment Directive could be relied upon directly by the individual employee. The court went further, however, and issued some wide-ranging statements of principle. Thus:

> 'Individuals may rely on an unconditional and sufficiently precise provision . . . against an undertaking in respect of which the state (understood as any body endowed with public authority, regardless of its relationship with other public bodies or the nature of the duties entrusted to it) has assumed responsibilities which put it in a position to decisively influence the conduct of that undertaking in any manner whatsoever (other than by means of general legislation) with regard to the matter in respect of which the relevant provision of a directive imposes an obligation which the member state has failed to implement in national law.[8]

This considerably simplifies the whole situation and means, arguably, that any employer outside the private sector may be caught by *Marshall*. Those advising in the public sector should therefore bear in mind the possibility at least of direct use of and horizontal effect of directives. Private companies will, of course, not be undertakings of the kind envisaged in *Foster v British Gas plc* and the directives could only have vertical effect in that context.

A working illustration of direct enforceability against public sector undertakings as above defined arises from the proceedings on discriminatory retiring ages, ie 65 for men and 60 for women, that were in issue in the *Marshall* case. This case decided that discriminatory retiring ages which were then permitted in unfair dismissal law[9] and under the Sex Discrimination Act 1975[10] were contrary to the EC Equal Treatment Directive.[11] As a result of the case, amending legislation was passed in the form of the Sex Discrimination Act 1986. However, between the date of *Marshall* (1986) and the coming into force of certain provisions of that Act (7 November 1987), private individuals, as a result of *Marshall*, became eligible to claim against employers in the form of the state or an emanation of the state and could rely directly upon the terms of the Equal Treatment Directive. Where the employer was in the private sector,

---

7 [1991] ICR 84, [1990] IRLR 353. On referral to the House of Lords this was implemented, the decision reported at [1991] ICR 463.

8 [1990] IRLR 353 at 363. See now *Doughty v Rolls-Royce plc* [1992] IRLR 126, *IDS Brief* 464, p 12 where it was held that Rolls-Royce did *not* fall within this definition.

9 EP(C)A s 64(1)(b).

10 Sex Discrimination Act 1975 s 6(4).

11 EEC Council Directive 76/207 of 9 February 1976, Art 5(1).

however, the employee had to wait until the Sex Discrimination Act 1986 came into force.[12]

Applying this to the Transfer Regulations, *if* it were ruled that the Transfer Regulations were in breach of the Acquired Rights Directive, could an individual rely on the terms of the directive against another individual in a domestic court *provided* the claim is against an employer who is either the state or state-controlled undertaking (as defined above)? By analogy with our working illustration in the field of sex discrimination, there seems to be no reason why not, although whether the directive is unconditional and sufficiently precise has never been tested.[13] Although this would not apply to many business transfer cases (which will in the majority of instances involve claims against private employers) it is an interesting possibility and one widened by the dicta in *Foster*, discussed above. It may be apparent, however, that the approach which is next discussed may be equally effective as a means of imposing European standards, and it also has the advantage of posing no distinction between the public and private sectors.

A third possibility, then, and an immensely important one in practice, is for an individual to base a claim squarely within the terms of the Transfer Regulations, but to ask the court or tribunal to interpret the regulations in areas of difficulty or ambiguity having regard to the aims and spirit of the directive and any more beneficial wording thereof. This has now been confirmed by the robust decisions of the House of Lords in *Pickstone v Freemans plc*[14] and *Litster v Forth Dry Dock & Engineering Co Ltd*.[15] A purposive interpretation must now be applied to domestic legislation in order to give effect to the aims of a directive on which it is based.[16]

---

12 See *Duke v GEC Reliance Ltd* [1988] AC 618, [1988] ICR 339.
13 See the interesting discussion by Hepple and Byre in 'EEC Labour Law in the United Kingdom – A New Approach' (1989) Industrial Law Journal 129 at pp 131–132.
14 [1988] ICR 697, [1988] IRLR 357.
15 [1989] ICR 341, [1989] IRLR 161. See also Docksey and Fitzpatrick: 'The duty of national courts to interpret provisions of national law in accordance with community law' (1991) Industrial Law Journal, p 113; Howells, (1991) Modern Law Review, p 456.
16 The only drawback to this dramatically helpful development is, as Hepple, in 'The Crisis in EEC Labour Law' (1987) ILJ 77 points out, that certain decisions of the ECJ on the interpretation of the Acquired Rights Directive leave the member states themselves to determine by national laws many crucial questions under the directive. A good example is the proviso to Art 4 (business transfer not to constitute grounds for dismissal) that 'Member states may provide that [this obligation] shall not apply to certain categories of employees who are not covered by the laws on practice of the member states in respect of protection against dismissal.' This, for example, may legitimise the exclusion of short-serving

Decisions of UK courts[17] have been based, however, on the proviso that, in order to apply this principle, the directive on which it is sought to place reliance must have pre-dated the defective domestic legislation concerned and the domestic legislation must have been intended to comply with the directive. Thus held the House of Lords in two emphatic decisions on this point, originally in *Duke v GEC Reliance Ltd*[18] and subsequently in *Finnegan v Clowney Youth Training Programme Ltd.*[19] This should not matter for our purposes, since the Transfer Regulations were clearly enacted subsequent to and in purported compliance with the Acquired Rights Directive.

Fascinatingly, however, in the European Court case of *Marleasing SA v La Commercial Internacional de Alimentacion SA*,[20] a company law referral to the European Court under Art 177 of the Treaty from a Spanish court, the European Court stated:

'. . . the obligations of member states under a directive to achieve its objects, and their duty by virtue of Art 5 of the Treaty to take all

---

workers from *Litster* (see Ch 7). Another example of the ruling that certain questions are a matter for the national courts of member states is the question of who is an employee within the terms of the protection contemplated by the directive: *Mikkelsen v Danmols Inventar A/S* [1986] 1 CMLR 316. For cases in this area, see *Lee Ting Sang v Chung Chi-Keung Construction and Engineering Co Ltd* [1990] 2 AC 374, [1990] IRLR 236; *O'Kelly v Trust House Forte plc* [1983] ICR 728, [1983] IRLR 369; *Nethermere (St Neots) Ltd v Taverna and Gardiner* [1984] IRLR 240. Although, as discussed in Ch 6, the definition of an employee under the Transfer Regulations is a little wider than the definition of employee in the EP(C)A, there are a large number of employees in atypical employment who will not satisfy the definition and, as Hepple and Byre in 'EEC Labour Law in the United Kingdom – a New Approach' (1989) ILJ 129 at 137 point out, this may have 'the result that Britain's growing "flexible" work-force is unlikely to benefit from the new "purposive" approach'. Finally, the European Court, in *Wendelboe v LJ Music Ap S* [1985] ECR 457 [1986] 1 CMLR 476 held the existence or otherwise of a contract of employment or employment relationship on the date of the transfer is a matter for national law (but subject to the directive, and in particular, Art 4(1)).

17 There have been other applications of this principle to date. See e g (in company law) *International Sales and Agencies Ltd v Marcus* [1982] 3 All ER 551 (Art 9(1) of the first EC directive on company law as an aid to interpretation of the predecessor to s 35 of the Companies Act 1985); see also, in the context of the Transfer Regulations and the Acquired Rights Directive, prophetic statements in *Secretary of State for Employment v Anchor Hotel (Kippford) Ltd* [1985] ICR 724; 1985 IRLR 452, EAT; *Secretary of State for Employment v Spence* [1987] QB 179; [1986] ICR 651, CA, and *Robert Seligman Corporation v Baker* [1983] ICR 770. None has been so emphatic and definitive as the 'twin' House of Lords decisions in *Pickstone* and *Litster* however.

18 [1988] IRLR 118.

19 [1990] ICR 462.

20 Case C 106/89 (13 November 1990, unreported).

necessary steps to ensure the fulfilment of that obligation, binds all authorities of member states, including national courts within their jurisdiction. It follows that in applying national law, *whether the provisions concerned pre-date or post-date the directive*, the national court asked to interpret national law is bound to do so in every way possible in the light of the text and aim of the directive to achieve the results envisaged by it and thus to comply with Art 189(3) of the Treaty.' (emphasis added)

The full ramifications of this decision need to be considered. We implied (above) that this decision may not be of importance to the subject of business transfers and employee rights because the Transfer Regulations *post*-date the directive concerned and therefore the principle of interpretation thereof is not affected by the rulings in *Duke* and *Finnegan*. But what of the EP(C)A provisions, which clearly pre-date the directive? Does *Marleasing* now mean *they* can be interpreted to give effect to the directive also? This possibility has been canvassed already in Ch 5. As there discussed, a unitary interpretation of the directive, the regulations and the EP(C)A provisions would make life much simpler and it cries out in its logic. *Marleasing* is an exciting decision for all labour lawyers, and its application in the UK, particularly in this area, is awaited with interest.

4 THE SCOPE OF THE TRANSFER REGULATIONS SUMMARISED

As has been discussed, the Transfer Regulations *do not apply to asset-only sales*, but only to transfers of undertakings.[1] A 'transfer' of an 'undertaking' is construed in a similar way as the 'transfer' of or 'change in ownership' of a business under the EP(C)A,[2] ie as the transfer of an undertaking *as a going concern*.[3] There are also other significant cases where the Transfer Regulations do not apply. The following is a checklist. Where a point is amplified in other chapters of the book this is indicated.

---

1 *Premier Motors (Medway) Ltd v Total Oil Great Britain Ltd* [1984] ICR 58, [1984] IRLR 471, EAT adopting, by implication, the reasoning in cases such as *Woodhouse v Peter Brotherhood Ltd* [1972] 2 QB 520, [1972] ICR 186, CA.
2 See *Premier Motors (Medway) Ltd v Total Oil Great Britain Ltd* [1984] ICR 58, [1983] IRLR 471, EAT.
3 As described in *Kenmir Ltd v Frizzell* [1968] 1 All ER 414, [1968] ITR 159.

(i)   The Transfer Regulations do not apply to *non-commercial* ventures (see Ch 4).[4]

(ii) The Transfer Regulations cover only *employees* and *not* workers engaged under contracts for services. The definition of employee in the Transfer Regulations (which is slightly wider than the definition of employee in s 153(1) of the EP(C)A[5]) is 'any individual who works for another person whether under a contract of service or apprenticeship or otherwise but does not include anyone who provides services under a contract for services and references to a person's employer shall be construed accordingly'.[6]

(iii) Regulations 8, 10 and 11 of the Transfer Regulations do not apply to employees ordinarily working outside the UK.[7]

(iv) The Transfer Regulations do not apply to employees on board a ship registered in the UK if the employment is wholly outside the UK or if the employee is not ordinarily resident in the UK.[8]

(v)   The Transfer Regulations do not apply to registered dock workers unless they are wholly or mainly engaged in work which is not dock work.[9]

(vi) Regulations 5 and 6 of the Transfer Regulations (automatic transfer of contracts of employment and collective agreements) do *not* apply to occupational pension schemes, for example, to transfer rights thereunder from the transferor to

---

4 Reg 2(1). The 1978 draft regulations did not include such a wide exclusion (see draft regs 3(4) and (5)). This exclusion is covered in Chapter 4 in more detail.

5 S 153(1) of the EP(C)A defines an employee as '. . . an individual who has entered into or works under (or where the employment has ceased, worked under) a contract of employment'.

6 Reg 2(1). The extended definition under the Transfer Regulations might therefore apply to workers under the type of 'sui generis' contract (ie neither employment nor independent contractor) in *Construction Industry Training Board v Labour Force Ltd* [1970] 3 All ER 220, DC (contract between contract workers and supplying agency). It is not clear whether any other workers traditionally excluded from the definition of 'employee' under employment statutes might be covered. It does *not* cover an equity partner in a firm, even if he provided services as a managing partner: *Cowell v Quilter Goodison & Co Ltd* [1989] IRLR 392.

7 Reg 13(1). The draft 1978 regulations were not so restrictive: see draft reg 3(2)(b).

8 Reg 13(2).

9 Reg 13(3). But see now the effect of the Dock Work Act 1989, which makes this proviso otiose.

the transferee, whether under the contract of employment or under a collective agreement (see Ch 7).[10]

(vii) Regulation 9 of the Transfer Regulations (transfer of recognition by transferor to transferee) does not apply unless the undertaking or part of the undertaking transferred maintains 'an identity distinct from the remainder of the transferee's undertaking' (see Ch 10).[11]

(viii) Regulation 5 of the Transfer Regulations does not transfer any liability of any person to be prosecuted for, convicted of, and sentenced for, any criminal offence (see Ch 7).[12]

(ix) The Transfer Regulations do not apply to an employee who is not employed in the undertaking or part undertaking transferred (see Ch 7).[13] References to a person employed in the undertaking or part thereof before the transfer mean 'immediately before' the transfer.[14] This will be a question of fact. Although an industrial tribunal in *Anderson v Kluwer Publishing Ltd*[15] held that an employee was employed in part of a business sold when he spent 80 per cent of his time there, the European Court in *Botzen v Rotterdamsche Droogdok Maatschappij*[16] adopted a different test. In the opinion of Slynn A-G an employee must be 'wholly engaged' in the part transferred subject only to the performance of other duties which can be regarded as *de minimis*. The court itself, in contrast, considered that:

> 'In order to decide whether the rights and obligations under an employment relationship are transferred under Directive 77/187 by reason of a transfer within the meaning of Article 1(1) thereof, it is therefore sufficient to establish to which part of the undertaking or business the employee was assigned.'

We cover this aspect more fully later in Ch 7. In the House of Lords decision in *Litster v Forth Dry Dock & Engineering Co Ltd*[17] it was, in the light of the Acquired Rights Directive,

---

10 Reg 7.
11 Reg 9(1).
12 An example would be a prosecution under the Health and Safety at Work Act etc 1974 or the Factories Act.
13 Reg 5(1).
14 Reg 5(3).
15 *Anderson v Kluwer* IT COIT 15068.85 *(IDS Employment Law Handbook No 36* p 45).
16 [1986] 2 CMLR 50.
17 [1989] ICR 341, [1989] IRLR 161.

decided necessary to deem included among those employed in the undertaking or part transferred those employees who would have been employed therein immediately before the transfer had they not been automatically unfairly dismissed within the meaning of reg 8 of the Transfer Regulations (see, in detail, Ch 7).

(x) The Transfer Regulations only apply to a transfer of an undertaking from one person to another. The Transfer Regulations do not apply to a take-over by way of a change in the ownership of share capital of a limited company. This excludes from the ambit of the regulations a common type of business take-over in the UK (see Ch 1).

(xi) The Transfer Regulations will usually not catch employees retained by the transferor whose contracts of employment would not otherwise be repudiated or terminated by the transfer. This follows from the wording of reg 5 which only applies in relation to employees whose employment would otherwise be terminated by the transfer. Thus if an employee is by genuine agreement, or by virtue of his contract of employment, lawfully retained by the transferring employer or held back from the business and deployed in other parts of the transferor's business, he could arguably be excluded. This needs to be treated with some caution but, again, is dealt with more fully later in this book in Ch 7.[18]

(xii) Finally, reg 3(4) of the Transfer Regulations provides that a transfer of an undertaking may be effected by a series of two or more transactions between the same parties subject to questions of time and intentions of the parties and all of the other circumstances. In other words, reg 3(4) with its concept of 'linked transactions' may be an effective anti-avoidance provision, preventing parties artificially fragmenting what is in reality a business transfer into a number of discrete and less identifiable transactions. This provision is referred to a number of times in the text, but, principally, in Chapter 4.

---

18 See e g *Direct Radiators Ltd v Howse* EAT 130/86; *Daisely v Leicester Light Transport Ltd* COIT 1504/83; *Secretary of State for Employment v J F Heiliwell & Sons Ltd* EAT 186/86; *Visionhire Consumer Electronics Ltd v Easton* EAT 20/87; *Mikkelsen v Danmols Inventar A/S* [1986] 1 CMLR 316.

Chapter 7

The Transfer Regulations and reg 5: the automatic transfer of employment obligations

1 INTRODUCTION

One of the most significant provisions of the Transfer Regulations is reg 5. This is set out in full as follows.

'(1) A relevant transfer shall not operate so as to terminate the contract of employment of any person employed by the transferor in the undertaking or part transferred but any such contract which would otherwise have been terminated by the transfer shall have effect after the transfer as if originally made between the person so employed and the transferee.

(2) Without prejudice to paragraph (1) above, on the completion of a relevant transfer:

    (a) all the transferor's rights, powers, duties and liabilities under or in connection with any such contract, shall be transferred by virtue of this regulation to the transferee; and

    (b) Anything done before the transfer is completed by or in relation to the transferor in respect of that contract or a person employed in that undertaking or part shall be deemed to have been done by or in relation to the transferee.

(3) Any reference in paragraph (1) or (2) above to a person employed in an undertaking or part of one transferred by a relevant transfer is a reference to a person so employed immediately before the transfer, including, where the transfer is effected by a series of two or more transactions, a person so employed immediately before any of those transactions.

(4) Paragraph (2) above shall not transfer or otherwise affect the liability of any person to be prosecuted for, convicted of and sentenced for any offence.

(5) Paragraph (1) above is without prejudice to any right of an employee arising apart from these regulations to terminate his contract of employment without notice if a substantial change is made in his working conditions to his detriment; but no right shall

arise by reason only that, under that paragraph, the identity of his employer changes unless the employee shows that, in all the circumstances, the change is a significant change and is to his detriment.'

So, on a relevant transfer under reg 3, reg 5(1) applies to transfer the employment relationship and reg 5(2) transfers all liabilities under in or connection with it.

This regulation is enacted in compliance with Art 3 of the Acquired Rights Directive which provides for the transfer of a transferor's rights and obligations arising from 'a contract of employment or from an employment relationship existing on the date of a transfer'. To be noted (see below) are the somewhat wider words 'employment relationship'. In so far as these add to the words 'under or in connection with [a contract]' it is submitted that reg 5 should be construed in the light of Art 3.

Another difference between the Transfer Regulations and the directive is that Art 3 stipulates that member states may provide that, in addition to a transferee, the transferor shall continue to be liable in respect of obligations which arise from a contract of employment or an employment relationship. This is not included in reg 5 but the provisions of Art 3 are permissive in this respect and the UK government decided not to legislate for joint liability of transferor and transferee. Finally, reg 5(5) (see below) is based on Art 4(2) of the Acquired Rights Directive.

The automatic transfer of contracts of employment and the definition of which contracts are caught by reg 5 is achieved by the rather cumbersome expression 'such contract which would otherwise have been terminated by the transfer'. This is a slight legal curiosity. For it can be argued that a transfer of itself does not terminate a contract of employment even if an employee is employed in the business transferred. The transfer, if it leaves him with no work to do for the original employer, may well be a repudiation of his contract entitling him to accept that repudiation as terminating the contract but, if the elective theory of termination of contracts (see below) is the correct one, a transfer would not, as is contemplated by reg 5, of itself terminate the contract of employment. This problem is referred to by Lord Oliver in *Litster v Forth Dry Dock & Engineering Co Ltd*[1] at p 362:

'To begin with, it is to be noted that the reference in regulation 5(1) to a "contract which would otherwise have been terminated by the transfer" is, strictly speaking, a misdescription. The reason why a contract

---

1 [1990] 1 AC 546, [1989] ICR 341.

of employment is said to "terminate" on a transfer of the employer's business is simply that such a transfer operates as a unilateral repudiation by the employer of his obligations under the contract and thus as a dismissal of the employee from his service. Because the relationship between employer and employee is of an essentially personal nature, the repudiation severs the factual relationship resulting from the contract, since the primary obligations on both sides are no longer capable of being performed. The contract itself, however, is not, strictly speaking, terminated but remains in being and undischarged so far as the enforcement of secondary obligations are concerned. . . . the necessary assumption in paragraph (1) of the regulation is that the contract of employment to which the consequence stated in the paragraph is to attach, is one which, apart from the transfer, would have continued in force and that what "terminates" it, or would, apart from the regulation, have terminated it, is the repudiatory breach constituted by the transfer. . . . the crucial question therefore, is what is meant by the reference to a contract being terminated "by" a transfer. . . . this could embrace a number of different possibilities. If nothing at all occurred to disturb the relationship of master and servant apart from the simple unannounced fact of the transfer of business by the employer, it is the transfer itself which constitutes the repudiatory breach which, apart from regulation 5(1), "terminates" the contract. If, however, the employer, contemporaneously with the transfer, announces to his workforce that he is transferring the business and that they are therefore dismissed without notice, it is, strictly, the oral notification which terminates the contract; yet it could not, as a matter of common sense, be denied that the contract has been "terminated by transfer" of the business, particularly when reference is made to the supplementary provisions of paragraph (2) of regulation 5 when read in conjunction with paragraph (3). . . . [in these circumstances then,] the contract can quite properly be described as having been terminated by the transfer.'

Lord Oliver, notwithstanding the niceties of contract law, clearly advocated a broad view of when a contract should be considered 'otherwise terminated by the transfer'. Such a broad view is necessary in order to bring employees naturally within the protection of reg 5 in accordance with the aims of the legislation. This point is, however, without prejudice to the possibility that employees who, under their contracts of employment, may be required, say, to work in other parts of the transferor's retained businesses, will not be employees whose contracts are 'terminated' by the transfer. In their case it may be argued that no repudiation occurs, and this point is canvassed subsequently in this chapter.

All this seems to contemplate employment subsisting at the time of transfer. The next problem, then, is which employees are liable to be transferred under reg 5(1) and how close to the transfer they have to be employed in order for employment obligations to be transferred; in other words, will any temporal interval in employment between dismissal by a transferor and transfer of the business mean that the contract of employment of the employee dismissed is not transferred to the transferee, or that the transferee is not liable for the transferor's duties and liabilities under the contract under reg 5(2)? It is important to note at the outset that as long as employment subsists (or is deemed to subsist) at the point of transfer, a transferee will be liable for all obligations in relation to a transferred employee whether these be accrued, actual or contingent statutory rights, arrears, or claims arising out of the acts of a transferor. The following discussion will also indicate that in most cases, employers cannot get round the requirement in the Transfer Regulations of subsisting employment by effecting pre-transfer dismissals for that purpose. The case in the UK law most influential in this conclusion is, again *Litster v Forth Dry Dock & Engineering Co Ltd*[2] around which much of this chapter (and indeed the book) must inevitably revolve.

2 THE REQUIREMENT OF EMPLOYMENT IN THE BUSINESS 'IMMEDIATELY BEFORE' THE TRANSFER

(i) Preliminary observations: a requirement allowing scope for abuse?

A dubious, but not uncommon, practice of some transferors and transferees is for dismissals of employees to be effected by the transferor prior to the transfer of the undertaking with the aim that the undertaking can be transferred to the transferee clean of employees; these employees will, in that case, it is planned, have their continuity of employment broken in order to be re-engaged, probably selectively, by the transferee in due course, but without acquisition of previously acquired rights. Whether this is possible in most cases depends upon the words in reg 5. Regulation 5 only bites when an employee is still employed in the undertaking 'immediately before' the transfer. Does this mean that, if the employee is not employed right up to the point of the transfer, i e is dismissed a short while before the transfer, the regulation will not apply so as to transfer this contract of employment to the transferee?

At first glance, common sense dictates that the transferor alone

---

2 [1989] IRLR 161.

should be liable for any transferor-initiated dismissal effected before the transfer date, and also that if the employee has been dismissed by the transferor immediately before the transfer date reg 5 should not bite so as to transfer the contract of employment and preserve continuity and so forth to the transferee.

This is, indeed, quite frequently (although not always, of course) the intention of some transferors and transferees when a business is sold. As mentioned in Chapter 5, whether through the process of hiving down or otherwise, it is not uncommonly arranged that the business is purchased free from employees who are then subsequently re-engaged on new terms and conditions by the transferee. An employee who was dismissed prior to the transfer in this way was, in the past, then left to claim a redundancy payment and make other claims for arrears of payments, unfair dismissal and the like, from the transferor. It can be argued that if the transferor and transferee intend that the transferor should pay these sums, then the court should give effect to this wish in their interpretation of reg 5. However, there are reasons in certain circumstances why an employee has an interest in making the transferee liable. One striking case is where the transferor is insolvent, and, where it would be beneficial to an employee to pursue a claim against a solvent transferee. It is true that the EP(C)A allows for reimbursement by the Secretary of State of certain debts due from an insolvent transferor, but not all debts are covered including, significantly, a compensatory award for unfair dismissal.[3] The injustice of this position, which left an employee with a fruitless claim for a compensatory award against an insolvent transferor, began to receive judicial attention.[4]

The Court of Appeal, in *Secretary of State for Employment v Spence*,[5] confirmed that employees must be employed up to the point of transfer to be transferred under reg 5. This legitimised attempts by vendors and purchasers to avoid the application of reg 5 by colluding to cause pre-transfer dismissals. All this has

---

3 Debts covered are: arrears of pay (up to eight weeks) (s 122(3)(a)); statutory minimum notice (s 122(3)(b)); holiday pay (up to six weeks, but only if due within 12 months of the insolvency (s 122(3)(c)); a basic award of compensation for unfair dismissal (s 122(3)(d)); a reasonable sum by way of reimbursement of an apprentice's or articled clerk's fee or premium (s 122(3)(e)).

4 *Pambakian v Brentford Nylons Ltd* [1978] ICR 665 (referred to on this point in the debate on the Transfer Regulations, 991 Hansard HL Deb col 689). The comments in this case are a harbinger of the concerns eventually expressed by the House of Lords in *Litster v Forth Dry Dock & Engineering Co Ltd* [1989] IRLR 161 (see later).

5 [1987] QB 179, [1986] ICR 651, CA.

changed fairly recently, however, because of the decision in *Litster v Forth Dry Dock & Engineering Co Ltd (in receivership)*, handed down by the House of Lords on 16 March 1989.[6] The effect of this case is that a transferee *may* be liable for pre-transfer dismissals even if the employees are not employed in the undertaking immediately before the transfer. This will be in a case where the dismissals are automatically unfair under reg 8 (see below) and are not for an economic, technical or organisational reason entailing changes in the workforce (reg 8(2)). In short, collusive dismissals will generally fall foul of reg 8 and, therefore, liability for such a collusive dismissal will pass to the transferee. The reason why a collusive dismissal falls foul of reg 8 (see below) is this. There will be a transfer-connected dismissal because the dismissal would not have taken place but for the transfer (reg 8(1)). And there may be difficulties in satisfying the employer's defence that there is an economic, technical or organisational reason entailing changes in the workforce (under reg 8(2)) in such a collusive dismissal, i e where the dismissals have taken place simply to break continuity of employment, or to ensure that a sale takes place, or to ensure that the business is more attractive to the purchaser, or to obtain a better price for the business.

Such dismissals may not involve a redundancy at all and therefore cannot be for an economic, technical or organisational reason. Put another way, even if there is, prima facie, an economic, technical or organisational reason, this has to be one *entailing* changes in the workforce and it has been held (see the discussion on reg 8 below) that the necessity for the dismissal must be related to the operational needs of the business and not simply to effect the sale or obtain a better price or to break continuity. Where employees are re-engaged after the transfer, or where new labour is engaged by the transferee at lower rates of pay then, patently, there seems to have been no need in terms of the requirements of the business to effect the dismissals and the dismissals should be automatically unfair. If so, liability will be transferred to the transferee. In other cases, that is to say, where either the dismissal is not connected with the transfer or where there has been a dismissal prior to the transfer and although a transfer-connected dismissal, it *is* for an economic, technical or organisational reason entailing changes in the workforce (because prior to the transfer there has been no direction from the transferee to dismiss and there is a genuine redundancy or inability to pay wages or such like, although this will be rare when a transfer follows shortly thereafter), the question of whether liability

6 [1989] IRLR 161.

for employees is transferred to the transferee depends on the rule in *Secretary of State for Employment v Spence*. This, as stated, provides that, in such cases, only employees employed in the business up to the point of (or immediately before the) transfer will be transferred under reg 5. In such cases of non-connected dismissals or connected pre-transfer dismissals that are for economic, technical or organisational reasons entailing changes in the workforce, all liabilities will therefore stay with the transferor. It is submitted that the best way of understanding the present position is by tracing its background historically.

(ii) The history

From the beginning, tribunals and courts were uneasy about an employer's ability to avoid the regulations by effecting termination of employment slightly before the transfer with a view to avoiding the effect of reg 5. One solution was to apply a broad interpretation to the words 'immediately before' in reg 5 in favour of employees. In *Apex Leisure Hire v Barratt*,[7] an early case now overruled by *Spence*, dismissals of employees took place on Friday 14 January and a transfer of the undertaking took place on 17 January. It was held that a dismissed employee was employed 'immediately before' the transfer, so that the transferee had to answer a complaint of unfair dismissal. Whether the employee was employed by the transferor immediately before the transfer was held to be a question of fact and degree in the circumstances. Because of this, considerable uncertainty began to arise as to who was liable – transferee or transferor – for redundancy payments or for unfair dismissal compensation. This uncertainty was shared not only by transferees of businesses but also by employees themselves, who were not certain whether, and if so against whom and when, to make claims for termination payments. By the time the employees had found out the answer, they might even have been too late, the limitation period for the appropriate claim having run out.[8]

None the less, decisions which concentrated upon the phrase

---

7 [1984] 3 All ER 795, [1984] ICR 452, EAT, also cited as *Alpha Fields v Barratt*.
8 As discussed in Ch 4, the confusion that can arise was illustrated in an industrial tribunal case, *Hansford v W Mumford Ltd and Graham Evans* COIT 16015/83, where (using Figure 3 in Ch 4) a business was sold from B to A, thence to C. It was found there was no relevant transfer to C, only from B to A. A effected the dismissal. Understandably confused by now, the employee sued B and C but not A, and therefore had no claim; by the time he found out he should have sued A, he was time-barred. See also *Croftward v Chandler* 17 October 1986, EAT 344/86, LEXIS transcript.

'immediately before' and confirmed that 'immediately before' was a question of fact and, therefore, of a flexible nature continued to appear. In an industrial tribunal case in *Ellison v R & J K Pullman (Retail) Ltd*[9] an employee was employed 'immediately before' the transfer when she was dismissed on 10 February, the transfer taking place the next day on 11 February. In *Kestongate Ltd v Miller*[10] an employee dismissed on 31 August before a sale on 14 September was held to be employed 'immediately before' the transfer in order that a claim could be brought against the transferee. In *Dickinson v Bryant*[11] an applicant who was dismissed on a Saturday, the transfer taking place on the following Monday, was employed 'immediately before' the transfer so that, again, liability for a redundancy payment and unfair dismissal passed to the transferee. On the other hand, a seven-day gap between a dismissal and transfer was held too long to be 'immediately before' the transfer in *Browne v Catlow and Pilling*,[12] as was a dismissal three days before in *Bannister v Brasway plc*.[13] But tribunals found little difficulty in making a transferee liable for a dismissal where the dismissal and transfer took place on the same day, provided the order was dismissal first and transfer second.[14]

It was said that this broad view of the Transfer Regulations was necessary to breathe life into the idea of transfer and safeguarding of acquired rights and continuity of working environment. For example, in *Secretary of State for Employment v Anchor Hotel (Kippford) Ltd*[15] Waite J (prophetically, it seems) emphasised that the construction of the Transfer Regulations might require a broader and more purposive view to be taken than perhaps was normal in order to give effect to the aims of the Acquired Rights Directive.[16]

And (referring to the problem of an employee left with only a claim against an insolvent transferor if a narrow view of

---

9 COIT 10988/83.
10 [1986] ICR 672, EAT, although this case proceeds on the assumption that transfer may have been 'a period of time' extending from exchange (20 August) to completion (14 September); but cf discussion below.
11 EAT 73/84 LEXIS transcript.
12 COIT 13862/41, IT.
13 *IDS Brief* (254/June 1983), p 7, IT.
14 *Lomax v David Search Ltd* COIT 1353/42; *Secretary of State for Employment v Anchor Hotel (Kippford) Ltd* [1985] ICR 724, [1985] IRLR 452, EAT; *Forth Estuary Engineering Ltd v Litster* [1986] IRLR 59, EAT.
15 [1985] ICR 724, [1985] IRLR 452, EAT.
16 Ibid at 454.

'immediately before' was taken) Hutchinson J thought, in *Dickinson v Bryant,*[17] that:

'. . . it has to be remembered that if the words of reg 5 are to be construed in the strictest sense . . . it would be very easy for a transferor without funds to agree with a transferee, for reasons convenient to them both, that employees should be dismissed a short time before transfer thus leaving them with a worthless remedy and so defeating the protection afforded by the Regulations.'[18]

(Again, it is interesting how, in 1984, this presages the concerns of the House of Lords in *Litster,* expressed later in 1989 (see infra).)

In *Bullard v Marchant*[19] the employee was dismissed on 21 June 1985 and the transfer took place on 24 June. Persuaded by the majority of opinion in EAT cases and particularly by the *Apex Leisure Hire* case, the EAT declined to interfere with the finding of an industrial tribunal that the transferee was liable for the dismissal effected by the transferor. However, the EAT in *Bullard* had some doubts about the received interpretation of reg 5 and invited an authoritative view from the Court of Appeal as a matter of urgency.

To add weight to this divergence of opinion, a parallel, but altogether different, interpretation of the way reg 5 was supposed to work had all along been mooted by some commentators, and this derived support from a handful of cases at least. One early case on the Transfer Regulations was *Premier Motors (Medway) Ltd v Total Oil Great Britain Ltd.*[20] There, it was found that there was a transfer of a business from Premier to Total Oil and thereafter a sale of the business to a Mr Lawrence. It was also found that there was no relevant transfer to Mr Lawrence transferring liability to him for the dismissal of an employee effected by Total, since at the time of this last transfer all recently dismissed employees were no longer employed in the undertaking: they had at the last minute been dismissed by Total. Another case which adopted a similar view was *Angus Jowett & Co Ltd v NUTGW.*[1]

Added to this, the Acquired Rights Directive, in Article 1(1), provides as follows:

'The transferor's rights and obligations arising from a contract of employment or from an employment relationship existing *on the date of a transfer* within the meaning of Article 1(1) shall, by reason of such transfer, be transferred to the transferee.' (emphasis added)

---

17 EAT 73/84 LEXIS transcript.
18 See also *Fenton v Stablegold Ltd* [1986] ICR 236, [1986] IRLR 64, EAT.
19 [1986] 3 CMLR 641, [1986] ICR 389, EAT.
20 [1984] ICR 58, [1983] IRLR 471, EAT.
 1 [1985] ICR 646, [1985] IRLR 326, EAT.

In other words, the directive contemplates subsisting employment at the date of the transfer at least (see below).

(iii) *Secretary of State for Employment v Spence*

This rather muddled state of affairs was clarified by the interpretation by the Court of Appeal of reg 5 in *Secretary of State for Employment v Spence*.[2] The facts in the case were that in November 1983 the employer went into receivership. At 11 am on Monday 28 November the workforce was dismissed and at 2 pm on the same day the business was sold to a company which subsequently re-engaged the dismissed workforce. The applicants claimed a redundancy payment from the transferor. Since the transferor was insolvent, a claim for reimbursement was made to the Secretary of State. He declined to pay, suggesting that any liability had been transferred to the transferee, in that the employees had been employed 'immediately before' the transfer. The industrial tribunal found in favour of the applicants and found that the transferor was liable and therefore the Secretary of State had to reimburse. This was because, first, in the opinion of the tribunal, there was only an asset sale. Second, the employees were not employed 'immediately before' the transfer. The EAT disagreed with the first point and, though doubting the second, decided not to reverse the industrial tribunal.

The Secretary of State appealed and, in ruling on the conflicting interpretations of reg 5, the Court of Appeal came out in favour of the narrow approach in *Premier Motors*. Since the employees had been dismissed prior to the transfer, however proximate that dismissal was to the transfer, they were no longer employed in the business immediately before the transfer. The reasoning of the court was that their employment had been terminated otherwise than by the transfer and, therefore, reg 5 did not operate to transfer their contracts. Regulation 5(3), which contains the proviso that reg 5 only applies to an employee employed in the undertaking or part transferred 'immediately before' the transfer, added, in the opinion of the court, nothing to reg 5(1) (although in some situations it might help to clarify reg 5(1)).[3] Nor did (as had been argued in some cases) reg 5(2) have any life independent of reg 5(1). As one division of the EAT put it, reg 5(2) deals only with the 'nuts and bolts' of reg 5(1) and only passes liability (such as

---

2 [1987] QB 179, [1986] ICR 651, CA.

3 And it might help to clarify, in a case where part only of an undertaking is transferred, whether an employee works in that part, or another part of the undertaking which is reserved from the sale (see later in the text).

dismissals) in relation to contracts transferred under reg 5(1), i e in relation only to contracts which would otherwise have been terminated by the transfer: *not* those which terminated before.[4]

In arriving at its decision the Court of Appeal was also fortified by European law and by the wording of the Acquired Rights Directive, which provides in Art 3(1) that:

> 'The transferor's rights and obligations arising from a contract of employment or from an employment relationship existing *on the date of a transfer* within the meaning of Article 1(1) shall by reason of such transfer be transferred to the transferee.'

And the European Court had decided the following reference from the Danish National Court in Case 19/83 *Wendelboe v L J Music ApS*,[5] that is:

> 'Whether the Council Directive of 14 February 1977 on the approximation of the laws of the member states relating to the safeguarding of employees' rights in the event of transfers of undertakings, businesses or parts of businesses requires member states to enact provisions in accordance with which the transferee of an undertaking becomes liable in respect of obligations concerning holiday pay and compensation to employees who are not employed in the undertaking *on the date of the transfer.*'[6] (Emphasis added.)

The court answered:

> 'The Council Directive No 77/187/EEC 14 February 1977 does not require the member states to enact provisions in accordance with which the transferee of an undertaking becomes liable in respect of obligations concerning holiday pay and compensation to employees who are not employed in the undertaking *on the date of the transfer.*' (emphasis added)

This ruling therefore supports the idea that employees must continue to be employed quite close to the point of transfer (certainly up to and including the date of the transfer) in order for reg 5 to bite. It could, however, be argued, even in the light of this European material, that where dismissal and transfer take place *on the same day*, an employee dismissed on the same calendar day as (but before) the transfer will none the less still be employed in the undertaking immediately before the transfer with the resultant

---

4 See Peter Gibson J in *Bullard v Marchant* [1986] 3 CMLR 641, [1986] ICR 389, EAT.
5 [1985] ECR 457, [1986] 1 CMLR 476.
6 [1986] 1 CMLR 476.

transfer of obligations to the transferee.[7] Both the terms of Art 3(1) of the Acquired Rights Directive and *Wendelboe*, it can be argued, are not inconsistent with this since they immediately refer to a non-application of the appropriate provisions in a case where the employees ceased to be employed earlier than the transfer *date*.

However, the Court of Appeal preferred to interpret reg 5 even more narrowly, suggesting that no distinction should even be made between the concept of *date* of transfer and *time* of transfer (thus disapproving *Secretary of State for Employment v Anchor Hotel (Kippford) Ltd*[8]). Although the decision of the European Court in *Wendelboe* referred to the *date* of transfer, the opinion of the Advocate-General[9] in that case had been that the obligation on member states to ensure rights and obligations were transferred applied only to employees employed at the *time* of transfer.[10] He repeated these views in Case 105/84 *Mikkelsen v Danmols Inventar A/S*[11] and the Court of Appeal in *Spence* adopted the Advocate-General's advice.

Thus, according to *Spence*, even if a dismissal occurred on the same day as, but before the transfer, reg 5, according to the Court of Appeal, would not apply. *Apex Leisure Hire v Barratt*[12] and *Fenton v Stablegold Ltd*[13] were, in the opinion of the Court of Appeal, wrongly decided.

An employee has, therefore, on the face of it to be employed in the undertaking up to and including the point of its transfer for obligations to be passed to the transferee under reg 5. Under *Spence*, if he is dismissed before the point of transfer, liability for the dismissal will remain with the transferor, provided the employee is dismissed before the transfer with *an effective date of termination before the transfer*.

It was thought that this authoritatively settled the question. Further, the Court of Session in Scotland in *Forth Estuary Engineering Ltd v Litster*[14] approved *Secretary of State for Employment v Spence* and held expressly that it made no difference that the pre-transfer dismissal was colluded at by the transferor and transferee and might be a blatant attempt to get round the Transfer

---

7 As was, in fact, held in the case of *Secretary of State for Employment v Anchor Hotel (Kippford) Ltd* [1985] ICR 724, [1985] IRLR 452, EAT.
8 [1985] ICR 724, [1985] IRLR 452, EAT.
9 Sir Gordon Slynn.
10 [1986] 1 CMLR 476 at 481.
11 [1986] 1 CMLR 316, ECJ.
12 [1984] ICR 452, [1984] IRLR 224, EAT.
13 [1986] ICR 236, [1986] IRLR 64, EAT.
14 [1988] IRLR 289.

Regulations. It still meant that the employee was not transferred to the transferee. Any interval between the pre-transfer dismissal and transfer was fatal to the application of reg 5.

Meanwhile, however, the European Court of Justice was thinking somewhat differently. In *P Bork International v Foreningen af Arbejdsledere i Danmark*[15] the lessees ('B') of a business were served with notice of termination of the lease by the lessor ('A'). The lessor (A) temporarily took the business back and thereafter sold it to a third party ('C'). The employees in the business ceased to be employed on surrender of the original lease by B. About half were re-engaged by C. A lapse of time took place between termination of employment by B and re-engagement by C. It was held that there could be a transfer of an undertaking under Art 1(1) of the Acquired Rights Directive in these circumstances. The problem was whether the re-engaged workers could invoke the Acquired Rights Directive to transfer their rights from B to C. This was because it was accepted that, ordinarily, only workers who have a current contract of employment at the date of transfer may invoke the directive.[16]

However, the European Court of Justice held that this was subject to the *mandatory* provisions of Art 4(1) of the Acquired Rights Directive which stipulates that 'the transfer of an undertaking . . . shall not itself constitute grounds for dismissal by the transferor or transferee'. This means that an employee unlawfully dismissed under Art 4(1) (our equivalent of reg 8; see the discussion on reg 8 below) (ie in connection with a transfer but where there was no economic, technical or organisational reason for dismissal entailing changes in the workforce – a defence not made out here because the workers were re-engaged) must be considered as still employed by the undertaking at the date of transfer. This meant, in effect, that employment obligations in relation to them were effectively transferred from transferor to transferee notwithstanding the interval between successive employments.

This obviously appeared to qualify the *Spence* case in the area of liability for automatically unfair pre-transfer transfer-connected dismissals if, indeed, it could be applied to English law for the purposes of interpreting the Transfer Regulations. So, under the European approach the following would have to be considered.

---

15 [1990] 3 CMLR 701, [1989] IRLR 41.
16 See Art 3(1) and *Mikkelsen v Danmols Inventar A/S* [1986] 1 CMLR 316; *Wendelboe v L J Music ApS* [1986] 1 CMLR 476, a position broadly equating to *Spence*.

(1) Is there a transfer-connected dismissal before the transfer?

(2) Is it automatically unfair (ie no 'eto' – economic, technical, or organisational reason)?

(3) If so, liability passes to the purchaser.

(4) Is it another kind of pre-transfer dismissal, ie one which is not automatically unfair?

(5) If so, *Spence* applies.

3   *LITSTER v FORTH DRY DOCK & ENGINEERING CO LTD*

Notwithstanding the above, because of the wording of the Transfer Regulations, which differs from the Acquired Rights Directive, it was not at all certain whether the Transfer Regulations could be construed to give effect to the *Bork* decision. The basis of Art 4(1) is that it prohibits transfer-connected dismissals where there is no eto and says, in effect, that they are nugatory. Hence, in the view of the European Court on the meaning of the directive, employees can be deemed still to be in employment at the point of transfer notwithstanding that unlawful dismissal. However, in the Transfer Regulations, there is no concept of prohibiting the dismissal. They simply provide that it is unfair. It does not follow naturally from the Transfer Regulations that the dismissal is deemed not to have taken effect. The natural reading is that such a dismissal has taken effect but it has to be compensated. So, in the light of that apparent problem and in view of the Court of Appeal decision in *Spence*, some doubt was expressed as to whether the *Bork* decision could be applied in the UK to interpret the Transfer Regulations. If that were the case, it would have meant that the Transfer Regulations as drafted were in breach of the directive as interpreted by the European Court. That, of course, would be a very unsatisfactory state of affairs.

However, in the House of Lords in *Litster v Forth Dry Dock & Engineering Co Ltd (in receivership)*[17] the House of Lords held that the Transfer Regulations had to be construed to give effect to our obligations under the directive, as interpreted by the European Court, and had to be read to the effect that an employee who is dismissed in connection with an impending transfer where there is

---

17 [1989] IRLR 161.

no eto is automatically transferred to the transferee whether or not there was an interval between dismissal and transfer.

The facts were that Forth Dry Dock & Engineering Co Ltd went into receivership in September 1983. Forth Estuary Engineering Limited was incorporated with a view to acquiring the business of Forth Dry Dock. At 3.30pm on 6 February 1984 the entire workforce of Forth Dry Dock were dismissed with immediate effect. The transfer was executed at 4.30pm. Within 48 hours of the dismissals it was learnt that Forth Estuary Engineering Limited was recruiting employees. A number of former employees applied for these jobs but only three were engaged. It materialised that the new company was recruiting at lower wages and ended up with a similar size workforce to that employed by the transferor, which was now in receivership. As will be seen to be very relevant, it is unlikely on those facts that this transfer-connected dismissal was for an eto *entailing* changes in the workforce. It looked collusive. In the words of Lord Oliver in the House of Lords in this case (see infra):

'It is difficult to resist the inference that the employer was not unmindful of the disadvantages which might flow under the regulations from the continuance of the employment of the existing workforce as compared with the advantages to be derived from the pool of unemployed tradesmen anxious for work on any available terms. . . the sequence of events and the secrecy with which they were enshrouded are such that they cannot rationally be accounted for otherwise than by the hypothesis that the dismissal of the existing workforce was engineered specifically with a view to preventing any liability for the obligations undertaken to their contracts of employment from attaching to [the purchaser], so as to leave them with nothing but a claim for redundancy on the redundancy fund under s 106 of the Act of 1978 and an illusory claim for unfair dismissal against an insolvent company.'

These facts, very obviously, can be seen to offend the principle in *Bork*.

In the industrial tribunal below the proceedings were prior to *Secretary of State for Employment v Spence* and although there had been a small interval between dismissal and transfer, the tribunal held none the less that the employees had been employed immediately before the transfer. This issue was not canvassed fully before the EAT but by the time the case reached the Court of Session the court had the benefit of reading *Spence* and decided to follow *Spence* and held that as the dismissal had occurred before the transfer, even though only an hour before, the employees were not employed near enough the point of transfer to be transferred to the transferee.

In the House of Lords however, argument was heard about the *Bork* case and it was concluded that unless the *Bork* case was applied, the Transfer Regulations would be in breach of the directive, a consequence that should be avoided if at all possible. It was certainly not possible, on a literal reading of the regulations, to give effect to the decision in the *Bork* case. However, an earlier decision of the House of Lords in *Pickstone v Freemans plc*[18] had held that a purposive construction had to be given to United Kingdom legislation that was intended to give effect to European legislation. Thus the way the House of Lords in *Litster* dealt with the situation was as follows. One solution was to say that the words 'immediately before the transfer' could be given a broad and flexible approach so that where there was a pre-transfer dismissal, the employee was employed immediately before the transfer. But that was not perfect and would lead to vagueness and uncertainty. Accordingly, reg 5(1), which refers to a person being employed immediately before the transfer, should now be read as if there were inserted immediately after those words words to the effect 'or would have been so employed if he had not been unfairly dismissed in the circumstances described in reg 8(1)'. As the employees were clearly dismissed contrary to reg 8 in this case (see above and in particular the quoted comments of Lord Oliver on the facts) it followed that liability for such dismissals passed to the transferee. Lord Oliver also stated:

> 'It follows from the construction that I attach to regulation 5(3) that where an employee is dismissed before and by reason of the transfer the employment is statutorily continued with the transferee by virtue of the regulations . . .'

a phrase the consequences of which will be returned to later in this chapter.

So, as previously discussed, in general terms this decision means that a pre-transfer dismissal, however long before the transfer (as long as it is connected) which is automatically unfair under reg 8 will result in liability passing to the transferee. Only in other cases will *Secretary of State for Employment v Spence* apply. The House of Lords held that there was no conflict between the finding in *Litster* and the facts of *Secretary of State for Employment v Spence*, because, on the facts in *Secretary of State for Employment v Spence*, the workforce had been dismissed before any transaction had been agreed and there was every possibility of the business not being sold at all. The receiver was under pressure from the bank to stop paying

---

18 [1989] AC 66, [1988] 2 All ER 803.

wages in any event and, for that reason, the pre-transfer dismissals took place. The business ceased trading two days before the sale. As it happened, a deal was concluded very shortly after the dismissals, but its fruition was by no means certain at the time of dismissal. Therefore, the House of Lords suggested, the dismissal in *Spence* was not automatically unfair. (It is not entirely clear why: presumably, either the dismissal was unconnected *or*, alternatively, if connected and prima facie caught by reg 8, was saved by reg 8(2), ie there was an eto.) So *Spence* is not overruled but its application to pre-transfer dismissal greatly restricted. To repeat our conclusions, the exercise which has to be followed now is this.

(a) Was the time between the dismissal and the transfer of so short a duration that the employee was employed immediately before the transfer? In effect was the employee employed actually at the point of transfer or as near as makes no difference (or rather, as Lord Oliver put it in *Litster*, where dismissal and transfer 'are so closely connected in point of time that it is, for practical purposes, impossible, realistically, to say that they are not precisely contemporaneous')?[19] If so, the contract of employment will be transferred to the transferee under reg 5. (Lord Oliver's comments should perhaps be treated with care: in reality employment may have to exist at the point of transfer. Thus, although it seems to have been envisaged by Lord Oliver that an interval between dismissal and transfer which is minuscule may be disregarded, the House of Lords approved the result in *Spence* where, it may be remembered, the interval was just three hours, ie over lunch, and as this was interpreted as a case of dismissal which was not automatically unfair, even that short an interval was fatal.)

(b) If the answer to the above is no, that is to say there is a pre-transfer dismissal which means there is some interval between a dismissal and the transfer, the next question to ask is was there a dismissal which was connected with the transfer so as to invoke reg 8(1) which makes such a dismissal prima facie automatically unfair? If the answer is yes, and reg 8 is invoked, does reg 8(2) apply (but see (1) below) which says that the dismissal shall not be automatically unfair if there is an economic, technical or organisational reason for the dismissal entailing changes in the workforce (the eto)? If there is no such eto, liability for the pre-transfer dismissal will pass to the transferee.

---

19 [1989] ICR 341 at 369.

(c) If there is a pre-transfer dismissal but it is either unconnected or, presumably, if connected, is for an eto (ie is not automatically unfair under reg 8) then, provided that the employee was not employed in the business immediately before the transfer (see (a)) liabilities will remain with the transferor and *Secretary of State for Employment v Spence* will apply.

4 PRACTICAL PROBLEMS AND QUESTIONS LEFT UNANSWERED BY *LITSTER*

Notwithstanding this revision of the law, many points that arise from *Litster* are not expressly dealt with in the opinions of the Lords. Only further case law can resolve these. A number of them are dealt with below.

(i) Transfer-connected dismissals

The House of Lords decision allows for automatic assignment to a transferee of liability for a pre-transfer dismissal where such dismissal falls foul of reg 8(1), ie is prima facie automatically unfair because it is in connection with the transfer. Some commentators have read the decision as meaning that as long as there is a transfer-connected dismissal, *any* transfer-connected dismissal liability will pass to a transferee. This is surely not the case. Although the words of the House of Lords could be interpreted as such, a dismissal which is prima facie automatically unfair under reg 8(1) ceases to be so if there is an economic, technical or organisational reason entailing changes in the workforce under reg 8(2). And it is submitted that only transfer-connected dismissals occurring before the transfer which are not for an eto will cause liabilities to pass to the transferee. In other cases *Spence* (see above) will apply. It is submitted that this is the meaning and intention of the European Court in the *Bork* case and, in fact, what the Lords were actually saying. The discussion below proceeds on that assumption. One way of reconciling these different views is that it will be relatively rare for a transfer-connected dismissal to be for an eto. If that practical point is taken on board, it will be seen that the distinction between reg 8(1) and 8(2) will often be blurred even if technically distinct. (See, too, the view of Van Gerven AG in *G d'Urso v Ercole Marelli Ellettromeccanica Generale SpA*[20] on Art 4 of the Directive.)

---

20 [1992] IRLR 136.

(ii) Qualifying employees

Does *Litster* apply only to those who have a qualifying period for unfair dismissal? This seems inherent from the use of the automatically unfair dismissal provisions of reg 8 to bring about the deemed continuation of contract to the point of transfer. That would seem unfair. Although, as with other areas of uncertainty about the scope of *Litster*, we shall have to wait upon case law, there is a strong moral argument for all employees to be covered irrespective of a qualifying period. On the other hand, Art 4(1) of the Acquired Rights Directive allows member states to provide that '[the prohibition against transfer-connected dismissals] shall not apply to certain specific categories of employees who are not covered by the laws or practice of the member states in respect of protection against dismissal'. It could therefore be argued that this unfortunately legitimises exclusion from *Litster* those employees with short service. (For the position of such employees in relation to statutory continuity of employment, see Ch 5.)

(iii) Section 57(3) cases

Does *Litster* apply not only to those unfairly dismissed under reg 8(1) but also to those unfairly dismissed under EP(C)A s 57(3) (eg when an eto has applied)? The answer here should be in the negative. Although, again, it is a point raised by some commentators, it is not one which is sustainable from a reading of *Litster*.

(iv) Continuation of the contract

Litster was concerned with liability for a pre-transfer dismissal, more precisely for *unfair dismissal* liability. Lord Oliver did, however, state (see above) that 'the employment is statutorily continued' (presumably to the point of transfer) where there has been a pre-transfer dismissal which is automatically unfair. The meaning of this approach has been the subject of some debate. At one extreme it is argued that such a dismissal is null and void. But the concept of nullity of a dismissal is alien to our domestic labour law: our law provides simply for automatic unfair dismissal liability when reg 8(1) is infringed. Whether that is effective enough a remedy is questionable; that may be a matter to be taken up by the EC Commission.[1]

---

1 See the principle of effectiveness of remedy under EC law expounded in *Von Colson and Kamann v Land Nordrhein–Westfalen* [1984] ECR 1891, [1986] 2 CMLR 430, discussed in more detail in Ch 6. See, however, the remedy under the proposed amendments to the collective redundancies directive (75/129), referred to in Ch 10.

But what are the consequences of deemed continuation of contract? Will a transferee also be liable for redundancy payments? Or for unpaid notice? Or for arrears of wages? These points are not dealt with by the decision but it seems arguable that a transferee would inherit these liabilities too. One view is that this means only such liabilities up to, and consequent on, dismissal, unless the dismissal *were* treated as null and void (see above). But it is possible that employment claims may also cover the period between dismissal and transfer too, i e until the eventual termination of statutorily continued employment at the instance of the *transferee* by refusing to employ. The *Bork* case itself concerned a claim for unpaid holiday pay. And suppose the employees were re-engaged after the point of transfer by the transferee. If the employment has been statutorily deemed to be continued to the point of transfer, will continuity be preserved? Again, although the point is not dealt with by the decision, the answer is, arguably, yes. (This emphasises how unfair it would be to restrict *Litster* only to those employees who qualify for unfair dismissal – see (ii) above.)

(v) The relevance of the eto

Assuming our view is correct (see (i) above), at the core of pre-transfer dismissal liability attaching to a purchaser under *Litster* is the automatically unfair dismissal under reg 8 and the scope of the eto. It is disappointing that there was no real discussion of this vital element, particularly the eto. A full discussion and in particular how reg 8 interfaces with *Litster* follows in Chapter 8.

(vi) Insolvency and *Litster*

Litster concerned an insolvent transferor, and has clear ramifications for insolvency practitioners. It clearly applies to sales by receivers and administrators. Will *Litster* also apply to sales by hiving down? What, therefore, is its relationship with reg 4? Regulation 4 and the mechanics of hiving down are, of course, discussed in detail in Chapter 9. As there explained, reg 4 facilitates hiving down by postponing the transfer under the Transfer Regulations that would otherwise arise on the hive down of the business to the subsidiary until either the disposal of the share capital of the subsidiary to a buyer or the subsidiary disposes of the business to a buyer. The question is whether a receiver may still dismiss employees for no other reason than this is required by the purchaser or that this may improve the sale price prior to the deemed postponed transfer under reg 4 (i e when the hived down company's business is sold or share capital sold) without imposing liability on a purchaser. The answer should, it is submitted, be no. Although this particular scenario was not envisaged by *Litster*, *Litster* should still apply because although dismissal is prior to an artificially postponed transfer, it is still a pre-transfer dismissal and, if not for an eto, should be caught by *Litster*. And remember, reg 4 is *not* in the directive. It should not really be in the regulations. If reg 4 might seem to diminish rights unless purposively construed, no doubt the courts will give effect to the aims of the directive and apply *Litster* to it. It is therefore argued in Chapter 9 that from an employment law perspective alone (this book is not concerned with the taxation or other legal aspects of business sales) there is no advantage in using hiving down and reg 4 as a means of disposal.

The next question is whether *Litster* applies to sales by liquidators and indeed, as speculated in Chapter 9, whether the Transfer Regulations apply at all in sales by liquidators. As explained later, under the EP(C)A a sale by a liquidator has attracted para 17(2) of Sch 13 to the EP(C)A without any question. And this must surely be sound.[2] Although it can be argued that a business sale is more likely to occur following a voluntary liquidation as opposed to a compulsory liquidation simply because the business is more likely in the former to have remained intact rather than disintegrate into a collection of assets, there seems no reason to distinguish between the two for business transfer legislation purposes.[3] Some doubt arises because the European Court in *Abels v Administrative Board of the Bedrigfsvereniging voor de Metaal-Industrie en de Electrotechnische Industrie*[4] has held that the *directive* does not apply to our equivalent of compulsory liquidation (see infra). The ramifications

---

2 *Thomsons Soft Drinks Ltd v Quayle* EAT 12/81 LEXIS transcript. This was a voluntary liquidation case, but the comments in the case are widely enough phrased to catch compulsory liquidations too (see Ch 9).

3 *Thomsons Soft Drinks Ltd v Quayle* EAT 12/81 LEXIS transcript. See also *Huggins v A & J Gordon (Aveley) Ltd* (1971) 6 ITR 164 (also a voluntary liquidation case). Both cases stress the need to return to first principles in atypical cases, ie to the test in *Kenmir Ltd v Frizzell* [1968] 1 All ER 414, [1968] 1 WLR 329.

4 [1987] 2 CMLR 406. The only development, as stated in Ch 9, since *Abels* in the European Court is that the court has ruled in the case of *G d'Urso v Ercole Marelli Elettromeccanica* (25 July 1991, unreported) that the directive may apply to the Italian procedure for special administration of major companies experiencing a crisis provided that there is a decision that the company's activities are to be pursued and as long as the company remains active. When the activities are ceased, the directive does not apply. This settles a dispute in Italy as to whether the Italian procedure was more akin to compulsory liquidation (as in *Abels*) or administration or receivership.

of this decision in the UK have still to be worked out. In the meantime, caution should be exercised.

Most (notwithstanding the above decision) assume compulsory liquidations are covered by the Transfer Regulations (see Ch 9). This is because the regulations are fairly widely drawn. And so it would certainly not be wise at this stage, at least, to advise a liquidator client or a client purchasing from a liquidator that the Transfer Regulations were inapplicable to compulsory liquidation until further judicial guidance is available. To repeat, however, the practical position may often render the above debate sterile. If there is a compulsory liquidation, although a business sale is perfectly possible, it is often found that there is no longer a business to run and assets are disposed of on a break-up basis.

As stated, a fuller discussion of insolvency and its aspects relevant to business transfers may be found in Chapter 9.

(vii) Remedies for dismissal

What about remedies for an automatically unfair pre-transfer dismissal? Will the remedy be purely compensation? Slynn A-G thought in *Wendelboe v LJ Music ApS*,[5] that:

> 'Whether the remedy for [the] dismissal consists in a court order declaring that dismissal to be a nullity or the award of damages or some other effective remedy is for the member states to determine. In any event the member states are required to provide for a remedy which is effective and not merely symbolic.'

The standard remedy for unfair dismissal is an order for compensation under s 72 of the Employment Protection (Consolidation) Act 1978. This comprises a basic award (EP(C)A s 73) and a compensatory award (EP(C)A s 74). However, an industrial tribunal may also make either a reinstatement or re-engagement order (EP(C)A s 69), an apparently much more effective remedy. And an industrial tribunal is, by virtue of s 68 of the EP(C)A, charged with the duty of examining the possibility of the remedy of reinstatement/re-engagement before the remedy of compensation. Notwithstanding this statutory emphasis, orders for reinstatement/re-engagement are relatively rare. It has been estimated they form only approximately 1 per cent of tribunal orders on remedy.[6]

---

5 [1985] ECR 457, [1986] 1 CMLR 476.
6 Source: *Employment Gazette*, May 1991 p 304. Out of 5,786 unfair dismissal cases proceeding to a hearing in 1988–1989 and 5,864 in 1989–1990, 58 resulted in reinstatement/re-engagement orders in 1988–1989 and 59 in 1989–1990, 1 per cent in each case. In both years this was 0.3 per cent of all (17,870 and 18,098 respectively) unfair dismissal applications.

It is submitted that tribunals should apply this order more readily in an automatically unfair dismissal case arising out of *Litster*, however. Such an order is the most effective way of implementing the prohibition against these types of dismissal contained in Art 4(1) of the directive. Section 69(4) of the EP(C)A specifically provides that a re-engagement order may be made against a successor of the original employer, and Lord Keith in *Litster* was anxious that employees in business transfer cases are not 'deprived of the remedy of reinstatement or re-engagement'.[7]

A reinstatement order under s 69 of the EP(C)A will ordinarily include an order for payment of loss of wages between a dismissal and reinstatement (EP(C)A s 69(2)), and this might also be the case with a re-engagement order (but in this case it is at the tribunal's discretion – EP(C)A s 69(4)). Of course, an employer may refuse to comply with a reinstatement or re-engagement order. If so, a tribunal may make an additional award of compensation under s 71 of the EP(C)A which is limited to maxima set out in s 71(2). This lack of power to enforce continued employment, leaving the employee with (albeit augmented) compensation is a defect in our unfair dismissal law. Mandatory reinstatement and re-engagement has therefore not been achieved in UK unfair dismissal law.[8]

On a different but not unrelated front, it has also been suggested that an injunction might be obtained against a vendor implementing a dismissal before a transfer or, alternatively, against a purchaser from requiring such a dismissal (on the basis of the tort of inducement of breach of contract) where the dismissal is contrary to reg 8 and because, under *Litster*, the employment is, notwithstanding the purported dismissal, deemed statutorily to continue. An

---

7 [1989] ICR 341 at 349.

8 The maximum that can be awarded under s 71 of the EP(C)A for failure to comply with a reinstatement/re-engagement order is, in addition to an award under ordinary principles, between 13 and 26 weeks' pay (save that where the dismissal was on account of race or sex discrimination the award is of an amount between 26 and 52 weeks' pay). Now an employee's loss of earnings, because of dismissal and the date specified in the order concerned, could well exceed this. To answer that point, the EAT in *Conoco (UK) Ltd v Neal* [1989] ICR 114, [1989] IRLR 51 suggested that an employee who was not reinstated in pursuance of a tribunal order might sue for arrears of pay in the county court or High Court in lieu of applying to the tribunal for a further order under s 71. Take a case like *Litster* where the lapse of time between dismissal and a reinstatement order (if granted) would have been about five years; the arrears available by virtue of *Conoco* would have been enormous! (The compensation claims in *Litster* were, incidentally, settled out of court.) *Conoco* was however overruled by the Court of Appeal in *O'Laoire v Jackel International Ltd* [1990] ICR 197, [1990] IRLR 70 which confirmed that the only remedy for breach of a s 69 order was an award by a tribunal under s 71.

alternative view is that statutory continuance of employment is for one purpose only, ie to supplement reg 5(3) and not otherwise; if so, an injunction would only lie if there was a breach of contract in the dismissal, e g summary dismissal with a payment in lieu of notice when the contract did not allow this. In either event, though, notwithstanding the possibility of an injunction in practice, this remedy is rarely granted in this type of case. In recent times, some employees have succeeded in obtaining injunctions to stop dismissals in breach of contract, particularly where breaches of procedure are concerned. The yardstick seems to be whether confidence in the employment relationship still exists. These cases are still, however, the exception rather than the rule.[9]

5 POSTSCRIPT ABOUT *SPENCE* CASES

Spence will not apply in a great many pre-transfer dismissal cases now and will certainly not apply in cases where the pre-transfer dismissal has been effected in an attempt to outflank the Transfer Regulations. None the less, as explained, where there is a pre-transfer dismissal which either is unconnected with the transfer, or, if connected, is for an eto, *Spence* (as explained above) will still apply. Where *Spence* does apply though, there are still problems in practice in applying it successfully.

(i) The requirement of a termination before the transfer

In order for liability to remain with the transferor, the employee will have to cease to be *employed* in the undertaking prior to the transfer. Just because an employee has been *dismissed*, this does not, of course, necessarily mean that he ceases to be *employed* prior to the transfer. If he is dismissed with notice and the period of notice straddles the transfer date, then he will, it seems, remain employed in the undertaking at the point of transfer and the contract of

---

9 See Hepple (1989) ILJ 129. See generally on injunctions *Hill v C A Parsons & Co Ltd* [1972] Ch 305, [1971] 3 All ER 1345; *Irani v Southampton and South West Hampshire Health Authority* [1985] ICR 590, [1985] IRLR 203, 590; *Powell v London Borough of Brent* [1988] ICR 176, [1987] IRLR 466; *Hughes v London Borough of Southwark* [1988] IRLR 55; *Ali v London Borough of Southwark* [1988] ICR 567, [1988] IRLR 100; *Kearney v NSPCC* IDS Brief 385 (November 1988) p 2; *Jakeman v South West Thames Regional Health Authority* [1990] IRLR 62; *Alexander v Standard Telephones and Cables Ltd* [1990] ICR 291, [1990] IRLR 55; *Wishart v National Association of Citizens' Advice Bureaux Ltd* [1990] ICR 794, [1990] IRLR 393; *Wadcock v London Borough of Brent* [1988] ICR 143.

employment and liability for the dismissal will pass to the transferee.[10] This will be so however distant the act of *dismissal* is to the point of transfer. Those advising employees apparently dismissed before the transfer in these circumstances should perhaps also scrutinise termination letters. Imprecise words by an employer, used orally or in a letter of dismissal, can occasionally lead a court to find that an employee has not been summarily dismissed with a payment in lieu, but, instead, has been simply put on paid leave over his period of notice. If such period of notice straddles the transfer date, the employee may therefore still qualify to be transferred.[11]

Also, finally, there is the possibility that an employee dismissed summarily, even with a payment in lieu of notice, may have been dismissed in breach of contract.[12] Such a breach, it has been held, does not of itself, at common law, end the contract of employment. An act of 'acceptance' by the injured party is needed to end the contract.[13] This 'elective' theory was first thought to apply only to breaches of the contract short of wrongful dismissal;[14] but in *Gunton v Richmond-upon-Thames London Borough Council*,[15] the Court of Appeal held it also applied to dismissals in breach of contract. The logical consequence is that an injured employee may refuse to accept a wrongful dismissal and may keep the contract alive for at least as long as the period of notice he was actually entitled to receive.[16] If summarily (and wrongfully) dismissed shortly before

---

10 It is fairly trite law that an employee remains employed during his period of notice, if notice is given.

11 For further guidance, see *Adams v GKN Sankey Ltd* [1980] IRLR 416; *Chapman v Letheby and Christopher Ltd* [1981] IRLR 440, EAT.

12 In *Konski v Peet* [1915] 1 Ch 530 it was suggested that dismissal with a payment in lieu of notice was lawful. But the modern view is that it is not: see Freedland *The Contract of Employment* pp 184 et seq and the cases cited therein here at note 16, p 154, below. This breach can be avoided by a provision in the contract allowing for a payment in lieu of notice (see below, text).

13 J McMullen 'A Synthesis of the Mode of Termination of the Contract of Employment' [1982] CLJ 110.

14 Ibid.

15 [1981] Ch 448, [1980] ICR 755, CA. And see *Hill v C A Parsons & Co Ltd* [1972] Ch 305, [1971] 3 All ER 1345, and, recently, *Irani v Southampton and South West Hampshire Health Authority* [1985] ICR 590, [1985] IRLR 203.

16 In *R v East Berkshire Health Authority, ex p Walsh* [1985] QB 152, [1984] ICR 743, CA Sir John Donaldson MR expressed a view that a wrongful dismissal must automatically end a contract at the point of dismissal but this has not been developed, and a later case, *Dietman v London Borough of Brent* [1987] ICR 737, [1987] IRLR 259, reaffirms the elective theory. In *Rigby v Ferodo Ltd* [1988] ICR 29, [1987] IRLR 516 the House of Lords was invited to rule that *Gunton* was wrong, but it declined to do so, having regard to the issues it had to decide. Cf here, though, *Micklefield v S A C Technology Ltd* [1991] 1 All ER 275, [1990] IRLR 218.

the transfer, even with a payment in lieu of notice (assuming this payment is made without the authority of the contract – see below),[17] such an employee could in theory keep his contract alive for the purpose of continuing to be employed at the point of transfer.

Another interesting point arises from the very facts of *Secretary of State for Employment v Spence*. As will be remembered, the employees in that case were dismissed at 11 am on the day of the transfer, the transfer taking place at 2 pm. The employees were subsequently re-engaged by the transferee. The Court of Appeal held that redundancy payments liability attached to the *former* employer (and hence the Secretary of State, as the former employer was insolvent) as the employees were not in employment at the point of transfer. Now, as has been seen, in many cases a pre-transfer dismissal in circumstances like these will attract *Litster* and the pre-transfer dismissal will be considered automatically unfair, with the consequence that employment obligations are imposed on the transferee. The House of Lords in *Litster* assumed that the facts in *Spence* did not give rise to that conclusion and, so, the dismissals were not automatically unfair. The reasons for this are explained above. In the very rare case that dismissal and transfer take place on the same day but *Spence is* held to apply because the employees' employment has terminated prior to the transfer, have the employees an additional argument?

Suppose, notwithstanding their employment came to an end before the transfer, they were paid to the end of the day. Could their employment not straddle the transfer because of that? The case of *Octavius Atkinson & Sons Ltd v Morris*[18] suggests not. An employee working on site away from home was dismissed at 2 pm. He travelled home, arriving at 4 pm. The question was whether his employment could be deemed to continue until the end of the day (this was an unfair dismissal case based in part on failure to offer alternative employment on redundancy: alternative work actually became available around 4 pm but was not offered to the employee – if he had still been in employment at that time the failure to offer such work would have been material to his case). The court held in that case that the summary dismissal was effective at once even if

---

17 As discussed at note 11, above, *Konski v Peet* suggests payment in lieu of notice without authority of the contract is lawful. But cf more recent cases such as *British Building and Engineering Appliances Ltd v Dedman Ltd* [1973] ICR 182, NIRC: affd [1974] 1 All ER 520, [1974] ICR 53, CA: *Dixon v Stenor Ltd* [1973] ICR 157, [1973] IRLR 28; *Robert Cort & Son Ltd v Charman* [1981] ICR 816, [1981] IRLR 437.

18 [1989] ICR 431, [1989] IRLR 158.

part way through the day, ie at lunchtime. However, the court remarked it had not heard argument on the question of whether the dismissal was a repudiation, and if so, whether it needed acceptance by an injured party in order for termination to occur. Thus: 'Nothing in this decision should be taken as regulating the position where an employee has not accepted the employer's repudiation.'

In *Robert Cort & Son Ltd v Charman*[19] and *Stapp v Shaftesbury Society*[20] the EAT and the Court of Appeal respectively held that a summary dismissal, even if wrongful at common law, was immediately effective when announced, so far as the effective date of termination of employment for the purposes of s 55(2)(a) of the EP(C)A was concerned. None the less, these cases were concerned with the effective date of termination for unfair dismissal purposes under statute, and it is theoretically possible that *Gunton* can still apply to the interpretation of whether the contract of employment is one 'otherwise terminated by the transfer' or whether the employee is 'employed' immediately before the transfer for the purposes of the Transfer Regulations, which is a different context. This, if correct, could give rise to great practical problems. For as discussed, rarely will the transferor be able to allow sufficient time after dismissals and before a transfer for a contract to terminate by expiry of full notice. This argument awaits full treatment by the courts.

We assumed (above) that dismissal with a payment in lieu of notice would be a breach of contract without the authority in the contract to make such a payment. However, it correspondingly follows that if a contract of employment specifically provides for discharge of notice liability by an employer, this *semble* will not be a breach of contract. Until the doubt raised here about the effect of summary dismissals is resolved, employers would be advised to include such a provision.[1]

But even then, a dismissal with less than the minimum period of notice under s 49 of the EP(C)A attracts, respectively, the provisions of s 55(5) and s 90(3) of the EP(C)A for the purposes of unfair dismissal and redundancy. Both these provisions stipulate that in such a case the effective date of termination of the employment will not be the date of summary dismissal but the date on which the statutory minimum period of notice *would have* expired,

---

19 [1981] ICR 816, [1981] IRLR 437.
20 [1982] IRLR 326, CA.
1 Many precedents of service agreements and contracts of employment contain such a clause. It may well be that the courts will strive to apply the reasoning in *Stapp* in this contractual context too; but a decision is awaited.

if given. It may be that these provisions are confined to particular purposes under the EP(C)A (for example to qualifying periods and basic award calculations (s 55(5));[2] but it is at least *arguable* that they could apply to the Transfer Regulations to help determine whether someone is still 'employed' in the undertaking prior to the transfer. This possibility too (if correct) would cause great problems if a summary dismissal occurred shortly before the transfer.[3]

(ii) 'Time' or 'moment' of transfer?

A related point which, again, is only applicable in the rare instances where a dismissal prior to the transfer on the same day as the transfer is not considered to be automatically unfair, and therefore governed by *Spence*, is this. *Spence* suggests employment must exist at the *time* or *moment* of transfer. This is supported by the House of Lords' view in *Litster* where, as discussed above, the result on facts of *Spence* was not disapproved (a three-hour interval was fatal in *Spence*). (The House of Lords in *Litster* seem to suggest that a *de minimis* interval can be ignored, but what this means is not clear (see above).) But the Acquired Rights Directive, in its English translation, refers to *date* of transfer. Lord Oliver in *Litster* refers to the '*date*' of transfer and '*time*' of transfer being interchangeable. But are they? In *Wendelboe v L J Music Aps*[4] the European Court referred to the date of transfer (although the Advocate-General talked of 'time' of transfer). Again in *Spence*, Balcombe LJ, considering *Wendelboe*, thought the two words meant the same thing, ie 'moment' of transfer (an expression used by the Advocate-General in *Mikkelsen v Danmols Inventar A/S*).[5] If date means *day* though, and we follow the English-language version of the directive, it would mean that even where the dismissal is not

---

2 In fact s 55(5) was applied by the EAT in *Charnock v Barrie Muirhead Ltd* [1984] ICR 641 in the context of a transfer of employment under para 18 of Sch 13 of the EP(C)A (see Ch 2). It may also be a relevant argument for the discussion in Ch 5.

3 Care here must also be taken about the mode of communication, if summary dismissal effective immediately is intended. In such cases, use of the postal service is not the wisest medium of communication. It has been held by the EAT in *Brown v Southall and Knight* [1980] ICR 617, [1980] IRLR 130 that a letter of dismissal is effective only when it arrives. Much safer would be the practice of hand delivery of dismissal notices. This causes special problems with those off sick, on maternity leave, or otherwise absent. Special enquiries will have to be made. Of course, one might cynically observe, if firing is becoming all that crucial to an employer, there might be a contrived dismissal with a sale in mind, thus bringing in *Litster*, and rendering all of the above academic!

4 [1985] ECR 457.

5 [1985] ECR 2639.

automatically unfair under reg 8, liability for a pre-transfer dismissal passes to a purchaser.[6] The answer lies surely in an over-view of the various member states' language versions. This exercise has not yet been carried out judicially. Anyway, as will be realised, the issue only arises in the few cases of pre-transfer terminations very close to the transfer that are not covered by *Litster*.[7]

(iii) The residual question of continuity of employment

Suppose the employment of an employee is terminated prior to the transfer but he is subsequently re-engaged by a transferee. Such facts will almost inevitably attract *Litster*. Only exceptionally will a dismissal by a transferor followed by transferee re-engagement be, it is submitted, a dismissal for an eto (see the discussion above).[8]

In the very rare event indeed that it could, in which case *Spence* may apply, so that reg 5 may not be applicable to preserve the employment contract, there is still the question of whether statutory continuity is broken here (for the purposes of EP(C)A para 17(2)). The detailed discussion in Chapter 5, to which the reader is referred here, shows that if a transferee re-engages an employee dismissed by a transferor the chances of acquiring him with broken continuity may be problematic in most cases and impossible in many.[9]

6 EXCLUSION OF EMPLOYEES FROM THE EFFECT OF REG 5: STRUCTURING THE DEAL TO AVOID THE APPLICATION OF THE TRANSFER REGULATIONS

It is possible for some transfers to fall outside the Transfer Regula-tions or at least for some employees involved to be excluded from their scope. Those acting on behalf of vendors and purchasers may wish to consider such avenues. At the outset, it must however be

---

6 There is an excellent discussion by Tony Kerr in *Acquired Rights of Employees* (Irish Centre for European Law, 1989) at pp 14–15.

7 As Tony Kerr points out in 'Implementation of Directive 77/187 into Irish Law and Case Law of the Court of Justice' in *Acquired Rights of Employees* (Irish Centre of European Law, 1989) the need for a uniform interpretation of Com-munity legislation requires proposals in one language version to be interpreted in the light of versions existing in other languages: see *Bestuur der Sociale Verzekeringsbank v Van der Vecht* [1967] ECR 345.

8 See the Department of Employment guidelines on etos in App D.

9 See Ch 5 and, in particular, *Teesside Times Ltd v Drury* [1978] ICR 822 and *Macer v Abafast* [1990] ICR 234, [1990] IRLR 137.

stated that courts will be vigilant about attempts to get round the Transfer Regulations, and this is especially so following *Litster* and its recognition that the Transfer Regulations must be construed to give effect to the aims of the directive, i e safeguarding of employee rights.[10]

(i) Where the sale is of a different character

(a) Asset only sales

The Transfer Regulations will not apply if assets only are being bought and sold.[11] The test of whether assets, as opposed to a business, are being sold is dealt with in detail in Chapter 4. Care must be taken on at least two fronts, however. First, it must be very carefully ascertained that only assets are being purchased. If there is something more to the sale, then a business (or part) may have been purchased and it matters not whether the parties have put the wrong label on the transaction. The reader is reminded that it has been held that if the parties assert they are transferring assets only, that will not bind an industrial tribunal if, in fact, they are transferring a business as a going concern.[12] Second, reg 3(4) should be considered, which allows multiple transactions to be linked if appropriate. Thus it is not possible to sell what is in reality a business by fragmenting the sale into a series of asset sales and sub-transfers in the hope that this will avoid the application of the Transfer Regulation.[13] None the less, upon a true asset sale, the Transfer Regulations do not apply and employees would be left with claims for redundancy payments and other matters against a transferor and an employee could be re-engaged by a purchaser of the assets with a break in continuity of employment and upon new terms and conditions of employment.[14] However, a purchase of assets only, by definition, usually carries over no goodwill or other aspects of enjoyment of a business as a going concern. If the latter is desired, then the structure of the deal may have to override any employment law considerations.

---

10 See Directive 77/187, preamble.
11 See Ch 4; *Woodhouse v Peter Brotherhood Ltd* [1972] 2 QB 520, [1972] 3 All ER 91; *Melon v Hector Powe Ltd* [1981] 1 All ER 313.
12 *Rencoule (Joiners and Shipfitters) Ltd v Hunt* (1967) 2 ITR 475 and see Ch 4.
13 See Ch 4 and Ch 6.
14 See Ch 4.

(b) Share sales

As already discussed,[15] by virtue of reg 3, the Transfer Regulations only apply to transfers of businesses from one person to another of an undertaking or part situated immediately before the transfer in the United Kingdom. They only apply, then, when a change of employer is involved. It is trite law that when there is a take-over of a company by purchase of share capital there is no change of employer at all. Should acquisitions therefore be structured towards share sales and not business transfers? At first glance there is little advantage from an employment law perspective in structuring an acquisition to involve acquisition of the share capital of a company which owns the target business. A purchaser of the share capital of the company will inherit contracts of employment and continuity of employment will also be unaffected. However, in two important respects, a purchaser of shares of a company is better placed than if he purchases the business of a vendor company. First, reg 8 of the Transfer Regulations does not apply so there is no risk of *automatically* unfair dismissals, express or constructive. Only the ordinary law of unfair dismissal applies.[16] Second, apart from consultation necessary in respect of redundancies under the Employment Protection Act 1975, there is no need to inform/consult with unions under reg 10, if there is a share sale as opposed to a business transfer. However, the same practical warning must be issued as under the preceding section. It must always be borne in mind that a decision on whether to buy a company's shares or its business may be influenced by tax factors or other corporate or legal considerations. Employment law issues should not be allowed to hold sway if the former are more important.

(ii) Where the Transfer Regulations prima facie apply because there is a business transfer

(a) *Non-transfer-connected dismissals*

As previously explained, not all pre-transfer dismissals attract *Litster*. Thus, if the employment of individuals has ended by virtue of a

---

15 See Ch 1.

16 A particular problem applicable to non-share sales, for example, in this context arises on imposed harmonisation of terms and conditions of the transferred workforce post-transfer. In that case it is difficult to establish an economic, technical or organisational reason for dismissal, thus avoiding the automatic unfairness of a constructive dismissal that may arise: *Berriman v Delabole Slate Ltd* [1985] ICR 546. This does not apply to share sales. See Ch 8.

pre-transfer dismissal that is not connected with the transfer or indeed, if connected, is for an economic, technical or organisational reason, *Litster* will not apply to their cases and therefore, by virtue of the principle in *Secretary of State for Employment v Spence*, unless they are employed in the business at the point of transfer, their employments will not be transferred. It is submitted that very few pre-transfer dismissals will fail to be covered by *Litster* but it could be argued that a pre-transfer dismissal for genuine redundancy reasons, certainly if no sale were in prospect, could fall under *Spence* and not *Litster*. The House of Lords in *Litster* approved the scenario in *Secretary of State for Employment v Spence* as comprising such a case. In that case the receiver was under pressure from the bank to stop paying wages in any event and for that reason the pre-transfer dismissals took place. The business ceased trading before the sale and although, as it happened, a deal was concluded very shortly after the dismissals, it was not concrete before the dismissals. The disadvantage of this approach is that to avoid the application of *Litster*, pre-transfer dismissals may have to take place almost immediately upon appointment of a receiver or liquidator or, at the very least, when no sale is in prospect, thus causing an inconvenient break in running of the business.

(b) Employees whose employment would not otherwise be terminated by the transfer: retained employees

Regulation 5 only applies to catch employees whose employment would otherwise be terminated by the transfer. It follows that employees whose employment is not affected by the transfer would not be caught by reg 5. Thus, if an employee is, by agreement, retained by an employer on other duties or held back from the business and deployed in other parts of the vendor's businesses, he could arguably be excluded from the operation of the Transfer Regulations. For example in *Direct Radiators Ltd v Howse*[17] the business was sold but a transferee did not require the employee's services. The employee stayed on over the transfer and for a short while thereafter with the transferor to help with some bookkeeping work relevant to the winding down of the transferor's activities. The EAT held that if the employee stayed on with the transferor under a contract of employment, then her contract would not be one which was otherwise terminated by the transfer and reg 5 would not transfer liability. (On the other hand, if the employee was not, after the transfer, working under the original contract of employment the

---

17 EAT/30/86; see also *Daisley v Leicester Light Transport Ltd* COIT 15044/83.

position might be different. So the case was remitted to find out whether, after the transfer, the employee stayed on with the transferor under a retained contract of employment or whether her contract of employment had in effect been terminated by the transfer and she was, thereafter, working under a contract for services.) For this to apply in the majority of cases though, a wide job description/mobility clause would have to be in place in the employment contract and redeployment effected before the transfer. If the employee has not, with his consent, been taken out of the business and redeployed elsewhere, his purported exclusion from the sale might seem to conflict with the general automatic effect of reg 5 that employees actually employed in the business at the time of transfer go over to the transferee.[18]

Cautious transferors and transferees would be advised to bring about an express agreement between transferor and employee to a change in terms of employment or even a novation with the employee in order that he stays with the transferor. Thus, in *Visionhire Consumer Electronics Ltd (t/a Visionhire) v Easton*,[19] Easton was an employee of the transferor who agreed to stay with the transferor for a week after the transfer. But the arrangement was that he would then join the transferee. An argument subsequently raised by the transferee that this was, because of the retention, a contract not otherwise terminated by the transfer, was rejected by the EAT, which stated:

'Apart from the fact that [the transferee's] argument would, in the view of the industrial members, cause immense difficulty as a matter of practice in industry and lead to grave disadvantages for the workforce, it does not in our view accord with what reg 5 says . . . If it is intended to retain part of the staff after a transfer, then that would have to be done by a novation of contract between the transferor and the employee before the transfer.'

Whether such a tripartite agreement (as opposed to one between the transferor and employee) is always necessary remains to be seen. But whatever arrangements were made, care would have to be taken to make sure they were genuine, a point stressed by Slynn

---

18 See *Secretary of State for Employment v J F Helliwell & Sons* EAT 186/86 – purported exclusion of employees in sale documentation ineffective.
19 EAT 20/87. The case is unreported: the quotations here are taken from the helpful summary in *IDS Employment Law Cases* 8.4.2; see, too, *Mikkelsen v Danmols Inventar A/S* [1986] 1 CMLR 316. The view in *Visionhire* seems supported by the recent European Court case of *G d'Urso v Ercole Marelli Ellettromeccanica Generale SpA* [1992] IRLR 136 confirming automatic transfer of employment *by virtue of the transfer alone*.

A-G in *Mikkelsen v Danmols Inventar A/S*[20] when he expressed the view:

> '. . . if an employee of one employer whose business is transferred genuinely and willingly agrees with that employer or the transferee of the business, that he will not be engaged under a contract of employment, or in an employment relationship with the transferee, then he cannot, as I see it, insist as against the transferee on the performance, as from the date of the coming into effect of the agreement, by the transferee of obligations arising under the previous contract of employment or employment relationship. In the absence of genuine express agreement to the contrary, however, his rights which had already accrued qua employee against the transferor will continue to be enforceable against the transferee. . . . It is obviously crucial for national courts to ensure that such agreement is *genuine* and *not tainted with duress.*' (emphasis added)

The court ruled that:

> '. . . Article 3(1) of Council Directive 77/187 of 14 February 1977 must be interpreted to mean that it does not cover the transfer of the rights and obligations of persons who were employed by the transferor at the date of transfer but who, *of their own free will*, do not continue to occupy a position as an employee with the transferee.' (emphasis added)

A similar point applies in relation to employees employed in a holding or service company supplying labour to another company which transfers its business. Regulation 5 will not apply in those cases as employees are not employed by the transferor company at all, and hence their employment contracts would not be affected.[1] For this to work without problems, however, it is arguable that the structure would have to be in place already and independently of the prospect of any sale – otherwise this might be regarded as a sham arrangement or a linked transaction (see below).[2] How this structure can appear is illustrated diagrammatically in Figure 4.

---

20 [1986] 1 CMLR 316. This decision was approved in *Marelli* (note 18, p 161).

1 A similar situation applied in *Banking Insurance and Finance Union v Barclays Bank plc* [1987] ICR 495, discussed in Ch 10.

2 What may be of note also is the possibility that the service company may be regarded as the *agent* of the trading company (or of a holding company) whether the structure was set up immediately before the transfer or was in existence for some while. In *Zabaxe Ltd v Nicklin* EAT 123/89 (LEXIS transcript) the employees provided services to Northminster Publishing Group Ltd but were paid through Northminster Holdings Ltd. The EAT remarked 'it was [what] . . . could be called an invoicing company and this was made perfectly clear to the

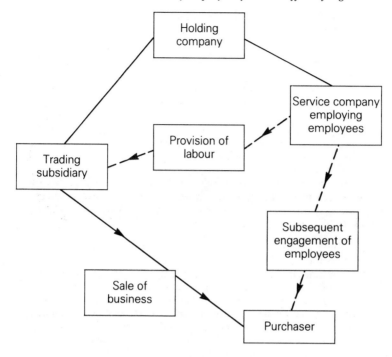

Figure 4 *Complex group structure where employees, although providing services to a transferor company, are not employed by it.*

(c) Employees excluded from the transfer by reason of their genuine wish not to work for the new proprietor

The discussion in section (b) above contemplates retention of an employee in the transferor's existing or retained business or businesses. There may also be occasions when an employee decides to work for *neither* transferor nor transferee. Can he validly elect to do so? It would seem a nonsense if he could not. Of course, a common scenario is that an expensive executive is compelled to resign and is 'bought off' in contemplation of an impending transfer. How valid

---

tribunal and the submission was that Holdings were merely *agents* for Northminster Publishing Group Ltd.' (emphasis added) Obviously this depends on the facts, but it is a risk to bear in mind. Company law authorities on disregard of separate corporate personality in this regard include *Smith, Stone & Knight Ltd v Birmingham Corpn* [1939] 4 All ER 116; *Hotel Terrigal Pty v Latec Investments Ltd (No 2)* [1969] 1 NSWLR 676; cf *Adams v Cape Industries plc* [1990] BCLC 479.

would that be? It is certainly not possible for a vendor to purport to exclude employees from a sale without more. In *Secretary of State for Employment v J F Helliwell & Sons Ltd*[3] the sale agreement purported to do just that. The EAT firmly stated this purported exclusion could *not* override the automatic effect of reg 5:

> 'Coming to the nub of the case, can the regulations be excluded by contract? In our view, the answer is unhesitatingly "No". These are mandatory provisions of law which operate upon the transfer of an undertaking and of course if they could be excluded contractually it would drive a coach and horses through the regulations and through the EEC Directive.'

On the other hand, this decision does not, it is submitted, preclude a genuinely negotiated 'exit' of an expensive individual who will not be required by the transferee. As the European Court in *Mikkelsen v Danmols Inventar A/S*[4] stated:

> '. . . the protection which the directive aims to ensure becomes pointless if the person concerned, as a result of a decision voluntarily taken by himself, does not continue the employment relationship with the new head of the undertaking after the transfer. This is the case where the employee in question terminates of his own free will, with effect from the transfer date, the contract of employment or employment relationship or if the contract or relationship is terminated, with effect from the transfer date by virtue of an agreement freely concluded between the employee and the transferor and the transferee of the undertaking. In a situation of that kind it must be concluded that Article 3(1) of the directive does not apply.'

An important factor is the *voluntary* nature of such an agreement. The case of *Logan Salton v Durham County Council*[5] (a case decided outside the context of business transfers) set out the principles under which the EAT thought that an agreement for termination of employment would not be impugned, i e where

> 'it was a contract separate from [the] contract of employment which was entered into:
>
> (a) willingly,
> (b) without duress and after proper advice,
> (c) for good consideration'.

The gist of these conditions is echoed by the comments of Slynn A-G in *Mikkelsen*,[6] cited in the preceding section.

---

3 EAT 186/86, LEXIS Transcript.
4 [1986] 1 CMLR 316.
5 [1989] IRLR 99.
6 [1986] 1 CMLR 316.

It is submitted that these principles should be adhered to as a minimum in negotiating with individuals for their exit from the business and 'exclusion' from the sale. And it should be noted that any agreement to forgo compensation under statute, e g for unfair dismissal, is not binding unless a conciliation officer from the Advisory Conciliation and Arbitration Service has 'acted' under s 134(3) of the EP(C)A.[7]

Finally, it must be stressed that any attempt to exclude statutory rights, including the Transfer Regulations, is covered by express anti-avoidance provisions, as referred to in section (e) below.

(d) Employees not wholly employed in the business transferred

An employer may employ employees working for his business as a whole. If he sells part only, reg 5 will not apply to employees who do not work in the part of the business transferred immediately before the transfer. This can cause some confusion where service, sales, administration or wages staff appear to have involvement in the part transferred even though they work generally elsewhere. One industrial tribunal in *Anderson v Kluwer Publishing Ltd*[8] held that an employee was employed in part of a business sold when he spent 80 per cent of his time there. The European Court in *Botzen v Rotterdamsche Droogdok Maatschappij*[9] posed a different, more conceptual, test. In the opinion of Slynn A-G, an employee must be 'wholly engaged' in the part transferred subject only to the performance of other duties which can be regarded as *de minimis*. The court itself coined another test, which, being the judgment of the court, is

---

7 A s 134(3) settlement occurs where no tribunal application has been submitted but where such a claim has been asserted. Where a tribunal claim alleging unfair dismissal has already been lodged, the section triggering conciliation is s 134(1). A conciliation officer of ACAS also has powers to act where other statutory rights are alleged to be infringed. A relatively recent practice of ACAS is to refuse to act where the parties have between themselves pre-agreed a settlement – such precludes real 'conciliation'. (See the ACAS Booklet, COT5, *How Conciliation Works*; this is a policy not without controversy, and see *Moore v Duport Furniture Products Ltd* [1982] ICR 84.) It is important therefore to bear this in mind in negotiations if a binding ACAS (COT3) agreement is desired. Any offers made must therefore be subject to negotiation and conciliation through ACAS for this purpose. Finally, it has been held that the concept of duress (which may vitiate consent and make an agreement voidable) can also apply to ACAS agreements (*Hennessy v Craigmyle & Co Ltd and Advisory, Conciliation and Arbitration Service* [1986] ICR 461, [1986] IRLR 300). Similar principles apply though: it must be shown that the employee had no alternative and his action was not voluntary. This is rarely applicable, it is submitted, where conciliation through ACAS has occurred.

8 COIT 15068/85.

9 [1986] 2 CMLR 50.

the one to be followed. The court held that employees of the transferring employer who were not *assigned* to the part transferred are not themselves transferred even if they have performed duties involving the transferred part's assets or have carried out duties from the employer's retained administrative department in relation to the transferred unit. The court stated:

> 'An employment relationship is essentially characterised by the link existing between the employee and the part of the undertaking or business to which he is assigned to carry out his duties. In order to decide whether the rights and obligations under an employment relationship are transferred under Directive 77/187 by reason of a transfer within the meaning of Article 1(1) thereof, it is therefore sufficient to establish to which part of the undertaking or business the employee was assigned . . . Directive 77/187 must be interpreted as not covering the transferor's rights and obligations arising from a contract of employment or an employment relationship existing at the date of the transfer and entered into with employees who, although not employed in the transferred part of the undertaking, performed certain duties which involved the use of assets assigned to the part transferred or who, whilst being employed in an administrative department of the undertaking which has not itself been transferred, carried out certain duties for the benefit of the part transferred.'

(iii) Anti-avoidance measures

A word of warning must be spoken at this juncture. The discussion above assumes *genuine* situations falling outside the scope of the Transfer Regulations. If *artificial* schemes are put in place there is an armoury of anti-avoidance approaches that can be taken by courts. First, reg 3(4) provides that linked transactions can be treated as one. It is not settled whether this catches arrangements between two parties alone or multiple parties but there are now increasing dicta to the effect that multiple party linked transactions can be covered as well as transactions between two parties (see Ch 6). Second, reg 12 of the Transfer Regulations restricts contracting out and makes void any provision of an agreement in so far as it purports to exclude or limit the operation of regs 5, 8 or 10, '*whether [such agreement is] in a contract of employment or not*' (emphasis added). Third, s 140 of the EP(C)A similarly makes void any agreement to preclude the operation of any EP(C)A right (e g unfair dismissal, redundancy, etc) again, '*whether in a contract of employment or not*' (emphasis added). Fourth, describing a transaction as an asset sale when it is not will not prevent an industrial tribunal examining the reality of the transaction: *Rencoule (Joiners & Shopfitters) Ltd v Hunt* (see Ch 4). Finally, it is clear from

European case law that we must consider the aims of the directive as expressed in its preamble, ie to *safeguard* employee rights. After *Pickstone* and *Litster* the tribunals may, it is submitted, approach a problem in this way and carefully scrutinise what might be artificial avoidance transactions.[10]

7 ENQUIRIES BEFORE CONTRACT, WARRANTIES AND INDEMNITIES

Bearing in mind the approach in *Litster* and the likelihood that ways of overtly avoiding the Transfer Regulations are now strictly limited, the most practical advice that can be offered to purchasers of businesses is, first, to make extensive enquiries before contract about employment obligations; second, to extract warranties of fact; third, to require undertakings of intention (eg to discharge payments); and finally, to seek indemnities against liabilities. Among the information that should be obtained as a minimum are details of identity of employees, dates of service, details of notice of termination, salary, wages and other benefits, pension details, commission, bonus scheme, profit-sharing scheme and share option scheme details, details of any recognised trade union, details of any collective agreement, Wages Council order, disputes with employees, pending or threatened litigation, enquiries, correspondence or contact with the Commission for Racial Equality and Equal Opportunities Commission, correspondence and contact with statutory authorities, details of out-workers, temporary workers and part-time labour, details of grievances and disciplinary

---

10 Gordon Stewart, in *Administrative Receivers and Administrators* (1987) (written before *Litster*) cites the unreported industrial tribunal decision in *Hinde v Permoid Ltd* COIT 18935/85 which approves the device of the 'put and call option' to avoid the effects of reg 5. Under this arrangement an option is given to a purchaser to call for an agreement for sale upon notice to the vendor. In *Permoid*, such a scheme was adopted, the employees being dismissed on the day of grant of the option. A sale agreement, pursuant to the option, took place a few days later. The industrial tribunal held the employees were not employed in the business immediately before the transfer (the date of the sale agreement) and so employment obligations relating to them were not transferred to the transferee. The industrial tribunal was, somewhat curiously, unimpressed by the argument that there was a series of transactions (the option/call/agreement) which could be linked and treated as one under reg 3(4) (see Ch 4 and Ch 6). It is submitted that, after *Litster*, this case would be unreliable authority for put and call options as a way round reg 5. The put and call option is, it is submitted, exactly the sort of artificial scheme liable to be exploded under the anti-avoidance provisions discussed in the text. I am grateful to Gordon Stewart for a copy of the *Permoid* decision.

cases in hand, and so forth. A little imagination and practical common sense can be employed to expand the list further. Warranties should include warranties that information disclosed is correct and remains correct at the time of completion and that obligations under s 99 of the Employment Protection Act 1975 and under s 100 of the same Act have been complied with, that consultation has taken place with trade unions, and indeed any other acts or steps required to be taken by the transferor have been taken. Indemnities should in the first instance include full cover against loss arising from breach of all warranties. It is then possible to negotiate a further indemnity against liability for all types of statutory liability, e g unfair dismissal and redundancy, and damages for breach of contract and pre-transfer obligations. The extent and range of such indemnities is, of course, a matter of bargaining between the parties. Examples of such enquiries, warranties and indemnities may be found in Appendix A.

8 CONCLUSIONS ON *LITSTER*

The recognition by the courts in the United Kingdom, significantly, in *Litster* that the aims of the Acquired Rights Directive ('to safeguard the rights of employees') must be taken into account in construing the Transfer Regulations, has certainly revised attitudes of those involved in buying and selling businesses. In many cases it will simply not be possible to ignore employee rights and in many cases a purchaser has no alternative but to respect those rights. In a situation where the deal is not naturally structured so as to fall outside the ambit of the Transfer Regulations this area is a classic case of *caveat emptor* or 'buyer beware'.

9 WHAT OBLIGATIONS AND LIABILITIES ARE CARRIED OVER TO A TRANSFEREE UNDER REG 5?

Assuming transfer of employment takes place either under the actual wording of reg 5 or as supplemented by *Litster*, what obligations are transferred?

Regulation 5(2) states:

'(2) Without prejudice to paragraph (1) above, on the completion of a relevant transfer:

(a) all the transferor's rights, powers, duties and liabilities under or in connection with any such contract, shall be transferred by virtue of this regulation to the transferee; and

(b) anything done before the transfer is completed by or in relation to the transferor in respect of that contract shall be deemed to have been done by or in relation to the transferee.'

Let us now see how the component parts of reg 5 operate.

(i) Dismissals (1): automatically unfair pre-transfer dismissals

As already discussed, the point of *Litster* is that a transferee will inherit liability for dismissals by a transferor contrary to reg 8(2). This would probably be by virtue of reg 5(2)(b). But, also, as in a *Litster* case employment is deemed statutorily to continue to the point of transfer for the purposes of reg 5(3) (see above), reg 5(2)(a) is also triggered and if there are any accrued employment obligations, the transferee will inherit these too (see (iii) below).

(ii) Dismissals (2): how a transferee becomes liable by refusing to employ

Suppose reg 5 applies and the transferor has done nothing to terminate the contracts of employment before the point of transfer. If that is the case, and if a transferee refuses to engage the employees covered by reg 5, he will have dismissed them, probably constructively.[11] He will be liable for redundancy and unfair dismissal and notice claims. (And, as discussed in (i) above such a transferee will also have to respect any accrued obligations under reg 5(2)(a) (see (iii) below).)

(iii) Other consequences of transfer of employment – transfer of employment-related obligations

(a) General

In the case of employees employed in the undertaking immediately before the transfer (and also in the case of employees deemed to be

---

11 See *Premier Motors (Medway) Ltd v Total Oil Great Britain Ltd* [1984] ICR 58, [1983] IRLR 471, EAT; *Batchelor v Premier Motors (Romford) Ltd* COIT 17295/82/LN (Chairman, Professor BA Hepple).

employed in the undertaking immediately before by virtue of *Lister*) reg 5(2)(a) transfers the contract and any rights, powers, duties and liabilities thereunder. It also provides that anything done before the transfer is completed by or in relation to the transferor in respect of that contract shall be deemed to have been done by or in relation to the transferee. The position is best viewed as an automatic 'novation' of matters related to the employment contract where the old employer drops out and is substituted by the new employer. It follows, it seems, that claims should, after the transfer, be pursued against the transferee and not the transferor. This is apparent from the directive and the Transfer Regulations and confirmed by the European Court in *Berg and Busschers v Besselsen*[12] wherein it was stated that:

> '. . . Article 3(1) of Directive 77/187 of 14 February 1977 must be interpreted as meaning that after the date of transfer, and by virtue of the transfer alone, the transferor is discharged from his obligations arising from the contract of employment or the employment relationship, even if the workers employed in the undertaking do not consent to or oppose that consequence, subject however to the power of the member states to determine that the transferor and transferee should be severally liable after the transfer.'[13]

By virtue of reg 5(2) it is clear that the following matters are transferred to a transferee.

(1) All contractual liabilities in relation to employees arising under or in connection with the contract of employment.[14]

---

12 [1990] ICR 396, [1989] IRLR 447. See also the proposed referral to the European Court in *Katsikas v Konstantinidis* (C–132/91), referred to below. In *Marelli* (note 18, p 161) the European Court robustly followed *Berg*, confirming automatic transfer of contracts by virtue of the transfer alone.

13 This power to provide for joint liability has not been used by the UK government in relation to the Transfer Regulations. There are views that any revision of the legislation should make joint liability mandatory.

14 This seems abundantly clear from reg 5(2). And the terms of all contracts of employment should therefore be scrutinised to ascertain the extent of transferred liabilities thereunder. Key problems are the extent of fringe benefits and length of the employee's notice period. A transferee should also beware of 'golden parachute' clauses in senior executives' service agreements (clauses which trigger liquidated sums of compensation on dismissal or even on other occasions, e g takeovers, and which are not subject to reduction (as are damages claims) on account of mitigation of loss). Sometimes compensation under golden parachutes can be triggered on take-overs such as business transfers – there is no reason why a *transferee* should not have to pick up the bill for this if the employee qualifies for transfer under reg 5. For interesting arguments on this point, see V Craig, 'Parachutes and the Transfer Regulations' (1989) *Scottish Law Gazette* p 82. On parachutes generally, see *Taupo Totara Timber Ltd v Rowe* [1978] AC 537, [1977] 3 All ER 123 and J McMullen, (1990) *Practical Law for Companies* p 15.

(2) Probably most statutory employment rights, e g accrued redundancy service, continuity of employment, eligibility for sex (including equal pay) and race discrimination protection[15] and the right to return to work after maternity leave (under EP(C)A s 45(1)).

(3) Liability to an employee in tort.[16]

(4) *Possibly*, liability to an *employee* on a complaint by him of non-payment of a protective award obtained by a trade union under EPA 1975 s 100.[17]

(5) Credit for an amount paid on account of redundancy by a transferor within the meaning of s 73(a) of the EP(C)A. (This may reduce a basic award for unfair dismissal for which a transferee is liable, the transferor taking the benefit, as it were, of the previous payment made by the transferor.[18])

But, the following matters it seems, are *not* transferred.

(1) An industrial training board levy.[19]

(2) A protective award in favour of a recognised *trade union* under s 101 of the EPA 1975.[20]

---

15 Unfair dismissal and redundancy payments liabilities have been assumed from the outset to be carried over (see e g *Apex Leisure Hire v Barratt* [1984] 3 All ER 795, [1984] ICR 452, EAT; *Premier Motors (Medway) Ltd v Total Oil Great Britain Ltd* [1984] ICR 58, [1983] IRLR 471, EAT). So should, on this basis, other statutory claims, such as race and sex discrimination protection (and see Hansard HL Deb col 1497, 10 December 1981 (Lord Lyell), and, logically, statutory continuity of employment under the EP(C)A (although on this see Ch 5).

16 *Secretary of State for Employment v Spence* [1983] QB 179, [1986] ICR 651, CA. The source of this point is the obiter remark (to be fair somewhat guarded) that, at p 662, 'the words "or [in respect of] a person employed in that undertaking or part" clearly can have the effect of transferring obligations other than contractual obligations; for example, as has been put in argument, they may well embrace obligations arising in tort'. It is submitted this is correct. And Art 3(1) of the Acquired Rights Directive refers to transfer not only of rights and obligations arising from contract of employment but also from 'an employment relationship'.

17 *Angus Jowett & Co Ltd v NUTGW* [1985] ICR 646, [1985] IRLR 326, EAT.

18 See *Walker v Dysch Rosen Shoes Ltd* EAT 341/90 LEXIS transcript.

19 *Plastics Processing Industry Training Board v Norsk Hydro Polymers Ltd* (3 December 1984, unreported), QBD.

20 *Angus Jowett & Co Ltd v NUTGW* [1985] ICR 646, [1985] IRLR 326, EAT.

(3) Rights under or in connection with an occupational pension scheme.[1]

(4) Criminal liability.[2]

In addition to contract-connected liabilities transferred, reg 5(2)(b) deems (if there is a transfer under reg 5(1)) anything 'done' by the transferor in relation to the contract to have been 'done' by the transferee. As discussed, these would include a dismissal. This means, for example, that a transferee would be liable for a pre-transfer dismissal by a transferor, for example either where the employee is still, notwithstanding the dismissal, on notice up to the point of transfer. And, of course, as discussed at length above, even if employment *has* ended prior to the transfer, where this was by reason of an automatically unfair pre-transfer dismissal liability for that unfair dismissal will likewise pass to the transferee (see *Litster*).

Also, it would seem possible, under reg 5(2)(b), for a transferee to inherit potential liability for the transferor's acts prior to the transfer which were short of a dismissal. For example, if there have been prior breaches of contract not yet affirmed, a transferee might assume liability for these if the employee were either to sue for breach of contract or to resign claiming constructive dismissal after the transfer. Also, if a prior breach was not repudiatory of itself it might, it seems, even be added to a subsequent breach committed by the transferee to count together as a constructive dismissal under the so-called 'last straw' doctrine.[3] Under this limb of Reg 5 a transferee might be liable for a host of matters, ranging from breaches of promise in the past to a transferor's sexual or racial harassment of an employee.[4] The possibilities are not finite.

(b) The width of reg 5(2) and the need for careful enquiries

If this view of the width of reg 5(2) is correct, a purchaser must make very careful enquiries, seek far-reaching warranties of fact

---

1 Reg 7. But the issue of pension does not end there. What are excluded are rights relating to an occupational pension scheme under the Social Security Pensions Act 1975 or the Social Security Pensions (Northern Ireland) Order 1975. If, for example, under the contract of employment, an employer had agreed to contribute to another scheme or indeed to contribute towards a personal pension plan, such obligations would, it is submitted, be transferred by virtue of reg 5 notwithstanding reg 7. See, in detail, *infra*.

2 Reg 5(4). An example might be criminal liability under the Health and Safety at Work Act 1974.

3 *Harvey on Industrial Relations and Employment Law* 11 para 177.

4 See, eg, *Porcelli v Strathclyde Regional Council* [1985] ICR 177, [1984] IRLR 467, EAT; affd [1986] ICR 564, [1986] IRLR 134, Ct of Sess.

(e g that no claims are known, or circumstances giving rise to such) and indemnities against possible claims. We have already mentioned the possibility of statutory claims such as race and sex discrimination and equal pay. The possibility of the existence of wider claims arising from discriminatory pay and benefit structures should not be underestimated. A widened risk is created by the possibility of equal pay claims arising out of Art 119 of the Treaty of Rome, directly enforceable by individuals irrespective of the domestic statute concerned (see Ch 6). We revert later to the possibility of transfer of claims or even potential claims under *Barber v Guardian Royal Exchange Assurance Group*[5] concerning unequal pension benefits between men and women. Unequal treatment in redundancy schemes, unjustifiable indirect discrimination (e g in relation to pay) in respect of part-time female workers or incremental pay due to seniority could otherwise give rise to other potential problems in the field of discrimination laws. Regulation 5(2) refers to transfer of rights 'under or in connection with [an employment contract]'. These words are fairly wide. If there is any doubt that statutory or treaty claims as discussed are not transferred, regard should be had to Art 3(1) of the Acquired Rights Directive which refers to Transfer of 'rights and obligations arising from a contract of employment *or from an employment relationship*' (emphasis added): truly wide drafting indeed!

(c) Problem cases – obligations tailored to a transferor's identity

The automatic transfer of the contract to a transferee and rights arising therefrom, such as employment protection rights and the release of the transferor may be comprehensible in the majority of cases.

But what of contractual matters in particular that are geared towards the transferor's identity? Arguably these are, literally, transferred too, but this may give rise to problems in the context of the changed identity of the employer. Suppose an employee caught by reg 5 has been given the title (and status) of director of the vendor company? How does the transferee comply with this, if its own structure does not envisage such individuals on the board (or indeed if the transferee is not a company). Not to confer that (or equivalent) status could give rise to a claim for breach of contract (at least if the right to be a director is considered to be part of the contract). Many other examples spring to mind. A few specific ones are dealt with below.

---

5 [1990] ICR 616, [1990] IRLR 240.

Restrictive covenants

It should surely follow that a restrictive covenant in an employment contract appertaining to the transferred business is transferred to a transferee so that, in theory, he can claim the benefit of it. But such covenants are enforceable only in so far as they are reasonable and necessary for the protection of the parties' interests.[6] What may have been reasonable in the context of the transferor's organisation may no longer look reasonable in the context of the transferee's organisation.

In *Initial Supplies Ltd v McCall*[7] McCall was a Sales Operations Manager, employed by a company called Pritchard Janitorial Supplies Ltd. His contract contained a restrictive covenant prohibiting the dealing with or soliciting of customers. Pritchard's business was then sold to Initial Supplies Ltd. Thereafter Mr McCall resigned from his position (now with Initial) to set up his own business. Initial sought an interim interdict to enforce the restrictive covenant they said was being broken. It is important to note that this was purely an interlocutory application and has not been fully reported. First, the petitioners put forward evidence that there was a 'relevant transfer' for the purposes of reg 5 upon the take-over. Second, however, the question arose, if so, was the benefit of the restrictive covenant transferred to Initial? The Court of Session (Lord Coulsfield) accepted that prima facie this might be so, but the question was not free from doubt: the question was complex and the conclusion 'far from obvious', and in the view of the court 'there [was] a prima facie case . . . but . . . it is one which may give rise to very difficult questions'. And Lord Coulsfield (and see below in relation to bonus schemes) mooted the idea that, in this difficult area, not all of the terms of the contract are necessarily transferred to a transferee under reg 5. (*Sed quaere*: although transfer of individualistic terms may cause problems, our view is that they are transferred – and if they are employee-oriented, an employer would have to compensate for non-observance – see below.)

The application for an interdict was refused on the basis of the possible doubt about transfer under reg 5 and about the wording of the clause itself (especially in the light of circumstances after the transfer (see below)). It is respectfully submitted, however, that although the question is indeed a difficult one, there is no reason why the benefit of a restrictive covenant should not *theoretically*

---

6 *Nordenfelt v Maxim Nordenfelt Guns & Ammunition Co* [1984] AC 535.
7 (1990) IRLIB 411, 19 October 1990, p 7. The quotes from the case are taken from *IDS Employment Law Cases*, 8.4.5. Otherwise the case is unreported.

pass to a transferee; but a transferee should not automatically assume that its terms will be reasonable in the light of the changed identity of the new employer.

Conversely, the transferor will lose the benefit of the covenant. While in most cases this will be of no moment as he has sold the business to which the covenant relates, he must realise that he will lose the benefit also of any covenant or term that purports to relate (subject to enforceability) to retained activities or, indeed, trade secrets. Will this mean that the right of action for past breaches of the implied duty of fidelity (eg concerning trade secrets) is also lost?[8] Logically, this should also follow!

Commission schemes

These also cause problems if tied, for example, to the vendor company's performance as opposed to the performance of the business transferred. It would not be feasible for the purchaser to honour such a scheme if not related to the business itself in isolation. In the case of *Initial Supplies Ltd v McCall* (discussed above) this subject was referred to (obiter) by Lord Coulsfield, who doubted that it followed that such rights always transferred. He said:

> 'Although reg 5 of the Transfer of Undertakings (sic) Regulations 1981 provides, taken shortly, that upon a transfer a contract of employment is to take effect as if it had originally been made between the new proprietor of the undertaking and the employee, it is, to my mind, far from obvious that it follows that the name of the new proprietor of the undertaking can be substituted for that of the former employer in every respect. It seems to me that there may be many situations in which the effect of such a substitution would be to make a radical alteration in the rights and obligations of the parties. For example, an employee whose remuneration included an annual bonus related to his employer's profits for the year would, on the petitioner's construction of the regulations, be entitled to claim a bonus related to the profits of the acquirer of the undertaking, if the acquisition had taken place during the year.'

Whatever the problems caused by such a transfer, again, it is submitted that the obligation is capable of transfer and if the transferee cannot replicate the bonus scheme, he would be in breach of contract. The only practical advice is that (apart from agreeing with the employee that the commission rights are cancelled or putting forward an alternative (on such agreements, see Ch 8) he should, as

---

8 See eg *Faccenda Chicken Ltd v Fowler* [1986] Ch 117, [1986] ICR 297.

a damage limitation exercise, install a scheme *similar* to that of the transferor providing similar remuneration or rewards for the employee transferred. If so this could reduce or extinguish damages that potentially flow from the breach of contract involved.

Stock option schemes

An employee is frequently, today, offered share options in respect of the share capital either of his employing company or of its holding company if his employer is part of a group. If an individual's right to share options were part of the contract of employment, it is arguable that this too would be transferred to a transferee by virtue of the Transfer Regulations. Such would cause enormous problems for a transferee who could not, of course, honour options over the shares either of the transferor company or its holding company. Presumably, similar rights would have to be granted by the transferee, a difficult task, since every company is different as to capital structuring and earning performance. The transferee might not even be a company with shares over which options might be granted!

However, the employee also faces a multitude of problems in asserting such a right against a transferee. A string of cases has made it apparently rather difficult for transfer of share option rights to occur in the manner speculated. In *Chapman and Elkin v CPS Computer Group plc*[9], for example, the Court of Appeal held that the transfer regulations had no application to share options because the share options concerned were not in a contract of employment but in another collateral contract granting the option.[10]

Second, in *Thompson v Asda-MFI Group plc*[11] it was provided in a group share option scheme that the options would lapse when the group sold off the company in which the employees were employed when as a result the employee ceased to be an employee of any

---

9 [1987] IRLR 462.
10 This, incidentally, enabled the plaintiffs who were employees of Data Entry International Ltd to exercise options in C P S Computer Group, the holding company of Data Entry upon the sale of Data Entry's business to another company. The options were exercisable upon the option holders ceasing to be an employee by reason of redundancy within six months following such cessation. The defendants had argued that the options were not exercisable because the Transfer Regulations applied and as a result the employees could no longer treat themselves as being redundant. However, as stated, the court indicated that, in its view, the Transfer Regulations had nothing to do with the collateral contract for the grant of the share options, only with the contract of employment. To be noted, however, is Art 3 of the Acquired Rights Directive which refers to transfer of rights both from the contract of employment and the 'employment relationship'. In this light, there is an area of doubt about *Chapman*.
11 [1988] Ch 241, [1988] IRLR 340.

company within the group. The court held that this prevented the employee from exercising the share options any further and it was not possible to imply into the rules of the scheme a term to the effect that the company would do nothing to cause the options to lapse or to cease to be exercisable under the rules.

In *Micklefield v SAC Technology Ltd*[12] it was common ground that the share option scheme rights *were* part of the contract of employment, but the employee faced a different problem. It was provided in the share option scheme that if the option holder ceased to be an executive for any reason he lost his right to exercise his share options and he was deemed to have waived any entitlement by way of compensation for loss of office or otherwise to any sum or other benefit to compensate him for the loss of any rights under the scheme. It was held that the clause was sufficiently clear effectively to enable the company to escape liability even if the individual were wrongly dismissed. Nor, held the court, was the clause in the share option scheme void under the terms of s 3 of the Unfair Contract Terms Act 1977. Excluded from s 3 is any contract so far as it relates to the creation or transfer of securities or of any right or interest in securities. Accordingly, so far as the contract related to his option to acquire shares it was excluded from the scope of the Unfair Contract Terms Act.[13]

It obviously makes sense for employees to insist that their share option rights are incorporated into a contract of employment, but they must, however, be alert to any exclusions of liability for damages for cessation of share option rights which may be contained in the share option scheme and thus also, by reference, incorporated into the contract.[14]

---

12 [1991] 1 All ER 275, [1990] IRLR 218.

13 Finally, reliance was placed on *Gunton v London Borough of Richmond-upon-Thames* [1980] ICR 755, [1980] IRLR 321 to the effect that the individual could elect to keep the contract alive and therefore keep the employment in force. The court, however, drew a distinction between the continuance of the contract and the continuance of the employment relationship. The scheme referred to the option holder ceasing to be employed. Therefore, the court held, whatever the status of the contract, even if kept alive by the doctrine of election, the individual had ceased to be 'employed'. On *Gunton*, however, contrast the cases discussed at note 15, p 154, which would not, probably, support this approach. To be contrasted, however, is *Chapman v Aberdeen Construction Group plc* [1991] IRLR 505 where a provision excluding loss arising from failure to exercise a share option *could* be void under the Unfair Contract Terms Act 1977, s 23, as it applied in Scotland. This case therefore suggests a difference between English and Scottish law on the point.

14 Fenton, in 'An Extra Leaving Gift', *Taxation*, 24 August 1989 p 614, argues such clauses are commonplace. They certainly make sense for employers.

Conversely, in the light of the above, any executive who considers that a business transfer may be on the horizon and who has share options that are presently exercisable but as yet unexercised should give rapid thought to their exercise and ascertain whether the scheme rules must be exercised before leaving the employment of the transferor or within a limited time thereafter.

(d) Pensions

Pensions, too are a logistical problem. But as will be seen below, mostly, these may be excluded from consideration.

Where the Transfer Regulations do not apply

There are several issues here. The first possibility is that there is a transfer of assets only, not constituting transfer of a trade, business or undertaking from one person to another. In such a case there will be a break in continuity of employment under statute and there will be no obligation on a purchaser of these assets to continue the contractual terms of any employee re-engaged by him. This, of course, includes liability to take on the pension scheme of the transferor. The transferee of assets would be quite entitled to ignore the pension rights of individuals re-engaged. Their rights against the transferor upon termination of their employment are discussed in brief at the end of this part.

A second situation is where the take-over is by way of acquisition of the issued share capital of the transferor by a transferee. In this case, all current contractual terms of the transferred employees are taken on by the transferee for there is no change in identity of the acquiring employer. However, the Transfer Regulations do not apply since there is, by virtue of there being no transfer of a business from one person to another, no change of identity in the employer. Accordingly, all rights are transferred, including current rights under the transferor's pension scheme. A detailed consideration of the take-over aspects of transferred employees' rights in this situation is outside the ambit of this book. However, this is not to say that there are no industrial relations or legal problems involved. These can include the treatment of surpluses arising from over-funding of a pension scheme and other questions of scheme management.[15] Legal control of the influence of a company over its pension scheme and benefits thereunder by use of its powers under the scheme rules has for some time been the subject of controversy.

---

15 See *Re Courage Group's Pension Scheme, Ryan v Imperial Brewing and Leisure Ltd* [1987] 1 All ER 528, [1987] 1 WLR 495.

Some judicial guidance is now available,[16] and as a fillip to employee rights in this area it has recently been held that a company's right to give or withhold its consent to increases in pension benefits in accordance with the scheme's rules is subject to the restriction that such right is not exercisable if it involves a breach of the implied obligation in every contract of employment that the employer will do nothing likely to destroy or seriously damage the relationship of confidence and trust between employer and employee.[17]

Another problem concerns the winding-up of the transferor's scheme and the imposed membership on employees of the transferee's scheme. This commonly happens upon acquisition of a wholly-owned subsidiary by an acquiring company. The labour law issues here seem to depend upon whether or not there has been a constructive dismissal by virtue of the winding-up of the transferor's scheme and the absorption of the employees into the transferee's new scheme. If the new scheme is less beneficial than the old scheme and imposition of membership thereof is a breach of contract then the employee may have the right to claim constructive dismissal and also unfair dismissal.[18]

Where the Transfer Regulations apply

The next situation concerns a business transfer covered by the Transfer Regulations. On a relevant transfer reg 5 would, unless otherwise qualified, protect all contractual terms, including pension rights, provided that the courts declared that membership of the pension scheme in question is a contractual right of the employee

---

16 It is a considerably complex legal question as to who owns the surplus in an employer's pension scheme for the benefit of employees although this question has recently been aired in the courts: *Re Imperial Food Ltd's Pension Scheme* [1986] 2 All ER 802, [1986] 1 WLR 717; *Ryan v Imperial Brewing and Leisure Ltd* [1987] 1 All ER 528, [1987] 1 WLR 495. The rules of the scheme will abso be relevant and, indeed, exactly what type of scheme it is; see also *Hosking's Pension Scheme and Retirement Benefits* (6th edn) p 94.

17 *Imperial Group Pension Trust Ltd v Imperial Tobacco Ltd* [1991] ICR 524, [1991] IRLR 66. The implied duty of maintenance of trust and confidence comes from *Woods v W M Car Services (Peterborough) Ltd* [1981] ICR 666, [1981] IRLR 347. The positive duty to provide information under the principle in *Scally v Southern Health and Social Services Board* [1991] 4 All ER 563, [1991] IRLR 522 is a step forward in the field. See also safeguards in the Social Security Act 1990.

18 See N Toulson *Managing Pension Schemes* Ch 28. Not uncommonly, a transfer to a new pension scheme is available. Negotiations then have to take place between vendor and purchaser over the transfer value of the employees' benefits that are to be transferred: see *Hosking* op cit. In *Stannard v Fisons Pensions Trust Ltd* [1992] IRLR 27 the CA held that trustees of an occupational pension fund must give properly informed consideration to the value of the fund in such circumstances.

concerned. It will be remembered that reg 5 operates to negate any termination of a contract of employment by virtue of a change in employer per se, and further, under reg 5(2) it is said that, on completion of a relevant transfer the transferor's rights, powers, duties and liabilities under or in connection with a contract of employment are transferred to the transferee and anything done before the transfer is completed by or in relation to the transferor in respect of the contract of employment transferred or a person employed in the undertaking shall be deemed to have been done by or in relation to the transferee.

Thus, at first glance, the transferred employee has nothing to fear; his pension rights might seem to be included in those automatically transferred to the transferee under reg 5 along with all other contractual rights. This is not so, however. It is provided in reg 7 as follows:

'Regulations 5 and 6 above shall not apply:

(a) to so much of a contract of employment or collective agreement as relates to an occupational pension scheme within the meaning of the Social Security Pensions Act 1975 or the Social Security Pensions (Northern Ireland) Order 1975; or

(b) to any rights, powers, duties or liabilities under or in connection with any such contract or subsisting by virtue of any such agreement and relating to such a scheme or otherwise arising in connection with that person's employment and relating to such a scheme.'

Thus, this provision takes away the benefit of reg 5 as far as a potential transfer of the employee's pension rights is concerned. This might seem to fly in the face of the general aims of the EC directive. But there is authority in the directive for putting such an exclusion into the Transfer Regulations. Article 3 provides an exclusion in relation to 'employees' rights to old age, invalidity or survivors' benefits under supplementary company or inter-company pension schemes in member states'. It is, thus, not possible to argue that the provisions of reg 7 contravene the directive.

In summary, the effect of reg 7 is to exclude occupational pension rights from the ambit of reg 5 and from the scheme of transfer of employment under the regulations.

In that respect, one commentator[19] argues, the Transfer Regulations are more detrimental to the employee than the existing law under the EP(C)A. The argument is as follows. But for the Transfer Regulations, transfer of employment would under the EP(C)A give

---

19 Elias (1982) Company Lawyer 147.

rise to a dismissal by reason of a redundancy. The transferee may, however, by virtue of the combination of s 82 and s 94 of the EP(C)A, have made an offer of alternative employment which, if suitable, and either accepted or unreasonably refused, would disqualify the employee from receiving the payment. Whether, first, this offer was suitable and whether, second, it had been unreasonably refused in the circumstances might hinge to a greater or lesser extent on whether or not the transferee was able to make a like or similar offer in relation to pension rights. If the pension rights within the transferee's undertaking were detrimental to the employee when compared with the transferor's pension scheme it could be that the employee might reasonably refuse this offer of employment made by the transferee. He/she would then be entitled to the redundancy payment after all. However, under the Transfer Regulations, upon a relevant transfer, reg 5 automatically transfers the contract of employment, even in a redundancy situation, and negatives any dismissal by virtue of change in identity of an employer so that the redundancy provisions discussed above do not apply. It is true that reg 5(5) states that automatic transfer is without prejudice to any right of an employee to terminate his contract without notice if a substantial change is made in his working conditions to his detriment, provided that he may not so terminate his contract by reason only of the change of identity of employer unless he can show that in all the circumstances the change is a significant one and to his detriment. But the problem here, it could be argued, is that, if reg 7 applies, the whole of reg 5 and reg 6 do not apply: if so reg 5(5) will have no application to the change in pension schemes operated by the different employer even if it is to the employee's detriment.[20]

So, in summary, employees may find that their employment rights are interrupted by non-continuance of their occupational pension schemes, either in the case of a simple transfer of assets *or* a business transfer. This is because in the former case there is no transfer of employment at all, and in the latter, although it is a business transfer to which the Transfer Regulations might otherwise apply, their rights are not transferred because reg 7 excludes reg 5. The rights of an employee in a business transfer may, then, be

---

20 Davies and Freedland, in *Transfer of Employment* (1982), suggest there could be a constructive dismissal when pension rights are changed, but this would be against the *transferor* since reg 5 would not apply, due to the blocking of pension claims against the transferee under reg 7. This theory has, however, to be tested. It is interesting to speculate whether there might also be a residual claim for breach of contract which survives transfer of employment. Again, this theory has to be tested.

little different from any other employee who is forced to leave his employer's pension scheme through termination of employment.[1] His rights as to the future will depend on what his new employer can or will offer him by way of transfer to the new employer's existing scheme, if one is in place or any new scheme which the new employer may be obliged to set up. This is usually covered by express provision in sale agreements. Legal and actuarial advice is usually necessary in drawing up such provisions.[2]

It is important to stress that all those involved in take-overs of businesses, whether employer advisers or employee advisers, should take specific and specialist advice upon the area of pensions. For the newcomer to the subject, there are excellent introductory guides giving some insight into pension benefits for those in employment and those suffering a transfer of employment. The reader should be aware, however, that pensions law is a dynamic area, subject to review from time to time.[3]

In cases where the transferor is insolvent, and there are arrears of employer contributions to the occupational pension scheme, s 123 of the EP(C)A provides for the Secretary of State in certain circumstances to pay sums into the scheme so that the employee is not prejudiced. Also, by s 386 of and Sch 3 to the Insolvency Act 1986, arrears of contributions within the meaning of Sch 3 to the Social Security Pensions Act 1975 are a preferential debt.

The European Court of Justice decision in *Barber v Guardian Royal Exchange Assurance Group*[4] adds another dimension. As is known, in this case the European Court declared that pension benefits could be considered as 'pay' for the purposes of Art 119 of the EEC Treaty.[5] As part of the duty to provide equality of pay

---

1 See *Hosking's Pension Scheme and Retirement Benefits* (above) Ch 8, 'Benefits on Leaving Service'; Higgins, 'Early Leavers from Pension Schemes' (1992) *LSG* 19 February, p 18. In *Warrener v Walden Engineering Co Ltd* (COIT 22672/91) an industrial tribunal accepted an employee's argument that Reg 7 did not apply to exclude transfer of rights under a *contracted out* scheme. If this were right it would revolutionise this area. But this decision is questionable even in the light of the directive itself.

2 See *Hosking* op cit and, in particular, Ch 19, 'Mergers, Acquisitions and Proposals'. Negotiations often revolve around the calculation of transfer value to be passed over to the transferee.

3 See *IDS Pensions Service Bulletin; Toulson* Ch 25.

4 [1990] ICR 616, [1990] IRLR 240.

5 As discussed above, Art 119 claims to have a limitation period, as in English law. The European Court did say that 'the direct effect of Art 119 of the Treaty may not be relied upon in order to claim entitlement to a pension with effect from a date prior to that of this judgment, except in the case of workers or those claiming under them who have before that date initiated legal proceedings or raised an equivalent claim under the applicable national law'. This limitation as to retro-

between men and women engaged on like work or work of equal value it will be necessary for all employers to equalise pension benefits and, in particular, establish equalisation of the ages of male and female workers at which pension benefits may be claimed. An interesting question is whether a potential or outstanding equal pay claim arising out of *Barber* against the transferor is a right under or in connection with an occupational pension scheme and hence not transferred to transferee, because of reg 7, or whether it is a statutory employment claim akin to race discrimination, sex discrimination or unfair dismissal that is a right 'under or in connection with the contract of employment' and hence transferred to a transferee under reg 5. If the latter is the case the transferee must make very careful enquiries of, and take full indemnities from, the vendor.

Finally, it is only rights under an occupational pension scheme within the meaning of the Social Security Pensions Act 1975 or the Social Security Pensions (Northern Ireland) Order 1975 that are excluded. If, under the contract of employment, an employer has agreed to contribute to some other type of scheme, or indeed to contribute to an employee's personal pension plan, it is submitted that such obligations would be transferred to a transferee. And, a purchaser must take care not only himself not to make any promises to individuals that pension rights will match up exactly to those in a former scheme, but also to enquire that no such promise has been made by a transferor; otherwise there might be liability for breach of contract, in the latter case by virtue of a transfer of a contractual liability under reg 5(2)(a).

10 CONSTRUCTIVE DISMISSAL AND REG 5(5)

It follows from reg 5 and the concept of automatic transfer of employment contracts that the change of identity of employer involved in a business transfer shall not of itself give an employee grounds for terminating the employment contract. As discussed in

---

activity is far from clear. Cases have, as a result, been referred to the ECJ for clarification of this issue and others (e g the obligations of trustees) (see *Coloroll Pension Trustees Ltd v Russell* [1991] IRLIB 431, p 8. The ambiguity for the future seems to have been settled at the EC summit at Maastricht, December 1991, through an agreed protocol that benefits of this kind are excluded from the Art 119 definition of pay if referrable to periods of employment prior to 17 May 1991 (the *Barber* judgment).

the Introduction to this book the contrary is the case, of course, at common law. There is one exception to this: in reg 5(5), it is stated that automatic transfer under reg 5

> 'is without prejudice to any right of an employee arising apart from these regulations to terminate his contract of employment without notice if a substantial change is made in his working conditions to his detriment; but no such right shall arise by reason only that, under that paragraph, the identity of his employer changes unless the employee shows that, in all the circumstances, the change is a significant change and is to his detriment.'

There are several points here. First, the earlier part of this sub-paragraph contains exactly the same trap as existed under the old redundancy payments legislation which referred to the right of the employee to terminate his contract *without notice* if he wanted to claim constructive dismissal. If he resigned *with* notice, however, he might have lost his right to claim constructive dismissal.[6] A better interpretation would be, however, that he has the right to claim constructive dismissal under the Transfer Regulations *whether or not* he gives notice, since this is the case under the existing constructive dismissal provisions of the EP(C)A. Further, the right to terminate generally (apart from change in identity of employer) is expressly limited to a case of substantial change in the employee's working conditions to his detriment. Again it would arguably be a diminution of employee rights if this condition were otherwise than descriptive or illustrative of the breaches of contract entitling an employee to resign.

This provision has been discussed on a number of occasions in connection with constructive dismissal claims arising out of changes of terms and conditions imposed by a transferee after transfer. These cases are discussed in Chapter 8 dealing with reg 8 and automatically unfair dismissals. In one of them, however, *Servicepoint Ltd v Clynes*,[7] Mr Clynes was employed by Wigfalls as a television engineer working in the Leeds area. The business of Wigfalls' service centres was then acquired by Servicepoint. Mr Clynes was then told to report for work in Manchester, and was given new terms and conditions which were different from his old ones. For example, there were changes to amount of shifts and hours of work and to certain bonuses and benefits. He decided to

---

6 See the Redundancy Payments Act 1965, s 3(1)(c); *Maher v Fram Gerrard Ltd* [1974] 1 All ER 449, [1974] ICR 31. The trap no longer exists in EP(C)A s 83(2)(c), the statutory successor to s 3(1)(c) of the 1965 Act.

7 EAT 154/88.

terminate his employment and claim constructive dismissal. It was held that there had been a repudiation of the contract which he was entitled to accept and therefore he was also entitled to terminate the contract without notice. It was also held there was a substantial change in his working conditions to his detriment within the meaning of reg 5(5). It was held, following the Court of Appeal decision in *Berriman v Delabole State Ltd*,[8] that this was automatically unfair under reg 8 (as no economic, technical or organisational reason entailing changes in the workforce could be made out). That aspect is discussed in Chapter 8. The importance of the case for present purposes is that the EAT appeared to be less than clear on the question whether, in a transfer of undertakings case, the only definition of constructive dismissal that is relevant is reg 5(5), as opposed to the general law on constructive dismissal.[9] Again, as discussed in Ch 8, *sed quaere* whether reg 5(5) is the only relevant provision. After all, there can be no unfair dismissal claim at all without a constructive dismissal, and surely, it is submitted, that must be a constructive dismissal as defined by the general law. Furthermore, it seems wrong if reg 5(5) is exhaustive because, on its terms, there is a possible disqualification for an employee who effects to terminate *with* notice and because the instances giving rise to the right to terminate under reg 5(5) are confined to instances of changes in working conditions.[10] All these are, as is submitted in Chapter 8, compelling reasons for the construction of the right to terminate under reg 5(5) as *descriptive* of the events which might give rise to a constructive dismissal, rather than being exhaustive of them.

In addition to the right to claim constructive dismissal by reason of a 'substantial change in working conditions to the [employee's] detriment', an employee may, exceptionally, resign and claim constructive dismissal by reason of the identity of the employer itself. This particular way out for an employee on change in identity of employer is, however, fraught with problems. One view holds that even if the employee were successful in claiming constructive dismissal by virtue of the change in identity of employer itself, he would not be able to avail himself of the full range of employment rights that would ordinarily be applicable under the EP(C)A. For example, there is a possibility that notwithstanding there might be a

---

8 [1985] ICR 546.

9 Eg s 55(2)(c) of the EP(C)A as interpreted by *Western Excavating (ECC) Ltd v Sharp* [1978] QB 761, [1978] 1 All ER 713, CA.

10 The general law is arguably much wider. Repudiatory breach of the implied duty of trust and confidence, for example, springs to mind.

constructive dismissal, he could be denied a redundancy payment (unfair dismissal is a separate issue). This is because, upon a change of employer and upon an offer by an employer to an employee of suitable alternative employment, it is specifically provided by virtue of s 94(4) of the EP(C)A that, in determining whether the offer is suitable or whether the employee's refusal of the offer is reasonable or unreasonable, any objection by the employee to the identity of the employer has to be ignored. Thus, ironically, although reg 5(5) does allow a limited way in which the employee can challenge the change of identity of employer (even though the Transfer Regulations ordinarily impose a change of employer on a transferred employee) if the employee exercises his right, his employment rights may be limited under the EP(C)A,[11] at least as far as redundancy payment is concerned.

Under reg 5(5), in determining whether 'in all the circumstances, the change is a significant change and is to [the employee's] detriment' the burden of proof seems to be on the employee. It is not clear what aspects of the employer's identity will be a significant change and to the employee's detriment. What if the employer does not recognise trade unions? What if there are different career structures within the transferee's undertaking? What if there are different employment prospects? What if the transferee has a bad record of industrial relations? It is submitted that this is a potential minefield of litigation. In the House of Commons debate on the regulations, the Under Secretary of State for Employment, Mr David Waddington, posited a narrow view of what all this meant. He thought:

'It is somewhat difficult to find examples of where a change could be significantly to the employee's detriment. When I asked those who advise me to give examples the only ones they could think of were

---

11 Elias (1982) Company Lawyer 147. It is true that the right to claim unfair dismissal would remain. But as there is a business transfer this might be defeated on ground of the business transfer/redundancy aspect (where tribunals tend very often to respect managerial prerogative, see infra). It is unclear whether reg 8 would make such dismissal automatically unfair. Also, mitigation of loss is important. If the new employer has made an offer to re-engage, failure to accept this might be a failing to mitigate loss, thus reducing compensation. However, if employer identity this would ipso facto be because the 'change' is a significant change and is to his detriment. If so, trust and confidence between employer and employee may have been lost, and (certainly at common law and probably in unfair dismissal law) an employee would then be entitled to refuse any offer of fresh employment by the contract breaker (*Shindler v Northern Raincoat Co Ltd* [1960] 2 All ER 239, [1960] 1 WLR 1038).

examples of new employers running off with their employees' wives or murdering their fathers.'[12]

But surely it is not as simple as that! Case law is bound to provide more helpful examples for us in due course.

---

12 Hansard HC Deb 7 December 1981, col 679. Finally, the issue of an employee's right to object to transfer of employment may be clarified by a referral to the European Court in *Katsikas v Konstantinidis* (C–132/91), *IDS Brief* Employment Law Supplement 63, p 84.

Chapter 8

Regulation 8 and automatically unfair dismissals

1 GENERAL

The provisions of reg 5, which cause automatic transfer of contracts of employment to a transferee, cannot, notwithstanding their dramatic effect, protect acquired rights in a complete way. For, if employers (whether they are transferors or transferees), either before or after the transfer of the undertaking, use the transfer as an excuse for redundancy or reorganisational dismissals, or as an opportunity unilaterally to impose changes of terms and conditions upon the workforce, the security of those transferred may be transient. It is true that, under the general law, both an express dismissal and a constructive dismissal may give rise to eligibility to make a claim for unfair dismissal. Industrial tribunals have been, however, on the whole, somewhat employer-oriented in their attitude to the exercise of managerial prerogative in the context of redundancy and reorganisation, and a dismissal in these circumstances (although it might attract a redundancy payment) will not *always* attract unfair dismissal liability.[1] In short, redundancy dismissals and reorganisational dismissals (which can be brought under the heading of 'some other substantial reason')[2] can be treated as fair if the employer satisfies the test of reasonableness in unfair dismissal law.[3] The fact that industrial tribunals are chary of interference with managerial prerogative in redundancy or unfair dismissal cases does not make reasonableness by any means an unrealistically high standard to satisfy.

Regulation 8 answers some of this concern by taking the protection of reg 5 further, making a dismissal in connection with a transfer *automatically unfair*. This radical provision is however

---

1 See Bowers and Clarke (1981) ILJ 34; *Richmond Precision Engineering Ltd v Pearce* [1985] IRLR 179, EAT.
2 Under s 57(1)(b) of the EP(C)A.
3 See Bowers and Clarke (1981) ILJ 34.

tempered by a 'defence' in reg 8(2) which may take away the automatic unfairness of these dismissals if certain conditions are fulfilled. Set out in full, reg 8 reads as follows:

'(1) Where either before or after a relevant transfer any employee of the transferor or transferee is dismissed, that employee shall be treated for the purposes of Part V of the 1978 Act and Articles 20–41 of the 1976 Order (unfair dismissal) as unfairly dismissed if the transfer or a reason connected with it is the reason or principal reason for his dismissal;

(2) Where an economic, technical or organisational reason entailing changes in the workforce by either the transferor or the transferee before or after a relevant transfer is the reason or principal reason for dismissing an employee:

   (a) para 1 above shall not apply to his dismissal;
   (b) without prejudice to the application of section 57(3) of 1978 Act or Article 22(10) of the 1976 Order (test of unfair dismissal), the dismissal shall for the purposes of section 57(1)(b) of that Act and Article 22(1)(b) of that Order (substantial reason for dismissal) be regarded as having been for a substantial reason of a kind such as to justify the dismissal of an employee holding the position which that employee holds.

(3) The provisions of this regulation apply whether or not the employee in question is employed in the undertaking or part of the undertaking transferred or to be transferred.

(4) Paragraph 1 above shall not apply in relation to the dismissal of any employee which was required by reason of the application of section 5 of the Aliens Restriction (Amendment) Act 1919 to his employment.'

Regulation 8, then, at first glance, makes a bold attempt to safeguard employee rights on transfers by creating a strong disincentive for a transferor or transferee to use the transfer as an excuse for redundancies. It makes a dismissal in connection with a transfer automatically unfair unless the dismissing employer can establish that there was an 'economic, technical or organisational' reason entailing changes in the workforce of either the transferor or the transferee before or after the relevant transfer. If that reason is established (which is then deemed to be a 'substantial' one justifying dismissal under s 57(1)(b) of the EP(C)A) the question of fairness of the decision falls to be decided under the general principles as to reasonableness under s 57(3) of the EP(C)A. Regulation 8 covers dismissals by transferors before but 'in connection with' the transfer and it also catches dismissals by transferees after they have acquired a business. It is to be noted that there is no limitation in time over which the dismissal might be regarded as 'in connection with' the transfer. It could be as much as months before or after the transfer (although the longer the interval before or after the transfer, the less easy it will be to establish the 'connection').

It will therefore be seen that reg 8 is important in general terms to restrain managerial prerogative to effect dismissals in connection with the transfer. However, following *Litster v Forth Dry Dock & Engineering Co Ltd*,[4] it has assumed another, massive, importance. For it is now a vital part of the test of when a transferee may be liable for pre-transfer dismissals effected by a transferor. As will be remembered, under *Secretary of State for Employment v Spence*,[5] employment has to exist at the point of transfer for it to be transferred under reg 5. How easy then for transferors and transferees to get round reg 5 by causing pre-transfer dismissals effective before the transfer. Not so now, since *Litster*, in which the House of Lords applied a purposive interpretation of the Transfer Regulations to make them conform to European law.[6] Now, as discussed at length in Chapter 7, where the pre-transfer dismissal is automatically unfair under reg 8, the employee will be deemed to be employed at the point of transfer notwithstanding the literal meaning of reg 5 and liability for the unfair dismissal will be passed to the transferee.[7] Regulation 8(2), with its defence to automatic unfairness if there is an 'economic, technical or organisational' reason for the transfer-connected dismissal, obviously becomes all-important to employers, even though, in many cases of pre-transfer dismissal, it will be very difficult to make out (see below).

So much for the background. What of the nuts and bolts? It must be stated, first, that it is for the employer to prove an 'economic, technical or organisational' reason. And he must adduce clear *evidence* in support of any argument that the reason for dismissal or at least the principal reason for dismissal was for an 'economic, technical or organisational reason'.[8] For example, an ulterior motive for dismissal would not be 'economic, technical or organisational' and the dismissal would then be automatically unfair.[9]

---

4 [1989] ICR 341, [1989] IRLR 161.
5 [1987] QB 179, [1986] 3 All ER 616.
6 See *P Bork International A/S v Foreningen af Arbejdsledere i Danmark* [1989] IRLR 41 and its interpretation of the mandatory effect of Art 4 of the Acquired Rights Directive.
7 The question of whether the *Litster* principle applies to all employees or only to those who *qualify* for unfair dismissal protection is discussed in Ch 7.
8 *May and Hassall (West) v Jansen* EAT 526/83 LEXIS transcript.
9 See e g *Fairweather v Gadhvi*; *Sinnot v Cleveland Truck Sales* ('wrong attitude'); but cf *Browne v Catlow and Pilling* (all cited in *IDS Brief* (254/June 1983) p 6).

But in spite of such points, 'economic, technical or organisational' is extremely wide, seemingly going much further than the traditional concept of redundancy. It was originally suggested that the defence is so wide that it might well, in most cases, remove the initial protection afforded by reg 8.[10] Even so, the employer having proved that the dismissal is for an 'economic, technical or organisational' reason, a tribunal has still to find that the dismissal was fair under s 57(3) of the EP(C)A. But, returning to a point already made, it has been argued that courts and tribunals are perhaps not willing enough more often to challenge the exercise of management prerogative in redundancies and business reorganisations.[11]

One early case, in particular, decided under the Transfer Regulations, illustrates this. In *Meikle v McPhail (Charleston Arms)*,[12] Mr McPhail took over the business of the 'Charleston Arms' public house in which Meikle was employed as a barmaid. The transfer was taken from the Scottish and Newcastle Breweries. It was a term of the agreement that McPhail would take over the employees. When he took control he thought that substantial economies would have to be made and the entire workforce, except for one barmaid, was dismissed. Meikle claimed her own dismissal was unfair. The dismissal fell under reg 8 of the regulations. However, it was held that there was an economic reason entailing changes in the workforce within the meaning of reg 8(2). Having so decided, it followed that, for the purposes of s 57 of the EP(C)A, the reason for dismissal was a substantial reason such as to justify the dismissal of an employee holding the position which that employee held.[13] The final question was therefore whether the dismissal was fair under s 57(3) of the EP(C)A.

It was held that, strictly speaking, the dismissal was not in the context of the present proceedings by reason of redundancy (because under the regulations it was deemed to be a substantial reason such as to justify dismissal – but see later in this chapter on possible entitlement of the employee to a redundancy payment notwithstanding). None the less, the considerations to be taken into account as to fairness were analogous to those applicable to redundancy dismissals.[14] Any question of fairness of course depends upon

---

10 Elias (1982) Company Lawyer 147 at 153.
11 *Hollister v NFU* [1979] ICR 542, [1979] IRLR 238, CA.
12 [1983] IRLR 351.
13 Reg 8(2)(b).
14 See also *Walker v (1) Dysch Rosen Shoes Ltd (2) Secretary of State for Employment* EAT 28.2.91 IDS Brief 445 May 1991 p 12 LEXIS transcript.

the facts of each individual case; precedents should not be followed.[15] In this case, it was argued strongly on behalf of the employee that the principles in *Williams v Compair Maxam Ltd*[16] (a case setting out certain recommended guidelines for a procedure in redundancy dismissals (discussed later)) had been departed from. In particular, it was alleged that the mere fact that trade unions had not been consulted under s 99 of the EPA made the dismissal unfair.[17] It was held, however, that in all the circumstances, having regard to the size and administrative resources of the employer, the employer had, on the facts, acted reasonably.[18]

2 DISMISSALS AND THE 'ECONOMIC, TECHNICAL OR ORGANISATIONAL' REASON FOR DISMISSAL – THE PROBLEM OF PRE-TRANSFER DISMISSALS

If reg 8(2) were as easy to satisfy as was feared by some commentators (see above), reg 8 would add little to our existing labour law. The following discussion indicates otherwise, however, particularly in the context of pre-transfer dismissals. But we start our discussion with two cases that, it is submitted, would now be regarded as plainly wrong. The following discussion too is especially important in the context of *Litster*, referred to above.

In *Anderson v Dalkeith Engineering Ltd*[19] Dalkeith Engineering Ltd went into receivership in 1983. The employee was made redundant on 11 March. Precision Machining (Edinburgh) Ltd purchased the assets on 18 March. On 21 March Precision Machining started up business and re-employed certain employees, but this did not include the applicant. It was held that reg 5 did not apply to transfer the employee's dismissal claim against Precision as he had not been employed immediately before the transfer (though the result would be different now, after *Litster* – see above). He therefore claimed unfair dismissal under reg 8 against the transferor who had dismissed him. It was held there was an 'economic, technical or organisational' reason entailing changes in the workforce and the

---

15 See *Martin v Glynwed Distribution Ltd* [1983] ICR 511, [1983] IRLR 198, CA.

16 [1982] ICR 156, [1982] IRLR 83.

17 In fact, breach of s 99 does not render a dismissal automatically unfair: *Hollister v NFU* [1979] ICR 542; *Hough v Leyland DAF Ltd* [1991] IRLR 194.

18 See also *Shipp v D J Catering* IDS Brief 245 (January 1983). An important factor though is the adherence of the employer to procedures before dismissal. A procedural lapse will ordinarily make a dismissal unfair: *Polkey v A E Dayton Services Ltd* [1988] AC 344, [1987] 3 All ER 974.

19 [1985] ICR 66, [1984] IRLR 429, EAT.

dismissal was not unfair automatically under reg 8. The fact that the dismissal was at the behest of the purchaser (and there was a contractual stipulation to that effect in the vending agreement) did not, according to the EAT, alter this; the reason was still economic.[20] The dismissal, as it turned out, was also not unfair under s 57(3). The vendor's compliance with the purchaser's request was not unfair unless there was an additional oblique motive. This decision was soon rightly criticised as it appeared to endorse the possibility of a vendor passively following the instructions of purchasers to dismiss without consideration of the interests of employees and the needs of the business for their dismissal.

However, in *Forth Estuary Engineering Co Ltd v Litster*[1] the EAT held, when considering s 57(3) in similar circumstances, that the transferor might not escape liability if he had not really considered whether the dismissals concerned were necessary. The distinguishing factor in *Litster* was that the transferor was not bound by any stipulation in the contract to dismiss, whereas in *Anderson v Dalkeith* there was such a contractual stipulation (although Lord Dunpark in the Court of Session in *Forth Estuary Engineering v Litster*[2] later doubted that the absence of a contractual stipulation necessarily made the employer's action unreasonable). Subsequent case law, of course, casts enormous doubt on the wiseness of a purchaser's actions in requiring dismissals in advance of the transfer, irrespective of the needs of the business. In fact, as we know, the House of Lords in *Litster* later ruled that this conduct would simply result in transfer of liability to the purchaser.

One of the essential problems with these cases is that in both *Anderson v Dalkeith* and *Forth Estuary Engineering Co Ltd v Litster* it was assumed that the pre-transfer dismissals could be for an 'economic, technical or organisational' reason entailing changes in the workforce, thus leaving a dismissal to be looked at *solely* under s 57(3). Subsequent cases, however, indicate that employers should fail at the *first* hurdle in this sort of case and that there may be greater likelihood of automatically unfair dismissals under reg 8 itself on those facts.

The first of such subsequent decisions is *Wheeler v Patel*.[3] The facts here were that on 12 December 1985 the employee was told

---

20 Contrast the law as it now stands under, e g, *Wheeler v Patel* [1987] ICR 631 where the opposite conclusion was reached – see infra.
1 [1986] IRLR 59, EAT: reversed on the issue of reg 5 by the Court of Appeal in the light of the subsequent decision in *Secretary of State for Employment v Spence* [1987] QB 179, [1986] 3 All ER 616, CA.
2 [1988] IRLR 289.
3 [1987] ICR 631, [1987] IRLR 211.

that the business in which she worked (a shop) had been sold and that she would be dismissed with effect from 17 January 1986. Contracts were exchanged on 6 January and completion took place on 20 January. The employee claimed unfair dismissal against both the vendor and purchaser. It was held that the Transfer Regulations did not apply to transfer her contract of employment over to the purchaser, rendering him liable for the unfair dismissal, because she had not been employed in the business immediately before the transfer (but again this would now be different after *Litster v Forth Dry Dock Engineering Co Ltd* (see Ch 7) and liability on those facts would now be transferred to a transferee). The transfer, according to the EAT, took place on completion, not on exchange of contracts and she had been dismissed before this.

But there then remained the question of liability for compensation for unfair dismissal against the vendor. The tribunal found that the reason for the dismissal was the vendor's desire to comply with the prospective purchaser's wishes and so reg 8(2) applied, and thus there was an 'economic, technical or organisational' reason entailing changes in the workforce. This meant the dismissal was not automatically unfair and only s 57(3) remained to be considered and this, in the circumstances, was also satisfied.

However, the EAT held that the word 'economic' in the phrase 'economic, technical or organisational reason entailing changes in the workforce' in reg 8(2) had to be construed *ejusdem generis* with the words 'technical' and 'organisational' and the word 'economic' had to be given a limited meaning relating to the conduct of the business. It did not include broader 'economic' reasons for dismissal such as the achievement of an agreement for sale. If the supposed economic reason advanced amounted to no more than a desire to obtain an enhanced price or achieve a sale, it would not be a reason which related to the conduct of the business.

This is a significant decision which increases the potential of employers for unfair dismissal liability if the dismissal is at the behest of the purchaser and for no other reason. And of course it will trigger *Litster* and the pre-transfer liability will be passed on to the purchaser. So dismissals to enhance the chances of a sale or simply because a purchaser requires them to occur may fall foul of reg 8 and be passed on to him under reg 5. The need for dismissals has, under this decision, to relate to the conduct of the business (like, perhaps, a considered redundancy exercise by the purchaser post-transfer).[4]

---

4 Interestingly, the EAT in *Bullard v Marchant* [1986] ICR 389 had already adopted this approach, although the significance of that decision had not been extensively commented upon at the time.

In parenthesis, *Forth Estuary Engineering Co Ltd v Litster* then went from the EAT to the Court of Session in Scotland.[5] This appellate decision adds nothing of value to our analysis. As has been stated (see Ch 7) this was an appeal mainly on reg 5, as in the EAT, it had been decided, pre-*Spence*, that the transferee took on the liability for unfair dismissal that primarily attached to the vendor when he had dismissed before the transfer. This was because it was held that the employees had been employed in the business immediately before the transfer. However, there had been a dismissal a short while before the transfer and after *Spence* (as it was then to be interpreted, prior to *Litster*) this decision could not stand. The Court of Session so held, deciding that, in fact, the vendor was liable for the pre-transfer dismissal (there had been an interval of three hours between dismissal and transfer). As such, it was not strictly necessary to comment upon reg 8 and s 57(3) since it was not in issue, at the appeal, whether there *was* an unfair dismissal liability. The issue was simply who was responsible *for* that unfair dismissal liability, assuming the liability arose. So the majority of the court expressed no view on reg 8. However, Lord Dunpark[6] seemed to suggest that the EAT had been correct in holding that the transferor had an 'economic, technical or organisational' reason for the dismissal (ie redundancy). As such, this conflicts with *Wheeler v Patel* and might, in isolation, cast some doubt on *Wheeler v Patel*. However, Lord Dunpark did say that *Wheeler* had not been cited or discussed in the court and his comments should be read accordingly.[7] (As a postscript, as we now know, in *Litster* in the House of Lords it was held that this dismissal *was* contrary to reg 8. Therefore liability for that dismissal should have passed to the transferee (see Ch 7).)

Moreover, the EAT in Scotland, in *Gateway Hotels Ltd v Stewart*,[8] followed the approach in *Wheeler v Patel*. In this case the employees were employed by Gateway Hotels Ltd at the Royal Hotel in the Bridge of Allan. The hotel was not doing well and Gateway decided to sell to a company called Lytpark Ltd. Lytpark insisted that the employees should be dismissed before the sale. This ultimately became a condition of the sale. On 14 February 1987 the employees were given notice of dismissal on grounds of redundancy although some were subsequently taken on by the purchasers. Those employees who were not taken on complained that

---

5 [1988] IRLR 289.
6 [1988] IRLR 289.
7 [1988] IRLR 289.
8 [1988] IRLR 287.

their dismissals were automatically unfair under reg 8 of the Transfer Regulations.

It was argued that the employees had been dismissed by reason of redundancy and that this was a reason falling under reg 8(2). However, the tribunal thought that the principal reason for dismissal was the condition in the contract of sale and that this did not amount to an 'economic, technical or organisational' reason under reg 8(2) and therefore the employees' dismissals were rendered automatically unfair. The EAT agreed and stated that to qualify under reg 8(2) an economic reason must be one which relates to the conduct of the business. This had not been established in the present case. Again (see above) this shows that any collusion between vendor and purchaser to make a condition of the sale that employees are dismissed before the sale could backfire on a transferee who may be liable for the resultant automatically unfair dismissal under the principle in *Litster* (see above).

What is the status of these cases? The relevant authorities under domestic law are all EAT and, in theory, another division of the EAT or another court could choose which case to follow. However, it is submitted that *Anderson* and *Litster* (EAT) are wrong on the issue of automatic unfairness. These cases ignore the issue of reg 8(1) and all too readily assume that, through reg 8(2), the situation revolves solely round s 57(3). *Wheeler v Patel* and *Gateway* are, it is submitted, correct in their reasoning on the issue of automatic unfairness.[9] Second, it is submitted that European law justifies and *requires* the approach taken in *Wheeler v Patel* to reg 8. *Wheeler v Patel*, it may be observed, is entirely consistent with the European Court's view of the mandatory effect of Art 4 of the Acquired Rights Directive which prohibits transfer-connected dismissals that are not for an eto. Thus, in *Abels v Bedrijfsvereniging voor de Metaal-Industrie en de Electrotechnische Industrie*[10] Slynn A-G stated:

'By Article 4(1), transfer of an undertaking is not to constitute in itself grounds for dismissal of employees by the transferor or the transferee, though such dismissals may take place "for economic, technical or organisational reasons entailing changes in the workforce". It is said that this exception will always be open on economic grounds in a liquidation, so that Art 4(1)'s first sentence is otiose. That does not seem to me to follow, since if a viable part of a business in liquidation is

---

9 And see also *Walker v Dysch Rosen Shoes Ltd* EAT 341/90, LEXIS transcript (IDS Brief citation at p 190, note 14).
10 [1987] 2 CMLR 406.

sold off, there may be no valid economic grounds for dismissing any of the staff employed in that part of the business.'

And in *Wendelboe v L J Music ApS*[11] he said:

> 'Where employees are dismissed, with a view to, and before, a transfer falling within the directive and are re-engaged immediately by the transferee thereafter, their dismissal must be regarded as contrary to Article 4(1) subject to the exceptions specified in that paragraph.'

Further, in *P Bork International A/S v Foreningen af Arbejdsledere i Danmark*[12] the European Court considered that, in determining whether there had been a dismissal in breach of Art 4(1), 'account must be taken of the objective circumstances in which the dismissal occurred and, in particular . . . the fact that it took place on a date close to that of the transfer and that the workers concerned were re-engaged by the transferee'. And finally, of course, implicit, if not express, support for *Wheeler* may be found in the fact that the dismissals in *Litster* were considered by the House of Lords to be automatically unfair when they occurred at the request of the transferee and in order to enable the transferee, the House of Lords surmised, to engage cheaper labour thereafter.

But there are at least two major problems about express dismissals under reg 8 after *Wheeler v Patel* that only further authority will satisfactorily answer. First, can express dismissals prior to a transfer but in connection with a transfer *ever* be for an economic, technical or organisational reason entailing changes in the workforce? The answer is, it is submitted, yes, if the economic ground relates to the conduct of the business as opposed to forming simply a motive to enhance the price of the sale or the chances of securing a sale. So a genuine redundancy could well be covered. But if there are dismissals prior to the transfer and wholesale, or even selective, re-engagement thereafter, how could this be an economic reason entailing changes in the workforce? Thus, employers buying and selling businesses must be very circumspect. What can such employers do in the face of a desire by the purchasers to shed labour? Perhaps one practical piece of advice would be to get the vendor to require documentation from the purchaser in addition to the vendor's own views about the manning of the business indicating *why* a reduction of the employees was necessary on economic grounds as opposed to grounds unrelated to the conduct of the business. But this will have to be genuine to succeed. Alternatively, the rationalisation could be effected prior to involvement of the

---

11 [1985] ECR 457, [1986] 1 CMLR 476.
12 [1990] 3 CMLR 701, [1989] IRLR 41.

purchaser and for business reasons. Only case law can unfold the scope of a purchaser's room for manoeuvre here.

One encouraging (albeit tribunal) decision for employers is *Sewell v DMG (Realisations) Ltd.*[13] This case arose out of the collapse of the Davies Magnet Group Ltd (DMG). Parts of the assets and undertaking of DMG were transferred to purchasers. Two of the transfers involved amounted to relevant transfers of parts of DMG's business for the purpose of the Transfer Regulations. Employees in those businesses were dismissed prior to the transfer. In at least one case this was at the request of the transferee. It was held, however, that the dismissals were for an economic, technical or organisational reason entailing changes in the workforce under reg 8(2). Among the factors concerned were that the receivers had intended to dismiss the remainder of the workforce in due course in any event, that the businesses were being moved to sites respectively 35 and 80 miles away[14] and

'as presently structured the two divisions of DMG were hopelessly uneconomic and could never be made otherwise. Their salvation lay only in a complete restructuring which included integrating them within the transferee's existing capacity . . . If the workforce could not be dismissed, the transfers could not go ahead because the businesses would be unrescuable.'

Although it cannot have the force of law, the Department of Employment's Guidance Notes on 'economic, technical or organisational reasons' are included in Appendix D. This may give some indication, especially to insolvency practitioners, of Department of Employment practice on acceptance of liability for pre-transfer claims when there has been a pre-transfer dismissal. As the notes rightly state however, they cannot be regarded as definitive of the law, and it is the prerogative of the parties always to have the facts of individual cases and the legal consequences thereof decided by an industrial tribunal.

In conclusion, then, pre-transfer dismissals with the involvement of a transferee involve great risks for the transferee. An alternative, of course, is for him to accept transfer of employment

---

13 IT, Case Nos 15486/89–15506/89; 13227/89–13254/89 and 13681/89; 5/6 February 1990.

14 The question of move of location is thought by the Department of Employment to be relevant to reg 8(2) in its Guidance Notes on the subject, referred to in the text below and Appendix D. On the other hand, Van Gerven AG in *Marelli* [1992] IRLR 146 controversially implied that Art 4 of the Directive (the equivalent of reg 8) cannot ever be relied upon when dismissals are as the result of a transfer. This seems questionable.

and then reduce the workforce after the transfer. This would arguably allow him then to plead an eto for the dismissal. But he must of course satisfy the test of fairness under EP(C)A, s 57(3). Such dismissals might ordinarily be by reason of redundancy (even though reg 8(2) dismissals are deemed to be for a 'substantial reason' under EP(C)A, s 57(1)(b)), and relevant case law may be consulted such as *Williams v Compair Maxam Ltd*;[15] *Meikle v McPhail (Charleston Arms)* (discussed above) is an example of this approach. When advising employers, *Polkey v A E Dayton Services Ltd*[16] is particularly relevant as to procedural matters as it is particularly tempting for corporate lawyers to cut corners and to forget about procedures in cases of business sales, such is the demand for secrecy and speed. This would be hazardous and bring back the possibility of unfair dismissal liability, this time under s 57(3). In *Polkey*, as is discussed in Chapter 10, it was stressed that procedural lapses, such as failure to follow guidelines of the kind formerly contained in the (now repealed) Industrial Relations Code of Practice, will ordinarily make a dismissal unfair without more.

Another matter to be borne in mind is that a dismissal involving selection for redundancy contrary to a customary or agreed procedure is, under s 59 of the EP(C)A, *automatically* unfair unless there are 'special reasons justifying a departure from that arrangement or procedure in [the employee's] case'.[17] This aspect is also covered in Chapter 10. It is argued in *Harvey on Industrial Relations and Employment Law*[18] that this rule may be inapplicable in a case of a dismissal falling under reg 8(2). This is because such dismissal is deemed to be for a 'substantial' reason for the purposes of s 57(1)(b) of the EP(C)A. *Ex hypothesi*, it is not by reason of redundancy and thus s 59, which deals with redundancies, cannot apply. However, this is, it is submitted, not necessarily the case. As explained later in this chapter, reg 8(2) cannot exclude the definition of redundancy under the EP(C)A and, if an employee is selected for redundancy as defined by the EP(C)A, it is submitted that s 59 is applicable if there is a customary or agreed procedure relating to redundancy selection notwithstanding that, for other purposes, dismissals under reg 8(2) are deemed, also, to satisfy s 57(1)(b) of the EP(C)A.

Of course we have been discussing, above, the express dismissal

---

15 [1982] ICR 156, [1982] IRLR 83, EAT.

16 [1988] ICR 142, [1987] IRLR 503.

17 *Harvey on Industrial Relations and Employment Law*, II, 909; II, 1073 et seq.

18 And, as discussed in Ch 10, a customary or agreed procedure is something that could be contained in a collective agreement which a transferee might inherit by virtue of reg 6 of the Transfer Regulations.

by a transferee of surplus staff, *following* a transfer, on genuine *redundancy* grounds. It is implicit from this discussion that it may be possible to satisfy reg 8(2) in such a case and make out an eto.

The next question to be asked is whether it will be possible to satisfy reg 8(2) in other post-transfer dismissal cases where the dismissals are transfer-connected. The chief example here is post-transfer, transfer-connected *reorganisational* dismissals. While cases generally,[19] and also in particular *Richmond Precision Engineering Ltd v Pearce*,[20] are favourable to employers who dismiss in the context of imposed reorganisational change outside the context of business transfers (the test of fairness under s 57(3) may be satisfied if the employer can show that appropriate procedures were followed and the terms were such that a reasonable employer could offer – injustice to the individual being only one factor, and not the primary factor), the same may not be so in a business transfer case. In the next section we argue that because of the wording of reg 8(2) transfer-connected reorganisational dismissals will usually be automatically unfair.

3 REORGANISATIONAL DISMISSALS, EXPRESS OR CONSTRUCTIVE, ARISING OUT OF AN IMPOSED HARMONISATION OF TERMS AND CONDITIONS

Possibly, an even greater dimension to the strength of reg 8 is its potential to control imposed harmonisation of terms and conditions of an acquired workforce with that of a transferee's existing workforce. A transferee is often tempted (or compelled in practice) to do this. If he does so without the employee's consent it may amount to a repudiatory breach and therefore a constructive dismissal. Alternatively he might dismiss expressly on the ground of an employee's refusal to accept new terms. The question is whether such dismissals, constructive or express, are transfer-connected (this is a question of fact and often this will be the case) and second, if so whether automatically unfair under reg 8 (ie whether or not justifiable as being for an eto under reg 2).

There seems no reason, in principle, why reg 8 should not apply to constructive dismissals as well as express dismissals (although, on

---

19 See *Banerjee v City and East London Area Health Authority* [1979] IRLR 147; *Evans v Elementa Holdings Ltd* [1982] ICR 323, [1982] IRLR 143; *Chubb Fire Security Ltd v Harper* [1983] IRLR 311.
20 [1985] IRLR 179.

the concept of constructive dismissal, the regulations (reg 5(5)) specifically refer to the 'right of an employee arising apart from these regulations to terminate his contract of employment without notice if a substantial change is made to his working conditions to his detriment . . .' (how this affects the ordinary law of constructive dismissal is discussed both in Chapter 7 and towards the end of this chapter).

The leading authority in this area (a constructive dismissal case, but the principles arising should also apply to express dismissals in similar circumstances) is *Berriman v Delabole Slate Ltd.*[1] Here the applicant was employed as a quarryman. His terms included a £100 guaranteed weekly wage. The quarrying business was owned by Mr Baker who in January 1983 transferred the undertaking to Delabole Slate. The applicant went over to Delabole Slate with the transferred business by virtue of reg 5. This was not disputed. But he was then offered fresh terms by his new employer at an hourly rate of £1.44 together with a bonus which altogether earned him slightly less per week and removed his guaranteed weekly wage. This was in breach of contract. In response, the employee resigned and claimed constructive dismissal. The industrial tribunal found that there had been a constructive dismissal. It also held that such dismissal was transfer-connected and so, prima facie, reg 8 applied. It went on to hold that this was not an automatically unfair dismissal under reg 8(1) because there was an economic, technical or organisational reason under reg 8(2) for the imposed harmonisation of terms and conditions. The industrial tribunal went on to find that the dismissal was fair under s 57(3) of the EP(C)A.

The EAT and the Court of Appeal held, however, that there was no economic, technical or organisational reason for the dismissal under reg 8(2). This was because an 'economic, technical or organisational reason' had, under the full terms of reg 8, also to entail a change in the workforce. In this case no change occurred in the workforce (as would usually occur in express workforce reduction dismissals) but merely in the terms and conditions enjoyed by the workforce. For a change in the workforce within the meaning of reg 8(2) there had to be a change in the composition of the workforce. Accordingly the dismissal was automatically unfair and s 57(3) of the EP(C)A did not arise for consideration. The Court of Appeal adopted the test that, for reg 8(2) to apply, there must be a change in the *numbers* of the workforce or, possibly, a change in their job *functions* which, although involving no overall reduction in

---

1 [1985] ICR 546.

numbers, involved a change in the individual employees which together made up the workforce.[2]

There are a few points worth mentioning in relation to the case. First, it is assumed that a change in *function* may entail a change in the workforce. Could a dismissal arising out of a more drastic change in terms than in the present case (e g issue of a completely new job description) entail a change in the workforce because of a change in function? It would seem wrong that an employee exposed to a more drastic change in terms (because his whole job function may be different) is less well protected than an employee faced with a more minor change in his terms. None the less, this distinction has been applied in subsequent cases. In *Lane v Dyno Rod plc*[3] an industrial tribunal held that an imposed change of terms and conditions on an area manager requiring him to change to a senior engineer was a dismissal for an economic, technical or organisational reason because a change in the entire job was involved and therefore the job *function*. And a similar conclusion was arrived at by the EAT in *Crawford v Swinton Insurance Brokers Ltd*.[4] There Mrs Crawford was originally employed to do typing and clerical work. The business was transferred to Swinton. She was told, after the transfer, that, in effect, the nature of her job would change from 'secretarial' to 'insurance salesman' (*sic*). She claimed constructive and unfair dismissal. The industrial tribunal held the dismissal was *not* automatically unfair under reg 8(1) and, further, that the dismissal was fair under s 57(3) of the EP(C)A because of the organisational need. The EAT confirmed that there did not always have to be a change in the identity of the workforce for reg 8(2) to apply. A change in job function amounted to the same thing (however the EAT remitted the case to the industrial tribunal on the general issue of fairness as it had failed to consider and identify the *principal* reason for dismissal as is required by reg 8(2)).

Second, the Court of Appeal in *Berriman* also disposed of two further arguments by the appellant, one technical and one of policy. It was mooted that the reason for dismissal in the present case *did* entail a change in the workforce since it entailed, in the first instance, the constructive dismissal of Mr Berriman, then the reduction of the workforce and, subsequently, a replacement of Mr Berriman by a newly recruited employee and so, as a result, a

2 The same result was arrived at by the EAT in a case pre-dating *Berriman* in the Court of Appeal, namely *May and Hassall (West) Ltd v Jansen* EAT 526/83 LEXIS transcript.

3 *Lane v Dyno-Rod plc* COIT 17833/85.

4 [1990] ICR 85, [1990] IRLR 42.

change in the composition of the workforce. This argument was, rightly it is submitted, rejected as fallacious. The correct approach to the burden of proof in establishing a reason for dismissal in this sort of case is to require the employer to show the reason for the employer's conduct which gave rise to the employee's resignation. Thus it was the reason for the conduct of the employer which was important, not the employee's response to that conduct. In this case, the reason for the employer's conduct was to standardise pay norms and not to reduce the workforce. Reduction of the workforce by one employee and his replacement by another was merely a consequence. Since the desire to standardise pay and conditions did not entail a change in the workforce, the dismissal was automatically unfair.[5]

Counsel had also argued that reg 8(2), as interpreted by the EAT, had undesirable effects on proposed employer reorganisation programmes. Employers might now be liable for larger sums if they unilaterally harmonised terms and conditions of those transferred with those already existing in the transferee's undertaking. The Court of Appeal rejected this argument too, even though it would have been in keeping with previously prevailing judicial attitudes to management reorganisation problems. The fact that unfair dismissal case law generally was sympathetic to business reorganisations could not prevail over subsequent legislation which had, as its express aim, the safeguarding of employee rights. Acquired terms and conditions of employment were, according to the Court of Appeal, one of the most important employee rights to be safeguarded.

This is an appropriately employee-oriented interpretation of the regulations in the light of the aim of the Acquired Rights Directive safeguarding employee rights, and one which is to be welcomed from that point of view. It effectively imposes a considerable restraint on transferees who intend to harmonise terms and conditions among employees inherited with their existing workforce. However, it seems only right to repeat our observation that it is odd that those dismissed as surplus to requirements will not be able to claim the automatic unfairness under reg 8 (since a change in the workforce will be entailed) whereas those kept on by the transferee but who suffer action short of dismissal by changes in their contract can. And as one commentator[6] has pointed out, it is surely also unjust that employees who resist such changes outside the context

---

5 See also the discussion on this point in *Servicepoint Ltd v Clynes* EAT 154/88, LEXIS transcript.
6 Collins [1985] ILJ 61.

of a business transfer may be less well off than employees who resist change when the Transfer Regulations apply.

These criticisms apart, it must be commented that striking a fair balance between the competing interests of employers and employees during a great many business reorganisations will always be a major problem. This case, to be fair, does seem to reset the balance previously tilted towards the employer. On the other hand, employers will regret this decision. It imposes a real restraint on unilateral harmonisation of terms and conditions. It might restrain purchasers from purchasing. Alternatively, it may affect the price a purchaser contracts to pay for a business in circumstances where employees are transferred and their terms are out of line with the purchaser's existing employees. Whatever the wider issues, an employer must now be cautious in embarking upon reorganisation programmes. If a purchaser perceives that he wants to reorganise and change the terms and conditions of employment, i e if the employees in the business to be transferred enjoy terms and conditions radically different from his own, then he may well insist that the employees are dismissed prior to the transfer so that he can re-engage thereafter, with the intention of avoiding liability, and offer new contracts as if the employees were newly recruited employees. But if he does so, this will be at his peril. As stated, such a scheme would rebound on the purchaser and he would inherit liability for dismissals by the vendor under the principles in *Litster v Forth Dry Dock & Engineering Co Ltd*[7] as such dismissals will be automatically unfair under the principles in *Wheeler v Patel*.[8] If the workforce is inherited under reg 5, there may be no real alternative but to seek to *agree* change with the transferred workforce. Regulation 8 may well therefore have altered the traditional management freedom referred to at the beginning of this chapter to effect such change.

Finally, there remains one point concerning the trigger to a constructive dismissal claim under reg 8 that we have discussed earlier in the text.[9] For an unfair dismissal claim based on a resignation to get off the ground there must be a constructive dismissal. Ordinarily this would be based on the definition in s 55(2)(c) of the EP(C)A, i e that:

'. . . the employee terminates [the] contract, with or without notice, in circumstances such that he is entitled to terminate it without notice by reason of the employer's conduct.'

---

7 [1989] ICR 341, [1989] IRLR 161.
8 [1987] ICR 631, [1987] IRLR 211. See the text, above.
9 See Ch 7.

In *Western Excavating (ECC) Ltd v Sharp*[10] it was held that the employee must show a repudiatory breach of contract on the part of the employer in response to which he has resigned, thereby accepting the breach as terminating the contract.

But reg 5(5) also provides for the possibility of such justified resignation. As a qualification to the idea of automatic transfer of employment, it states:

'Paragraph (1) above is without prejudice to any right of an employee arising apart from these regulations to terminate his contract of employment without notice if a substantial change is made in his working conditions to his detriment; but no such right shall arise by reason only that, under that paragraph, the identity of his employer changes unless the employee shows that, in all the circumstances, the change is a significant change and is to his detriment.'

As discussed in Chapter 7, the question arises whether reg 5(5) is descriptive of the circumstances giving rise to the right to allege constructive dismissal after a business transfer, or exhaustive. As will have been seen above,[11] in *Servicepoint Ltd v Clynes*,[12] this matter was raised in the EAT on appeal from the industrial tribunal, albeit rather obliquely. But the EAT did say,

'It may be that the regulations should be read as a whole and that where the regulations have clear wording, then they should be applied without necessary reference to the principles of constructive dismissal.'

Whether this means the EAT thought that, in a Transfer Regulations case, the only definition of constructive dismissal that is relevant is reg 5(5), not the general law, or whether the terms of reg 5(5) are *wider* than the ordinary law of constructive dismissal, is not entirely clear (the industrial tribunal found there had been both a repudiation at common law *and* a case failing under reg 5(5)). As suggested in Chapter 5, if reg 5(5) were to be looked at as providing the *only* definition of constructive dismissal for the purposes of this subject there are grounds for saying it would narrow, rather than enlarge, an employee's options. For reasons discussed in Chapter 7, it is submitted that the better view is that reg 5(5) is descriptive and not exhaustive of the circumstances giving rise to the right to allege constructive dismissal: in other words the preferred approach would be to say that it *supplements* an employee's rights.

---

10 [1978] QB 761, [1978] 1 All ER 713.
11 Ch 7.
12 EAT 154/88.

4 SOLUTIONS TO THE *BERRIMAN*/REG 8 PROBLEM

Are there ways of avoiding automatic unfair dismissal liability arising out of constructive or express dismissals in connection with imposed harmonisation? The following are some suggestions.

(i) Post-transfer harmonisation by agreement

One practical alternative to incurring this liability for automatic unfair dismissal is to seek to impose change by agreement. This should be done by negotiation and ultimate agreement of new terms. Sometimes this can be achieved without financial conse-quences; in other cases it may be necessary to 'buy out' the offending terms by, say, offering a single sum in consideration of the employee giving up those terms. Such an arrangement, by virtue of contract law, should be effective.

The question arises whether any such agreement could be attacked as an attempt to contract out of the Transfer Regulations. This may seem unduly restrictive at first sight. The issue came before the European Court in *Foreningen af Arbejdsledere i Danmark v Daddy's Dance Hall*.[13] In this case, following a relevant transfer that occurred on the change-over of lessees of a restaurant (see Ch 4) the restaurant manager re-engaged by the new lessee was offered new terms. At the employee's request, these included a trial period of three months during which either side could give fourteen days' notice. The manager was then dismissed under that provision. The proceedings brought by the manager in the Danish court con-cerned the period of notice he was entitled to. Under his arrange-ments with the old employer he would have been entitled to three months' notice. Was that overridden by the agreement with the new employer to receive only 14 days' notice?

As will be seen from Chapter 4, the European Court decided there was a transfer of an undertaking covered by the directive on the change-over of lessee. The other question referred to the court was:

'Can an employee who enters into an agreement with the purchaser of a business waive rights under the directive where by so doing he obtains certain advantages so that his conditions of employment, taken as a whole, are not altered in such a way as to leave him in a worse position?'

---

13 [1988] ECR 739, [1989] 2 CMLR 517.

The submission on behalf of the United Kingdom in this case was that if it were possible to waive such rights against the former employer, it should be possible, to the same extent, against the new employer. If accepted, this submission would allow agreed harmonisation as discussed above. And the court in its judgment stated: 'This argument must be upheld.'

Of course, it was not possible to contract out of the directive. Thus:

> 'It follows that employees are not entitled to waive the rights conferred on them by the directive and that those rights cannot be restricted even with their consent. This interpretation is not affected by the fact that, as in this case, the employer obtains new benefits in compensation for the disadvantages resulting from an amendment to his contract of employment, so that, taking the matter as a whole, he is not placed in a worse position than before . . .
>
> However, the directive can be relied on only to ensure that the employee is protected in his relations with the transferee to the same extent as he was in his relations with the transferor under the legal rules of the member state concerned . . . consequently, in so far as national law allows the employment relationship to be altered in a manner unfavourable to employees in situations other than the transfer of an undertaking . . . such an alteration is not precluded merely because the undertaking has been transferred in the meantime and the agreement has therefore been made with the new employer. Since by virtue of Art 3(1) of the directive the transferee is subrogated to the transferor's rights and obligations under the employment relationship, that relationship may be altered with regard to the transferee to the same extent as it could have been with regard to the transferor, provided that the transfer of the undertaking itself may never constitute the reason for that amendment.'

This therefore allows a consensual variation of terms with the transferee to the same extent as allowed for under domestic law with the transferor. It should therefore permit the parties to come to terms on the question of alteration of contracts.[14]

---

14 A residual area of doubt concerns the phrase 'provided that the transfer of the undertaking itself may never constitute the reason for [the] amendment'. But surely this would, literally, more or less always be the case here. If this proviso were interpreted to mean that, in any circumstances where a transfer was the start (however long ago) of the chain of events leading to an amendment, the parties cannot subsequently consensually vary terms, the decision of the court would be unduly restrictive. Surely it was not intended to rule out post-transfer agreements freely entered into for good consideration? More clarification of the court's proviso and indication of when, in point of time and in what circumstances it is to apply would obviously have been helpful (to be contrasted is the more robust opinion of the court in favour of voluntary agreements by employees not to join

(ii) 'Red circling'

Another practical solution is for workers' rights to be maintained but for their conditions to be 'red circled'. This expression comes from equal pay discrimination law and means that the transferee could continue to honour the higher-paying conditions of transferred employees but freeze them by awarding no pay increases until such time as the terms and conditions of the existing workforce have caught up. This would seem to be permissible provided that there is no contractual entitlement to a pay increase or award. Of course, in practical terms, this presupposes that the exercise of harmonisation through red circling can be completed within a reasonable time. There may be industrial relations problems if increases in respect of the transferred workers are frozen for too long.

(iii) Delaying the harmonisation

The *Berriman* principle only applies to transfer-connected dismissals. There is no limitation in time as to when dismissals will be connected with the transfer. It is obviously a question of fact and degree. The more time that elapses since the transfer the less likely there will be a connnection with that transfer. Unfortunately, it is not possible to predict how long a purchaser will have to wait before a court will decide that his actions are no longer connected with the transfer.

(iv) Vendor dismissals

The purchaser's liability can theoretically be avoided if the vendor brings about the transfer-connected dismissals, either express or constructive, in connection with harmonisation. However, since this whole discussion presupposes that transfer-connected dismissals arising out of imposed harmonisation will generally be automatically unfair under reg 8 of the regulations, it would seem likely that a purchaser's request to a vendor to effect changes in this manner would largely be futile and would simply have the boomerang

---

the transferee at all – see *Mikkelsen v Danmols Inventar A/S* [1986] 1 CMLR 316, Ch 7). Of course, under *Daddy's Dance Hall*, the workers' rights may only be altered to the same extent as was possible before the transfer. If, for example, a transferee acquired an employee with accrued continuity of service, it would not be possible to agree, say, to contract out of the statutory minimum period of notice under s 49 of the EP(C)A 1978 by agreeing a shorter period of notice than the statutory minimum. The same applies to any other statutory right in respect of which contracting out is prohibited by statute. Whether this was ultimately the deciding factor under *domestic law* in *Daddy's Dance Hall* is not clear from the judgment of the European Court.

effect of passing liabilities on to the purchaser by virtue of the principle in *Litster*.

(v) Short-serving workers

It seems likely, as the law stands at present, that only those employees with a qualifying period for unfair dismissal may claim automatically unfair dismissal under reg 8. Therefore it seems possible that changes can be effected with relative impunity in the case of short-serving workers. Two caveats must, however, be made here. First, it must be noted that if an employee has been acquired by virtue of a relevant transfer, reg 5 will pass over to the transferee previously acquired continuous service and this must also be taken into account in assessing whether an employee has attained a qualifying period. Second, there is a common law dimension which is not dependent upon a qualifying period in connection with imposed harmonisation. If an employer at common law unilaterally changes terms and conditions he runs the risk that the employee may treat this as a repudiation. This of course may lead to a constructive dismissal, but the employee is not obliged to trigger a constructive dismissal. If, for example, the repudiation consists of an attempted variation of pay he may simply resist that change and assert his rights under the contract. He is not obliged to accept a repudiatory breach as terminating the contract. As long as he keeps his rights alive, he may sue for his wages under his original contract. Such was the case in *Rigby v Ferodo Ltd*[15] where it was held that an employer cannot evade this principle by giving notice of the change. Such would be, simply, a notice of intended breach of contract. To avoid this scenario an employer would have to give full notice of termination of the contract of employment in accordance with its terms and couple it with an offer of a new contract containing the changed terms to take effect on its expiry which of course the employee can accept or reject. Such would amount to a dismissal in law and could, in theory, give rise to an unfair dismissal claim. But we turn full circle here as this could not be pursued unless the employee had attained the appropriate qualifying period (see above). As present, the qualifying period for unfair dismissal stands at two years. This has, however, been liable to change in the past.[16]

---

15 [1987] ICR 457.
16 The period was originally set at two years, reduced to 26 weeks, increased to one year, and has now stood at two years for some time (Unfair Dismissal (Variation of Qualifying Period) Order 1985, SI 1985/782). The qualifying period does not apply to dismissals for trade union membership or non-membership or activities nor to race or sex discrimination claims.

(vi) Changing the employees' functions

If one applies the obiter dictum in *Berriman* which has been applied subsequently in both *Lane v Dyno Rod* in the industrial tribunal and in *Crawford v Swinton Insurance Brokers* in the Employment Appeal Tribunal one can state that the law seems to be that as long as there is a change in the job functions of the workforce this may be a dismissal entailing changes in the workforce. The irony that a more drastic change involves less protection for employees than a more minor change in terms and conditions has been remarked on above. None the less, this seems available to employers as a way of getting round the automatic unfairness in reg 8. If an employer is able completely to revise the jobs of employees concerned he may therefore be able to avoid the automatic unfairness and be left with justifying a change under the general principles of s 57(3). It is to be remarked, however, that the upshot of the *Berriman* case and the distinction between a minor change of terms and conditions and a change of the entire job function is that the reg 8 defence of an economic, technical or organisational reason is only likely to succeed in this context where the dismissal satisfies the definition of redundancy. Clearly, when there are express workforce reductions this will satisfy the definition of redundancy and will of course be a dismissal 'entailing changes in the workforce'. Second, if the entire job function changes this too could satisfy the definition of redundancy. An example is *Murphy v Epsom College*[17] where a plumber was dismissed and replaced by a heating technician. Notwithstanding that the employee had been replaced and that there was no workforce reduction it was held that the plumber had been dismissed by reason of redundancy because the employer's requirements in respect of work to be performed had radically changed. The qualities possessed by a heating technician were so fundamentally different from the skills possessed by the plumber that the new job created was substantially different from the old one. The job *function* had changed. The definition of redundancy was satisfied. The requirement of work of a particular kind had ceased or diminished. An industrial tribunal will, however, be keen to expose a sham exercise on the part of employers who purport to change job functions but who are really making cosmetic changes. To be contrasted, therefore, is *Vaux and Associated Breweries Ltd v Ward*[18] where an employee was dismissed from her post as barmaid when

---

17 [1985] ICR 80.
18 (1970) 5 ITR 62. See, too, in this area *Robinson v British Island Airways Ltd* [1978] ICR 304; *Hall v Farrington Data Processing Ltd* (1969) 4 ITR 230; *Denton v Neepsend Ltd* [1976] IRLR 164.

her employers wanted to turn the pub in which she worked into a modern roadhouse with a younger and more attractive barmaid. The court ruled that there was no redundancy. There was still work of a particular kind required to be done, i e that of a barmaid. The new job holder was not performing work of a substantially different kind.

In view of the genuineness of a change in job function required, it may be that wholesale change in job functions is not a practicable exercise for employers to embark on.

(vii) Conclusions on avoidance of reg 8

Regulation 8 is not intended to be avoided and quite rightly so. The aim of the Acquired Rights Directive is to protect acquired rights of employees. Many of the above suggestions ring of artificiality. A purposive approach will be applied to constructions of the Transfer Regulations and to the actions of employers. One can only conclude that the only realistic mode of effecting immediate change is to agree this with the employees concerned for an appropriate consideration. Indirectly, therefore, reg 8 highlights the need for, and raises the status of, individual and collective consultation and bargaining in the process of reorganisational change.

5 THE INTER-RELATIONSHIP BETWEEN REDUNDANCY ENTITLEMENTS AND DISMISSALS UNDER REG 8

A redundancy payment may also be due to an employee even if his dismissal falls under reg 8 as long as the statutory definition of redundancy is satisfied. This conclusion may seem trite, but earlier decisions tended to cast some doubt on the issue. The doubt arose because if the employer *does* succeed in persuading the industrial tribunal that there is an 'economic, technical or organisational' reason for the dismissal, this is, according to the Transfer Regulations, treated as a 'substantial' reason for the purpose of s 57 of the EP(C)A (unfair dismissal). Would this therefore mean that there is, *ex hypothesi*, no dismissal for *redundancy* for the purpose of decided entitlement to a redundancy payment?

In a Scottish EAT case, *Canning v Niaz and McCloughlin*,[19] it was decided that an employee *was* thereby excluded from entitlement to a redundancy payment. In this case, Mrs Canning was employed

---

19 [1983] IRLR 431.

by the first respondent. The first respondent sold his business to the second respondent, but the latter did not wish to employ Mrs Canning. She claimed a redundancy payment from the second respondent. But reg 8 seemed to apply, and the question of unfair dismissal was raised. The employer succeeded in showing that there was an economic, technical or organisational reason entailing changes in the workforce and that the dismissal was also not unfair under EP(C)A, s 57(3). Having failed to be awarded compensation for unfair dismissal the employee asked the tribunal to award her a redundancy payment.[20] Both the industrial tribunal and the EAT considered that, because the economic, technical or organisational reason 'defence' applied to the reg 8 unfair dismissal claim, the reason was deemed to be 'some other substantial reason'; *ex hypothesi* the employee had not been dismissed by reason of redundancy and was therefore not entitled to a redundancy payment.[1]

But this is surely wrong. With respect, a finding of the reason for the purposes of s 57 (unfair dismissal) should not adversely affect rights under the redundancy payments provisions of the EP(C)A. It cannot have been intended that, where an eto applies, it takes away the right to a redundancy payment that would arise on the facts under the definition in the EP(C)A. The better view is that a redundancy payment may also be payable even if the employer has demonstrated that he has an eto reason for dismissal and therefore a 'defence' to a claim of automatic unfairness under reg 8, provided the definition of redundancy in s 81 of the EP(C)A is satisfied.[2] Fortunately, the EAT in England in *Gorictree Ltd v Jenkinson*[3]

---

20 It is, of course, perfectly possible to be awarded both a redundancy payment and unfair dismissal compensation in addition thereto, because the redundancy dismissal was unfair: *Midland Foot Comfort Centre Ltd v Moppett* [1973] 2 All ER 294, [1972] ICR 219.

 1 Although it has been argued that, in *Canning*, the definition of redundancy was not satisfied anyway, as the employee, it seemed, was being replaced by a member of the new employer's family (Collins (1985) ILJ 61 at 63). And if the facts arose now, there would be a distinct likelihood that the dismissal would have been automatically unfair under reg 8. It would now be hard to establish an economic, technical or organisational reason for dismissal entailing changes in the workforce when the employee was being replaced by another employee of the new employer's choice: see *Wheeler v Patel* [1987] ICR 631, [1987] IRLR 211; *Gateway Hotels Ltd v Stewart* [1988] IRLR 287; *Litster v Forth Dry Dock & Engineering Co Ltd* [1989] ICR 341, [1989] IRLR 161, HL. As is stated elsewhere in the text, many cases decided before *Litster* and *Wheeler v Patel* have to be looked at afresh on their facts.

 2 See *Skilling v Reed* COIT 26417, IT; see also, in a different context, *Chapman v CPS Computer Group plc* [1987] IRLR 462 (entitlement to exercise of share option in a redundancy situation once business sold).

 3 [1985] ICR 51, [1984] IRLR 391, EAT.

subsequently disapproved the *Canning* decision and the EAT in Scotland in *Anderson v Dalkeith Engineering Ltd*[4] declined to follow it. These later decisions are to be preferred.

Accordingly, in conclusion, if there is a dismissal in connection with the transfer it may, prima facie, be automatically unfair under reg 8(1). But if there is an economic, technical or organisational reason entailing changes in the workforce under reg 8(2), the case falls to be decided as to fairness in the usual way, according to general principles under s 57(3) of the EP(C)A. In that case, the reason for dismissal is *deemed* to be a 'substantial' reason under s 57(1)(b) for the purposes of unfair dismissal only. However, economic, technical or organisational reasons can include both reorganisation *and* redundancy, and if, for the purposes of the redundancy payments provisions, the facts actually satisfy the statutory definition of redundancy, the applicant should be entitled to a redundancy payment irrespective of any rights to unfair dismissal compensation.

---

4 [1985] ICR 66, [1984] IRLR 429, EAT.

Chapter 9

Insolvency and business transfers, receivership and hiving down

1 GENERAL

Insolvency can have a traumatic impact on employees. Its legal impact on contracts of employment also has consequences, but the extent of these depends on the type of insolvency situation that arises and the position is complex and often incompletely clarified by court decisions.

2 THE EFFECT OF APPOINTMENT OF A RECEIVER, ADMINISTRATOR OR LIQUIDATOR ON CONTRACTS OF EMPLOYMENT[1]

Receivership will not ordinarily result in termination of the contracts of employment of employees, at least where the receiver is a receiver and manager who, after 1986, is called an 'administrative receiver' (see s 29(2) of the Insolvency Act 1986). He is expressly deemed to be an agent of the company (Insolvency Act 1986 s 44(1)(a)).[2] There should not, of course, be a relevant transfer to the receiver under the Transfer Regulations on the simple appointment of that type of receiver. Finally, he has authority to continue the business of the company and to sell it (Insolvency Act 1986 s 42(1) and Sch 1).

The same applies to the appointment of an administrator under

---

1 See Freedland *The Contract of Employment* pp 330–350.
2 *Griffiths v Secretary of State for Social Services* [1974] QB 468; [1973] 3 All ER 1184. Perhaps not, however, when he is not a manager (*Kerr on Receivers* (10th edn) p 154); or if continued employment cannot, in practice, take place (see *Re Mack Trucks (Britain) Ltd* [1967] 1 All ER 977, [1967] 1 WLR 780); and see G Lightman and G Moss *The Law of Receivers of Companies* (1986) p 201.

the Insolvency Act 1986. His appointment likewise will not terminate contracts of employment.[3] By virtue of the Insolvency Act 1986 s 14(5) he is also expressly made an agent of the company and, again, there will be no transfer of a business to him by reason of his simple appointment. Obviously, too, he has authority to both run and sell the business on behalf of the company (Insolvency Act 1986 s 14 and Sch 1).

A liquidator appointed following a voluntary liquidation is considered also to be an agent of the company and again his appointment does not terminate contracts of employment.[4] As above, he may cause disposal of the business of the company.

However, a more complicated scenario arises when a liquidator is appointed by the court. This type of liquidator, by contrast, is an agent of the court and not the company. It is therefore argued that his appointment automatically terminates contracts of employment.[5] If he wishes to continue employment of employees involved thereafter he must do so personally. But, if so, what happens when this liquidator then causes a disposal of the business? If he does employ the employees personally, then unless the liquidator is also the transferor of the business, reg 5 will not protect the employees concerned. But, at first glance, the liquidator does not own the business, and so cannot be the actual transferor, even if he brings about the transfer. And reg 5 will only protect employees of the transferor. One solution would be that the liquidator himself took a transfer of the business before its onwards disposal. But it would seem odd, at first glance, to say that there has been a transfer of the business to the liquidator on his appointment and adoption of employees. Certainly there would be no formal transaction effecting such a transfer. Nor, undoubtedly, would the liquidator intend or invite it. This loophole could be closed by a number of methods. First, it could be argued that there *could* be a transfer to the liquidator, before the ultimate sale and upon his employing the workforce, especially as the law (underpinned by European Court decisions – see Ch 4) does not require, on a relevant transfer, a change of absolute ownership, but simply a change in the employer employing employees in the business who takes on employment obligations in respect of such employees (see Ch 4). Alternatively, it is also arguable that reg 3(4) (linked transactions) (see Ch 6, Part 4) might allow the disposal of the business (even if treated as a transfer otherwise than by the liquidator) and transfer of the employees to be

---

3 See Lingard *Corporate Rescues and Insolvencies* (2nd edn, 1989) Ch 13.
4 *Reigate v Union Manufacturing Co (Ramsbottom) Ltd* [1918] 1 KB 592.
5 *Re Oriental Bank Corpn* (1886) 32 Ch D 366.

treated as one transaction. In any event, it is vital for employees that courts to strive to find a relevant transfer on the ultimate disposal in this type of situation. Perhaps the decision in *Litster*, applying a purposive approach to the Transfer Regulations to make them conform with the aims of the Acquired Rights Directive in safeguarding employee rights, would be useful in this regard. (The application of the Transfer Regulations and the directive in principle to compulsory liquidation aside from this technical point is considered below.) Similar problems, which need not be repeated in full here, apply also to a *receiver* appointed by the court.[6]

3 THE APPLICATION OF THE BUSINESS TRANSFER LEGISLATION TO INSOLVENCY SITUATIONS

Many business sales arise from insolvency situations. *Secretary of State for Employment v Spence*[7] and *Litster v Forth Dry Dock & Engineering Co Ltd*,[8] two of the leading cases on transfer of undertakings, are good examples. There is no doubt, it is submitted, that the Transfer Regulations (and the EP(C)A provisions) apply to sales during the course of a creditors' or members' voluntary winding up, a receivership and an administration, whether through the use of the mechanism of hiving down (see below) or a more orthodox and direct transfer. The statutory provisions are, it is suggested, perfectly widely enough drawn to allow this, and anyway, the Transfer Regulations specifically *refer* (in reg 4: see below) to such situations. Nor has it ever been seriously disputed that a sale arising from a compulsory liquidation falls within the ambit of the business transfer legislation, at least as far as EP(C)A Sch 13 para 17(2) is concerned (although there may be technical problems, referred to above).[9] Some doubt arises in relation to the Transfer Regulations,

---

6 *Reid v Explosives Co Ltd* (1887) 19 QBD 264.
7 [1987] QB 179, [1986] ICR 651.
8 [1989] ICR 341, [1989] IRLR 161.
9 In *Thomsons Soft Drinks Ltd v Quayle* EAT 12/81, LEXIS transcript (although this was a *voluntary* liquidation case) May J made generally directed comments thus: 'In our opinion, although the fact that a sale is by a liquidator and may not be expressed to comprise the goodwill as well as the assets of the vendor is a factor to be taken into account, *this is by no means conclusive*' (emphasis added) (see Ch 7). On the other hand, once a company has gone into compulsory insolvent liquidation it is less likely (although not impossible) that there will be anything by way of a business as a going concern to sell. But the matter is a question of fact as with a sale in any other context (see *Huggins v A & J Gordon (Aveley) Ltd* (1971) 6 ITR 164 and Ch 7). See also *Hall v Carjill Manufacturing Ltd (in liquidation)* COIT 1432/121.

however, because of a decision of the European Court on the Acquired Rights Directive in *Abels v Administrative Board of the Bedrifsvereniging voor de Metaal Industrie en de Electrotechnische Industrie*.[10] There the European Court held that the directive does not apply to the transfer of undertakings, businesses or parts of businesses which occur in the context of insolvency proceedings instituted with a view to the liquidation of the assets of the transferor under the supervision of the competent judicial authority. It is thought that this means, in the UK, a compulsory winding-up on the ground of insolvency (or, in the case of an individual, personal bankruptcy). In fact Slynn A-G would also have excluded a 'surséance van betaling' (judicial suspension of debts) under Dutch law from the directive (the nearest equivalent of administration under UK law). But the ECJ, as stated, went no further than excluding the equivalent of compulsory liquidation (and individual bankruptcy) (see above). This has yet to be tested here but to be noted is the view of Hamilton J in the Irish High Court, on application by the liquidator of Castle Brand Ltd (in liquidation) for directions, that SI 1980/306, the European Communities (Safeguarding of Employees' Rights on Transfer of Undertakings) Regulations 1980 (the Irish SI implementing the directive) did not cover insolvent compulsory liquidation in the light of the *Abels* decision.[11] However, as discussed in Chapter 7, the wording of the Irish Regulations differs from that of the Transfer Regulations. And the Irish Regulations expressly provide in Art 2(2) that 'a word or expression that is used in these regulations and is also used in the Council directive shall, unless the context otherwise requires, have the meaning in these regulations that it has in the Council directive'. The Transfer Regulations are reasonably widely drawn, and it is generally *assumed* that they *do* apply to compulsory liquidations (and it is permissible for member states to make more favourable provision for employees than in the directive (see Art 7)).[12] More recently the European Court of Justice has ruled on the applicability of the Acquired Rights Directive to the Italian procedure for the special administration of major companies experiencing a crisis. In *G d'Urso v Ercole Marelli Elettromeccanica*[13] the court held that the directive applies to such procedure as long as there is a decision that the company's activities are to be pursued and as long as the

---

10 [1987] 2 CMLR 406.
11 See *Acquired Rights of Employees* pp 66–73.
12 See P L Davies 'Acquired Rights, Creditors' Rights, Freedom of Contract, and Industrial Democracy' in (1989) 9 *Yearbook of European Law* p 21.
13 ECJ, (25 July 1991, unreported).

company remains active. Such will not be the case if the activities are ceased. This decision seems to settle the dispute as to whether the Italian procedure is really akin to liquidation as in *Abels* or to a *surseance*. This lends indirect support for the inclusion in the Transfer Regulations of administration at least and also, arguably, receivership (although these two procedures were not under discussion in the European Court). As discussed above however the position is academic under the Transfer Regulations as it is argued that receivership and administration are expressly included anyway.

On the other hand, it has been urged that the government should use the *Abels* decision to legislate to restrict the Transfer Regulations in this area, excluding transfers arising out of compulsory liquidations.[14] The government has, however, no plans to do this at present.[15]

It may now be appropriate to deal in more detail with the subject of receivership and administration and other insolvency situations as they interface with the business transfer legislation and, in particular, with the practice of hiving down and its treatment in reg 4 of the Transfer Regulations.[16]

4 HIVING DOWN AND REG 4 OF THE TRANSFER REGULATIONS

The concept of hiving down has been touched upon in discussion elsewhere in this book, but it will now be appropriate to discuss in detail the provisions of reg 4 of the Transfer Regulations which deals with this specialised aspect of sales of businesses. Regulation 4 states as follows:

'(1) Where the receiver of the property or part [or the administrator of a company appointed under Part II of the Insolvency Act 1986] or, in the case of a creditors' voluntary winding-up, the liquidator of a company transfers the company's undertaking, or part of the company undertaking (the "relevant undertaking") to a wholly owned subsidiary of the company, the transfer shall for the purposes of these regulations be deemed not to have been effected until immediately before:

---

14 See M Homan *Financial Times* 22 June 1989.
15 Letter to the author from the Department of Employment.
16 See, in detail, Davies and Freedland 'The Effects of Receiverships upon Employees of Companies' (1982) ILJ 95.

(a) the transferee company ceases (otherwise than by reason of its being wound up) to be a wholly-owned subsidiary of the transferor company; or

(b) the relevant undertaking is transferred by the transferee company to another person;

whichever first occurs and, for the purposes of these regulations the transfer of the relevant undertaking shall be taken to have been effected immediately before that date by one transaction only.

(2) In this regulation "creditors' voluntary winding-up" has the same meaning as in the Companies Act 1948, or, in Northern Ireland, the Companies Act (Northern Ireland) 1960; and "wholly-owned subsidiary" has the same meaning as it has for the purposes of s 150 of the Companies Act 1948 and s 144 of the Companies Act (Northern Ireland) 1960.'[17]

Hiving down is a practice followed by liquidators, receivers and administrators of insolvent companies in an attempt to facilitate the sale of the company's undertaking or part thereof. Whether, following *Litster v Forth Dry Dock & Engineering Co Ltd*, it is really worth, from an employment law point of view, structuring a sale from a receiver, administrator or liquidator via a hive down (see below) remains to be seen. But, if so, the mechanics are as follows.[18]

The following discussion assumes the appointment of an administrative receiver by the debenture holder or of an administrator under the Insolvency Act 1986. These will be the most common cases in practice.

In receivership examples such as the one envisaged above, if the business is to be sold as a going concern and if hiving down is to be applied, the receiver of the insolvent company (and this may be applied, *mutatis mutandis*, to an administrator etc) usually creates a wholly-owned subsidiary company (B) to which the business to be sold is transferred. The employees necessary to continue the business as a going concern are retained by (A) and lent out to (B) in order to perform the work required to be done by

---

17 The words in square brackets were added by the Transfer of Undertakings (Protection of Employment) (Amendment) Regulations 1987, SI 1987/442, reg 2. The definition of 'wholly-owned subsidiary' in the 1948 Companies Act was re-enacted by s 736 of the Companies Act 1985. (A new definition, using the expression 'subsidiary undertaking' was included by virtue of the Companies Act 1989 s 21 (Companies Act 1985 s 258) but this would not seem to apply for the purposes of interpretation of reg 4 without amendment of reg 4.) The definition of 'creditors' voluntary winding-up' is now contained in the Insolvency Act 1986, ss 84, 90.

18 There is also a description of hiving down in *Pambakian v Brentford Nylons Ltd* [1978] ICR 665 at 668–670.

the business. In due course a purchaser (C) either acquires the share capital of (B) or takes a transfer of the business from (B). (B), of course, has no employees. They have simply remained employees of the parent (A). This is illustrated by Figure 5 below.

(1)

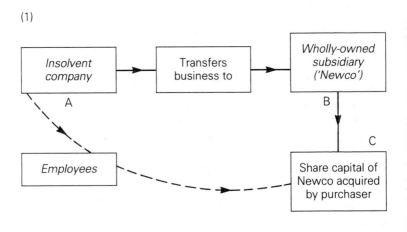

(2)

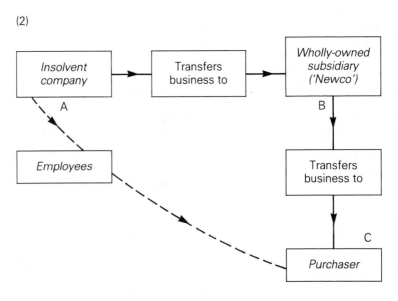

Figure 5 *Possible hiving down transactions*

Shortly prior to the acquisition of (B) or its business by (C) the receiver will have dismissed those employees. Part or all (usually only part) of that workforce may, in due course, be offered fresh employment with (C). Before *Litster* it was assumed that they went over to (C) having suffered a break in employment rights. If that were the case their contracts would not be transferred and their continuity of employment would be broken. They would, in that event, make their claims for notice payments, redundancy payments, arrears of wages and so forth against the insolvent parent. If that company were unable to pay, reimbursement would be made by the Secretary of State under s 122 of the EP(C)A.[19]

By this method, the receiver could, in theory, sell the business free of employees. The Transfer Regulations, at first glance, would have inhibited the effectiveness of hiving down. Indeed, the 1978 draft of the regulations contained no equivalent of reg 4. Nor, importantly, does the Acquired Rights Directive (see below). As such, there would no longer have been any point in hiving down the business from (A) to (B) for, under the wording of reg 5, as drawn, employees would automatically be transferred with it.

On the other hand, one interpretation of the effect of sales by a receiver of the undertaking on contracts of employment is that the sale by a receiver of the undertaking of a company in receivership does not of itself terminate contracts of employment. If this is so, then reg 4 would cease to be relevant at all. On this view, the transfer of the undertaking to the wholly-owned subsidiary would not terminate contracts of employment, and so the contract would not be, for the purposes of reg 5, 'otherwise terminated by the transfer'. Although the case of *Re Foster Clark Ltd's Indenture Trusts*[20] is commonly cited in favour of the proposition that a sale of the undertaking amounts to dismissal, as Davies and Freedland[1] point out, that really only applies when the sale also amounts to cessation of employment. In hiving down, the employment is specifically reserved by the receiver and maintained, and, *sed quaere*, upon transfer of the wholly-owned subsidiary, whether there are contracts which 'would otherwise have been terminated by the transfer'. If so, there is no need for reg 4 at all. Either for the

---

19 But, as pointed out in *Litster v Forth Dry Dock & Engineering Co Ltd* [1989] ICR 341, [1989] IRLR 161, there would still be some claims not met, e g an unfair dismissal compensatory award. See *Angus Jowett & Co Ltd v NUTGW* [1985] ICR 646, n 3, p 220.
20 [1966] 1 All ER 43, [1966] 1 WLR 125.
1 Davies and Freedland *Transfer of Employment* (1982).

avoidance of doubt or otherwise, the legislator, as Davies and Freedland comment, thought differently.[2]

So, in response to insolvency practitioners' representations, this perceived problem was dealt with by the introduction in the present regulations of reg 4. This postpones the effect of the regulations, and a relevant transfer is deemed not to take place until either the wholly-owned subsidiary (B) leaves the control of the parent (A) or the business is disposed of by the subsidiary (B). Unashamedly, the intention of this obviously was that, as long as the receiver dismissed employees before the disposition of the business to the purchaser (C), and made sure that the effective date of termination of these employees was before the disposition of the business to (C), the purchaser could, in the light of *Secretary of State for Employment v Spence*[3] acquire the business free of employees, as described above. (B) would only have assumed the liabilities of the employees employed by (A) if they were employed by (A) immediately before this postponed transfer of the business from (A) to (B); and the receiver would make sure this did not happen. Regulation 4 therefore, on the face of it, allows hiving down to operate successfully from an employment law point of view and *Secretary of State for Employment v Spence* gave the receiver the opportunity safely to carry on employment of the employees up to just before the point of transfer before he needed to dismiss them to avoid transfer of their contracts of employment and obligations in connection therewith under reg 5. Receivers certainly regarded this opportunity as valuable, since continued employment of employees until very close to the point of transfer meant the business was kept going and was more attractive for sale.

But as will be seen, of course, *Secretary of State for Employment v Spence* is qualified by *Litster*. Therefore, the law about pre-transfer dismissals and transfer of employment obligations in the context of reg 4 should, it is submitted, be no different from non-insolvency situations. That is, a pre-transfer (including a postponed transfer under reg 4, it is submitted) dismissal which is automatically unfair under reg 8 will give rise to transfer of liability to a transferee. It has been suggested that reg 4 is unaffected by *Litster* and hiving down may still be a way of getting round transfer of employment contracts. This is hardly tenable. *Litster* holds that a purposive

---

2 Ibid.
3 [1987] QB 179, [1986] ICR 651, CA. See *Angus Jowett & Co Ltd v NUTGW* [1985] ICR 646 where the EAT considered that employees were excluded from the protection of the Transfer Regulations when they had been dismissed prior to the postponed transfer under reg 4 (at p 658).

interpretation must be applied to the Transfer Regulations in order to make them conform to the Acquired Rights Directive. As already stated the directive contains no equivalent of reg 4. It is quite clear too that reg 4 as applied prior to *Litster* would diminish employee rights (ie by inhibiting transfer of their employment contracts). It is submitted that a court or tribunal must construe reg 4 in such a way as not to defeat the aims of the directive. As with other areas, then, *Litster* is a potent restraint on the ability of receivers and administrators to sell a business free of employees. As a result of *Litster*, there would seem, from an employment law perspective at least, no material advantage in selling under a hiving down scheme over and above a direct sale: the principles deriving from *Litster* apply to both.[4]

As mentioned above, the Insolvency Act 1986 created the concept of an 'administrator' of a company. Broadly, he may be appointed by resolution of the company in a potential insolvency where a liquidation has not occurred.[5] As discussed above, the appointment of an administrator should have the same effect as that of a receiver and manager appointed as agent of the company.[6] An administrator has also, it would seem, available to him the mechanism of hiving down as a way of selling the undertaking or part thereof.[7] Regulation 4 was amended to include reference to this new concept and to make it apply, *mutatis mutandis*, to sales by an administrator.[8] And as stated above, the hiving down provisions in reg 4 are also applicable to hive-downs by liquidators appointed as a result of a creditors' voluntary winding-up, but not, presumably, to one appointed as a result of a compulsory winding-up (reg 4(1)). In the light of *Litster v Forth Dry Dock & Engineering Co Ltd*, however, it is questionable, as stated above, whether hiving down has any advantages in employment law for a transferor, whether such transferor is in liquidation, receivership or administration.

Finally, included in Appendix D are two documents of interest to

---

4 Although Hepple and Byre, 'EEC Labour Law in the United Kingdom – A New Approach' (1989) ILJ 129 regard the question of whether the supplemented version of Reg 5(3) applies to Reg 4 as far from cut and dried. It is questionable whether, morally, too, it is right to seek expressly to avoid the employment rules under the regulations. See the criticism by the House of Lords of the circumstances in *Litster*. See too *Re Opera Ltd* [1891] 2 Ch 154; *Larsen v Henderson* [1990] IRLR 512.

5 Insolvency Act 1986 Pt II.

6 Insolvency Act 1986 s 14(5) deems an administrator to be an agent of the company.

7 See *Lingard* and the specimen hive down agreements included therein.

8 See the Transfer of Undertakings (Protection of Employment) (Amendment) Regulations 1987, SI 1987/442.

those involved in this area and of use to insolvency practitioners. One is the Department of Employment's Guidance Notes on 'Economic, Technical or Organisational Reasons' for dismissal and the Department's views on when it will accept liability for compensation payments when there are pre-transfer dismissals. As stated in Chapter 8, these obviously cannot be taken as a definitive statement of the law but it provide an insight into the department's own thinking at least. The second document is the Employment Department Redundancy Payments Service questionnaire in business transfer cases which shows the department's reasoning in the form of questions asked of insolvency practitioners in order to determine whether there is a case falling under *Litster* or *Spence*.

Space does not permit consideration of other problems of liquidation, receivership and administration in relation to employees. There is, however, excellent detailed material which can provide further thought.[9] One thing must, however, be stated. The subject area of corporate rescues following insolvency raises, not for the first time in this book, a complex interaction between rights of employees to a continuous and undisturbed work environment, and the economic argument, that, although hiving down (as it was originally intended to operate) would involve dismissal, selective re-engagement, and perhaps also an imposed revision of terms of employment on those re-engaged, it would at least allow the creation of some new jobs. Would purchasers be as much attracted to the purchase if they had to inherit all of the work-force or could not change terms and conditions? This is a commercial approach which may indeed have its merits.[10] But it is at the expense of the Acquired Rights Directive's aim of safeguarding employee rights on transfer. The alternative, it is said, would be to have no new jobs at all as no purchaser would want the business in its old form. Davies and Freedland suggest[11] the interests of employees are best protected by a broad employee-oriented approach rather than a commercially defined approach. And there is comparatively little empirical, as opposed to anecdotal, evidence that a more employee-oriented approach in this area would deter purchasers from purchasing or deter employers from hiring; only when there is such evidence should there be adopted, perhaps, without reservation, the

---

9 Davies and Freedland 'The Effects of Receiverships upon Employees of Companies' (1980) ILJ 95. And see *Lingard* and *Lightman and Moss*, op cit.
10 It is strongly argued in Floyd 'Saving Businesses and Companies – Formal and Informal Procedures' (a report from the sixth annual congress of the Association Européenne des Practiciens des Procédures Collectifs (AEPPC)) (1987) *Insolvency Law & Practice* 2.
11 Davies and Freedland *Labour Law: Text and Materials* (2nd edn, 1984).

insolvency practitioners' view that it is necessary to subordinate the concept of the transfer of acquired employee rights to the exigencies of selling an ailing business.[12] It is submitted that, in many cases, a purchaser's fears about enlarged liability for employment obligations on sale are satisfied by his negotiating indemnities from the vendor (though this is difficult in practice where, say, a receiver is involved) or, alternatively offering a lower price to compensate for the risk, or by agreeing a reserve for meeting potential claims. To be fair, insolvency practitioners, on the whole, seem not to be impressed by such arguments and regard the *Litster* decision as something not far short of a disaster.[13]

Finally, it has been mentioned that an employee's claims against the insolvent company will be met by the Secretary of State. While largely satisfactory as far as most debts are concerned, this can cause hardship because, inter alia, unfair dismissal compensatory awards are not among the claims met. As is seen from the more detailed discussions about *Litster* elsewhere in the book this is mitigated now by the effect of that decision: a compensatory award arising from a pre-transfer, transfer-connected dismissal which is automatically unfair under reg 8 will be the responsibility of the transferee, who, in all likelihood, will be solvent and able to pay it. But what of compensatory awards arising from pre-transfer dismissals not automatically unfair under reg 8 but, say, simply under EP(C)A 1978 s 57(3), where *Litster* does not apply? The Secretary of State cannot reimburse that particular award and nor will a transferee inherit the liability. What of other avenues? Could the receiver himself be liable? After all, he will have effected the dismissals. But he did dismiss, surely, as agent of the company only. And until relatively recently, the receiver, provided he was an agent of the company, would *not* be liable himself for employment obligations simply by continuing existing contracts (as opposed to personally entering into new ones).[14]

Some change in this area was brought by the Insolvency Act 1986. Under s 44(1)(b) and (2) of that Act an administrative receiver,[15] although now expressly deemed to be an agent (see above), may be personally liable on contracts of employment he 'adopts' after 14

---

12 An employer/receiver-orientated view (and a justification for reg 4) may be found in Mr David Waddington's introduction of the Transfer Regulations in the House of Commons (991 Hansard HC Deb col 678).

13 Literally, it seems, from one major accountancy firm's publication (Cork Gully's 'Phoenix feature' 1991 p 10, 'The *Litster* Effect – A Recipe for Disaster'.

14 *Nicoll v Cutts* [1985] BCLC 322, CA.

15 See Lightman and Moss, op cit, p 202 for the position other receivers appointed out of court.

days of his appointment. What does this mean? One commentator has expressed the view that a receiver does not 'adopt' a contract simply by continuing it.[16] But this may be far too sanguine,[17] adding little to the position prior to the 1986 Act[18] and being inconsistent with previous authorities on the concept of 'adoption' (which seem to imply non-repudiation).[19] A receiver may, therefore, have to repudiate (dismiss) on appointment and enter into fresh contracts or, in the view of one commentator, indicate within 14 days that he does not 'adopt' the contracts which are still the company's responsibility.[20] In the unreported case of *Re Specialised Mouldings Ltd*,[1] Harman J appears to have been disposed to approve the latter course of action, ie that a receiver simply has to inform employees that contracts are not adopted. It is therefore some authority against the so-called theory of 'adoption by omission'. But further and definitive case law is awaited.

What if the contract *is* adopted (which surely will be rare)? Will the receiver's liability be limited to wages after the period of adoption, or will he also be liable for dismissal compensation on termination? The former may often cause no problem in practice, whereas the latter probably would. For as two commentators have put it:

> 'There are few circumstances in which a receiver would wish to take the benefit of an employee's continuing services and deny him payment. A liability for redundancy payments and any other employee rights, on the other hand, could easily sweep up all the available assets leaving the debenture holder and other creditors with no return at all and the receiver with a personal liability that had not been of his own making.'[2]

A debate currently ensues as to whether a receiver who adopts a contract of employment is liable for accrued salary etc or, additionally, termination payments.[3] Legislative amendment may

---

16 *Lingard* p 77 para 6.23.
17 Cf *Lightman and Moss* p 206.
18 *Nicoll v Cutts* [1985] BCLC 322, CA.
19 See eg *Re Diesels and Components Pty Ltd* (1985) 9 ACLR 825; *Airlines Airspares Ltd v Handley Page Ltd* [1970] Ch 193, [1970] 1 All ER 29n; Mayson and French *A Practical Approach to Company Law* (8th edn) p 591.
20 *Mayson and French* p 591. See also *Tolley's Company Law*, para 15566.
 1 *Insolvency Law and Practice* July/August 1987, p 122.
 2 Withall and Conquest *Insolvency Law and Practice* ibid.
 3 The Insolvency Service of the Department of Trade and Industry, canvassed with interested parties in June 1991 the possibility of amendment of s 44 to provide for liability of a receiver for income of employees from the date of the receiver's appointment until the receivership has been completed, but not otherwise.

be necessary to settle the legal ambiguities in this area, whatever the solutions and views in practice.[4]

5 INFORMATION AND CONSULTATION OBLIGATIONS

As will be seen from Chapter 10, if there is a recognised trade union, certain information and consultation rights apply in respect of any proposed transfer. These apply also, if submitted, to transfers from insolvent companies. Where hiving down takes place (see above) there is a suggested technical problem in imposing the duty to inform/consult on a liquidator, receiver or administrator in this regard because of the wording of reg 4 of the Transfer Regulations. This matter is dealt with more fully in Chapter 10, but briefly, as will be seen from that chapter, the safer view is that (especially in view of *Litster*, as there is no equivalent of reg 4 in the Acquired Rights Directive (see above)) the duty applies in these circumstances just as in any other case.

---

4 In *Lightman and Moss* (at p 206) the authors seem to think that liability will attach only in relation to the period of adoption (ie presumably not for dismissal compensation), but this is not a natural reading. It is more likely dismissal liability would also attach. Finally, problems will arise as to why the draftsman in s 37(1)(a) and s 44(1)(b) dealing respectively with receivers and administrative receivers placed words allowing a receiver to exclude his personal liability close to the part dealing with ordinary contracts but *not* contracts of employment. Administrators may not have this problem. They are simply declared to be agents of the company (Insolvency Act 1986 s 14(5)).

Chapter 10

Business transfers and collective employment law

1 INTRODUCTION

In addition to potential liability to individuals on business transfers, the vendor and the purchaser must also be aware of obligations owed to recognised trade union representatives of individual employees involved.

Information and consultation obligations may be owed to such trade unions either under reg 10 of the Transfer Regulations or, if there are redundancy dismissals, additionally under s 99 of the EPA. These are discussed later in this chapter. An important reminder is also included at the end of this chapter (see Part 5) that failure to inform and consult on redundancies, whether with employees or their representatives, may have an effect on unfair dismissal liability to individual employees.[1]

But there are also two other collective employment law considerations involved if the Transfer Regulations apply. They are, under reg 6, the transfer of any existing collective agreement from the transferor to the transferee, and, under reg 9, the transfer of recognition by an employer of an independent trade union. The automatic transfer of these two matters parallels the automatic

---

1 Non-compliance with collective obligations can frequently affect an employer's liability in individual cases, particularly, for example, in the context of any procedure for handling redundancies. For failure to consult with an appropriate trade union may be one factor (not necessarily conclusive) which is relevant as to whether an individual dismissal is fair. See, in detail, Part 5 of this chapter and *Williams v Compair Maxam Ltd* [1982] ICR 156, [1982] IRLR 83, EAT; nb also, however, *Hollister v NFU* [1980] IRLR 196; *Hough v Leyland DAF Ltd* [1991] IRLR 194 (breach of an employer's obligations under s 99 does not automatically render an individual redundancy dismissal unfair). Also, under s 59 of the EP(C)A selection of an individual for redundancy in contravention of a customary or agreed procedure may make a redundancy dismissal automatically unfair (again, see Part 5 of this chapter). The customary or agreed procedure might well be contained in a collective agreement referred to in this chapter (see Part 2).

transfer of contracts of employment in the case of individuals.[2] The two issues of transfer of collective agreements and of recognition are linked, in that the trade union party to the collective agreement to be transferred under reg 6 must also be a recognised trade union.[3] Further, rights under the EPA to information and consultation on redundancies and under reg 10 of the Transfer Regulations (matters discussed in Ch 8) only apply in favour of a recognised trade union. Employment protection law, in the main, generally ignores any kind of employee representative other than a representative of a recognised trade union.[4] The concept of transfer of recognition may be, therefore, for that purpose at least, important.

2 THE TRANSFER OF COLLECTIVE AGREEMENTS

Regulation 6 of the Transfer Regulations provides that where, at the time of a relevant transfer, there exists a collective agreement made by or on behalf of the transferor with a trade union recognised by the transferor in respect of any employee whose contract is preserved by reg 5, the agreement, in its application to the employee, shall, after the transfer, have effect as if made by or on behalf of the transferee with the trade union. Also, anything done under or in connection with the agreement by or in relation to the transferor before the transfer shall, after the transfer, be deemed to have been done by (or in relation to) the transferee.[5] Discussion of this provision here falls into two parts. First, it must be examined whether the provision is of any real practical significance, having regard to the precarious legal status of collective agreements. Second, assuming that the provision is, in given cases, of practical significance, the drafting of the provision in the regulations poses a

---

2 And both depend on there being a relevant transfer under the Transfer Regulations.

3 Transfer Regulations reg 6(a).

4 All 'collective' rights under the EPA and the EP(C)A apply to independent trade unions or their representatives, eg disclosure of information (EPA s 17); procedure on handling redundancies (EPA ss 90–107); time off (EP(C)A s 27); information and consultation on transfers of undertakings (Transfer Regulations regs 10 and 11); cf the Collective Redundancies Directive (75/129) and the Acquired Rights Directive (77/187) which refer respectively to worker and employee 'representatives' (see respectively, Arts 2 and 6; but this means 'representatives' according to the laws or practice of member states (Acquired Rights Directive Art 2(c))).

5 Reg 6(a); the language is redolent of reg 5 concerning the consequence of transfer of contracts of employment.

number of questions as to whether its intention can fully be put into effect.

First, however, it is doubtful whether, on one level, this provision has any major practical significance in that, in all probability, a collective agreement may not be legally enforceable as between the parties to it (at least at the time of writing; a Green Paper: 'Industrial Relations in the 1990s' (HMSO, Cm 1602, July 1991) raised a possibility of change in this area in the future, however). The first pointer to the question of legal enforceability of a collective agreement should be s 18 of the Trade Union and Labour Relations Act 1974 (TULRA), in which there is a presumption that, in the case of a collective agreement entered into before 1 December 1971 or after 15 September 1974, it is not legally enforceable.[6] This presumption can be rebutted under s 18(1) if the agreement is in writing and also contains a provision which (however expressed) states that the parties do intend that the agreement shall be a legally enforceable contract.[7] This provision has been held to be a substantive rather than procedural matter so that, where the presumption under s 18 against enforceability applies, any agreement arrived at between the parties will not simply be an unenforceable contract, as one might expect, but not even a contract at all.[8] In labour law this last refinement will, for most purposes, be academic: it is enough that the contract is not *enforceable* to exclude legal action on the collective agreement.[9]

A contrary presumption applies to collective agreements entered into between 1 December 1971 and 15 September 1974. That is to say, the agreement is presumed to be legally *enforceable* unless there is a provision to contrary effect. In fact, during this period, which was governed by the Industrial Relations Act 1971 (IRA), the norm was for collective agreements to include what is referred to by some[10] as a 'TINALEA' clause ('this is not a legally enforceable agreement'). This characterised the concern of the trade unions at that time, both to show that they were not seen to be co-operating with the spirit of the IRA, and to ensure, beyond doubt, that these sort of agreements were not legally binding contracts. The legacy of the IRA has not been entirely forgotten. On occasions one can find the odd collective agreement entered into after 15 September 1974 which contains a TINALEA clause, even

---

6 TULRA s 18(1). *National Coal Board v NUM* [1986] ICR 736, [1986] IRLR 439.
7 TULRA s 18(1)(a) and (b).
8 *Monterosso Shipping Co Ltd v International Transport Workers' Federation* [1982] 3 All ER 841, [1982] ICR 675, CA.
9 TULRA s 18.
10 See Elias Napier and Wallington *Labour Law: Cases and Materials* (1980) p 85.

though, strictly speaking, such a clause is not necessary, since the parties may after 1 September 1974 rely upon the *presumption* against enforceability without express provision against enforceability.

Some collective agreements might not be covered by the presumption. The presumption only applies to collective agreements defined by s 30 of TULRA. The legal enforceability of agreements outside s 30, therefore, depends upon common law rules. The common law position as to the enforceability of collective agreements might be thought to be academic, now that TULRA retrospectively assumes pre-1971 agreements to be covered by the presumption against enforceability. But, despite, this, there could be a considerable number of modern agreements not governed by the statutory presumption. As stated, the statutory presumption under s 18 of TULRA applies only to a 'collective agreement' as defined by TULRA. In s 30 of TULRA, a collective agreement is defined as being 'any agreement or arrangement by or on behalf of one or more trade unions and one or more employers or employers' associations and relating to one or more of the matters mentioned in s 29(1)' of TULRA. The matters mentioned in s 29(1) are as follows:

'(a) terms and conditions of employment, or the physical conditions in which any workers are required to work;
(b) engagement or non-engagement, or termination or suspension of employment or the duties of employment, of one or more workers;
(c) allocation of work or the duties of employment as between workers or groups of workers;
(d) matters of discipline;
(e) the membership or non-membership of a trade union on the part of a worker;
(f) facilities for officials of trade unions; and
(g) machinery for negotiation or consultation, and other procedures, relating to any of the foregoing matters, including the recognition by employers or employers' associations of the right of a trade union to represent workers in any such negotiation or consultation or in the carrying out of such procedures.'

If the agreement does not deal with any of the above matters, it will not be covered by the statutory presumption against enforceability and the common law will apply. For example, an agreement concerning the way in which an employer might apply his capital resources, development of the business and so forth may be outside s 29 and, therefore, such an agreement would be a collective agreement not governed by the statutory presumption of non-enforceability. The common law position, therefore, merits consideration, even today.

At common law, the legal position of collective agreements is not clear. The leading case is *Ford Motor Co Ltd v Amalgamated Union of Engineering and Foundry Workers*.[11] In the context of the particular agreement considered by the court, the then prevailing academic opinion against enforceability and the particular aspirational wording of that agreement itself dissuaded the court from saying the agreement was legally enforceable. This may well be what a court would decide when looking at most agreements today, but the finding in the case is not conclusive[12] of the law and it cannot be *assumed* that the agreement will always be unenforceable. If it were non-aspirational in its wording and related to clear and specific matters, the collective agreement could take on the appearance of a commercial agreement and, therefore, be enforceable between the parties.[13] *A fortiori*, of course, if it were to contain a provision to that effect.

Much of this, though, might seem academic in relation to reg 6, for, as will be remembered, reg 6 only applies to transfer a *collective agreement*. A collective agreement under the regulations is defined as a collective agreement as defined in s 29 of TULRA, and an agreement outside the subject matter of s 29 (even if it were enforceable) would not be covered by reg 6. As to agreements satisfying the definition in TULRA, pre-1971 and post-1974 collective agreements will, as stated, be subject to a presumption against enforceability under s 18 of TULRA which, in practice, is rarely rebutted within the terms of s 18(1). Collective agreements entered into between 1971 and 1974 that fall under s 30 of TULRA are presumed to be enforceable but are, none the less, likely to have a TINALEA clause rebutting that presumption. In practice, then, most agreements, either by the wish of the parties or by legal presumption, will not be enforceable contracts. For those reasons, reg 6 may well have limited practical significance on the level of legal enforceability between the parties. And if a collective agreement is not enforceable, a transferee may, in theory, simply resile from its terms, with or without notice, with impunity.[14]

---

11 [1969] 2 QB 303, [1969] 2 All ER 481; see also *Stuart v Ministry of Defence* [1973] IRLR 143.

12 Hepple [1970] CLJ 122; Selwyn (1969) MLR 377.

13 See *Elias Napier and Wallington* p 82; the common law presumption of the intention to create legal relations in commercial agreements is discussed in Cheshire Fifoot and Furmston *The Law of Contract* (12th edn, 1991) p 116.

14 See also the repeal of the provisions in the EPA 1975 concerning enforcement of recognition claims discussed in Part 3 below, see pp 234–236. A good example of

On another, more practical level however, an employer should be aware of two possible consequences of a transfer under reg 6. First, a collective agreement, even though unenforceable as a contract between the parties, might confirm *recognition* of the trade union for collective bargaining purposes. This is a matter not dependent on a contract. If the agreement does therefore confirm recognition of the union, the union will probably still be recognised at the point of transfer itself and reg 9 will then apply, transferring recognition to a transferee (even though a transferee may subsequently resile from recognition) – see Part 3 below. Transfer of recognition would also trigger, if applicable, obligations under s 99 of the EPA (see also below) if there were a proposal by the transferee to implement redundancies (again before recognition had been withdrawn from by the new employer). Second, the collective agreement may contain redundancy selection procedures. Even if not enforceable by the union against the employer, these could comprise 'a customary arrangement or agreed procedure relating to redundancy' under s 59 of the EP(C)A. As will be explained in Part 5, s 59 of the EP(C)A modifies the general law of unfair dismissal by making redundancy dismissals in breach of such arrangement or procedure *automatically unfair* unless there are special reasons for justifying departure. Again, a purchaser should be careful of, and make full enquiries about, the terms of collective agreement lest he proceeds, wrongly, on the assumption he is free from such constraints in the future.[15]

And finally there is the individual employment law dimension. Even if collective agreements are unenforceable between the parties, they are not devoid of *all* legal significance. They may be a source of terms for an individual contract of employment.[16] This is so even if the collective agreement providing the source has expired

---

a post-1974 agreement which none the less contained an *express* rebuttal of legal intentions may be found in *Marley v Forward Trust Group Ltd* [1986] ICR 891, [1986] IRLR 369, CA.

15 In *Alexander v Standard Telephones & Cables Ltd (No 2)* [1991] IRLR 286 it was held that a redundancy selection procedure before the court was not incorporated into the individual contract of employment, thus preventing enforcement of its terms by the individual employee (see note 18, below). But this does not affect the point made about the relevance of the existence of the procedure for statutory unfair dismissal rules (s 59 of the EP(C)A) made in the text.

16 See Smith and Wood *Industrial Law* (4th edn) p 149 et seq. In so far as the Court of Appeal in *Gascol Conversions Ltd v Mercer* [1974] ICR 420, [1974] IRLR 155 suggested that because a collective agreement was binding in honour only it could not provide a source of terms for an individual contract, this is now thought to be wrong (see Elias Napier and Wallington *Labour Law: Cases and Materials* p 414 and *Marley v Forward Trust Group Ltd* [1986] ICR 891, [1986] IRLR 369, CA).

or been resiled from.[17] All this is subject to the suitability of terms in the collective agreement for transfer into the individual contract[18] and a legal 'bridge' existing between the collective agreement and the individual contract.[19] But it would seem that reg 6 is unnecessary to effect transfer of the terms so incorporated from a collective agreement into an individual contract from a transferor to a transferee, since reg 5 transfers any individual contract from the transferor to the transferee in circumstances where reg 6 applies (reg 6

---

17 *Morris v Bailey Ltd* [1969] 2 Lloyd's Rep 215, CA; *Burroughs Machines Ltd v Timmoney* [1977] IRLR 404; *Gibbons v Associated British Ports* [1985] IRLR 376; *Marley v Forward Trust Group Ltd* [1986] ICR 891, [1986] IRLR 369, CA.

18 See *Young v Canadian Northern Railway Co* [1931] AC 83; *British Leyland (UK) Ltd v McQuilken* [1978] IRLR 245; *Tadd v Eastwood and Daily Telegraph Ltd* [1983] IRLR 320; affd [1985] ICR 132, [1985] IRLR 119, CA (on different grounds), *Gallagher v Post Office* [1970] 3 All ER 712; *Camden Exhibition and Display Ltd v Lynott* [1966] 1 QB 555, [1965] 3 All ER 28, CA. In general, the courts are more likely to hold that substantive provisions of a collective agreement such as terms about hours and pay are more appropriate for incorporation than procedural or collective matters. One of the more recent discussions on the question of suitability of terms for incorporation is *National Coal Board v National Union of Mineworkers* [1986] ICR 736, [1986] IRLR 439. That case arose from the formation of the breakaway trade union, the Union of Democratic Mineworkers. The UDM then claimed the right to negotiate directly with the NCB, cutting out the NUM in certain areas. A 1946 agreement granted exclusive recognition rights to the NUM. The NUM sought to enforce the exclusive rights granted by the 1946 agreement. The court held, however, that the 1946 agreement was a collective agreement caught by s 18 of TULRA (and in any event it had been terminated by the NCB). The NUM then argued that the relevant provisions of the 1946 agreement were incorporated into individual employees' contracts and so enforceable by them. The court held that although provisions of a collective agreement incorporated into individual contracts could survive termination of the collective agreement, the procedural provisions of the 1946 agreement, including the recognition provision, were intended to resolve industrial disputes between employer and union and thus were not intended to be enforceable between the NCB and its individual employees. As stated above (note 15), in *Alexander v Standard Telephones and Cables Ltd (No 2)* [1991] IRLR 286 Hobhouse J held that a redundancy selection procedure with provisions respecting seniority in the collective agreement under consideration was not incorporated into individual contracts of employment so as to create a contractual right to 'last in first out' on redundancy. The learned judge considered that because the selection criterion was included in the context of a procedure agreement it was not appropriate for incorporation. The decision is not, however, above criticism (see [1991] IRLR p 282 (editorial)).

19 See *Edwards v Skyways Ltd* [1964] 1 All ER 494, [1964] 1 WLR 349; *Land v West Yorkshire Metropolitan County Council* [1979] ICR 452; [1979] IRLR 174, EAT per Kilner Brown J; revsd [1981] ICR 334, [1981] IRLR 87, CA (on a different issue); cf *Singh v British Steel Corpn* [1974] IRLR 131; *National Coal Board v Galley* [1958] 1 All ER 91, [1958] 1 WLR 16, CA; *Gascol Conversions Ltd v Mercer* [1974] ICR 420, [1974] IRLR 155, CA.

only applies in respect of any employees whose contract of employment is preserved by reg 5 – see below).

When reg 6 applies, whether or not the collective agreement is legally enforceable between the parties (and, as discussed, the agreement will usually not be enforceable between the parties) the position is as follows. The collective agreement would be transferred from the transferor to the transferee and would be deemed to be made as if between the transferee and the appropriate trade union. It is to be noted here that reg 6 applies to an agreement between an *employer* and a *trade union*. For the regulation to apply, this must be a trade union *recognised* by the employer (*recognised* here meaning recognised for the purpose of collective bargaining, i e for one or more of the matters set out in s 29 above for recognition – see the discussion in Part IV below).

If reg 6 bites, how effective is it in transferring an agreement to a transferee? It is stated[20] that the agreement shall be transferred in its application in relation to an employee whose contract is preserved by reg 5(1).

Does this mean that the provisions of the collective agreement are enforceable against the transferee only in so far as they relate to matters concerning the *individual* employment relationship? In other words, if there are procedural or collective matters, would they not be covered by reg 6? If that is right, reg 6, even if applicable, adds very little to reg 5. This restrictive view is at least a possible interpretation of reg 6 because of the emphasised words '*its application in relation to the [transferred] employee*'. This would denude reg 6, if correct. But surely, even *collective* matters can relate to an individual employee (albeit sometimes indirectly, e g the duty to inform and consult with trade unions over dismissals, redundancy planning, and so forth). So, a better view would be that reg 6 can apply to a provision of a collective agreement, even if it is not incorporated into an individual contract of employment. Another explanation of the emphasised words is that they merely *identify* the employees to whom the transferred agreement relates, i e those employees transferred under reg 5.

One question that therefore arises from that point is whether the collective agreement transferred has application *only* to employees transferred under reg 5 or whether it is wider and covers any subsequently recruited employees even if they are engaged on different terms. In fact, as stated, reg 6 provides that the collective agreement is only transferred in its application in relation to an employee

---

20 Reg 6(a).

whose contract is preserved by reg 5 and not in relation to other, subsequent, employees.

That this was the intention of Art 3 of the Acquired Rights Directive seems to be confirmed by the European Court decision of *Landsorganisationen i Danmark v Ny Molle Kro*.[1] In that case there was, in 1981, a transfer covered by the domestic business transfer legislation in Denmark (Law No 111 of 21 March 1979) which, in compliance with the directive, transfers, inter alia, a subsisting collective agreement from a transferor to a transferee. A new employee, Mrs Hansen, was engaged by the business two years later, in 1983. She was engaged under terms which were less favourable than those which operated under the collective agreement which had been transferred in 1981. Did the terms of the collective agreement which were transferred to the transferee in 1981 apply to cover the employee who was not engaged until 1983? Article 3(2) provides 'the transferee shall continue to observe the terms and conditions agreed in any collective agreement on the same terms applicable to the transferor under that agreement'. It was held this must be interpreted as meaning that the directive does not require the transferee to continue to observe the working conditions agreed under a collective agreement with regard to workers who are not employees of the undertaking at the date of transfer. As Mrs Hansen was recruited two years later, the employer did not have to apply the terms of the inherited collective agreement in her favour. It seems, therefore, that reg 6 of the Transfer Regulations is in line with our European obligations.

Finally, it is provided that reg 6(b) transfers any 'order' made in respect of a collective agreement in its application in relation to an employee transferred. This presumably is a reference to any possible order by the Central Arbitration Committee under the now repealed Sch 11 to the EPA (which extended collectively agreed terms and conditions in some situations to all employers in an 'industry' in a 'district').[2] Since this provision has now been repealed, reg 6(b) has limited, or no, effect unless any comparable provision is now or subsequently enacted.[3]

3 TRANSFER OF RECOGNITION

Under reg 9 of the Transfer Regulations it is provided that, upon a relevant transfer, and provided that the undertaking or part of the

---

1 [1989] ICR 330, [1989] IRLR 37.
2 Sch 11 to the EPA.
3 Repealed by the Employment Act 1980.

undertaking transferred maintains an identity 'distinct from the remainder of the transferee's undertaking', recognition of an independent trade union is transferred from the transferor to the transferee, in respect of any description of employees who in consequence of the transfer become employees of the transferee. It is expressly provided that any agreement for recognition may be varied or rescinded after the transfer (reg 9(2)(b)).

Regulation 9 seems wider than reg 6, in that recognition is transferred in relation to all employees of such description who, *in consequence* of the transfer, become employees of the transferee. It does not follow from reg 9 that they have to be employees protected by reg 5, ie employed actually (or deemed to be so by virtue of *Litster v Forth Dry Dock & Engineering Co Ltd* (see Ch 7)) at the time of transfer (although, conversely, it can also be argued that an employee who, 'in consequence of the transfer', becomes an employee of the transferee probably does so in the same circumstances as envisaged by reg 5 as explained in *Litster*; if so, the point made here involves a distinction without a difference).

However, at first glance, it can be argued again that this provision, as with reg 6, has limited practical effect. For there is now no means of enforcing recognition by an employer of an independent trade union following the repeal of ss 11–16 of the EPA 1975 by the Employment Act 1980.[4] Under those now repealed provisions, ACAS had a statutory function whereby it might recommend recognition, following which an employer might legally be obliged to recognise an independent trade union.[5] As this is now no longer the law, an employer can, with legal impunity, resile from an express recognition agreement or from an understanding, express or implied, concerning recognition.[6] Also, very frequently it may not be possible to establish that the transferred undertaking maintains a distinct identity from the rest of the transferee's undertaking, especially when harmonisation after the transfer not only of employee terms and conditions but also trading methods etc is common. This question will be, presumably, a question of fact.

However, although this regulation is far from perfect, it may vitally protect and preserve the rights of an independent recognised

---

4 Employment Act 1980 s 19. And reg 9(2)(b) (referred to above) expressly allows variation or rescission of the transferred agreement.

5 A recognition award made by ACAS was enforceable by the imposition of employees' collective claims by order of the Central Arbitration Committee in the event of employer non-cooperation.

6 The phenomenon of derecognition is observed by Hepple and Byre [1989] ILJ 129 and Towers [1988] IRJ 181. Cf Morris and Archer *Trade Unions, Employers and the Law* para 5.26, n 4.

trade union to be consulted and informed under s 99 of the EPA[7] on business transfer dismissals which take place more or less at the time of or at the point of transfer itself. At the point of transfer, a potential transferee would, it is submitted, in practice, have no time to resile from the transferred recognition agreement and would, if dismissals were effected at that time, have to observe the information and consultation provisions concerned (EPA s 99), at this stage at least.

4 INFORMATION AND CONSULTATION UNDER THE TRANSFER REGULATIONS

A business transfer caught by the Transfer Regulations triggers information and possibly consultation obligations in favour of any independent recognised trade union. Under the Transfer Regulations, long enough before[8] a relevant transfer[9] to enable consultation to take place between an employer and representatives of an independent recognised[10] trade union, the employer has, under reg 10(2), to inform representatives of:

(a) the fact that the relevant transfer is to take place, when, approximately, it is to take place and the reasons for it; and

---

7 For example, redundancy dismissals may be proposed by the transferee once he has acquired a new workforce.

8 'Long enough before' is not defined. It is obviously a question of fact. Perhaps a reasonable period may be implied. Some help may be gained from an analogy with *NUT v Avon County Council* [1978] ICR 626, [1978] IRLR 55, a case on s 99 of the EPA (see below). Art 6 of the Directive (in the light of which reg 10 should be construed) provides for performance of the obligation 'in good time'.

9 'A relevant transfer' involves the question of when this takes place. The timing of a relevant transfer is relevant to the condition that information must be supplied 'long enough before' the transfer to allow consultation to take place (see note 8, above). As will be seen from Ch 4, the weight of judicial opinion favours *completion* of a transfer as opposed to a preceding exchange of contracts. Caveats to that are that the event of a transfer is a question of fact and particularly following *Dabell v Vale Industrial Services (Nottingham) Ltd* [1988] IRLR 439 it can occur without completion of legal formalities if a factual assumption of responsibilities for management has taken place; and, second, the interpretation of reg 10 by the EAT in *Banking Insurance and Finance Union v Barclays Bank plc* [1987] ICR 495 means that the duty under reg 10 involves a proposed or planned transfer even if it eventually does not take place (see below).

10 See discussion at pp 254–255 below.

(b) the legal, economic and social implications[11] of the transfer for the affected employees; and

(c) the measures which he envisages he will, in connection with the transfer, take in relation to those employees, or if he envisages that no such measures will be taken, that fact; and

(d) if the employer is the transferor, the measures which the transferee envisages he will, in connection with the transfer, take in relation to such of those employees as by virtue of reg 5 above, become employees of the transferee after the transfer or, if he envisages that no measures will be so taken, that fact.[12]

It is not express in reg 10 that the information has to be supplied in *writing* (cf the obligations under s 99 of the EPA, discussed in Part 5 (multiple redundancies)). But in view of the provisions of reg 10(4) which state:

'The information which is to be given to the representatives of a trade union under this Regulation shall be delivered to them, or sent by post to an address notified by them to the employer, or sent by post to the union at the address of its head or main office,'

this is surely to be implied.[13]

The obligation to inform and consult does not apply to non-business transfers, i e sales of companies by way of disposal of share capital.[14] Nor does it apply in relation to companies which are associated with the company selling its business. So union representatives of employees employed by a holding company, or a service company, which lends out those employees' services to a subsidiary, do not have to be informed or consulted when the business of that subsidiary is sold. The non-application of the Transfer Regulations and (therefore also reg 10) to certain complex transfers within a group of companies is well illustrated by *Banking Insurance and Finance Union v Barclays Bank plc*.[15] In this case Barclays Bank plc decided to set up a new bank, Barclays De Zoete Wedd (BZW), to which Barclays' business activity in Barclays

---

11 In *NALGO v British Waterways Board* COIT 11548/88/LN/A the industrial tribunal considered that the union was, under this head, entitled to sufficient information about the new employer to enable it to assess its worth.
12 Reg 10(2).
13 To be noted is the industrial tribunal decision in *NALGO v British Waterways Board* COIT 11548/88/LN/A where the view of the tribunal was that the information had to be supplied in writing.
14 *TGWU v BICC Bryce Capacitors Ltd* COIT 33462/84.
15 [1987] ICR 495.

Merchant Bank Ltd (BMB) and other subsidiaries would be transferred. But the employees working for BMB were not employed by BMB, but by Barclays. And they were, in any event, transferred to a new service company formed to lend their labour to BZW, called Barclays de Zoete Wedd (Services) (BZW/S). It was held that there was no relevant transfer on their transfer to BZW/S and their trade union need not be consulted. The union's argument that reg 10 applied in its favour when the business of associated companies was transferred was not accepted (there was probably a business transfer from BMB to BZW and these companies were, it is presumed, associated with Barclays and BZW/S).

At least one potential loophole in reg 10 was plugged in *Banking Insurance and Finance Union v Barclays Bank plc*, however. One industrial tribunal had previously taken the view that, because reg 10(2)(a) requires information to be given about the fact that the transfer *is* to take place, the information obligation (and, therefore, also the consultation obligation if measures are envisaged, discussed later) was not triggered until the actual transfer *had* more or less taken place.[16] Such an interpretation would have rendered the regulation almost impotent and would have meant there would be no sanction for failing to inform (and consult) about a *proposed* transfer that, in the end, happened not to take place. But the EAT in *Banking Insurance and Finance Union v Barclays Bank plc* held that the duty to inform applies also to a 'proposed' transfer.[17]

It is relevant to note that the duty to inform applies to trade union representatives of any 'affected employee', ie not only those employees employed in the undertaking or the part of the undertaking to be transferred but also to those employees who may be affected in some other way by the transfer or by measures taken in connection with it.[18] The duty is on an 'employer',[19] and this may be either a transferor or a transferee. Although, commonly, the transferor will be the employer charged with performing the duty, a transferee could also be required to observe certain aspects of the obligations concerned. For example, the duty could extend to information to trade union representatives about existing employees of a transferee's own business who may be affected by an acquisition; and, under reg 10(3), a transferee has to give the transferor information to enable the transferor to provide the information under (d) above.

---

16 *NATTKE v Rank Leisure Ltd* COIT 1388/134.
17 [1987] ICR 495.
18 Reg 10(1).
19 Ibid.

In addition to the information obligation, where an employer of any affected employees envisages that he will, in connection with the transfer, be taking 'measures' in relation to any such employees of a description in respect of which the independent trade union is recognised, he has to enter into consultations with that trade union.[20]

In the course of those consultations, the employer has to consider any representations made by the trade union and to reply to those representations and, if he rejects any of those representations, state his reasons. A 'special circumstances' defence similar to that under s 99 of the EPA applies.[1] Under this, the employer has both to show that there were special circumstances which rendered it not reasonably practicable for him to perform the duty *and* that he took all such steps towards its performance as were reasonably practicable in those circumstances.[2] But it seems to be for the employer to prove the 'special circumstances' defence if appropriate.[3] The case law on 'special circumstances' under s 99 of the EPA (multiple redundancies) would seem to be relevant. The 'special circumstances' defence in relation to s 99 of the EPA is discussed in Part 5. It will be seen that it is sparingly applied in relation to s 99. It remains to be seen, however, whether the defence will be applied more willingly in favour of employers in a business transfer situation due to the speed with which such transfer can take place and because, often, of the fact that it is to occur is surrounded by secrecy.

An industrial tribunal in *NATTKE v Rank Leisure Ltd*[4] suggested that the speed and urgency with which a transaction had to be completed *could* be a special circumstance under reg 10(7) (although on the facts of that case, the employer had still not taken all the steps reasonably practicable in the circumstances towards compliance). Could secrecy be a special circumstance also? A defaulting employer could argue that the circumstances of a business transfer, as opposed to a general redundancy exercise outside the context of a business transfer, made the need for secrecy a special circumstance. On the other hand, if the defence of secrecy were accepted as a general principle, it would arguably be applicable in many cases and therefore emasculate reg 10. The courts might not be willing to allow that. And, interestingly, Millett J in

---

20 Reg 10(5).
 1 Reg 11(2).
 2 Reg 11(2)(a), (b).
 3 Regs 11(2) and 11(3).
 4 COIT 1388/134.

Institution of Professional Civil Servants v Secretary of State for Defence[5] considered that a transferee could not supply information to a transferor for the purposes of allowing a transferor to communicate information to unions about a transferee's measures (reg 10(3)) under cover of confidentiality to prevent the information being published.[6] Also, there is no equivalent of the 'special circumstances' defence in the Acquired Rights Directive. The purposive approach to the Transfer Regulations marked by *Litster* (see Ch 7) should, it is submitted, require the courts to treat the defence with some circumspection as it clearly diminishes the rights envisaged by the directive.

Unfortunately, in contrast to the EPA 1975, in the context of multiple redundancies, there is no minimum period over which consultation has to take place (the EPA provides for 90 days in the largest cases, 30 days in smaller cases and at the earliest opportunity in any event). The EAT in *NUT v Avon County Council*[7] did consider that, for the purposes of the EPA, consultation had also to be 'meaningful'. It would be helpful if this gloss were imported into provisions of the Transfer Regulations. Finally, as stated towards the end of this discussion, Art 6(2) of the directive requires consultation 'with a view to *seeking* agreement'. This is a further, persuasive, argument for putting some flesh on the skeleton of reg 10.[8]

Also, under the Transfer Regulations (and again in contrast to the EPA) there is only a duty to consult where the employer envisages he will *take measures*. If none is proposed, then no consultation need take place.[9] This restrictive interpretation was assumed to be correct by Millett J in *Institution of Professional Civil Servants v Secretary of State for Defence*.[10] He was, however, critical of it. For, in his view, unions might well wish to be consulted as much when measures were not envisaged as when they were. Unfortunately unions in such a position are not catered for by reg 10.

The *Institution of Professional Civil Servants* case also provides some useful viewpoints on the scope of words such as 'measures'

---

5 [1987] 3 CMLR 35, [1987] IRLR 373.
6 In *NALGO v British Waterways Board* COIT 11548/88/LN/A the industrial tribunal considered that failure to supply dates of birth and length of service of members of staff on grounds of confidentiality could not be excused as a 'special circumstance'.
7 [1978] ICR 626, [1978] IRLR 55. The test adopted by the industrial tribunal in *NALGO v British Waterways Board* COIT 11548/88/LN/A included the glosses 'effective' and 'meaningful' consultation.
8 See Ch 6.
9 *NATTKE v Rank Leisure Ltd* COIT 1388/134. And see Art 6(2) of the directive.
10 [1987] 3 CMLR 35, [1987] IRLR 373.

and other matters. This was a case arising under the Dockyard Services Act 1986 (see Ch 4) involving the privatisation of two royal dockyards at Rosyth and Devonport which were placed under commercial management on 6 April 1987 by the transfer of the dockyards to private concerns.

The Dockyard Services Act 1986 more or less repeated the provisions of reg 10 of the Transfer Regulations about consultation and information. The trade union brought an action in the High Court complaining that the minister had not complied with his duty to inform and consult under the Dockyard Services Act. As the case concerns wording similar to reg 10 of the Transfer Regulations it is useful for the purposes of interpreting that regulation.

The outcome of the case was that the learned judge concluded that the Secretary of State had taken all reasonable steps to inform the workforce and their representatives and to consult the unions on the introduction of commercial management and had not confined himself to the bare performance of his statutory obligations. If it were the case that any consultation was incomplete it was due to the obstructive attitude of the unions to the transfer to commercial management. The union's claim therefore failed.

In the course of his judgment, Millett J passed comment on a number of matters. First, as stated above, it was confirmed that there is only a duty to consult when measures are envisaged. Illogical though this was, it was a natural reading of the Act (and, hence, the Regulations). What, then, did 'measures' mean?[11] 'Measures' according to Millett J was a

'. . . word of the widest import, and includes any action, step or arrangement, while "envisages" simply means "visualises" or "foresees". Despite the width of these words it is clear that manpower projections are not measures at all; though positive steps to achieve planned reductions in manpower levels otherwise than through natural wastage would be.'[12]

The learned judge was also of the view that for the need to consult to arise the employer must have formulated some definite plan or proposal which it had in mind to implement. And this could be a

---

11 On 'measures' see, by way of illustration, *NALGO v British Waterways Board* COIT 11548/88/LN/A.

12 [1987] 3 CMLR 35. It is also interesting to speculate whether an employer would have to consult about measures a transferee envisages in relation to pension rights, which are invariably affected by a change of employer. One argument is that as reg 7 excludes regs 5 and 6 in respect of occupational pension schemes there is no need to consult. Another view (see here *MSF v RHP Bearings Ltd* COIT/603/80 (although by concession)) is that reg 7 has no bearing on the words of reg 10. The latter is certainly arguable.

developing situation: for reasons beyond an employer's control measures might only be envisaged at a late stage. In that case, if there was then insufficient time for effective consultations to take place before the transfer, an employer could not be criticised.

Is consultation confined to the subject matter of the proposed measures? The information required to be provided is quite wide-ranging (see paras (a) to (d)). Does an employer also have to consult about these items as well as any measures that the transferee is proposing to take? The legal doubt arose because the preamble to the list of information that had to be provided under the Dockyard Services Act (and the same is the case under reg 10 of the Transfer Regulations, *mutatis mutandis*) reads:

'(6) Long enough before the transfer to enable consultations to take place between the Secretary of State and the representatives of the independent trade unions recognised by him in respect of the employees, the Secretary of State shall, in accordance with sub-section (13) below, inform those representatives of –'.

Did this mean that consultation also has to take place about items (a) to (d) as well as any measures proposed? Surely not, Millett J said:

'Parliament could hardly have intended to compel the employer in the private sector to consult the unions on the desirability of the transfer itself or the sufficiency of the reasons for it. These are matters of business policy for the transferring employer to decide and the unions cannot expect to participate in the decision.'

What about the insertion of the word 'consultation' here though? Millett J added:

'The reconciliation in my view is this: the consultations referred to in the opening words of sub-s (6) [see reg 10(2) of the Transfer Regulations] are *voluntary* consultations which the unions may seek on any topic once they have the requisite information, but which the transferring employer is not compelled to grant if he chooses not to do so. The only consultations which he is *obliged* by law to enter into are those referred to in sub-s (8) [see reg 10(5) of the Transfer Regulations].'

(I e when measures are proposed: see reg 10(5) of the Transfer Regulations.)

Compensation for breach is also more modest than under the EPA. This cannot, under the Transfer Regulations, exceed *two weeks' pay* for each employee in question, but has to be, within that maximum, such sum as the tribunal considers just and equitable having regard to the seriousness of the failure of the employer to comply with his duty.[13] A considerably greater maximum applies under the EPA.[14] Any compensation awarded to an employee under reg 11 reduces the amount payable to him under the EPA.[15] It also reduces any liability of an employer under or in respect of a breach of the contract of employment in respect of a period falling within the protected period under an EPA award.[16] Conversely any remuneration payable[17] and any payment made to an employee by an employer under, or by way of damages for breach of the employment contract[18] reduces the amount of compensation due for breach of reg 10, under reg 11. This, it can be seen, is hardly generous. All in all these provisions appear anodyne when compared with those under s 99 of the EPA, which themselves are far from perfect.[19]

If the default relates to the failure to inform or consult concerning the measures which the transferee might take in relation to the transfer, the transferor may, after he has given notice to the transferee of this, join the transferee into the industrial tribunal proceedings. And, if the industrial tribunal considers that it was not reasonably practicable for the transferor to comply with his obligations because of lack of information supplied by the transferee, the industrial tribunal may require the transferee to pay the appropriate compensation instead of the transferor.[20]

The comments made above on the weakness of the information/consultation provisions lead naturally to the question of what is the effect, if any, of *Litster v Forth Dry Dock & Engineering Co Ltd*[1] and its purposive approach to the Transfer Regulations on the consultation and information obligations generally? In the main, the obligations under reg 10 are regarded as ineffectual and far from impressive. This is partly due to the weakness inherent in the drafting of regs 10 and 11. But the wording of reg 10 differs from the Acquired Rights Directive in a number of respects. First, as stated, the directive contains no 'special circumstances' defence. Second, the poor financial remedy is hardly in keeping with the spirit of the directive. The principle in *Von Colson and Kamann v Land Nordrhein-Westfalen*[2] that the effective transposition of a

---

13 Reg 11(11).
14 EPA s 101.
15 Reg 11(7)(a).
16 Reg 11(7)(a).
17 Reg 11(7)(b).
18 Reg 11(7)(b).
19 See Freedland (1976) ILJ 24.
20 Reg 11(3) and (4).
 1 [1989] ICR 341, [1989] IRLR 161.
 2 [1984] ECR 1891, [1986] 2 CMLR 430.

directive requires also effective remedies seems clearly transgressed by reg 11.[3] Third, the failure to allow consultation in favour of worker representatives other than recognised trade unions in an age of de-recognition by employers is also, arguably, a departure from the intention of the directive.[4]

Another point, as mentioned above, is that consultation, under Art 6(2) of the directive, has to be *with a view to seeking agreement*. It has been thought that this implies at the very least a duty to bargain in good faith and it certainly seems to involve a higher duty than under the Transfer Regulations which do not expressly oblige the employer to consult with any view to reaching agreement.

After *Litster*[5] and *Pickstone v Freemans plc*,[6] discussed at length earlier (see Ch 7) it seems that a court or tribunal hearing a case under the information and consultation provisions of the Transfer Regulations is entitled to give the regulations a purposive construction. Could it, for example, read into the Transfer Regulation words such as 'with a view to seeking agreement' that appear in the directive in order to marry them with our European obligations? If this were the case, the employers' obligations under reg 10 would certainly be more real than they are at present.

The duty on employers in hiving down cases

The concept of hiving down has been discussed in Chapter 9. In that chapter we adverted to a possible problem in applying reg 10 in such

---

3 How can the award of two weeks' pay be an effective remedy? And, as stated, this is a maximum. In *NALGO v British Waterways Board* COIT 11548/88/LN/A the award was £25 per affected employee, notwithstanding a number of breaches of the provisions of reg 10 on the part of the employer.

4 The collective obligations to inform/consult are, under the directive, applicable to employee 'representatives'. But if there are under the UK system no representatives because of the absence of compulsory recognition, it is hard to see how compliance with the directive can occur. (On the debate on de-recognition, see p 235, n 6.) Against this, however, is Art 3 of the directive, which states: 'Member states may provide that where there are no representatives of the employees in an undertaking or business, the employees concerned must be informed in advance when a transfer within the meaning of Art 1(1) is about to take place.' The permissive nature of this provision does suggest that it was contemplated that there could be an aristocracy of employees with employee representatives entitled to information/consultation and others not, unless member states choose to provide otherwise. On the future of recognition in UK law see Ewing (1990) ILJ 209. As a pointer to change, there is currently a proposal to amend Directive 75/129 on redundancies (p 246, n 13). It is likely that change will correspondingly be proposed, in due course, to Directive 77/189.

5 [1989] ICR 341, [1989] IRLR 161.

6 [1989] AC 66, [1988] 2 All ER 803.

circumstances.[7] The problem is this.The effect of reg 4 when the business of an insolvent company is transferred to a subsidiary company (the sale vehicle) is to postpone the transfer that would obviously otherwise take place until the point when either the share capital of the subsidiary is sold or the subsidiary itself transfers the business. But the obligation to inform/consult only applies to an 'affected employee' of either the transferor or transferee. By the time of this deemed postponed transfer, the employees may not be employed by the subsidiary which has the power to dispose of the business having been kept back by the receiver and employed by the insolvent company. It is therefore at least arguable that as the transferor (the subsidiary) is not the employer of the employees, no obligation to inform or consult applies in relation to the receiver of the insolvent company. If this interpretation were correct it would deny the effect of reg 10 in favour of trade unions where a receiver, administrator or liquidator was selling the business via the process of hiving down. However, it must be borne in mind that after *Litster*[8] the courts will take a purposive approach to the Transfer Regulations, including reg 4 (which has no parallel in the Acquired Rights Directive) and therefore it is submitted that this argument, though ingenious, would be unsafe to rely upon if advising a receiver, administrator or liquidator on his obligations under reg 10.

The inter-relationship between reg 11 and reg 5 of the Transfer Regulations

Finally, it remains to be considered whether liability for an award under reg 11 of the Transfer Regulations is likely to be inherited by a transferee by virtue of the automatic transfer of employment obligations under reg 5 of the Transfer Regulations. As will be considered below, in *Angus Jowett & Co Ltd v National Union of Tailors and Garment Workers*,[9] the EAT (Beldam J presiding) held that liability to a trade union in respect of a protective award for breach of s 99 was not automatically transferred to a transferee under reg 5. The question whether an employee's individual entitlement under such award was not in question before the EAT. The possibility of transfer of individual entitlement under an award is discussed in Part 5 and the conclusion reached that transfer might

---

7 The argument is rehearsed in *IDS Employment Law Handbook* 47, *Transfer of Undertakings* pp 164–165.
8 [1989] ICR 341, [1989] IRLR 161.
9 [1985] ICR 646, [1985] IRLR 326.

be possible. The same principles should apply in relation to reg 10. Liability to the trade union under reg 11 should, according to the EAT, not be passed to a transferee because the matter is a collective one and *not* one 'under or in connection with [an employment] contract'. *Quaere*, however, whether this would prevent individual employee entitlement under that award passing to a transferee.

5 INFORMATION AND CONSULTATION OBLIGATIONS ON REDUNDANCIES UNDER THE EMPLOYMENT PROTECTION ACT 1975

If, before or after a transfer of a business, a transferor or transferee implements redundancy dismissals, the provisions of s 99 of the EPA concerning information to and consultation with trade unions may be triggered.[10] If the Transfer Regulations apply on the sale of the business, there will be no dismissals merely by reason of the transfer *itself*. But dismissals often occur prior to or after the sale as a cost-cutting or re-organisational exercise. Of course, on or before a transfer of a business to which the Transfer Regulations apply, reg 10 of the Transfer Regulations, concerning information to, and consultation with, trade unions on transfers may apply;[11] but that is a different matter and one which has already been discussed. In this part we discuss the EPA information/consultation obligations on dismissal, the duty to notify the Department of Employment in such circumstances, and the inter-relationship between the duty to inform and consult and the question of fairness of redundancy dismissals for the purposes of unfair dismissal.

(i) Information and consultation obligations in favour of trade unions

The Employment Protection Act 1975 requires an employer to inform and consult with representatives of an independent recognised trade union before implementation of redundancies.[12] These provisions are intended to implement the EC Council Directive 75/129 of 17 February 1975 (the 'Collective Redundancies Directive').[13]

---

10 EPA ss 99–107.
11 Transfer Regulations regs 10 and 11.
12 EPA s 99.
13 See Freedland (1976) ILJ 24, for comment. After *Litster v Forth Dry Dock & Engineering Co Ltd* [1989] ICR 341, [1969] IRLR 161 it should be open for a

Under s 99 of the EPA, an employer proposing[14] to dismiss as redundant any employee of a description in respect of which an

---

tribunal or court to construe s 99 in the light of Directive 75/129 where necessary. Finally the EC Commission submitted a proposal in November 1991 for a directive amending Directive 75/129. Briefly, the changes made are to ensure that information and consultation obligations apply where decisions on redundancies in one member state are taken by a controlling body based in a different member state (providing also that it will be no defence that failure to supply information was because the controlling body has not supplied the information in time); and to extend information and consultation rights to crews of sea-going vessels. Also, member states need not, under the proposal, provide for workers' representatives in establishments ordinarily employing fewer than 50 workers but in such cases the employer would be required to supply the information direct to the workers. Finally (and controversially for the UK) member states are, under the proposal, to make available judicial procedures for declaring null and void any dismissals effected in breach of the directive's requirements. It would seem only logical to make appropriate proposals for amendment in due course to Directive 77/187 and it is thought that this is likely.

14 'Proposing to dismiss' means something approaching a decision to dismiss. The narrow view of 'proposal' means that consultation does not have to begin until a fairly advanced stage of the exercise. See also *NALGO v National Travel (Midlands) Ltd* [1978] ICR 598; *Association of Patternmakers and Allied Crafts v Kirvin Ltd* [1978] IRLR 318; *NUPE v General Cleaning Contractors* [1976] IRLR 362; *USDAW v Leancut Bacon Ltd* [1981] IRLR 295. The EC Collective Redundancies Directive 75/129 which s 99 implements refers to a duty to consult employee representatives arising when collective redundancies are *contemplated* (Art 2). (This contrasts with the duty to inform the public authorities of *projected* redundancies (Art 3).) It is argued in *Harvey on Industrial Relations and Employment Law* (III, 373) that the decision of the European Court in *Dansk Metalarbejderforbund and Specialarbejderforbundet i Danmark v Nielsen & Søn, Maskinfabrik A/S (in liquidation)*: 284/83 [1986] 1 CMLR 91 seems to support a view that the duty under Art 2 to consult when redundancies are *contemplated* arises at an earlier stage than it has been interpreted as arising in domestic law under s 99 (which refers to a *proposal*). Principally, this is because the Advocate-General (Herr Carl Otto Lenz), when discussing the distinction between the obligation to inform the authorities of *projected* redundancies under Art 3 and the obligation to inform the employee representatives where redundancies are *contemplated* under Art 2, concluded that notice to the authorities must be given where an employer 'actually plans to make redundancies' whereas representatives of workers must be consulted 'at an earlier stage'. How much earlier is not clear. But if the meaning of the directive is wider than the interpretation in case law under s 99 so far it is probable that future cases could take into account that wider view and apply it to our domestic law. It is necessary to interpret English legislation enacting European legislation to make it, whenever possible, conform with European legislation: *Pickstone v Freemans plc* [1989] AC 66, [1988] 2 All ER 803, HL; *Litster v Forth Dry Dock & Engineering Co Ltd* [1989] 1 All ER 1134, [1989] IRLR 161, HL. Notwithstanding these arguments, in the latest domestic case on this subject (*Hough v Leyland DAF Ltd* [1991] IRLR 194), the EAT endorsed the narrower approach above referred to, Knox J holding the view that (for the purposes of s 99) matters should have reached the stage whereby a specific proposal has been formulated.

independent trade union is recognised by the employer has to consult with representatives of that trade union about the dismissal.[15]

Consultation has in any case (even if it is proposed that only one person is to be dismissed as redundant) to begin at the earliest opportunity. In larger redundancies, a minimum period is set down. Thus, if the employer proposes to dismiss as redundant 100 or more employees at one establishment within a period of 90 days or less the consultation period must begin at least 90 days before the first of those dismissals takes effect. Where an employer proposes to dismiss as redundant ten or more employees at one establishment within a period of 30 days or less, the period of consultation must commence at least 30 days before the first of those dismissals takes effect.[16]

For the purposes of consultation required by the EPA the employer has to disclose in writing to trade union representatives the following information:

(a) the reasons for his proposals;

(b) the numbers and descriptions of employees whom it is proposed to dismiss as redundant;

(c) the total number of employees of any such description employed by the employer at the establishment in question;

(d) the proposed method of selecting the employees who may be dismissed; and

(e) the proposed method of carrying out the dismissals with due regard to any agreed procedure including the period over which the dismissals are to take effect.[17]

This information has to be given to trade union representatives by delivery to them or sent by post to an address notified by them to the employer or sent by post to the union at the address of its head or main office.[18]

To comply with the consultation element of the obligations under the EPA, the employer has to consider any representations made by

---

15 EPA s 99(1) (see, for recognition, infra).
16 EPA s 99(3), [1988] IRLR 10, EAT (consultation required even though one employee involved).
17 EPA s 99(5).
18 EPA s 99(6).

trade union representatives and also to reply to those representations; and if the representations are rejected, state the reasons for rejection.[19]

The duty is fairly strict but if there are 'special circumstances' which render it not reasonably practicable for the employer to comply with any of the requirements of supply of information and consultation, the employer has to take all such steps towards compliance with that requirement as are reasonably practicable in the circumstances.[20] It is for the employer to prove in any tribunal proceedings complaining of infringement of the section that there were such 'special circumstances' which rendered it not reasonably practicable for him to comply with any requirement of s 99 and, also, that he took all such steps towards compliance with that requirement as were reasonably practicable in these circumstances. If the industrial tribunal is satisfied that there were special circumstances and that steps as described above were taken it may find there was no infringement of the provisions by the employer. But special circumstances are not easy to establish and it should not be assumed that this defence will easily be satisfied.[1]

In the event of infringement of the consultation and information obligations, the appropriate trade union may present a complaint to an industrial tribunal.[2] If the complaint is well founded the tribunal makes a declaration to that effect and it may also make a 'protective award'.[3] This is an award covering such employees as may be specified in the award being employees who have been dismissed or whom it is proposed to dismiss as redundant and in respect of whose dismissal or proposed dismissal the employer has failed to comply with s 99.[4] It is an order for the payment of remuneration to these

---

19 EPA s 99(7). It is to be noted that the obligation is restricted to information and consultation – there is no duty to accommodate the views of the trade union. But the EC Collective Redundancies Directive 75/129 provides that consultation should be 'with a view to reaching an agreement' (Art 2) (cf Directive 77/187 where the words are 'with a view to seeking agreement'). After *Pickstone v Freemans plc* [1989] AC 66, [1988] 2 All ER 803, HL and *Litster v Forth Dry Dock and Engineering Co Ltd* [1989] 1 All ER 1134, [1989] IRLR 161 it is arguable that s 99 may have to be construed in this light. If so, this would greatly sharpen the provisions of s 99.

20 EPA s 99(8). See below. There is, however, no equivalent of this defence in Directive 75/129. Again, the purposive approach in *Litster* should restrict its application.

1 EPA s 101(2) see *Clarks of Hove Ltd v Bakers' Union* [1979] 1 All ER 152, [1978] ICR 1076 and the fuller discussion infra.

2 EPA s 101(1).

3 EPA s 101(3), (4).

4 EPA s 101(4).

employees for a 'protected period'.[5] The protected period is a period of 90 days in a case where the minimum period of consultation was to be 90 days; 30 days where the minimum period of consultation was to be 30 days; in any other case, 28 days; and in all cases, 'beginning with the date on which the first of the dismissals to which the complaint relates takes effect, or the date of the award, whichever is the earlier'.[6] These are maxima and it is possible that a smaller (or nil) award may be made by the tribunal even though the employer has breached the provisions. This will depend on what the tribunal determines to be just and equitable in all the circumstances having regard to the seriousness of the employer's default in complying with the requirements of the provisions.[7]

Notwithstanding the language of the statute, there has been some confusion about the expression 'beginning with the date on which the first of the dismissals . . . takes effect' (see above), and when the protected period (and hence payment under the award) commences.[8] In more recent cases the view seems to be favoured that it commences on the date on which the first dismissal to which the complaint related was *proposed* to take effect, not when it *actually* occurred.[9]

Under s 102, if the industrial tribunal has made a protective award under s 101, an employee included in the description of employees to which the award relates is then entitled to be paid remuneration by the employer for the protected period as specified in the award.[10] The rate of remuneration payable under the award is a week's pay for each week of the protected period and, if remuneration has to be calculated for less than one week, the

---

5 EPA s 101(5).

6 EPA s 101(5).

7 EPA s 101(5). For a full discussion on the considerations to be taken into account on the issue of what is 'just and equitable' see *Harvey* III 1443–1458. See too, recently, *Sovereign Distribution Services Ltd v TGWU* [1990] ICR 31, [1989] IRLR 334.

8 *E Green & Son (Castings) Ltd v ASTMS* [1984] ICR 352, [1984] IRLR 135. Compare *GKN Sankey Ltd v National Society of Metal Mechanics* [1980] ICR 148, [1980] IRLR 8. See also *GMWU (MATSA) v British Uralite Ltd* [1979] IRLR 413; *NUT v Avon County Council* [1978] ICR 626, [1978] IRLR 55; *TGWU v RA Lister & Co Ltd* [1986] IRLIB 21 May 1989, p 11, EAT.

9 *TGWU v Ledbury Preserves (1928) Ltd* [1986] ICR 492, [1986] IRLR 412, EAT, preferring *E Green & Sons (Castings) Ltd v ASTMS* over *GKN Sankey Ltd v National Society of Metal Mechanics*. However, this is a matter of some controversy and there are certainly strong arguments in favour of the commencement date being after the first dismissal actually took place: *Harvey* III, 1430, 1442.

10 EPA s 102(1).

amount of a week's pay is reduced proportionately.[11] At first glance this seems to allow for a substantial bonus to affected employees but they will not necessarily, in all cases, receive *additional* remuneration from the employer, even if covered by the protective award. For it is provided that any payment made to an employee by an employer under his contract of employment or by way of damages for breach of that contract in respect of the period falling within a protected period shall go towards discharging the employer's liability to pay remuneration under the protective award in respect of the protected period. Conversely, any payment of remuneration under a protective award in respect of a period under which the employee should have been paid or was entitled to notice shall go towards discharging the employer's liability for remuneration under, or in respect of, any breach of contract on his part during that period.[12]

There are further provisions for reduction of the protective award. For example, an employee ceases to be entitled to remuneration under the award when he is fairly dismissed by his employer during the period of the protective award for a reason other than redundancy,[13] or in a case where the employee unreasonably terminates his contract of employment over this period.[14] Also, in dismissal cases, the employer may make the employee an offer before the ending of his employment under the old contract to renew his contract or to re-engage under a new contract so that the renewal or re-engagement will take effect before or during the protected period. If the terms and conditions of the new contract do not differ from the old contract or if they do, the offer constitutes an offer of suitable employment in relation to the employee,[15] then, if the employee unreasonably refuses the offer, he is not entitled to any remuneration under a protective award in respect of any period during which, but for the refusal, he would have been employed. This latter point is subject to the enjoyment of a trial period on the part of the employee and the provisions concerning the trial period here mirror the provisions concerning a trial period in the redundancy payments provisions of the EP(C)A (see above Ch 5).[16]

---

11 EPA s 102(2).
12 EPA s 102(3). It seems that an *ex gratia* payment such as an augmentation of a statutory redundancy payment should not be liable to be deducted from payments due under a protective award: *Watts v Cape Insulation Ltd* (1987) IRLIB 330, 2 June, p 10.
13 EPA s 102(5)(a).
14 EPA s 102(5)(b).
15 EPA s 102(6).
16 EPA s 102(7)–(11).

An employee who is not paid remuneration under a protective award to which he is entitled may complain to an industrial tribunal. If successful he is entitled to an order that the employer pays him the amount of remuneration which the industrial tribunal finds is due under the award.[17]

As already suggested in relation to the Transfer Regulations, it is interesting to consider whether an employer's liability to a trade union for not informing and consulting may be in any way transferred to a transferee of the business, if it were sold. If this were to occur at all, it would be under reg 5 of the Transfer Regulations which provides, on a relevant transfer, that 'all the transferor's rights, powers, *duties and liabilities* under or in connection with [a transferred contract of employment]' are, by virtue of reg 5(2)(a), transferred to a transferee.

However, as discussed above, it has been held in *Angus Jowett & Co Ltd v NUTGW*[18] that the liability of an employer under a protective award made under s 100 of the EPA cannot be passed to a transferee under reg 5 of the Transfer Regulations, as it is not an obligation 'under or in connection' with a contract of employment transferred under reg 5. The EAT in that case did not expressly have to decide whether an employee's individual entitlement following a tribunal order that he was entitled to remuneration under a protective award would be carried over under reg 5. The better view should be that such individual entitlement under the *employee's* industrial tribunal order *would* be a duty or liability 'under or in connection with a contract of employment' and so would be transferred to a transferee upon a transfer of an undertaking. Although there are, as yet, no decided cases, it seems that the above points should apply, as discussed, likewise to the question of transferability of entitlement under a compensation award where this award is made under reg 11 of the Transfer Regulations as opposed to s 100 of the EPA (see above). Even if individual entitlement *can* be transferred, liability for an individual employee's entitlement under a tribunal protective award (or the equivalent under the Transfer Regulations) will, however, not be passed to a transferee where the employee concerned was not employed in the business transferred 'immediately before' the transfer. This will not, of course, apply where there was a pre-transfer dismissal which was automatically unfair under reg 8 of the Transfer Regulations under the principle in *Litster v Forth Dry Dock & Engineering Co*

---

17 EPA s 103(1).
18 [1985] ICR 646, [1985] IRLR 326, EAT.

Ltd.[19] In that case the liability (if capable of transfer) *should* be transferred to the transferee.

Finally, some brief discussion of some of the nuts and bolts of the information and consultation provisions may be helpful.

(a) Establishment

First, information and consultation under the EPA has to take place in respect of redundancies proposed at the same *establishment*. What is an establishment seems to be a question of fact for the industrial tribunal. Generally, it has been said that the concept of 'establishment' denotes some degree of permanence perhaps of buildings, administration, centralisation of records and tools and equipment.[20]

An employer should not be able artificially to fragment his undertaking into temporary but separate establishments for the purposes of getting round the provisions of the EPA. An industrial tribunal should see through such a sham and aggregate the employees involved in the various bogus 'establishments' and count them as falling within one true establishment. However, the provisions of the EPA apply only to *one employer*. If a number of associated employers *genuinely* operate at the same establishment, each separate employer's redundancy programme has to be considered separately, and the number of redundancies proposed as a whole by separate (even though associated) employers at that establishment cannot be aggregated for the purposes of enlarging the consultation period.[1]

An employer might also be tempted artificially to stagger his redundancy programme in order that he might implement redundancies in small consecutive groups, thus, in each case, attracting less onerous information and consultation periods in respect of each group of dismissals. It is submitted here, too, that if this is plainly a sham the industrial tribunal could look behind this arrangement and decide that the redundancy programme was connected;[2] but the EPA scheme is regrettably not entirely safe from possible abuse by employers operating dubious fragmentation exercises.

---

19 [1989] ICR 341, [1989] IRLR 161. Otherwise see *Secretary of State for Employment v Spence* [1987] QB 179, [1986] ICR 651, CA.
20 See *Barley v Amey Roadstone Corpn Ltd* [1977] ICR 546, [1977] IRLR 299; *Barratt Developments (Bradford) Ltd v UCATT* [1978] ICR 319, [1977] IRLR 403; *Clarks of Hove Ltd v Bakers' Union* [1979] 1 All ER 152, [1978] ICR 1076, CA.
1 *E Green & Son (Castings) Ltd v ASTMS* [1984] ICR 352, [1984] IRLR 135, EAT.
2 *TGWU v Nationwide Haulage Ltd* [1978] IRLR 143. See also EPA 1975, s 99(4).

(b) Special circumstances

The special circumstances 'defence' has already been mentioned. It is unwise to generalise about the type of circumstances which might give rise to 'special circumstances', e g insolvency, receivership, sudden reduction of the order book and so forth. The circumstances must be 'special' in each case. In other words neither an insolvency, nor, for example, a sudden falling-off of orders might be special circumstances per se; it would depend on the facts. A case commonly cited to illustrate the narrowness of the special circumstances 'defence' is *Clarks of Hove Ltd v Bakers' Union*.[3] In that case the company had been in financial difficulty for some time and had long been seeking assistance. Eventually, all avenues proved to be impossible and meanwhile the company underwent serious losses. It was decided that the company should cease trading immediately and over 300 employees were summarily dismissed. A receiver was appointed very shortly thereafter. It was held that, while it was not reasonably practicable to comply with the consultation provisions since the proposal to dismiss and the actual dismissals were simultaneous, there were no special circumstances absolving the company from the duty to inform and consult. In the view of the industrial tribunal, special circumstances were 'something out of the ordinary run of events',[4] such as, according to the tribunal, the destruction of the plant, a general trading boycott or a sudden withdrawal of supplies from the main supplier.[5] The industrial tribunal did decide that insolvency of itself was not a special circumstance. This decision was approved by the Court of Appeal and has considerable weight.[6] However, exceptionally, if there is genuine uncertainty as to whether, for example, the employer might lose a vital contract, or when a contract might end, and so there was a genuine difficulty in predicting when redundancies might have to be proposed, this could amount to special circumstances if inaction over the period of uncertainty postponed the start of consultation and thereby caused a breach of the EPA.[7]

---

3 [1979] 1 All ER 152, [1978] ICR 1076, CA.

4 Ibid.

5 Ibid at 368. It is interesting to speculate whether urgent action by a receiver or administrator, to make a business saleable, would also justify departure from s 99 (but see the caveat at n 7).

6 Ibid at 368.

7 Further illustrations of the courts' approach can be found in *Association of Patternmakers v Kirvin Ltd* [1978] IRLR 318, EAT; *USDAW v Leancut Bacon Ltd* [1981] IRLR 295, EAT; *Armour v ASTMS* [1979] IRLR 24. As mentioned

(c) Recognition

Finally, the rights under s 99 apply only to a recognised independent trade union. The discussion of recognition here may also be of assistance in connection with reg 10 of the Transfer Regulations: see Pt 4 above. Recognition can arise in several ways. It can arise from a collective agreement but, in this case, it does not, of course, matter whether the agreement itself is legally enforceable.[8] It can also arise informally and it can even be implied from a previous course of dealing.[9] According to the cases, the question is a mixed one of fact and law.[10]

Recognition has to be recognition 'for the purposes of collective bargaining', i e in relation to one or more of the matters specified in s 29 of TULRA (see the discussion on collective agreements in Pt 2 above). It has been held that, for the purposes of recognition, this must be recognition in relation to *negotiating* rights as opposed to merely *representational or consultation* rights. However, it seems that the grant of partial negotiation rights to a trade union would be sufficient to count as recognition.[11] Recognition has to be 'to any extent' and, therefore, if there is partial recognition covering say one or two only of the matters set out in s 29, this will count for the purposes of rights to consultation and notification over redundancies etc.[12] This contrasts with the rule relating to disclosure of information to a recognised trade union for collective bargaining purposes under s 17 of the EPA. Under that provision, where there is only partial recognition by the employer, the employer need only disclose such information as relates to the terms of the partial

---

earlier the purposive approach marked by *Litster* may make strict application of the special circumstances defence suspect in view of its absence from Directive 75/129.

8 *Amalgamated Society of Boilermakers, Shipwrights, Blacksmiths and Structural Workers v George Wimpey ME & Co Ltd* [1977] IRLR 95.

9 *NUGSAT v Albury Bros Ltd* [1978] ICR 62, [1977] IRLR 173; affd [1979] ICR 84, [1978] IRLR 504. Although in the view of the Court of Appeal, since recognition is a serious matter for the employer, it seems that an agreement or conduct from which agreement can be implied must be clear and unequivocal.

10 *NUTGW v Charles Ingram & Co Ltd* [1978] 1 All ER 1271, [1977] ICR 530; cf *TGWU v Dyer* [1977] IRLR 93.

11 *NUGSAT v Albury Bros Ltd* [1978] ICR 62, [1979] IRLR 173; affd [1979] ICR 84, [1978] IRLR 504.

12 *NUGSAT v Albury Bros Ltd* [1978] ICR 62, [1977] IRLR 173; affd [1979] ICR 84, [1978] IRLR 504; *R v Central Arbitration Committee, ex p B T P Tioxide Ltd* [1981] ICR 843, [1982] IRLR 60.

recognition.[13] But partial recognition seems to suffice for a trade union to enjoy information and consultation under s 99.

(ii) Notification to the Department of Employment

Until 1984, an employer intending to dismiss any employee by reason of redundancy had to give advance information of that dismissal under the Redundancy Rebate Regulations. The Redundancy Rebate Regulations 1984[14] abolished that requirement and, anyway, the right to rebate was altogether finally abolished by the Employment Act 1989.[15] Therefore the sole advance notification provisions are now those under s 100 of the EPA.[16] It is important to note that the obligations under s 100 are *not* dependent on there being a recognised trade union: they apply to all multiple redundancies as defined by s 100.

Under s 100 of the EPA the duty to notify the Secretary of State arises where 100 or more employees are to be made redundant within a period of 90 days or less or where ten or more employees at one establishment are to be made redundant within a period of 30 days or less. Unlike the s 99 obligations, no duty arises where fewer than ten employees are to be made redundant. The period of notification to the Secretary of State is, respectively, 90 days and 30 days.[17] A copy of the notice under s 100 of the EPA has to be given to union representatives if the notice relates to employees of any description in respect of which an independent trade union is recognised by the employer.[18] A special circumstances defence, similar to that under s 99, may apply.[19] If there is default under the section, the Department of Employment may take criminal proceedings.[20]

---

13 See e g *R v CAC, ex p B T P Tioxide Ltd* [1981] ICR 843, [1982] IRLR 60. See, too, Employment Act 1989, s 14, which limited the range of duties for which time off with pay is allowed to officials of an independent recognised trade union to the scope of the union recognition granted by the employer (EP(C)A, s 27(1), as amended), along lines similar to s 17 of the EPA.

14 SI 1984/1066.

15 Section 17.

16 The Wages Act 1986 denied the right to claim rebate to employers who had more than nine employees, and the Employment Act 1989 (s 17) then abolished the right to rebate altogether.

17 Section 100(1).

18 Section 100(4).

19 Section 100(6).

20 Section 105.

(iii) The inter-relationship between collective obligations to inform and consult and liability to individual employees for unfair dismissal

In addition to informing and consulting with representatives of independent recognised trade unions, consultation with individuals is extremely important. This is only good industrial relations practice. In any event, consultation with both trade unions and employees may help an employer to avoid unfair dismissal liability.[1] Information and consultation should occur in relation to individual dismissals, whether by reason of redundancy or otherwise. If there is a transfer of an undertaking, and the Transfer Regulations apply, a transfer of the undertaking will not result in a dismissal per se. But dismissals effected by the transferor or the transferee prior to or subsequent to the transfer may attract unfair dismissal claims, and imposed reorganisational changes on or after transfers may result in express or constructive dismissals, which may or may not be unfair. Some of these dismissals may be automatically unfair under reg 8 of the Transfer Regulations (if they are in connection with the transfer but subject to reg 8(2), see Ch 8), but others will not (either because of reg 8(2) or because they are not connected), and in those cases, an industrial tribunal will have to decide on the reasonableness of the employer's actions. Information and consultation will be an important factor in that.[2]

The Industrial Relations Code of Practice 1972 (now repealed)[3] had laid down guidelines about redundancy procedures and how to apply good industrial relations practice:

> '44 Responsibility for deciding the size of the workforce rests with management. But before taking the final decision to make any substantial reduction, management should consult employees or their representatives, unless exceptional circumstances make this impossible.
>
> 45 A policy for dealing with reductions in the workforce, if they become necessary, should be worked out in advance so far as practicable and should form part of the undertaking's employ-

---

1 See the (now repealed) Industrial Relations Code of Practice (1972) paras 65 et seq. See also para 45.
2 *Polkey v A E Dayton Services Ltd* [1988] AC 344, [1988] ICR 142.
3 Under the Employment Codes of Practice (Revocation) Order 1991 SI 1991/1264 the 1972 Industrial Relations Code of Practice was repealed on the ground of obsolescence. As mentioned in Ch 1 this is not sound reasoning (see Ch 1, note 10, p 18). For paras 44–46 on redundancy were never been replicated in a subsequent statutory code (see note 4, below). The guidelines in the 1972 Code about redundancies are still sound, and so repeated here.

ment policies. As far as is consistent with operational efficiency and the success of the undertaking, management should in consultation with employee representatives seek to avoid redundancies by such means as:

(i)   restrictions on recruitment;
(ii) retirement of employees who are beyond the normal retiring age;
(iii) reductions in overtime;
(iv) short-time working to cover temporary fluctuations in manpower needs;
(v)   retraining or transfer to other work.

46 If redundancy becomes necessary, management in consultation, as appropriate, with employees or their representatives, should:

(i)   give as much warning as is practicable to the employees concerned and to the Department of Employment;
(ii) consider introducing schemes for voluntary redundancy, retirement, transfer to other establishments within the undertaking and a phased rundown of employment;
(iii) establish which employees are to be made redundant and the order of discharge;
(iv) offer help to employees in finding other work in co-operation, where appropriate, with the Department of Employment, and allow them reasonable time off for the purpose;
(v)   decide how and when to make the facts public, ensuring that no announcement is made before the employees and their representatives and trade unions have been informed.'

A code of practice is not a code of legally enforceable obligations and failure to observe it does not of itself render a dismissal unfair. But its provisions have to be taken into account by an industrial tribunal.[4] This 1972 Code has now been abolished (see above). But the ACAS Advisory booklet 'Redundancy Handling' could be a useful reference point in the alternative.

---

4 As emphasised in the Industrial Relations Code of Practice (1972) (Introduction) (now abolished). This is also the position under the more widely known *ACAS Code of Practice 1: Disciplinary Practice and Procedures in Employment* (1972) (EPA 1975 s 11) which does not relate as such to pure redundancy dismissals. An attempt to revise the ACAS code was made in the mid-1980s. A consultative document on a draft code of practice was produced by ACAS in November 1985. The draft was rejected by the government as a replacement of the code. In due course, ACAS issued an advisory handbook *Discipline at Work* (1988). This does not have the status of a code, but its advice is sound and its content likely to be influential. As stated in the text, another ACAS advisory booklet *Redundancy Handling* (1989) may also be useful; it too, though, does not have the status of a code.

Other guidance on proper procedures in redundancy and related cases may be found in case law. It is perhaps only with caution that one should cite guidelines in decided cases about unfair redundancies under s 57(3) of the EP(C)A. In recent cases it has been emphasised that reasonableness is a question of fact for the industrial tribunal, and tribunals are exhorted only to 'drink the pure waters of the statute',[5] and dicta to like effect abound.[6]

None the less a slightly older authority, *Iceland Frozen Foods Ltd v Jones*,[7] summarises guidelines in certain EAT cases and the points made therein are still useful to bear in mind. The EAT said in that case:

'Since the present state of the law can only be found by going through a number of different authorities, it may be convenient if we should seek to summarise the present law. We consider that the authorities establish that in law the correct approach for the industrial tribunal to adopt in answering the question posed by s 57(3) of the Act of 1978 is as follows:

(1) the starting point should always be the words of s 57(3) themselves;

(2) in applying the section an industrial tribunal must consider the reasonableness of the employer's conduct, not simply whether they (the members of the industrial tribunal) consider the dismissal to be fair;

(3) in judging the reasonableness of the employer's conduct an industrial tribunal must not substitute its decision as to what was the right course to adopt for that of the employer;

(4) in many (although not all) cases, there is a band of reasonable responses to the employee's conduct within which one employer might reasonably take one view, and another quite reasonably take another;

(5) the function of the industrial tribunal, as an industrial jury, is to determine whether in the particular circumstances of each case the decision to dismiss the employee fell within the band of reasonable responses which a reasonable employer might have adopted. If the dismissal falls within the band, the dismissal is fair: if the dismissal falls outside the band it is unfair.'[8]

---

5 Per Waite J in *Anandarajah v Lord Chancellor's Department* [1984] IRLR 131.
6 *Bailey v BP Oil (Kent Refinery) Ltd* [1980] ICR 642, [1980] IRLR 287; *Thomas and Betts Manufacturing Ltd v Harding* [1980] IRLR 255; *Anandarajah v Lord Chancellor's Department* [1984] IRLR 131; *O'Kelly v Trusthouse Forte plc* [1984] QB 90, [1983] IRLR 369, CA; *Varndell v Kearney & Trecker Marwin Ltd* [1983] ICR 683, [1983] IRLR 335, CA; *UCATT v Brain* [1981] ICR 542, [1981] IRLR 224, CA; *Gilham v Kent County Council (No 2)* [1985] ICR 233, [1985] IRLR 18, CA.
7 [1983] ICR 17, [1982] IRLR 439, EAT.
8 Ibid.

In *Williams v Compair Maxam Ltd*,[9] Browne-Wilkinson J formulated general principles concerning reasonableness in a redundancy context:

'. . . there is a generally accepted view in industrial relations that, in cases where the employees are represented by an independent union recognised by the employer, reasonable employers will seek to act in accordance with the following principles:

(1) The employer will seek to give as much warning as possible of impending redundancies so as to enable the union and employees who may be affected to take early steps to inform themselves of the relevant facts, consider possible alternative solutions and, if necessary, find alternative employment in the undertaking or elsewhere.

(2) The employer will consult the union as to the best means by which the desired management result can be achieved fairly and with as little hardship to the employees as possible. In particular, the employer will seek to agree with the union the criteria to be applied in selecting the employees to be made redundant. When a selection has been made, the employer will consider with the union whether the selection has been made in accordance with those criteria.

(3) Whether or not an agreement as to the criteria to be adopted has been agreed with the union, the employer will seek to establish criteria for selection which so far as possible do not depend solely upon the opinion of the person making the selection but can be objectively checked against such things as attendance record, efficiency at the job, experience or length of service.

(4) The employer will seek to ensure that the selection is made fairly in accordance with these criteria and will consider any representations the union may make as to such selection.

(5) The employer will seek to see whether instead of dismissing an employer he could offer him alternative employment.

The lay members stress that not all these factors are present in every case since circumstances may prevent one or more of them being given effect to. But the lay members would expect these principles to be departed from only where some good reason is shown to justify such departure. The basic approach is that, in the unfortunate circumstances that necessarily attend redundancies, as much as is reasonably possible should be done to mitigate the impact on the workforce and to satisfy them that the selection has been made fairly and not on the basis of personal whim.'[10]

---

9 [1982] ICR 156, [1982] IRLR 83, EAT.
10 Ibid.

These points began to be applied in many cases.[11] But the guidelines fell out of favour somewhat when the EAT had to correct industrial tribunals which rather too slavishly followed the guidelines, applying them in circumstances where they might not have been appropriate.[12] None the less, the concept of consultation and other procedures before dismissal has always been considered important.[13]

The question is *how* important, especially where the procedural failure was relatively technical. As early as 1972, in *Earl v Slater and Wheeler (Airlyne) Ltd*[14] Sir John Donaldson, commenting on the case of an employee dismissed without being given the opportunity of a hearing, said:

> '. . . whilst we do not say that in all circumstances the employee must be given an opportunity of stating his case, the only exception can be the case where there can be no explanation which could cause the employers to refrain from dismissing the employee. This must be a very rare situation.'[15]

The emphasis on the requirement of procedures before dismissal was approved by the House of Lords in *W Davis & Sons Ltd v Atkins*.[16] However, as Davis and Freedland[17] traced, the years following *Davis v Atkins* saw 'an erosion of the procedural dimension of fairness'.[18] Cases such as *A J Dunning & Sons (Shopfitters) Ltd v Jacomb*[19] and *Bailey v BP Oil (Kent Refinery) Ltd*[20] indicated that procedural matters were but one small part of fairness, and a mere procedural irregularity of itself would not make the dismissal unfair. This was compounded by a rule which became attributed to

---

11 E g *Grundy (Teddington) Ltd v Plummer and Salt* [1983] ICR 367, [1983] IRLR 98; *Robinson v Carrickfergus Borough Council* [1983] IRLR 122, NICA. See, more, recently *Walls Meat Co Ltd v Selby* [1989] ICR 601.
12 See *Rolls-Royce Motors Ltd v Dewhurst* [1985] ICR 869, [1985] IRLR 184, EAT; *A Simpson & Son (Motors) v Reid and Findlater* [1983] IRLR 401; *Gray v Shetland Norse Preserving Co Ltd* [1985] IRLR 53.
13 Other cases emphasising consultation include *Holden v Bradville Ltd* [1985] IRLR 483; *Graham v ABF Ltd* [1986] IRLR 90; *Dyke v Hereford and Worcester County Council* [1989] ICR 800; *Huddersfield Parcels Ltd v Sykes* [1981] IRLR 115; *Freud v Bentalls Ltd* [1983] ICR 77, [1982] IRLR 443 and *Walls Meat Co Ltd v Selby* [1989] ICR 601.
14 [1973] 1 All ER 145, [1972] ICR 508.
15 [1972] ICR 508 at 512.
16 [1977] IRLR 314.
17 *Labour Law: Text and Materials* (2nd edn).
18 Ibid at p 480.
19 [1973] ICR 448, [1973] IRLR 206.
20 [1980] ICR 642, [1980] IRLR 287.

the case of *British Labour Pump Co Ltd v Byrne*,[1] but which originated in the EAT case of *Lowndes v Specialist Heavy Engineering Ltd*.[2] This was that, notwithstanding a failure to observe procedures, an employer could, *ex post facto*, justify what would otherwise have been an unfair dismissal by persuading an industrial tribunal that, on the balance of probabilities, the defect in procedure made no difference and that, if the proper procedure had been followed, the employer would have reasonably decided to dismiss in any event. The 'no difference' or '*British Labour Pump*' rule became even more established when endorsed by the Court of Appeal in *W & J Wass Ltd v Binns*.[3] Some judicial disquiet or qualification was subsequently expressed.[4] But it was not until the ruling of the House of Lords in *Polkey v A E Dayton Services Ltd*[5] that the position became clear. The House of Lords overruled *British Labour Pump*: the reasonableness of the employer's action had to be judged at the time of dismissal, not with the benefit of hindsight. A failure to follow procedures before dismissal would not *necessarily* make a dismissal unfair, but ordinarily, a procedural failure may of itself make a dismissal unfair. There are exceptions if following procedures is pointless. Thus, Lord Mackay thought:

'If the employer could reasonably have concluded in the light of the circumstances known to him at the time of dismissal that consultation or warning would be *utterly useless* he might well act reasonably even if he did not observe the provisions of the code.' (emphasis added)[6]

This was echoed by Lord Bridge who thought:

'. . . if the tribunal is able to conclude that the employer himself, at the time of dismissal, acted reasonably in taking the view that, in the exceptional circumstances of the particular case, the procedural steps normally appropriate would have been *futile*, could not have altered the decision to dismiss and therefore could be dispensed with, in such a case the test of reasonableness under s 57(3) may be satisfied.'[7] (emphasis added)

---

1 [1979] ICR 347, [1979] IRLR 94.
2 [1979] ICR 1, [1976] IRLR 246. See also *British United Shoe Machinery Co Ltd v Clarke* [1978] ICR 70, [1977] IRLR 297.
3 [1982] ICR 486, [1982] IRLR 283.
4 See *Sillifant v Powell Duffryn Timber Ltd* [1983] IRLR 91; *Dunn v Pochin (Contractors) Ltd* [1982] IRLR 449; *Murray McKinnon v Forno* [1983] IRLR 7; *Henderson v Granville Tours Ltd* [1982] IRLR 494; *Siggs & Chapman (Contractors) Ltd v Knight* [1984] IRLR 83.
5 [1988] ICR 142, [1987] IRLR 503.
6 [1987] IRLR 503 at 504.
7 [1987] IRLR 503 at 508.

Obviously, though, this will be rare. However, if there is a purely 'technical' unfair dismissal, unfair because of a procedural defect that may well have made no difference, while this cannot be an excuse for an employer on the merits, it may qualify or restrict the remedy obtainable. For a tribunal may only award such a sum under a compensatory (as opposed to basic) award for unfair dismissal as is 'just and equitable'.[8] Compensation in cases where the procedural defect would have made no difference might even be nil[9] or confined to a period equivalent to the period over which consultation etc would have run its course, perhaps a number of weeks in some cases, but depending on the facts,[10] ie the additional period over which the employee would have been employed had the dismissal been fair.

Other relevant factors, apart from lack of consultation, which might make a dismissal unfair under s 57(3) include unfair selection[11] and failure to consider alternative employment.[12] On a different dimension, an employer must be careful, as already stated, (see Part 2) not to infringe a customary arrangement or agreed procedure for selection for redundancies under s 59 of the EP(C)A, breach of which could give rise to an *automatically* unfair redundancy dismissal unless there are 'special reasons justifying a departure from that arrangement or procedure in [the employee's] case'.[13] On a business transfer it could be argued that reg 6 of the Transfer Regulations (transfer of collective agreements – see Part 2) could transfer such a redundancy selection procedure agreement, if it were in a collective agreement, to a transferee of a business. Any transferee would, therefore, be well advised to include enquiry

---

8 EP(C)A s 74(1).
9 *Polkey v A E Dayton Services Ltd* [1988] ICR 142, [1987] IRLR 503 per Lord Bridge.
10 *Mining Supplies (Longwall) Ltd v Baker* [1988] ICR 676, [1988] IRLR 417; *Abbotts v Wesson-Glynwed Steels Ltd* [1982] IRLR 51.
11 *Williams v Compair Maxam Ltd* [1982] ICR 156, [1982] IRLR 83.
12 EP(C)A s 59(b). The onus is on the employer if he seeks to assert such special reasons: *Tilgate Pallets Ltd v Barras* [1983] IRLR 231. And as to guidelines see *Cross International v Reid* [1985] IRLR 387. To be noted is the interesting argument, based in part on the discredited case of *Canning v Niaz and McLoughlin* [1983] IRLR 431, which is rehearsed in *Harvey on Industrial Relations and Employment Law* II 909; II 1073 et seq, that s 59 cannot apply to a selection for redundancy apparently in breach of s 59 arising in conection with a transfer under the Transfer Regulations. This argument, which, it is submitted, is not well founded, is more fully canvassed in Ch 8. There is considerable case law on s 59, including on what amounts to a customary arrangement or agreed procedure in *Harvey* II 920 et seq.
13 *Vokes Ltd v Bear* [1974] ICR 1, [1973] IRLR 363.

of the existence of such agreements, whether formal or informal, when making requisitions of the transferor.[14]

It finally remains to be determined what, if any, is the direct inter-relationship between a failure to inform and consult a representative of a recognised trade union under s 99 of the EPA and under reg 10 of the Transfer Regulations (if relevant, since there will usually be no dismissal arising out of the transfer itself), and liability for unfair dismissal. In law, it has always been thought that s 99 (and, presumably, by analogy, also reg 10) was independent from the question of fairness of dismissal of an individual employee. It certainly must be the case that failure to consult for the purposes of s 99 or reg 10 cannot per se render an individual dismissal unfair.[15] None the less, failure to consult a recognised trade union or indeed an individual may be one factor (not necessarily conclusive) in deciding the fairness or otherwise of an individual dismissal. This should be so whether or not s 99 or reg 10 actually apply, and may be regarded simply as good industrial relations practice.[16]

---

14 See Appendix A (Warranties and Indemnities). See also, *Alexander v Standard Telephones and Cables Ltd (No 2)* [1991] IRLR 286, n 15, p 231.

15 *Hollister v NFU* [1979] ICR 542, [1979] IRLR 238, CA; *Ladbroke Courage Holidays Ltd v Asten* [1981] IRLR 59; *Hough v Leyland DAF Ltd* [1991] IRLR 194.

16 *Williams v Compair Maxam Ltd* [1982] ICR 156, [1982] IRLR 83; *Grundy (Teddington) Ltd v Plummer* [1983] ICR 367, [1983] IRLR 98.

Chapter 11

Promises and reassurances: contracts, estoppels and representations

As has been seen, statutory continuity of employment on change of employer is, generally, only preserved if the provisions of Sch 13 to the EP(C)A apply (principally, paras 17 and 18 thereof).[1] Otherwise, on any change of employer, continuity is broken. Similarly, unless the Transfer Regulations apply, an employment contract will not be carried over to a new employer, however proximate the old employment to the new, and however similar the old working environment to the new. In summary, unless these statutory provisions apply, a new owner of the business need not honour any acquired rights of a transferred employee.

Sometimes, however, employers reassure employees about their rights on transfer. If the statutory provisions apply, this is legally unnecessary to effect a transfer of acquired rights.[2] Good industrial

---

1 See also, though, Sch 13 para 12 and, elsewhere, s 45(1) of the EP(C)A (right of an employee to return to work after maternity leave with the successor of an employer); s 69(4) of the EP(C)A (industrial tribunal order of re-instatement or re-engagement with dismissing employer or his successor); reg 4 of the Labour Relations (Continuity of Employment) Regulations 1976, SI 1976/660 (re-instatement or re-engagement of an employee by successor of dismissing employer after presentation of unfair dismissal complaint (reg 3(a)), after a claim under a designated dismissal procedure permitted by the EP(C)A (reg 3(b)) or after a conciliated settlement under the auspices of ACAS (reg 3(c)).

2 On the other hand, even if the statutory provisions (the EP(C)A and the Transfer Regulations) apply they do not, themselves, transfer all matters. For example occupational pension scheme rights are excluded from the Transfer Regulations (reg 6); and it has been held that share option schemes may not be caught by reg 5 if contained in a collateral contract (*Chapman and Elkin v CPS Computer Group plc* [1987] IRLR 462; but see the discussion in Ch 7). An employer's promise that an employee may join a transferee's pension or share option scheme may therefore be actionable along the lines discussed in the text below (see contractual promises). All this pre-supposes a promise made by a transferee. The interesting question remains whether a transferee could be made liable for a collateral promise by a transferor by virtue of reg 5 of the Transfer Regulations. There is the argument that such matters are collateral and outside the employment contract and therefore not caught by reg 5 (see *Chapman and Elkin*). But that cannot be stated with any certainty, especially since the question of whether the

relations practice and other considerations may, however, make such assurance desirable or appropriate.[3] But, sometimes, assurances that previous employment will be respected are given when the statutory safeguards do not apply, principally, for example, when there has been no transfer of a business or undertaking within the meaning of the legislation. Often the reassurance is given by the new employer. This is often a promise that previously acquired statutory continuity will be honoured for the purposes of any future claims against the new employer. What is the legal status of such assurances?

Justice would require that these promises were effective. An employee may, of course, totally rely upon such a promise, particularly where, for example, *factual* continuity of employment was unbroken on the change of employer. As a result, he may have failed properly to claim a redundancy payment in time from his old employer (which is the action he should have taken if there was no transfer of business). Consider also his position if he is dismissed by the new employer at a later date: can he count a period of service with a former employer towards his continuous service with the new employer simply because the new employer has at some time assured him that he may?

1 PROMISSORY ESTOPPEL

The courts first tried to find a solution by applying the doctrine of promissory estoppel. It seems now, however, that this cannot apply to help an employee in this situation. In arriving at this conclusion,

---

words in reg 5 defining the in connection with [employment] contract' – could be interpreted broadly in the light of the corresponding words in the directive which include '. . . rights and obligations arising from [an employment contract] or from an *employment relationship* . . .' (emphasis added) has not yet been fully considered. This therefore highlights the need (discussed in Ch 7) for the purchaser to make careful enquiries of what might have been said by a vendor to employees before a transfer.

3 And reg 10 of the Transfer Regulations obliges a transferee to inform/consult recognised trade unions about a transfer, and some relevant information may emerge then. Section 1 of the EP(C)A requires an employer to issue a written statement of main terms and conditions of employment not later than 13 weeks after the beginning of an employee's employment. Such a statement has to identify the employer (s 1(2)(a)). On change of employer, a new employer should issue a fresh statement. Or, if the identity of the employer is changed in circumstances such that continuity of the employee's period of employment is not broken (and provided no other changes in employment terms are involved) the employer must, within one month of the change, inform the employee of the nature of the change by written statement under EP(C)A, s 4(4).

it is perhaps helpful to discuss the doctrine of estoppel. Not all promises are legally effective. In the law of contract only those promises which are supported by consideration (ie something of value whether in money terms or otherwise) are binding.[4] If A assures B that A will do a certain thing for B, it will not always be the case that A's assurance is supported by consideration provided by B. Thus, if a new employer promises an employee that his previous continuous employment will be preserved if he joins the new employer's concern, the employee will not necessarily have given consideration for that promise. If he has, there may be a binding contract between A and B. The possibility of such a contract to honour previous employment is discussed later in this chapter. If there is consideration, it is most likely to be in the form of an undertaking by the employee to go and work for the new employer in circumstances where he is otherwise under no legal obligation so to do (and that would be valid consideration in law). Alternatively, it could comprise some financial inducement, such as improved terms (again, valid consideration in law).

But an assurance made by the new employer to the newly engaged employee about continuity could be without consideration. If the contract of engagement has already been concluded and the employee is given a subsequent assurance about previous employment, there will be no consideration provided by the employee for the assurance. As the main contract would have already been concluded, an act of the employee in entering that contract cannot be good consideration for a subsequent promise by the employer about continuity. The law would say that any consideration would be 'past' consideration and, therefore, not valid consideration.[5]

Contract law developed estoppel to cover this type of situation in contexts other than business transfers. It is, of course, most unfair if a person promises another a certain thing, understanding that the promisee will act upon this in reliance, that the promisor is allowed later to renege without legal remedy. But, in fact, the promisee has no legal remedy for breach of contract if no consideration was provided for the promise to him. This is where the concept of promissory estoppel[6] comes in. In the case of *Central London Property Trust Ltd v High Trees House Ltd*[7] (the *High Trees* case) it

---

4 Cheshire, Fifoot and Furmston *The Law of Contract* (12th edn, 1991) Ch 4.
5 *Roscorla v Thomas* (1842) 3 QB 234; *Re McArdle* [1951] Ch 669, [1951] 1 All ER 905, CA.
6 On which see, generally, *Cheshire, Fifoot and Furmston* pp 90–105.
7 [1947] KB 130.

was established that if a person relies upon the promise of another and changes his position accordingly, then the promisor should not be allowed to renege upon his promise, notwithstanding that it is not supported by consideration. The *High Trees* case was controversial when first decided in 1947 and, to a certain extent, remains so. None the less, it has received (at times grudging) acceptance from the courts and has, over the years, been extensively applied.[8]

So, if a new employer promises an employee that he will honour previous employment, can promissory estoppel apply? One major problem here is that promissory estoppel may only be used as a 'shield' and not as a 'sword'.[9] In other words, the doctrine of promissory estoppel may only be used defensively, usually to defend a claim made against the promisee by the promisor in breach of the promise. But the issue in transfer of employment cases usually concerns an employee who makes a claim either for statutory notice, unfair dismissal or redundancy where, perhaps, length of employment is in question. As the employee is the one making the claim, it seems that promissory estoppel should not apply. But there seemed to be an ingenious route through in cases of *redundancy*, and in any other case where *continuity* of employment was disputed. In these cases there is a *presumption* of redundancy or continuity under statute in favour of the employee, which then has to be rebutted by the employer.[10] Accordingly, the argument went, if there was a statutory presumption that a statutory right applied, then, unless otherwise disproved by an employer this made the employer, as it were, the wielder of 'the sword' when he challenged the statutory presumption and made out a case for its non-application. In such a case, an employee raised the employer's promise as a means of defending this attack on the statutory

---

8　See *Cheshire, Fifoot and Furmston* pp 97 et seq, and the cases cited there in note 14, and later in the text.

9　*Combe v Combe* [1951] 2 KB 215, [1951] 1 All ER 767, CA; *The Proodos C* [1981] 3 All ER 189. Other problems include the issue of whether estoppel can arise when no pre-existing legal relationship or contract exists between the parties (*Chitty on Contracts* 26th edn, Vol 1, para 210) and the conclusion that estoppel cannot create new rights (*Chitty* para 217).

10　EP(C)A Sch 13 para 1(3) (continuous employment); EP(C)A s 91(2) (redundancy; see *Willcox v Hastings* [1987] IRLR 298, CA). It is also possible to argue that a similar presumption could apply in relation to unfair dismissal, where it is for the employer under s 57 of the EP(C)A to show a permissible reason (under s 57(1)(b) or s 57(2)) for dismissal. In other words, the burden of proof is on the employer at this stage. However, *sed quaere* whether there is a presumption in the sense referred to in the text for unfair dismissal purposes, since there is no express statutory *presumption* of unfairness of the dismissal. So, in practice, in this examination, the scope of EP(C)A Sch 13 para 1(3) will be most important.

presumption. Thus viewed, the doctrine of promissory estoppel could be used by the employee truly as a shield and not a sword, even though in fact he was *making* a statutory claim, probably for redundancy or unfair dismissal.

This initially attractive analysis runs into immediate problems, though, when successive employers are involved. And this, of course, will be the case in a transfer of employment situation. For it is now virtually certain that the presumption as to continuity of employment does not apply to successive employers, as opposed to employment with the one employer only (see below).[11] And, if so, for the reasons above, it would be equally questionable whether the doctrine of estoppel would apply in favour of the employee in such a case.

None the less the first decision to tackle such problems was *Evenden v Guildford City Association Football Club*.[12] In this case the employee was employed by the supporters' club of Guildford City Association Football Club. He accrued a number of years' service with the supporters' club. Subsequently he was taken on by the football club itself. But there was no transfer of a business on this change of employer under para 17(2) of Sch 13 to the EP(C)A, (or, rather, its predecessor), nor any provision under the Schedule which would have preserved continuity. Strictly then, the employment was broken on the change of employer and a claim should have been made at that time against the supporters' club. The football club, however, assured the employee that his previous service would be honoured so far as statutory continuity and any potential claim against the football club in the future were concerned. Eventually, when subsequently dismissed by the football club, the employee claimed a redundancy payment against the football club based on his entire length of service with both the football club and the supporters' club. It was held by the Court of Appeal that the football club was estopped from denying its promise to honour previous continuity of employment and, accordingly, for the purposes of calculating the size of a redundancy payment due from the football club, the employee's service with both the supporters' club and with the football club counted. The Court of Appeal in *Evenden* applied promissory estoppel in favour of the employee making the claim for a redundancy payment, because the presumption of continuity, which the court assumed

---

11 See EP(C)A Sch 13 para 1(3) and compare it with para 17(1) which says: 'the foregoing provisions of this Schedule relate only to employment *by the one employer*' (emphasis added). And see Ch 5 above.

12 [1975] QB 917, [1975] ICR 367, CA.

was relevant, meant that the employee was using the doctrine as a shield and not a sword.[13] And the Court of Appeal thought that the presumption of continuity[14] applied to employment not only by one employer but also to employment with successive employers (but see below).[15] Accordingly, the second employer was estopped from denying continuity accrued with the first employer, notwithstanding that there had been no transfer of a business between the first and second employer nor any other saving provision under (what are now) paras 17 or 18 of Sch 13 to the EP(C)A.

However, in *Secretary of State for Employment v Globe Elastic Thread Co Ltd*,[16] the House of Lords subsequently rejected the estoppel argument. In that case the employee, Mr Wijaszko, worked for a company called Heathcoats from 1948 onwards. In 1970 he went over to the Globe Elastic Thread Co. There was, in this case, no transfer of a business nor any other example of facts under paras 17 or 18 which might have preserved his continuity of employment. However, the second employer (Globe Elastic Thread Co) promised that his previous continuous employment would be honoured. It seemed that the principle decided in *Evenden v Guildford City Association Football Club* was applicable and that, if so, Mr Wijaszko might count both periods of employment towards his period of continuous employment. An industrial tribunal thought, in fact, that this was the case and found an estoppel against the second employer and awarded a redundancy payment based on the entire length of service with both employers. However, when the second employer put in a claim for rebate from the Secretary of State in respect of the redundancy payment,[17] the Department of Employment made the point that, under the provisions of the

---

13 Ibid.

14 EP(C)A Sch 13 para 1(3).

15 See Lord Denning MR [1975] ICR 367, 372. Cf *Chapman v Wilkinson* (1967) 3 ITR 39; *Evenden v Guildford City Association Football Club* [1974] ICR 554, [1974] IRLR 285, EAT. Note now, though, the opposing view of Lord Wilberforce in *Secretary of State for Employment v Globe Elastic Thread Co Ltd* [1979] ICR 706 at 711 and see now *Secretary of State for Employment v Cohen* [1987] ICR 570, [1987] IRLR 169 where the EAT firmly held (Scott J presiding) that the presumption applied to employment with the one employer only, *not* in cases of successive employers. See text below.

16 [1980] AC 506, [1979] ICR 706, HL.

17 An employer originally received a rebate from the redundancy fund in respect of a redundancy payment made by him under s 104 of the EP(C)A. However from August 1986 this provision was curtailed in its application to employers who employed no more than nine employees (Wages Act 1986 s 27(3); McMullen (1987) ILJ 266; EP(C)A s 104A). Section 17 of the Employment Act 1989 (effective 16 January 1990) repealed ss 104 and 104A (and Sch 6) of the EP(C)A thus abolishing the rebate altogether.

statute, there had been a break in continuity and why, therefore, should the Department of Employment pay a rebate otherwise than in accordance with a redundancy payment calculated in terms of the statute? The Department of Employment alleged that it was not party to any such estoppel even if the doctrine applied. The House of Lords agreed, and held that any estoppel (if there was one) did indeed not bind the Secretary of State for Employment in relation to his duty to make rebate to a second employer. Accordingly, rebate was only payable on the redundancy payment that would have been made on the basis of the employee's period of service with the Globe Elastic Thread Co.

Although this case is concerned with the Secretary of State's liability to make a rebate to an employer who has dismissed by reason of redundancy, the decision goes further than this. The House of Lords further held that an estoppel could *not* affect any rule concerning continuity of employment under the EP(C)A. In other words, if employment was broken under the terms of the statute, an estoppel could not rectify this for the purposes of a statutory claim.

As a final nail in the coffin of the estoppel argument, Lord Wilberforce dealt with the question of whether the presumption of continuity of employment could apply in a case of successive employments. He considered it would not.[18] And in *Secretary of State v Cohen*[19] (EAT) Scott J emphatically stated that the presumption of continuity applied to employment with the one employer only, not to successive employments.

In short, it will not now be possible for an employee to use promissory estoppel in a statutory claim before an industrial tribunal to prevent an employer denying continuous employment, even where that employer has promised that continuity will be honoured. Only the statutory provisions can determine whether employment is continuous and whether the provisions of Sch 13 to the EP(C)A apply.

2 THE RESIDUAL AREA OF ESTOPPEL OF FACT

There may be one other area of 'estoppel' which is relevant to a book on transfer of employment. This is estoppel by representation

---

18 [1979] ICR 709 at 711. Although because of the finding that any estoppel (if there was one) did not bind the Secretary of State, it was not necessary to decide the question whether the presumption of continuity under statute applied to successive employers. The obiter remark is, however, important for this area and also for the discussion in Ch 5.

19 [1987] ICR 570, [1987] IRLR 169.

of fact.[20] In *Smith v Blandford Gee Cementation Co Ltd*,[1] an employee who understood he was employed by the NCB received a written statement of terms and conditions under the then Contracts of Employment Act 1972 (now s 1 of the EP(C)A) to the effect that Blandford Gee were his employers. He subsequently relied upon that. In the end, he made a statutory claim (for a redundancy payment) and he made this claim against Blandford Gee. Blandford Gee claimed that the NCB were the employers and the claim was wrongly addressed. But it was held that the employee was entitled to claim all statutory rights against Blandford Gee. Blandford Gee were estopped from denying that they were employers by virtue of their statement issued under the Contracts of Employment Act 1972 (now EP(C)A, s 1). The estoppel of fact prevented the employer from going back on a statement that a particular state of affairs was correct.

This may be relevant, on occasions, to situations of transfers of businesses. There can be some complex situations involving groups of companies or multi-site employers, where the employee may genuinely be confused as to who is his employer. Sometimes he will not necessarily be employed or paid by the company for which he works. An employee may be entitled, it could be argued under *Smith v Blandford Gee Cementation Co Ltd*, to rely upon the fact that the employer referred to in the statutory statement of terms and conditions of employment is the employer against whom statutory claims must be made, even if another employer is the *actual* employer. If this case is right, and also has the consequence here discussed, employers should take considerable care in the preparation of written statements if they wish to ensure that the right company in the group will be responsible for statutory claims.

One possible drawback for an employee in this area is that the doctrine of estoppel could work *against* an employee. For could the doctrine of estoppel of fact be used against him if inaccurate terms as to payments, benefits etc are included in the written statement? If the employee does not react when he is handed a statement with inaccurate information, could he later be deemed to be estopped from denying the provisions of the written statement, even though they are not as he understood them to be? This is indeed a possible danger, but it is submitted that the courts should be slow to find that an employee is estopped from denying matters in the written statement detrimental to him; he, arguably, has less opportunity and insight (in view of complex restructurings of which he may not

---

20 Treitel *The Law of Contract* (8th edn) Ch 3.
1 [1970] 3 All ER 154.

always be aware) to correct the error. A court should be more likely to find as a matter of policy that an employer could be estopped from denying matters of fact the denial of which could be prejudicial to an employee; after all, the employer prepared the statement and, in fact, to prevent an employee challenging an inaccurate statement would conflict with the employee's right to go to an industrial tribunal under s 11 of the EP(C)A to challenge inaccurate particulars. All these factors should make cases where an employee is bound by an inaccurate statement rare.[2]

A good example of this occurred recently in the case of *Clifford v Union of Democratic Mineworkers*.[3] In 1985 the Nottingham area of the National Union of Mineworkers declared itself independent from the NUM and became the UDM. The employee brought a claim for unfair dismissal against the UDM arising out of a dismissal in 1986. It was important for her to show that her employment prior to 1985 was with the Nottingham area of the NUM rather than the NUM in London as para 17(2) of Sch 13 may have applied to cover the transfer from the Nottingham area to the UDM, thus allowing her to qualify for unfair dismissal. An industrial tribunal held she had been employed by the Nottingham area notwithstanding she had a document issued in 1983 headed 'Particulars of Employment between [the NUM and Clifford]'. The industrial tribunal felt able to ignore the statement of the employer as it did not, in the light of all the other evidence (including the existence of control by the Nottingham area), reflect the truth of the situation. The Court of Appeal declined to interfere with that conclusion.

In *Lumley Insurance Consultants Ltd v Pruddah*,[4] it was suggested by the EAT that a statement in the *terms and conditions* of a transferred employee, that on the business transfer previous employment did not count, where the true situation was that continuity had been preserved, would be void under s 140 of the EP(C)A.[5] The same should apply if erroneous assertions to like effect are included in a *written statement*.

3 BREACH OF CONTRACT

It seems to have been assumed in the *Globe Elastic Thread Co Ltd* case (see above) that the employer's promise might have

---

2 See e g *System Floors (UK) Ltd v Daniel* [1982] ICR 54, [1981] IRLR 475.
3 [1991] IRLR 519, CA.
4 EAT 150/83 LEXIS transcript.
5. And perhaps under reg 12 of the Transfer Regulations?

constituted a contract, under which Mr Wijaszko could have sued the Globe Elastic Thread Co in the county court. If so, it may be suggested that although he could not then have succeeded in the industrial tribunal to claim his full redundancy payment on the basis of service with two employers, he might, none the less, have sued and claimed damages equivalent to the amount of the shortfall of the redundancy payment in the county court on the different ground of breach of contract. (At that time, industrial tribunals had no jurisdiction to entertain claims for breach of contract. At the time of writing this is still the case. However, s 131 of the EP(C)A contains power to confer jurisdiction on industrial tribunals in respect of damages for breach of contract. There are now proposals for the exercise of this power but no instrument has yet been published.)

How would such a contract arise? As stated above, a contractual promise requires consideration. But this can arise in a transfer of employment situation. The employee may have joined the new employer on the express condition[6] that previous continuous employment was honoured. This could amount to a contractual promise. The consideration for this type of promise would be the employee's promise to go and work for the new employer in circumstances where he was not otherwise obliged to do so. This promise could be part of the main contract of engagement itself or, possibly, contained in a secondary contract implied by the court from certain actions and conduct by the parties.[7] (Although, an employee seeking to rely upon such an assurance would be well advised to seek legal advice and have a written document drawn up in which the consideration is recited.)

If the assurance became part of a contract, the employee might sue the new employer for breach of contract if he failed to claim a statutory payment based on continuous service with the old employer and the new employer. Damages for breach of contract in this sort of case would be an amount equivalent to the loss of any accrued rights in respect of any previous employment, subject to mitigation of loss. That is, there would be damages for loss of chance to claim a redundancy payment, a basic award for unfair dismissal or any other statutory award based on previous continuity of employment which arose as a result of the second employer's breach of promise.[8] Contract law mostly looks to see what would

---

6 *Cheshire, Fifoot and Furmston* Ch 6.

7 As, for example, in *Shanklin Pier Ltd v Detel Products Ltd* [1951] 2 KB 854, [1951] 2 All ER 471.

8 On damages for loss of chance, see the case of *Chaplin v Hicks* [1911] 2 KB 786, CA; *Laverack v Woods of Colchester Ltd* [1967] 1 QB 278, [1966] 3 All ER 683; *Manubens v Leon* [1919] 1 KB 208; Treitel, op cit, p 845.

have happened if a promise had been fulfilled. In such a case, if the contract were fulfilled, previous continuity would have been honoured by the second employer and would have been reflected in a higher redundancy payment, payment in lieu of statutory minimum notice or unfair dismissal basic award, than was actually due under the statutory rules.[9]

4 MISREPRESENTATION

It could, in theory, be possible that an assurance given by a second employer to a re-engaged employee that the employee's continuity of employment will be preserved might also be a representation to him which induces the formation of the second contract of employment. If the assurance were not honoured, it might seem that the employee could sue for misrepresentation, intentional or negligent, under the Misrepresentation Act 1967. Misrepresentation has been successfully argued in employment law, albeit in a totally different context from transfer of employment.[10] But successful action might not be likely under misrepresentation in transfer of employment cases, since a representation must be a statement of *fact* and not 'a statement of intention or of opinion or of law'.[11] A representation that continuity etc *will* be honoured is probably a statement of intention.

---

9 *Hadley v Baxendale* (1854) 9 Exch 341.
10 *McNally v Welltrade International Ltd* [1978] IRLR 497.
11 See *Cheshire, Fifoot and Furmston* p 270; *Maddison v Alderson* (1883) 8 App Cas 467. Cf *Edgington v Fitzmaurice* (1885) 29 Ch D 459, CA, per Bowen LJ at 483. It is difficult to tell whether there is a difference if the representation is that continuity *is* preserved; is this a statement of fact or law?

Conclusions

Perhaps the most significant recent development in the field of business transfers and employee rights since the last edition of this book has been the purposive interpretation of reg 5 of the Transfer Regulations by the House of Lords in *Litster v Forth Dry Dock & Engineering Co Ltd (in receivership)*.[1] Clearly, recognition of the case law of the European Court (for example of *P Bork International A/S v Foreningen af Arbejdsledere i Danmark*[2]) and of the concept, following *Pickstone v Freemans plc*,[3] that a purposive interpretation must be applied to legislation intended to enact a European Community directive, in this case, the Acquired Rights Directive, is of fundamental importance. In justifying the adoption of this jurisprudence in relation to the Transfer Regulations the House of Lords in *Litster* declared that it could not have been the intention of Parliament to enact legislation which fell short of the terms of the Acquired Rights Directive, hence the need to supplement our defective legislation. As has been pointed out elsewhere in this book, in view of the originally stated reluctance of the government to introduce the Transfer Regulations in the first place,[4] one might be excused if one attributes some irony to this end result.

But whereas this interpretative analysis gives force to the aims of the directive in respect of transfer of employment, the issue of discrepancies between the Transfer Regulations and the more far-reaching obligations in the directive is not yet over. It is clear that after *Litster* and *Pickstone v Freemans plc* it is open to argument in any court or tribunal that the Transfer Regulations as a whole must be given a purposive construction necessary to marry them with our European obligations if the Transfer Regulations fall short of them.

---

1 [1989] ICR 341, [1989] IRLR 161. See Ch 7.
2 [1990] 3 CMLR 701, [1989] IRLR 41. See Ch 4.
3 [1988] ICR 697, [1988] IRLR 357.
4 See Ch 6.

It should therefore be remembered (see Ch 6) that there are a number of instances where this is the case. For example there is no requirement in the Acquired Rights Directive that an undertaking has to have the character of a commercial venture (cf reg 2(1)); and there is no provision in the directive allowing for hiving down (cf reg 4 – see Ch 9 above). As far as information and consultation obligations are concerned, there is no 'special circumstances' defence in the directive (cf reg 10(2)); consultation under the directive has to be with a 'view to seeking agreement' (Art 6(2)) whereas no such enjoinder appears in the Transfer Regulations. After *Litster*, however, it is open to invite a tribunal or court to take a purposive approach to the Transfer Regulations and construe them to bring them more in line with the directive. The effect of such an approach on the discrepancies above will be interesting to observe. Finally, compensation under the Transfer Regulations, as discussed in Chapter 10, is, under reg 11, a maximum of two weeks' pay. This is a remedy which is far from an incentive to employers to comply with the consultation provisions of the regulations and is arguably in breach of the principle expounded by the European Court in *Von Colson and Kamann v Land Nordrhein–Westfalen*[5] that 'the transposition of [a] directive must . . . produce *effective* results' (emphasis added). This has been interpreted to mean that compensation or other remedies enacted under domestic law must be such as to ensure appropriate and effective redress. Regulation 11 hardly achieves this. Again, the courts' approach to these problems in the light of *Litster* will be interesting.

Of course, this type of discussion generates tension. Shortly after *Litster* was reported a commentator in the *Financial Times* warned that a possible consequence of the ruling might be that it would now be more difficult for receivers (and other lenders) to sell businesses and, if so, this would at the end of the day be at the expense, ironically, of continuing the employment of the employees involved.[6] This is because of the special impact *Litster* was in negating artificial schemes to avoid the Transfer Regulations. Whether this fear is justified remains to be seen, and a final conclusion can only be made once empirical evidence is to hand. It may be, though, that an overhaul of the area, particularly as it interfaces with insolvency law, is necessary.[7]

---

5 [1984] ECR 1891, [1986] 2 CMLR 430. See also Hepple and Byre (1989) ILJ 129 for further examples and discussion.

6 M Homan, *Financial Times*, 22 June 1989; Floyd, *Insolvency Law and Practice* (1989), p 177.

7 See the valuable critique by Collins (1989) ILJ 144.

Litster for example, rather unsatisfactorily, failed to deal with the European Court case of *Abels v Administrative Board of the Bedrifsvereniging voor de Metaal Industrie en de Electrotechnische Industrie*[8] where it was held that the Acquired Rights Directive does not apply to transfers in the context of insolvency proceedings instituted with a view to the liquidation of the assets of the transferor under the supervision of the competent judicial authority, ie presumably, in the UK context, compulsory winding-up on insolvency grounds. It has always been assumed, however, that the Transfer Regulations are wider and cover transfers in all cases of insolvency: a definitive ruling is awaited.

But consideration of such reform apart, it is necessary to remind ourselves that the UK submitted to a number of measures promulgated by the European Community under the Social Action Programme, including the Acquired Rights Directive,[9] and we cannot now complain when we are reminded by both the European Court and by our own House of Lords that full, and not optional, compliance therewith is necessary.[10] The response of the European Court answers in some ways the comment of Lord Wedderburn in the House of Lords debate on the introduction of the regulations in 1981 and cited in the first edition of this book, that:

'[The regulations] snatch away the rights which were intended by the directive, like some bicycle thief snatching purses in the night.'[11]

There are some residual areas of concern. First, it it has always been highly unsatisfactory that there exists lack of uniformity between the provisions of the EP(C)A and the Transfer Regulations. At the next available opportunity, revision of the law relating to business transfers should be undertaken and the law put into one harmonious and understandable code. This surely would eliminate many of the technical problems and pitfalls highlighted in the text. At least some steps forward may have been taken since the first edition. As will have been seen from Ch 4, the EAT in *Macer v*

---

8 [1987] 2 CMLR 406.

9 See Hepple and Byre (1989) ILJ 129.

10 In *Re Collective Redundancies: EC Commission v Belgium (Case 215/83)* [1985] 3 CMLR 624 the European Court stated, in deciding a case on the Collective Redundancies Directive (75/129/EEC of 17 February 1975 on the approximation of the laws of the member states relating to collective redundancies): 'The court has consistently held that the member states must fulfil their obligations under Community directives in every respect and may not plead provisions, practices or circumstances existing in their legal system in order to justify a failure to comply with those obligations.'

11 Hansard HL Deb 10 December 1981, Col 1490.

Abafast Ltd[12] advocated a commonsense unitary approach to provisions in the EP(C)A and the Transfer Regulations affecting pre-transfer dismissals and transfer of employment rights. It is our view that it can only be in the interests of all concerned, whether employees or vendors or purchasers of businesses, that the law is straightforward and comprehensible and that further advances to this end should be made.

Second, there is a strong argument for extending the scope of the law relating to business transfers to other types of disposition of business associations, principally to company take-overs by acquisition of share capital. In particular it seems only fair that provisions, for example, relating to information to and consultation with trade unions and to automatic unfairness of dismissals in connection with a transfer should apply not only to business transfers from one person to another, but also to other types of company take-over, ie by way of acquisition of share capital. On any change in ownership of a business, whether it is by way of a business transfer or by way of acquisition of share capital, a new proprietor will inevitably consider redundancies and harmonisation of terms and conditions of employment. There seems no good reason why an employee dismissed in connection with the change of ownership of a company's share capital should be less well protected than an employee employed in a business transferred from one person to another. Also, recognised trade unions ought to have the same information and consultation rights against the employer in share capital acquisition cases as in business transfers.

A related problem is the right of employees to information and consultation in undertakings with complex structures. On a broad level, this raises policy matters such as industrial democracy and consultation and information in domestic companies and groups and multi-nationals. The original draft EC Fifth Directive on Industrial Democracy and the 'Vredeling' proposal for an EC Directive on consultation with and information to employees in undertakings with complex structures both met with opposition from the UK government. On the EC agenda at present are the proposed European Company Statute (with various possibilities of worker participation), the latest version of the Fifth Directive, and the recent 'Proposal for a directive on the establishment of a European Works Council' in community-scale undertakings or groups of undertakings for the purposes of informing and consulting employees (29 November 1989). The eventual outcome of these

---

12 [1990] ICR 234, [1990] IRLR 137.

proposals is still awaited.[13] Focusing on existing provisions, we may expect (see Ch 10) changes to Directive 75/129 on redundancies, to enlarge the consultation obligations to cover transnational undertakings; it is likely that consequent changes to consultation provisions of the Acquired Rights Directive will follow in due course. There is also need, it is admitted, for further reform in connection with the consultation provisions as they operate in the context of domestic undertakings with complex structures. Take a group of companies with a holding company at the head and a number of subsidiaries. It is not uncommon practice these days for many employees to be employed by a holding company or even by a specific subsidiary service company, either of which lends out the services of employees to an active manufacturing or trading subsidiary. If the manufacturing or trading subsidiary sells its undertaking or part thereof, the Transfer Regulations do not apply to protect the employees in the service or holding company. It is true that the right of trade unions to information and consultation under reg 10 applies not just to employees transferred but also employees of either the transferor or transferee who might be affected by the transfer whether or not they are employed in the undertaking transferred. But employees in the service or holding company will not be employed either by the transferor or transferee and although affected in reality, will not have the right to be informed or consulted through the trade unions. Nor will their dismissals be automatically unfair under reg 8. Again this is an area crying out for reform.[14]

Finally, we mentioned in Chapter 6 the possibility of scrutiny by the EC Commission of infringement by the UK of the obligations under the Acquired Rights Directive. And, at the time of writing, it is reported that the EC Commission is in the process of drafting a revised version of the Acquired Right Directive.

In short there is no reason to suppose that developments during the life of this edition will be any less eventful than those which took place during the life of the last edition. Business transfers and employee rights remains one of the most complex and developing areas in labour law and one of the best examples of the impact of European law on domestic employment law.

---

13 See *Farrar's Company Law* (3rd edn, 1991). On the European Works Council proposal referred to in the text, see the Department of Employment Consultative Document of February 1991 and government comments thereon. Otherwise, see E Tabachnik, 'Minimum Standards of Democracy', in *Corporate Law – The European Dimension* (Butterworths, 1991); Boyle (1992) *Co Lawyer* p 6.

14 See *Banking Insurance and Finance Union v Barclays Bank plc* [1987] ICR 495, and the Take-overs and Mergers (Employee Protection) Bill 1987 (Appendix F).

Appendix A

Enquiries, disclosures, warranties and indemnities and other practical aspects

This book is not a textbook on the procedure for contracting and completing sales and purchases of businesses and companies; it only deals with the effects of such transactions on employee rights. None the less, a basic understanding of certain aspects of business sales can help our appreciation of the employer's position and the way in which employers may seek, inter se, to share responsibility in financial terms. There are many excellent books which deal with the subject of business sales itself. Those books point out the desirability of at least two basic steps. First, there is the exercise of due diligence by the investigation into the business, assessing its worth and potential liabilities. Apart from accounting and financial investigations and assessments, enquiries before contract and requirements for disclosures are essential. This appendix offers a brief guide to the employment law side of that investigation. Second, increasingly, it is difficult or often impossible for a purchaser to plan, in advance, with the vendor to avoid inheritance of employment obligations. This follows from the case of *Litster v Forth Dry Dock & Engineering Co Limited (in receivership)*.[1] It is therefore prudent to apportion liability for employee claims between the vendor and purchaser by agreement, through the use of a disclosure letter, warranties and indemnities.[2]

In practice, personnel managers, trade unionists and employees never get involved in, or even see, this aspect of a transaction, which is invariably handled by lawyers skilled in the practice of sales and purchases of companies and businesses. Most lawyers have their own precedents of warranties and indemnities suitable for apportioning liability for employee claims on business transfers and, if they do not, there are useful books which provide them.[3]

The following, however, is a simplified guide.

---

1 [1989] ICR 341, [1989] IRLR 161.
2 See Knight *The Acquisition of Private Companies* (5th edn, 1989); Wine *Buying and Selling Private Companies and Businesses* (3rd edn, 1986). A useful practical guide is afforded by Howard, 'Buying a Business: Negotiating the Sale Agreement' *Practical Law for Companies*, July 1991, p 23.
3 See e g *Knight* op cit; Sinclair *Warranties and Indemnities on Share Sales* (2nd edn, 1990) (this book, although expressed to be about warranties and indemnities on share sales, is also a useful guide as to how warranties and indemnities might look when applied *mutatis mutandis* to sales of businesses). Other precedents can be found in 9 Forms and Precedents (4th edn) and *Longmans Practical Commercial Precedents*, e g Precedent D5, D5020, D5-124-127.

A DISCLOSURE LETTER

A disclosure letter is commonly written by the purchaser to the vendor. It may deal with enquiries made by the purchaser during the course of negotiations. It also provides an opportunity for the vendor to qualify (subject to negotiation) the extent of any warranty that he might be asked to enter into. The following questions (at least) should ideally be dealt with in a disclosure letter about employment matters on a business transfer.

1 The names, addresses, sex and age of all employees.

2 The dates of commencement of service of all employees.

3 Details of notice required to terminate each employee's contract of employment.

4 The salary, wages and other benefits of each employee stating whether overtime is contractual or voluntary.

5 Pension details in relation to each employee.

6 All other fringe benefits and perquisites in relation to each employee whether believed to be contractual or otherwise including any arrangement or facility granted to an employee even if believed to be collateral to the contract of employment.

7 The names of all trade union or other employee representatives with the name of the trade union, the position and how long the position was held.

8 Details of any significant terms of every contract of employment of all employees (including service agreements for directors) or of any written statement under the EP(C)A.

9 Details of any commission or bonus schemes, contractual or discretionary in relation to all employees.

10 Details of any profit-sharing scheme applicable to employees and the names of employees to whom it applies.

11 Details of any share option scheme of which any employee is a member.

12 Details of any trade union recognised by the vendor, giving details of the recognition agreement and date of agreement and how long recognised.

13 Details of any other collective agreement with any trade union giving dates, contents and other surrounding circumstances and details of any disputes thereunder.

14 Details of any other agreement whatsoever, whether plant, local or national, with any union or other body of employee representatives.

15 Details of any Wages Council order applicable to the employment of any employee.

16 Details of any dispute whatsoever with any employee whether brought under the company's disciplinary or grievance procedure or otherwise or any matters which might give rise to such.

17 Details of any litigation threatened or pending against the vendor including, without limitation, any county court claims, High Court claims or industrial tribunal or arbitration claims or any matters which might give rise to such.

18 Details of any enquiry, correspondence, or contact between the vendor and the Commission for Racial Equality and the outcome thereof.

19 Details of any enquiry, correspondence or contact between the vendor and the Equal Opportunities Commission and any outcome thereof.

20 Details of any enquiry, correspondence or contact between the vendor and any officer appointed by the Secretary of State under s 20 of the Wages Act 1986 (enforcement of Wages Council orders) and any outcome thereof.

21 Details of any enquiry, correspondence or contact between the vendor and the Health and Safety Inspectorate and any outcome thereof.

22 Details of any enquiry, correspondence or contact between the vendor and the Inland Revenue concerning employees and any outcome thereof.

23 Details of all individuals in the undertaking working on training, work experience or similar schemes.

24 Details of any complaints currently pending under the company's grievance procedure.

25 Details of any complaints currently pending under the company's disciplinary procedure.

26 Details of any current appeals against dismissal.

27 Details of any recent changes of terms and conditions in relation to any employee.

28 Full particulars of the vendor's pension scheme including details of trust deed and rules and full particulars of retirement ages and benefits on retirement.

29 Details of names of all trustees of the vendor's pension scheme(s) and dates of appointment.

30 Details of any employee about to exercise or who has given notice to exercise or who has exercised a right to maternity leave and who, it may be possible, may elect to return to work after such leave.

31 Details of any current industrial tribunal award, county court order or High Court judgment in respect of any employee dispute.

The disclosure letter should comprise, therefore, a comprehensive schedule of information. This should be underpinned from the purchaser's point of view by warranties extracted from the vendor that, at the time of completion, all matters referred to in the disclosure letter are accurate and true as at the time of completion.

Conversely, a vendor may wish to use a disclosure letter, to a certain extent, to his own advantage, in qualifying the extent of warranties and indemnities extracted from him. In view of the normal extent of warranties and indemnities, if in doubt, a vendor should disclose. On the other hand, however, he must realise that, if this is done before contract, the disclosure of discouraging information may influence the purchaser not to proceed or to negotiate a reduction in the price to be paid for the business. However, that is a risk that has to be taken if warranties are sought to be qualified.

B WARRANTIES

Under the law of misrepresentation (save in the context of a contract entered into under the utmost good faith) non-disclosure is not actionable misrepresentation. The function of warranties is to fill this gap in the law. That is to say, the purchaser seeks to extract express representations from the vendor upon which the purchaser might sue if they prove to be wrong. These can be potentially unlimited in the size of claim thereunder. However, it is conventional for a vendor to negotiate a limitation of liability by excluding small claims, capping the total liability, specifying the time within which a claim should be brought and restricting warranties to matters within the vendor's own knowledge; and the disclosure letter itself can limit exposure, if warranties are subject to the disclosures.[4] To shorten the verbiage that can arise in vending agreements, the first warranty may be that the contents of the disclosure letter remain correct at the time of completion, thus:

1 All matters and facts and circumstances in the disclosure letter dated
[   ] are true and remain true at the time of completion and
that there are no other matters or details or information whatsoever of
the same or similar nature to the matters or details or information disclosed in the disclosure letter which have occurred since the date of the
disclosure letter.

Other warranties might usefully be as follows. It is important to note that these are merely suggestions and are not exhaustive. Nor should they be used as precedents for all cases, as every deal is different. They are purchaser-oriented and may need amplification in special cases.

2 There are no claims whatsoever pending or threatened against the
vendor within the jurisdiction of an industrial tribunal or any facts that
might give rise to the same.

3 There are no claims within the jurisdiction of a county court or the High

---

4 Howard *Practical Law for Companies* (1991) p 23.

Court in being or threatened against the company or any facts that might give rise to the same.

4 [Where recent redundancies have taken place] All notices required by EPA s 100 have been issued.

5 [Where recent redundancies have taken place] All information has been provided to and all consultations taken place with trade unions under the requirements of EPA s 99 and under reg 10 of the Transfer Regulations and that the requirements of EPA s 99 and under reg 10 of the Transfer Regulations have been complied with.

[6 [Where [redundancy] dismissals have taken place [but NB footnote 5]] If notices of dismissal of any employees have been issued the effective date of termination, whether by actual expiry of due contractual notice or under EP(C)A s 49 or otherwise, of all such employees has taken place before the transfer date and that before the time of transfer there are no employees whatsoever employed in the undertaking otherwise than as disclosed.][5]

7 There are no current industrial disputes or claims for recognition by any trade union or any facts which might give rise to the same.

8 All notices have been issued under the Social Security Act 1975.

9 There have been no claims whatsoever from employees between exchange of contracts and the completion date or any facts which might give rise to the same.

10 Nothing has occurred prior to the transfer which might give rise to a claim for constructive dismissal.

11 No arrangement has been made with or facility afforded to or understanding reached with (whether or not such has been regarded by the vendor as part of the contract of employment) with any employee otherwise than has been fully disclosed.

12 The salaries and wages and other benefits of all employees employed up to dismissal prior to the transfer have been paid or discharged in full.

13 There are no enquiries instituted by the Equal Opportunities Commission or by the Commission for Racial Equality or by any officer appointed by the Secretary of State under s 20 of the Wages Act 1986

---

5 *A note of extreme caution needs to be made here.* The purchaser should avoid all involvement in pre-transfer dismissals. If a purchaser has insisted on pre-transfer dismissals, these will usually be automatically unfair (*Litster v Forth Dry Dock & Engineering Co Ltd* [1989] ICR 341, [1989] IRLR 161). Liability for such dismissals will pass to the purchaser along with other employment obligations. Even if a vendor unilaterally dismissed employees prior to the transfer there is always the risk that the dismissals offend reg 8 and, again, bring in *Litster*. An indemnity is essential here against all pre-transfer dismissal liabilities. See Chs 7 and 8.

currently pending or threatened or any facts which might give rise to the same.

14   No employment conditions of employees employed in the undertaking nor anything that has occurred prior to the transfer will give rise to any claim for sex discrimination or equal pay either under domestic United Kingdom or European Law or for race discrimination.

C INDEMNITIES

The practice has grown up by purchasers not only to require warranties from a vendor in a vending agreement but also to extract indemnities from him. In company share sales, indemnities in relation to taxation matters are often obtained under a separate deed of indemnity, frequently obliging the selling shareholders in a company to indemnify the target company (ie the company being acquired) itself.[6] However, indemnities are required on general matters both in share sales and in sales of businesses by a purchaser direct from a vendor. Very exceptionally, a vendor will be able to extract an indemnity from a purchaser when selling. But such a vendor would have to be in an extremely strong bargaining position vis-à-vis the purchaser; since, commonly, the vendor is in a weaker position than the purchaser, the purchaser being either a more powerful predator or the vendor in a weak financial position, indemnities will almost always be purchaser-oriented. One exception to this might be upon a sale by a receiver/administrator, since such a transferor may be unwilling to enter into indemnities in favour of the purchaser.

Nothing can take the place of a considered drafting of indemnities according to the facts of each case and the precedents set out below should not be slavishly used without consideration for what is intended to be done. Again these are purchaser-oriented and would clearly have to be altered for a vendor (for, although the emphasis is on a purchaser's indemnity, a vendor, were he strong enough, would correspondingly need advice on indemnities from the purchaser, especially in respect of post-completion matters). Note too that the following clauses assume a transfer within the meaning of the Transfer Regulations takes place on *completion*. In fact, this seems to be the position on the balance of case law.[7] However, the clauses

---

6 See *Sinclair*. The reason for a deed of indemnity in share sales is that the selling shareholders and the target company are not otherwise in privity of contract; the vending agreement is between the selling shareholders and the *acquiring* company/person.

7 As discussed in Ch 4, many (though of course not all) sales of business take place by exchange of contracts after which there follows a period whereafter completion takes place. In favour of exchange are *Kestongate Ltd v Miller* [1986] ICR 672 (EAT); *Kennedy Brookes Hotel Catering Ltd v Reilly and Cook* EAT 53/82; and *Wright v A W Smith (Gosport) Ltd* COIT 17923/86. In favour of the view that transfer takes place on completion are *Batchelor v Premier Motors (Romford) Ltd* COIT 17295/82; *Dickinson v Bryant* EAT 73/84; *Field v Barnett*

will have to be altered/adapted if case law were to change on this issue. And, very importantly, it should be borne in mind that in cases in the European Court it has quite clearly been indicated, in the context of the Acquired Rights Directive, that the question of whether there is a business transfer does not depend on whether there has been a change of ownership but whether the operation of the business is continued or resumed by a new employer carrying on the same or a similar business. In other words, as discussed in Ch 4, it is possible for a transfer to take place prior to a formal completion of a transaction.[8] A good example of this in operation is *Dabell v Vale Industrial Services (Nottingham) Ltd*.[9] Basically, the question of when there is a business transfer is a question of fact and advisers should endeavour to make sure that if the transaction is formally to be arranged to take place on completion, the parties in fact behave in such a manner that is consistent with this. In other words, letting the purchaser into occupation prior to the proposed legal date for completion could give rise to difficulties and to a de facto transfer prior thereto.[10] A non-exhaustive and subjective sample of indemnity clauses for different situations is set out below.

(i) Where all employees' contracts are adopted by the purchaser

The below-mentioned indemnity assumes that the Transfer Regulations apply in respect of all employees taken on by the purchaser. The question arises what sort of indemnity, if any, ought to be extracted from the vendor. Arguably the vendor ought to be responsible for all outgoings in respect of employees up to the date of completion. Furthermore, it might be prudent to provide that the vendor should indemnify the purchaser against any constructive dismissal that might arise out of an objection by an employee to the identity of the new employer (see reg 5(5)). As discussed, this line of objection on the part of the employee is fairly limited. Reg 5(5) only allows this where there is change of identity and the employee can show that 'in all the circumstances, the change is a significant change and is to his detriment' – none the less this contingency should be provided for. Of course constructive dismissals may arise after the transfer if the purchaser attempts unilaterally to harmonise terms and conditions of the transferred

---

EAT 761/84; *Secretary of State for Employment v Spence* [1987] QB 179, [1986] 3 All ER 616; *Wheeler v Patel* [1987] ICR 631, [1987] IRLR 211; *Secretary of State for Employment v Galbraith* EAT 107/87 (82/97); and *Brook Lane Finance Co Ltd v Bradley* [1988] ICR 423, [1988] IRLR 283 (although to be noted is the failure of the EAT in *Macer v Abafast Ltd* [1990] ICR 234, [1990] IRLR 137 to correct an industrial tribunal's view that completion took place on exchange).

8 See *Foreningen af Arbejdsledere i Danmark v Daddy's Dance Hall A/S* [1988] ECR 739, [1988] IRLR 315; *Berg and Busschers v IM Besselsen* [1989] IRLR 447; *Landsorganisationen i Danmark v Ny Molle Kro* [1989] IRLR 37; *P Bork International A/B v Foreningen af Arbejdsledere i Danmark* [1989] IRLR 41.

9 [1988] IRLR 439.

10 See *Mohammed v Delaney* (12 December 1986) EAT 606/86 and the discussion in Ch 4.

employees. An indemnity could be extracted by a purchaser from a vendor in respect of those claims too. But it would arguably be unfair to do so.

'1 (a) In respect of the transferring employees, the purchaser will use all reasonable endeavours to allow the contracts of employment with the vendor to continue with the purchaser by virtue of the Transfer of Undertakings (Protection of Employment) Regulations 1981 but the vendor shall indemnify and hold harmless the purchaser against all claims, costs and demands liabilities and expenses whatsoever (including legal expenses on an indemnity basis) arising out of any constructive dismissal of any such employees following any objection by such employees to the identity of the purchaser.

(b) The purchaser may at its entire discretion defend or settle or compromise any such claim and the vendor shall upon demand indemnify and hold harmless the purchaser against all claims, costs, demands, liabilities and expenses whatsoever (including legal expenses on an indemnity basis) arising out of, or in connection with, so doing.

2 The vendor will be responsible for all outgoings and accrued liabilities in respect of the employees including without limitation all wages, holiday pay, bonuses, commissions, payment of PAYE, National Insurance contributions, pension contributions and otherwise up to the date of the transfer. The purchaser shall be responsible for all such outgoings (excluding pension contributions) after the date of transfer.

3 (a) The vendor will indemnify and hold harmless the purchaser against all claims, costs, demands, liabilities and expenses (including legal expenses on an indemnity basis) arising from any claim whatsoever by any employee having its origin, cause or causes prior to the date of completion including without limitation any claim for breach of contract, wrongful dismissal, unfair dismissal, race discrimination, sex discrimination or equal pay (whether under United Kingdom law or European law) or otherwise. The vendor shall also indemnify and hold harmless the purchaser against all claims, costs, demands, liabilities and expenses whatsoever (including legal expenses on an indemnity basis) in connection with any investigation by the Equal Opportunities Commission, Commission for Racial Equality or by an officer appointed by the Secretary of State under s 20 of the Wages Act 1986 or any other statutory or common law claim by any third party (which shall include any person, firm or company or governmental or statutory or local authority or commission) having its origin/cause in circumstances before the transfer.

(b) The purchaser may at its entire discretion defend or settle or compromise any such claim and the vendor shall upon demand indemnify and hold harmless the purchaser against all claims, costs demands, liabilities and expenses whatsoever (including legal expenses on an indemnity basis) arising out of, or in connection with, so doing.'

(ii) Where the purchaser has required the vendor to terminate the employment of certain employees prior to the transfer as he wishes only selectively to acquire the workforce or not at all

Here the position is fraught with danger for the purchaser as the principle in *Litster* will apply. In other words, if a purchaser requests a vendor to terminate the employment of individuals prior to the transfer, in all likelihood this will rebound upon the purchaser who will, under the principle in *Litster*, be liable. (This is because such dismissals will be automatically unfair under reg 8 and therefore the employment of such individuals will be deemed statutorily to continue to the point of transfer, thus triggering reg 5 in their cases. If he does none the less insist on proceeding in this manner, an indemnity is essential. As this is a very clear risk, he must make sure that the vendor is good for the indemnity that he has given and here, as in other cases where he is in doubt about the ability of the vendor to comply with the indemnity, a retention from the purchase price should be considered (or perhaps a personal guarantee from the owners of the business or from a holding company of a vendor company):

'(a) The vendor has terminated the employment of all employees whose names appear in Schedule 1 to this Agreement and has ensured that the effective date of termination of such employees has taken place prior to the transfer. The vendor in respect of such employees will indemnify and hold harmless the purchaser against all claims, costs, demands and liabilities and expenses whatsoever (including all legal expenses on an indemnity basis) arising out of any contract of employment or any termination of such contract of employment including, without limitation any claim within the jurisdiction of an industrial tribunal or at common law or otherwise.

(b) The purchaser may at its entire discretion defend or settle or compromise any such claim and the vendor shall upon demand indemnify and hold harmless the purchaser against all claims, costs demands, liabilities and expenses whatsoever (including legal expenses on an indemnity basis) arising out of, or in connection with, so doing.'

(iii) Indemnity in respect of trade union information/consultation obligations

'(a) The vendor shall indemnify the purchaser against all proceedings, claims, costs and demands, liabilities and expenses whatsoever (including legal expenses on an indemnity basis) arising out of any claim made by any trade union under section 99 of the Employment Protection Act 1975 or under regulation 11 of the Transfer of Undertakings (Protection of Employment) Regulations 1981 for an award under either statutory provision or in respect of any individual employee's entitlement under such award under the Employment Protection Act 1975 or the Transfer of Undertakings (Protection of Employment) Regulations 1981 arising either from the transfer itself or from any dismissal of any employee of the vendor whether employed in the business transferred hereunder or not.

(b) The purchaser may at its entire discretion defend or settle or compromise any such claim and the vendor shall upon demand indemnify and hold harmless the purchaser against all claims, costs demands, liabilities and expenses (including legal expenses on an indemnity basis) arising out of, or in connection with, so doing.'

This might equitably be made subject to proper supply of information from the purchaser as required by reg 10(3) of the Transfer Regulations.

D PRECEDENTS OF LETTERS

It is probably pointless to try and suggest a precedent of every single letter that might arise out of a business transfer but a few specimen letters may be of assistance. To assist in the application of these and of the sample enquiries, warranties and indemnities, the following factual example is posed.

Factual example

Conglomerate Limited is a light engineering company. It is in some financial difficulty. It has two divisions, one division manufacturing components for the automotive industry, and another division making lawnmowers. Due to financial circumstances it has to sell the lawnmower division in order to allow survival of its remaining activities. The directors have also considered that, for some time, the lawnmower division is an activity inconsistent with the main activities of the company.

Acquisitive Limited is interested in buying the lawnmower division. It investigates the company and one of its conclusions is that it is seriously overmanned.

There is a recognised trade union, the National Union of Lawnmower Operatives (NULMO). There is a collective agreement between NULMO and Conglomerate Limited governing terms and conditions of employment and redundancy planning. Conglomerate Limited also employs a fair amount of part-time and casual labour. Acquisitive Limited will either want to consider taking on some but not all of the workforce or, alternatively, taking on all of the workforce but undertaking a harmonisation of terms and conditions of the employees in the lawnmower division with those of Acquisitive's other employees. It is expected that the lawnmower division will retain its identity as a discrete division within Acquisitive's main field of activity.

Notes

Obviously comprehensive enquiries should be made of the vendor by the purchaser. Particular points to note are the existence of a collective agreement, the terms of which may be transferred to the purchaser. If there is a redundancy planning clause in the collective agreement this may set down a customary or agreed procedure for selection of redundancies. The existence of many part-time and casual workers should also be borne in mind in the question of selection for redundancies in view of the possibility of sex discrimination claims.

The trade union will have to be consulted under reg 10 of the Transfer of Undertakings (Protection of Employment) Regulations 1981. A draft letter is set out below. Also, if redundancies are effected prior to or subsequent to the transfer, it is likely too that the provisions of s 99 of the Employment Protection Act 1975 will also have to be observed. Although it is possible for a purchaser to resile from the fact of recognition of the trade union, this would have to be done fairly promptly and redundancies to follow subsequently, for the rights under s 99 of the EPA to be excluded. Accordingly, a draft letter to trade unions concerning s 99 of the EPA 1975 as well as a draft letter to individuals concerning their redundancies are also set out below. It is to be noted that once a proposed purchaser is on the scene and he indicates to a vendor that redundancies ought to be made, there is the risk that *Litster* will apply. Most pre-transfer dismissals at the request of a purchaser will ordinarily fall foul of *Litster* and liability in respect of those will fall upon the purchaser himself because such dismissals will be automatically unfair under reg 8 of the Transfer Regulations. It is arguable that a genuine redundancy selection exercise prior to the transfer, even if it involves the purchaser's directions, might fall outside *Litster* and might result in dismissals which are not automatically unfair under the Transfer Regulations because they are for an economic, technical or organisational reason entailing changes in the workforce but, notwithstanding the favourable view of the facts of *Spence* in the House of Lords in *Litster*, this cannot be relied upon. A surer way of avoiding automatic unfair dismissal is for the purchaser to effect redundancy dismissals after the transfer although of course it would pick up the bill for the redundancy payment. Either way, the purchaser may seek to have an indemnity in respect of the redundancy costs from the vendor. The indemnities described above may assist in that regard. Finally, an alternative scenario is that the workforce is acquired without redundancies. An employer may wish to seek to change terms and conditions of acquired employees to marry up with those operating in favour of already existing employees. Unless this is done with agreement, this could result in constructive dismissals which would be automatically unfair. This should be borne in mind as a potential cost in acquisitions. The only sure way of avoiding this potential risk is for an employer to agree with employees for the consensual variation of their terms and conditions. Sometimes a one-off payment can induce such agreement. The legal position concerning agreement is discussed in Chapter 8. A sample letter is included in that regard. Finally, a sample letter follows concerning a communication to employees indicating that their terms and conditions will be honoured and previous continuous service honoured.

1 Letter to trade union from the vendor under reg 10 of the Transfer Regulations

'Dear Sir

Proposed disposal of the lawnmower division of
Conglomerate Limited to Acquisitive Limited

I am writing to inform you that it is proposed that the lawnmower division will be sold to Acquisitive Limited. In advance of this proposed transfer I am informing you of certain matters as required under regulation 10(2) of the Transfer of Undertakings (Protection of Employment) Regulations 1981.

(a) I have informed you that this transfer is proposed to take place. It is proposed that completion will be on or about the end of [
        ]. The reasons for it are the continuing financial difficulties that the Company faces in operating a number of divisions and the fact that the activities of the lawnmower division do not logically harmonise with the main activities of the company. It is hoped that the disposal will result in a sounder future for the employees of the division;

(b) The legal implications of the transfer are that it is intended that the Transfer Regulations apply to transfer the contracts of employment and statutory continuity of employees concerned to Acquisitive Limited who will honour such matters. It is not envisaged that there will be any economic or social implications of the transfer for employees [save that, as you are aware, such employees' membership of our pension scheme will cease after the transfer and while it is hoped that Acquisitive will be able to provide satisfactory benefits under its own scheme, some financial adjustments will be inevitable];

(c) We are informed that Acquisitive intends no measures will be taken in connection with transferred employees. I believe that Acquisitive Limited will be contacting you regarding the question of continuing recognition and future bargaining issues.

[As neither we nor Acquisitive envisage any measures will be taken in relation to the transfer, it seems there are no consultations necessary but if that position changes we shall of course let you know with a view to entering into consultations in relation to the same.]

you have any queries arising out of this letter.

als to be transferred from the vendor

s company will complete the sale of its lawnmower
you are employed, to Acquisitive Limited. As you
ted, difficult trading conditions have made it neces-
any to make savings. This, combined with the fact
of the lawnmower division have been increasingly
he activities of the group as a whole has necessitated
vision for the purposes of preservation of its goodwill
mployment of its employees.

you to join them and your case is governed by the
dertakings (Protection of Employment) Regulations
ich your continuous employment and contractual rights
are transferred automatically. Acquisitive intend to honour your
employment terms. An exception to that, as you will understand, is
your rights under the Conglomerate pension scheme of which you will
cease to be a member after the transfer. An alternative scheme is
operated by Acquisitive, of which it is expected you will be invited to
become a member.

You may expect to hear from Acquisitive shortly.

Yours sincerely'

3 Letter from the purchaser to individuals acquired concerning existing contracts and continuity

'Dear [   ]

As you know, Acquisitive has signed heads of terms for the
completion of the acquisition of the lawnmower division of Conglomerate Limited in which you are presently employed. It is envisaged that completion will take place on [   ]. Upon that date
by virtue of the Transfer of Undertakings (Protection of Employment) Regulations 1981 you will become an employee of Acquisitive.
Acquisitive intends to honour your existing terms and conditions of
employment save in relation to your current pension rights. Pension
matters are excluded from the Transfer Regulations as being capable
of transfer to an acquiring employer. But I envisage that shortly after
the transfer you will be invited to join the pension scheme currently
operated by Acquisitive Limited and the pension trustees of your old
scheme will, at your request, make any necessary arrangements for

the transfer of any accrued right capable of transfer to Acquisitive's scheme. I will be letting you have further details in due course.

I am also able to assure you that the effect of legislation is to preserve your continuity of employment on your transfer of employment to us and we shall observe and respect such continuity and the statement of terms and conditions that we will issue to you in due course showing us as the employer will also confirm that your continuous employment runs from the date it commenced with Conglomerate Limited.

Yours sincerely'

4 Letter from purchaser to purchaser's existing employees

'Dear [   ]

I am writing to inform you that on [   ] we will acquire the lawnmower division currently owned by Conglomerate Limited.

This will obviously necessitate some integration of staff from the acquired business with staff from our own group. I do not envisage any major disturbance for existing staff and no change in terms and conditions of employment of existing staff will be involved.

[Unfortunately, it may arise that following integration of new staff, redundancies will be needed. It is to be hoped this can be avoided. But if it does arise, full consultations will take place and other alternative measures considered.]

Yours sincerely'

5 Letter to trade union pursuant to s 99 of the EPA 1975 (transferee employer)

'Dear Sir

Following the acquisition of the lawnmower division from Conglomerate Limited it has become clear to us that to ensure the survival of this business as a going concern, certain cost-saving exercises need to be undertaken, including dealing with the serious overmanning problem in the division as we have now seen.

Accordingly, it is proposed that a number of redundancies take place. It is proposed out of the 200 works staff, 40 individuals are made redundant. Of these, 4 are apprentices, 30 skilled labour and 6 unskilled labour. Out of the 100 staff employees, it is proposed to make redundant 30 employees of whom 10 are secretarial/clerical and 20 managerial.

The proposed method of selection of employees is in accordance with the collective agreement between NULMO and Conglomerate Limited which, as we have informed you already, we are prepared to honour, that is to say the following factors:

(1) Consideration of the balance of skills within the workforce;

(2) Performance ability and time-keeping;

(3) All things being equal, last in first out.

It is proposed that after a period of consultation between us of 30 days from the date of this letter, the first dismissal will take effect. It is proposed that selected employees will work for 2 weeks of their notice period (which will run from the expiry of our 30-day consultation period) and will then leave with the balance of any notice monies due to them, being discharged with a payment in lieu of notice.

I am enclosing a copy of Form HR1 sent to the Department of Employment under section 100 of the Act. I am also informing you that today I am posting a notice regarding the above proposals on to the works noticeboard.

I look forward to hearing from you with any representations you may wish to make upon the above proposals in order that consultation can now ensue.

Yours sincerely'

6 Letter from the purchaser to employees transferred recording agreed change to terms and conditions following harmonisation

'Dear [   ]

As you know, following our acquisition of the lawnmower division from Conglomerate Limited it has been necessary for economic reasons to harmonise the terms and conditions of our present staff with those that you enjoyed with Conglomerate Limited. As we have informed you in our various discussions, it is no longer feasible to operate the split shift system that you previously enjoyed with Conglomerate Limited. As a result, it is necessary to abolish the shift premium payments for the third night shift which will be abolished with effect from [   ]. Furthermore, in respect of the quarterly bonuses, these will now be based upon the performance of individual departments as opposed to the performance of the undertaking as a whole which may or may not affect your ability to recover a bonus at the end of each quarter.

In consideration to your agreeing to these changes we have agreed that you will be made a single premium payment of £750 which will appear in your monthly pay statement on [   ]. Therefore you have agreed to vary your terms and conditions of employment and a revised statement of terms and conditions recording these new terms is enclosed.

I would be grateful therefore if you could now sign the statement of terms and conditions and record your assent to the terms of this letter on the attached pro forma return slip and return it to me by [   ]. This will enable me to authorise payment to you of the single premium above referred to by [   ].

Yours sincerely'

Appendix B

List of qualifying periods for main statutory employment rights

The following is a list of the main qualifying periods for statutory claims. As well as having a general awareness of these matters when dealing with employees, a purchaser should, of course, work out lengths of service of employees he may inherit, particularly in relation to unfair dismissal and redundancy. It is also important to note that many statutory rights (sex and race discrimination and equal pay, for example – there are others too) do not require *any* qualifying period.

	Right	*Qualifying Period*
1	Redundancy payment (EP(C)A s 81(4))	2 years
2	Unfair dismissal (in the case of employees commencing employment on or after 1 June 1985) (EP(C)A s 64)	2 years[1]
3	Sex discrimination, race discrimination and equal pay (Sex Discrimination Act 1975 s 63; Race Relations Act 1976 s 54; Equal Pay Act 1970 s 2(1))	None
4	Written statement of reasons for dismissal (EP(C)A s 53(2) (as amended by Employment Act 1989, s 15(1))	2 years
5	Maternity pay and right to return to work after confinement (EP(C)A ss 36, 56)	2 years before beginning of 11th week before expected week of confinement
6	Guarantee payment (EP(C)A, s 12)	1 month ending with the day before payment is claimed, or more than 3 months if engaged on a fixed term or specific task contract for 3 months or less

---

1 However, importantly, unfair dismissal claims relating to trade union membership (EP(C)A, s 58(1)) require *no* qualifying period (EP(C)A, s 64(3)).

Right	Qualifying Period
7 Written statement of terms and conditions (EP(C)A s 1)	None, but has to be supplied within 13 weeks
8 Time off for union officers, union members or for public duties (EP(C)A ss 27–29)	None
9 Wages Act 1986 (deductions from pay)	None
10 Claim for remuneration under protective award (EPA s 103) or under an award made following breach of reg 11 of the Transfer Regulations	None
11 Time off for safety representatives or ante-natal care (SI 1977/500; EP(C)A s 31A)	None
12 Itemised pay statement (EP(C)A s 8)	None
13 Remuneration on suspension on medical grounds (EP(C)A, s 19)	One month ending on day before suspension begins or more than 3 months if engaged on a fixed term or specific task contract for 3 months or less
14 Complaint of action short of dismissal on trade union grounds (EP(C)A, s 23)	None
15 Time off to look for work under notice of redundancy (EP(C)A, s 31)	Two years
16 Statutory sick pay (Social Security and Housing Benefits Act 1982; Statutory Sick Pay Act 1991)	None
17 Statutory maternity pay (Social Security Act 1986)	26 weeks before beginning of 14th week before expected week of confinement
18 The right to return to work after pregnancy	2 years before beginning of 11th week before expected week of confinement

This list is not exhaustive. For more detail a specialist work such as Hepple and O'Higgins *Encyclopaedia of Labour Relations Law* should be consulted.

Appendix C

A note on compensation levels for redundancy payments and unfair dismissal

All the following figures apply from 1 April 1991 and will apply until 31 March 1992. Subject to approval by Parliament, new, mostly increased, figures will apply from 1 April 1992. These are included in brackets after the 1991/2 figures. Figures tend to be reviewed annually.

A REDUNDANCY PAYMENTS

The maximum amount of a redundancy payment is £5,940 (20 × 1 × £198) (£6,150 (20 × 1 × £205)). The rules on how to calculate this payment (which is based on age, length of service and the amount of a week's pay) are in Schs 4, 13, and 14 of the EP(C)A.

B UNFAIR DISMISSAL

(i) Ordinary cases

The maximum basic award is £5,940 (£6,150). The maximum compensatory award is £10,000 (unchanged). The additional award for failure to reinstate/re-engage will vary from £2,574 (£2,665) to £5,148 (£5,330) (ie 13–26 weeks' pay) (ordinary cases) or £5,148 (£5,330) to £10,296 (£10,660) (ie 26–52 weeks' pay) (discrimination cases).

(ii) Other cases

In the case of s 58 dismissals and s 59(a) (for union membership or activities) the *minimum* basic award (s 73(4)(a)) is £2,650 (£2,700) and the maximum award is £5,940 (£6,150). The maximum compensatory award is as stated in (i) above. The minimum and maximum for a special award where there is no order for reinstatement or re-engagement (provided one of these orders have been sought) (s 75A) are £13,180 (£13,400) and £26,290 (£26,800) respectively.

The minimum for the special award where there has been an order for reinstatement or re-engagement which has not been complied with (s 75A(2)) is £19,735 (£20,100), *but there is no maximum in this case* as the award is 156 weeks' pay without limit to the amount of a week's pay (normally £198 (£205)) to be taken into account.

Notes

These figures are taken from the Unfair Dismissal (Increase of Compensation Limit) Order 1991, SI 1991/466; the Employment Protection (Variation of Limits) Order 1991, SI 1991/464 and the Unfair Dismissal (Increase of Limits of Basic and Special Awards) Order 1991, SI 1991/467. The bracketed figures for 1 April 1992 are taken from the Draft Employment Protection (Variation of Limits) Order 1992 and the Draft Unfair Dismissal (Increase of Limits of Basic and Special Awards) Order 1992, both requiring approval from Parliament at the time of writing. It is important to note that when it is stated that new figures will apply from 1 April 1992, these will apply where the effective date of termination of employment (or relevant date in redundancy cases) falls on or after 1 April 1992.

Labour law textbooks should be consulted for details of other statutory claims.

Appendix D

Department of Employment documents

PART 1: DEPARTMENT OF EMPLOYMENT GUIDANCE ON 'ECONOMIC, TECHNICAL OR ORGANISATIONAL' REASONS[1]

(Reprinted with the permission of the Department of Employment. The notes to this text are not from the document, but are those of the author.)

1   Given the dearth of traditional authority, it is difficult to provide any firm guidance on the meaning of 'economic, technical or organisational reason', bearing in mind that the leading case, ie *Wheeler v John Golding Group of Companies* [1987] IRLR 211, was in effect concerned with defining what was *not* an economic, technical or organisational reason. However, the following may provide some general guidance but it should be borne in mind that what follows represents no more than the opinions of the Department of Employment and does not represent a definitive view of the law. In cases of doubt, the question of whether Regulation 8(2) applied would be a matter for an industrial tribunal to determine on the facts of the particular case.

2   First of all it seems to the Department that where there is a 'genuine redundancy' within the meaning of section 81(2) of the Employment Protection (Consolidation) Act 1978, this will be likely to fall within the meaning of 'economic, technical or organisational reason entailing changes in the workforce'. However, not all dismissals which appear to be by reason of redundancy will necessarily fall within Regulation 8(2). If, for example, there was a clause in the transfer agreement requiring the transferor to dismiss the employees before completion, even if that were held to be a redundancy within the meaning of section 81(2), it would not necessarily fall within Regulation 8(2) because it would not be a reason which related to the conduct of the business (see *Wheeler v*

---

1   These notes cannot, of course, be treated as a definitive view of the law. But they are a helpful insight into the thinking of the Department of Employment about *Litster* and pre-transfer dismissals.

John Golding Group of Companies, referred to above, and also *Gateway Hotels Ltd v Stewart* [1988] IRLR 287).

3   Subject to the caveat referred to in paragraph 1 above, the following considerations may be of some assistance to insolvency practitioners in coming to a view as to whether Regulation 8(2) applies:–

(a) Dismissals which are not connected with the transfer of the whole or part of a business do not fall within Regulation 8 and liability will fall to be determined by the application of the principles set out in *Secretary of State for Employment v Spence* [1986] IRLR 248. Where such dismissals take effect prior to the transfer being completed claims will generally fall to be paid by the Redundancy Fund, subject to the satisfaction of the other relevant conditions.

(b) An example of an 'economic' reason might be where demand for the company's product has fallen to such an extent that the company's profitability will no longer allow staff to be employed and the staff have to be dismissed. In effect, it seems that a dismissal in such circumstances would normally entail a dismissal by reason of redundancy within the meaning of section 81(2).

(c) An example of 'technical' might be where a company has been employing staff on manually operated machines and the new owners wish to use only computerised machinery, with the result that the employees of the transferor company might not have the technical skills necessary to be employed by the transferee. Once again, this might well fall within the statutory definition of redundancy in section 81(2), particularly section 81(2)(b).[2]

(d) An example for 'organisational' might be where a company at one location is taken over by a purchaser at a distant location. In such a case, it might be appropriate to dismiss the staff on the grounds that it is not practical to relocate them. Once again, depending upon the facts of any particular case, this might well be a redundancy falling within section 81(2)(a) in so far as the employer had ceased to carry on the business in the place where the employee was employed.[3]

(e) Any argument that an employee has been dismissed for an economic, technical or organisational reason will not usually be sustainable where the employee continues to work for the transferee.

---

2 See *Murphy v Epsom College* [1984] IRLR 271 and Ch 8.
3 See *Sewell v DMG Realisations*, IT, Case Nos 15486/89–15506/89; 13227/89–13254/89 and 13681/89; 5/6 February 1990 and Ch 8.

PART 2: EMPLOYMENT DEPARTMENT REDUNDANCY PAYMENTS SERVICE INSOLVENCY QUESTIONNAIRE

(Reprinted with the permission of the Department of Employment and Her Majesty's Stationery Office.)

Emloyment Department	Redundancy Payments Service

Redundancy: information from employer's representative

All notes in this form are for guidance only. They are not a full and authoritative statement of the law.

What is this all about?
We need information from you to help us decide whether the former employees of an insolvent employer are entitled to payments from the National Insurance Fund.

What if I don't know, or am not sure about the answers to some of the questions?
Please answer them all to the best of your knowledge, or give your opinion based on the available information.
The final responsibility for deciding entitlement to a payment rests with us, not with you.

The forms seek a lot of information. Why?
We need more information in cases where:
- there has been, or will be, a transfer of assets, of all or part of the insolvent business; **and/or where:**
- employees have been dismissed since the date of insolvency.

The form invites you to skip past these sections if neither event occurred.

Why do you need the extra information in those cases?
We need to decide whether any dismissals of employees during the period of insolvency are within the scope of the House of Lords' judgement in the Litster case.* For that, we need to find out whether such dismissals were or were not related to a transfer of business.

We also need to identify dismissals which are related to a business transfer but which are for economic, technical or organisational reasons entailing changes in a workforce, within the meaning of the Transfer of Undertakings (Protection of Employment) Regulations 1981 - referred to in this form as "the Regulations." **(Note:** references in this form to "Regulation 8(2)" mean Regulation 8(2) of those Regulations.)

Litster and Others v Forth Dry Dock and Engineering Co. Ltd. and Another 1989. IRLR 161.

What happens next?
We will pay the claims if we are satisfied that your opinion - that the employees are within the scope of categories A or B (see page 4 of this form) - is well founded.

How can employees get more information?
Our free booklet, PL718 "Employees' rights on Insolvency of employer" is available from Jobcentres.

Notes:
- where boxes appear that give you a choice of answer(s), please tick those that apply;
- if there is not enough space for your answer, please continue on a separate sheet of paper and attach it to this form. Please mark each continuation sheet so that is clear to which part of the form it relates.

Details of Insolvent company

1. Name of company

2. Address of registered office

3. Trading address (if different from 2)

Postcode

Postcode

4. Company number

5. Date incorporated

6. Nature of business

7. Who were the directors of the company?

Inits	Surname (CAPITALS please)	Sex (M/F)	Inits	Surname (CAPITALS please)	Sex (M/F)

8. Are any of the directors claiming redundancy payments as employees of the company? Yes ☐ No ☐ ▶ go to question 10

9. Please give details of the shareholders and their shareholdings:

Name of shareholder	Shares held	Name of shareholder	Shares held

IP 14 ——————————— 1 ——————————— Over ▶

Details of associated companies

10. Are there any legally associated companies of the Insolvent company? Yes ☐ No ☐ ▶ go to question **15**

11. Please give details of the associated companies:

Name of associated company	Registered no.	Name of associated company	Registered no.

12. Why do you consider these companies to be legally associated?

13. Did the associated companies offer to employ any of the insolvent company's employees? Yes ☐ No ☐ ▶ go to question **15**

14. Please give details of the offer:

Date	Time	Was the offer made:		Who made the offer?		
		in writing? ☐	orally? ☐	Name (CAPITALS please)	Position	

Details of employees

15. How many people were employed by the company on the date it became insolvent?

16. Are any employees claiming continuity of employment prior to the date of incorporation? Yes ☐ No ☐ ▶ go to question **20**

17. Please give details of that employment:

Name of employer (CAPITALS please)

Address

Postcode

18. Should that employment be treated as continuous employment? Yes ☐ No ☐ ▶ go to question **20**

19. Why do you think it should be treated as continuous employment?

20. To your knowledge, have there ever been any official or unofficial strikes? Yes ☐ No ☐ ▶ go to question **22**

21. Please give dates of the strikes:

- from [ ] to [ ]   • from [ ] to [ ]
- from [ ] to [ ]   • from [ ] to [ ]

22. Who should we contact for details of the employees' wages records?

Name (CAPITALS please) [ ]   Telephone [ ]

Address

Postcode

Details of the Insolvency/action taken

23. On what date did the business formally become insolvent?

24. What type of insolvency is it (such as "compulsory liquidation", "creditors' voluntary liquidation")?

25. Has there been, or will there be, a transfer of:

● **assets only?** ▶ Please enclose a copy of the contract of sale or other instrument of transfer. Please say why you think this is **not** a relevant transfer within the meaning of the Regulations:

● **the whole business?** ▶ Please enclose a copy of the sale agreement or other instrument of transfer.
● **part of the business?** If none, please give details of the transfer here:

● **none of the above?** ▶ go to question **30**

26. To whom was the transfer made?
Name of person or company (**CAPITALS** please)

Address

27. On what date was the transfer made?

28. On what date did negotiations begin?

Postcode

29. Which of the following have been transferred?

● the goodwill of all or part of the business   ● the customer list

● the work in progress   ● any premises

● the intellectual property rights

30. Have any employees of the Insolvent business gone to work for any employer to whom all or part of the business has been transferred?   Yes   No

31. Have there been any dismissals since the date of Insolvency?   Yes ▶ please enclose copies of any dismissal letters   No ▶ go to 'Declaration'

32. Were the dismissed employees given any notice?   Yes   No ▶ go to question 34

33. Please give details of the notice given:

Date given	Was notice given:		Who gave it?	
	in writing?	orally?	Name (**CAPITALS** please)	Position

Notes: • in our view, dismissals which occurred after the start of negotiations for the sale of all or part of the business are likely to be dismissals in connection with the transfer;
• where an employee is re-engaged by a transferee employer, it is unlikely that any dismissal in connection with the transfer will have been for an economic, technical or organisational reason;
• claims which properly fall under 34 **A** or **B** will be paid by this Department.

34. Please give below details of employees, dismissed since the date of Insolvency, who you consider to be within the scope of either category **A** or **B** below. Take care to ensure that you include each employee in the correct category. Use continutation sheets as necessary.
If groups of employees are to be dismissed at staged intervals, please send us a separate form for each group as the dismissals occur.

A Employees whose dismissals were not connected with the transfer of all or part of the business within the meaning of the Regulations

Line no.	Inits	Surname (CAPITALS please)	Sex (M/F)	Dismissed on: Date	Time	Line no.	Inits	Surname (CAPITALS please)	Sex (M/F)	Dismissed on: Date	Time
1						8					
2						9					
3						10					
4						11					
5						12					
6						13					
7						14					

How many continutation sheets for category **A** are attached?

What were the reasons for these dismissals?

B Employees whose dismissals were connected with the transfer of all or part of the business but which were for economic, technical or organisational reasons entailing changes in a workforce (within the meaning of Regulation 8(2)) - such as genuine redundancy dismissals

Line no.	Inits	Surname (CAPITALS please)	Sex (M/F)	Dismissed on: Date	Time	Line no.	Inits	Surname (CAPITALS please)	Sex (M/F)	Dismissed on: Date	Time
1						8					
2						9					
3						10					
4						11					
5						12					
6						13					
7						14					

How many continutation sheets for category **B** are attached?

Why do you think that these dismissals are within the scope of Regulation 8(2)?

Declaration

I declare that: • the information given in this form and in any attachments is correct and complete to the best of my knowledge;
• for any answers where I have given my opinion, I have done so to the best of my ability and having taken account of all the available evidence.

Signed

Date

Address

Name (CAPITALS please)

Telephone

Postcode

0001829010000 8/91 30,000

Appendix E

Relevant statutory materials

INTRODUCTION

There follows a selection of relevant statutory materials in five sections. Section one includes legislation contained in the Employment Protection (Consolidation) Act 1978 covering statutory continuity on change of employer (both in the case of business transfers and other instances), miscellaneous bridging provisions and redundancy liability on change of employer. The latter (redundancy liability) provisions will generally be otiose if the Transfer of Undertakings (Protection of Employment) Regulations 1981 (see p 324 below) apply. But as explained in the text (Ch 3) there could none the less be cases where the Transfer Regulations are inapplicable and the EP(C)A provisions applicable (e g in the case of transfer of an undertaking not in the nature of a commercial venture).

Section two contains provisions from the Employment Protection Act 1975 concerning the procedure for handling multiple redundancies. Section three contains extracts from the general provisions in the EP(C)A relating to unfair dismissal. Section four comprises the Transfer of Undertakings (Protection of Employment) Regulations 1981. Section five includes a selection of European materials.

SECTION ONE

Continuity of Employment, Miscellaneous Bridging Provisions and Redundancy

(a) Continuity

151 Computation of period of continuous employment

(1) References in any provision of this Act to a period of continuous employment are, except where provision is expressly made to the contrary, to a period computed in accordance with the provisions of this section and Schedule 13; and in any such provision which refers to a period of continuous employment expressed in months or years a month means a calendar month and a year means a year of twelve calendar months.

(2) In computing an employee's period of continuous employment any question arising as to—

> (*a*) whether the employee's employment is of a kind counting towards a period of continuous employment, or
>
> (*b*) whether periods (consecutive or otherwise) are to be treated as forming a single period of continuous employment,

shall be determined in accordance with Schedule 13 (that is to say, week by week), but the length of an employee's period of employment shall be computed in months and years of twelve months in accordance with the following rules.

(3) Subject to the following provisions of this section, an employee's period of continuous employment for the purposes of any provision of this Act begins with the day on which he starts work and ends with the day by reference to which the length of his period of continuous employment falls to be ascertained for the purposes of the provision in question.

(4) For the purposes of section 81 and Schedule 4 an employee's period of continuous employment shall be treated as beginning on his eighteenth birthday if that date is later than the starting date referred to in subsection (3).

(5) If an employee's period of continuous employment includes one or more periods which, by virtue of any provision of Schedule 13, do not count in computing the length of the period but do not break continuity, the beginning of the period shall be treated as postponed by the number of days falling within that intervening period or, as the case may be, by the aggregate number of days falling within those periods.

(6) The number of days falling within such an intervening period is—

> (*a*) in the case of a period to which paragraph 14(3) of Schedule 13 applies, seven days for each week within that sub-paragraph;
>
> (*b*) in the case of a period to which paragraph 15(2) of (4) of that Schedule applies, the number of days between the last working day before the strike or lock-out and the day on which work was resumed;
>
> (*c*) in the case of a period to which paragraph 16(1) of that Schedule applies, the number of days between the employee's last day of employment before service under Part I of the National Service Act 1948 and the day on which he resumed employment in accordance with Part II of that Act.

NOTE
This section was substituted by the Employment Act 1982, s 20, Sch 2, para 7(1).

*   *   *

EMPLOYMENT PROTECTION (CONSOLIDATION) ACT 1978
(c 44)

SCHEDULE 13

COMPUTATION OF PERIOD OF EMPLOYMENT

*   *   *

Change of employer

17.—(1) Subject to this paragraph and [paragraphs 18 and 18A], the foregoing provisions of this Schedule relate only to employment by the one employer.

(2) If a trade or business or an undertaking (whether or not it be an undertaking established by or under an Act of Parliament) is transferred from one person to another, the period of employment of an employee in the trade or business or undertaking at the time of the transfer shall count as a period of employment with the transferee, and the transfer shall not break the continuity of the period of employment.

(3) If by or under an Act of Parliament, whether public or local and whether passed before or after this Act, a contract of employment between any body corporate and an employee is modified and some other body corporate is substituted as the employer, the employee's period of employment at the time when the modification takes effect shall count as a period of employment with the second-mentioned body corporate, and the change of employer shall not break the continuity of the period of employment.

(4) If on the death of an employer the employee is taken into the employment of the personal representatives or trustees of the deceased, the employee's period of employment at the time of the death shall count as a period of employment with the employer's personal representatives or trustees, and the death shall not break the continuity of the period of employment.

(5) If there is a change in the partners, personal representatives or trustees who employ any person, the employee's period of employment at the time of the change shall count as a period of employment with the partners, personal representatives or trustees after the change, and the change shall not break the continuity of the period of employment.

18. If an employee of an employer is taken into the employment of another employer who, at the time when the employee enters his employment is an associated employer of the first-mentioned employer, the employee's period of employment at that time shall count as a period of employment with the second-mentioned employer and the change of employer shall not break the continuity of the period of employment.

[18A.—(1) If an employee of one of the employers described in sub-paragraph (2) is taken into the employment of another of those employers, his period of employment at the time of the change of employer shall count as a period of employment with the second employer and the change shall not break the continuity of the period of employment.

(2) The employers referred to in sub-paragraph (1) are the governors of the schools maintained by a local education authority and that authority.]

NOTE
Para 18A was added by the Employment Act 1982, s 21, Sch 3, para 2(3).

(b) Miscellaneous bridging provisions

(i) *Pregnancy and the right to return*

EMPLOYMENT PROTECTION
(CONSOLIDATION) ACT 1978
(c 44)

45 Right to return to work

(1) The right to return to work of an employee who has been absent from work wholly or partly because of pregnancy or confinement is, subject to the following provisions of this Act, a right to return to work with her original employer, or, where appropriate, *his successor*, at any time before the end of the period of twenty-nine weeks beginning with the week in which the date of confinement falls, in the job in which she was employed under the original contract of employment and on terms and conditions not less favourable than those which would have been applicable to her if she had not been so absent.

(2) In subsection (1) "terms and conditions not less favourable than those which would have been applicable to her if she had not been so absent" means, as regards seniority, pension rights and other similar rights that the period or periods of employment prior to the employee's absence shall be regarded as continuous with her employment following that absence [but subject to the requirements of paragraph 5 of Schedule 5 to the Social Security Act 1989 (credit for the period of absence in certain cases).]

*   *   *

NOTES
Emphasis added.
See below for definition of "successor".
Sub-s (2) was added by the Social Security Act 1989, s 23, Sch 5, para 15 from a date to be appointed (probably 1 January 1993).

(ii) Reinstatement or re-engagement after unfair dismissal

EMPLOYMENT PROTECTION
(CONSOLIDATION) ACT 1978
(c 44)

69 Order for reinstatement or re-engagement

*   *   *

(4) An order for re-engagement is an order that the complainant be engaged by the employer, *or by a successor of the employer or by an associated employer*, in employment comparable to that from which he was dismissed or other suitable employment, and on making such an order the tribunal shall specify the terms on which re-engagement is to take place including—

   (*a*) the identity of the employer;
   (*b*) the nature of the employment;
   (*c*) the remuneration for the employment;
   (*d*) any amount payable by the employer in respect of any benefit which the complainant might reasonably be expected to have had but for the dismissal, including arrears of pay, for the period between the date of termination of employment and the date of re-engagement;
   (*e*) any rights and privileges, including seniority and pension rights, which must be restored to the employee; and
   (*f*) the date by which the order must be complied with.

*   *   *

NOTES
Emphasis added.
See below for definition of "successor".

(iii) Reinstatement or re-engagement following conciliated agreement

LABOUR RELATIONS (CONTINUITY OF
EMPLOYMENT) REGULATIONS 1976
(SI 1976 No 660)

NOTES
Made: 27 April 1976.
Authority: Trade Union and Labour Relations Act 1974, Sch 1, para 30(3) (now Employment Protection (Consolidation) Act 1978, Sch 13, para 20).
Statutory references to legislation now consolidated into the Employment Protection (Consolidation) Act 1978 have not been amended, but Sch 15, para 4 (above, para 380) requires such references to be construed as references to the corresponding provisions of the 1978 Act. Corresponding provisions are therefore noted at the end of each Regulation.

1 Citation, commencement and revocation

(1) These Regulations may be cited as The Labour Relations (Continuity of Employment) Regulations 1976 and shall come into operation on 1st June 1976.

(2) As from that date the Industrial Relations (Continuity of Employment) Regulations 1972 shall cease to have effect.

2 Interpretation

(1) The Interpretation Act 1889 shall apply to these Regulations as it applies to the interpretation of an Act of Parliament and as if these Regulations and the Regulations hereby revoked were Acts of Parliament.

(2) In these Regulations, unless the context otherwise requires—

"the 1965 Act" means the Redundancy Payments Act 1965;
"the 1974 Act" means the Trade Union and Labour Relations Act 1974;
"the 1975 Act" means the Employment Protection Act 1975; and
"the effective date of termination" has the same meaning as in paragraph 5(5) of Schedule 1 to the 1974 Act.

NOTES
"Para 5(5)": now s 55(4) of the Employment Protection (Consolidation) Act 1978.
See, now, for Interpretation Act 1889, Interpretation Act 1978.

3 Application

These Regulations apply to any action taken in relation to the dismissal of an employee which consists—

    (*a*) of the presentation by him of a complaint under paragraph 17 of Schedule 1 to the 1974 Act, or

    (*b*) of his making a claim in accordance with a dismissals procedure agreement designated by an order under paragraph 13 of that Schedule, or

    (*c*) of any action taken by a conciliation officer under paragraph 26(4) of that Schedule.

NOTES
"Para 17": EPCA, s 67(1).
"Para 13": EPCA, s 65(1)–(3).
"Para 26(4)": EPCA, s 134(3).

4 Continuity of employment where employee re-engaged

(1) The provisions of this Regulation shall have effect to preserve the continuity of a person's period of employment for the purposes of Schedule 1 to the Contracts of Employment Act 1972 and for the purposes of that Schedule as applied by the 1965 Act, the 1974 Act and the 1975 Act.

(2) If in consequence of any action to which these Regulations apply a dismissed employee is reinstated or re-engaged by his employer or by a successor or associated employer of the employer the continuity of that

employee's period of employment shall be preserved and, accordingly, any week falling within the interval beginning with the effective date of termination and ending with the date of reinstatement or re-engagement, as the case may be, shall count in the computation of the employee's period of continuous employment.

NOTE
"Schedule 1": now EPCA, Sch 13.

5 Exclusion of operation of sections 24 and 24A of the 1965 Act where redundancy or equivalent payment repaid

(1) Where in consequence of any action to which these Regulations apply a dismissed employee is reinstated or re-engaged by his employer or by a successor or associated employer of the employer and the terms upon which he is so reinstated or re-engaged include provision for him to repay the amount of a redundancy payment or an equivalent payment paid in respect of the relevant dismissal, sections 24 or 24A of the 1965 Act (which require the continuity of the period of employment to be treated as broken where a redundancy payment or an equivalent payment is paid and he is subsequently re-engaged) shall not apply if those provisions are complied with.

(2) For the purposes of this Regulation the cases in which a redundancy payment shall be treated as having been paid are cases mentioned in paragraphs (*a*) and (*b*) of section 24(3) of the 1965 Act.

NOTES
"Ss 24, 24A": now EPCA, Sch 13, para 12.
See below for definition of "successor"

(iv) Definition of "successor"

EMPLOYMENT PROTECTION (CONSOLIDATION) ACT 1978
(c 44)

153 Interpretation

(1) In this Act, except so far as the context otherwise requires—

*   *   *

"successor" has the meaning given by section 30(3) and (4) of the Trade Union and Labour Relations Act 1974.

*   *   *

TRADE UNION AND LABOUR RELATIONS ACT 1974
(c 52)

30 General provisions as to interpretation

*   *   *

(3) Subject to subsection (4) below, in this Act "successor", in relation to the employer of an employee, means a person who, in consequence of a change occurring (whether by virtue of a sale or other disposition or by operation of law) in the ownership of the undertaking or of part of the undertaking for the purposes of which the employee was employed, has become the owner of that undertaking or of that part of it, as the case may be.

(4) Subsection (3) above shall have effect (subject to the necessary modifications) in relation to a case where—

> (*a*) the person by whom an undertaking or part of an undertaking is owned immediately before a change is one of the persons by whom (whether as partners, trustees or otherwise) it is owned immediately after the change, or
>
> (*b*) the persons by whom an undertaking or part of an undertaking is owned immediately before a change (whether as partners, trustees or otherwise) include the persons by whom, or include one or more of the persons by whom, it is owned immediately after the change.

as that subsection has effect where the previous owner and the new owner are wholly different persons; and any reference in this Act to a successor of an employer shall be construed accordingly.

*   *   *

(c) Redundancy

EMPLOYMENT PROTECTION
(CONSOLIDATION) ACT 1978
(c 44)

PART VI

REDUNDANCY PAYMENTS

Right to redundancy payment

*   *   *

82 General exclusions from right to redundancy payment

[(1) An employee shall not be entitled to a redundancy payment if he has before the relevant date attained the following age, that is to say—

> (*a*) in a case where—
>
> > (i) in the business for the purposes of which he was employed there was a normal retiring age of less than sixty-five for an employee holding the position which he held, and
> >
> > (ii) the age was the same whether the employee holding that position was a man or a woman,
>
> that normal retiring age; and

(*b*) in any other case, the age of sixty-five.]

(2) Except as provided by section 92, an employee shall not be entitled to a redundancy payment by reason of dismissal where his employer, being entitled to terminate his contract of employment without notice by reason of the employee's conduct, terminates it either—

- (*a*) without notice, or
- (*b*) by giving shorter notice than that which, in the absence of such conduct, the employer would be required to give to terminate the contract, or
- (*c*) by giving notice (not being such shorter notice as is mentioned in paragraph (*b*)) which includes, or is accompanied by, a statement in writing that the employer would, by reason of the employee's conduct, be entitled to terminate the contract without notice.

(3) If an employer makes an employee an offer (whether in writing or not) before the ending of his employment under the previous contract to renew his contract of employment, or to re-engage him under a new contract of employment, so that the renewal or re-engagement would take effect either immediately on the ending of his employment under the previous contract or after an interval of not more than four weeks thereafter, the provisions of subsections (5) and (6) shall have effect.

(4) For the purposes of the application of subsection (3) to a contract under which the employment ends on a Friday, Saturday or Sunday—

- (*a*) the renewal or re-engagement shall be treated as taking effect immediately on the ending of the employment under the previous contract if it takes effect on or before the Monday after that Friday, Saturday or Sunday; and
- (*b*) the interval of four weeks shall be calculated as if the employment had ended on that Monday.

(5) If an employer makes an employee such an offer as is referred to in subsection (3) and either—

- (*a*) the provisions of the contract as renewed, or the new contract, as to the capacity and place in which he would be employed, and as to the other terms and conditions of his employment, would not differ from the corresponding provisions of the previous contract; or
- (*b*) the first-mentioned provisions would differ (wholly or in part) from those corresponding provisions, but the offer constitutes an offer of suitable employment in relation to the employee;

and in either case the employee unreasonably refuses that offer, he shall not be entitled to a redundancy payment by reason of his dismissal.

(6) If an employee's contract of employment is renewed, or he is re-engaged under a new contract of employment, in pursuance of such an offer as is referred to in subsection (3), and the provisions of the contract as renewed, or of the new contract, as to the capacity and place in which he is

employed, and as to the other terms and conditions of his employment, differ (wholly or in part) from the corresponding provisions of the previous contract but the employment is suitable in relation to the employee, and during the trial period referred to in section 84 the employee unreasonably terminates the contract, or unreasonably gives notice to terminate it and the contract is thereafter, in consequence, terminated, he shall not be entitled to a redundancy payment by reason of his dismissal from employment under the previous contract.

(7) Any reference in this section to re-engagement by the employer shall be construed as including a reference to re-engagement by the employer or by any associated employer, and any reference in this section to an offer made by the employer shall be construed as including a reference to an offer made by an associated employer.

NOTES
Sub-s (1) was substituted with savings by the Employment Act 1989, ss 16(1), 29(6), Sch 9, para 3. The substitution does not apply where the relevant date was before 16 January 1990.

* * *

84 Renewal of contract or re-engagement

(1) If an employee's contract of employment is renewed, or he is re-engaged under a new contract of employment in pursuance of an offer (whether in writing or not) made by his employer before the ending of his employment under the previous contract, and the renewal or re-engagement takes effect either immediately on the ending of that employment or after an interval of not more than four weeks thereafter, then, subject to subsections (3) to (6), the employee shall not be regarded as having been dismissed by his employer by reason of the ending of his employment under the previous contract.

(2) For the purposes of the application of subsection (1) to a contract under which the employment ends on a Friday, Saturday or Sunday—

    (*a*) the renewal of re-engagement shall be treated as taking effect immediately on the ending of the employment if it takes effect on or before the Monday after that Friday, Saturday or Sunday, and

    (*b*) the interval of four weeks referred to in that subsection shall be calculated as if the employment had ended on that Monday.

(3) If, in a case to which subsection (1) applies, the provisions of the contract as renewed, or of the new contract, as to the capacity and place in which the employee is employed, and as to the other terms and conditions of his employment, differ (wholly or in part) from the corresponding provisions of the previous contract, there shall be a trial period in relation to the contract as renewed, or the new contract (whether or not there has been a previous trial period under this section).

(4) The trial period shall begin with the ending of the employee's employment under the previous contract and end with the expiration of the

period of four weeks beginning with the date on which the employee starts work under the contract as renewed, or the new contract, or such longer period as may be agreed in accordance with the next following subsection for the purpose of retraining the employee for employment under that contract.

(5) Any such agreement shall—

(*a*) be made between the employer and the employee or his representative before the employee starts work under the contract as renewed or, as the case may be, the new contract;

(*b*) be in writing;

(*c*) specify the date of the end of the trial period; and

(*d*) specify the terms and conditions of employment which will apply in the employee's case after the end of that period.

(6) If during the trial period—

(*a*) the employee, for whatever reason, terminates the contract, or gives notice to terminate it and the contract is thereafter, in consequence, terminated; or

(*b*) the employer, for a reason connected with or arising out of the change to the renewed, or new, employment, terminates the contract, or gives notice to terminate it and the contract is thereafter, in consequence, terminated,

then, unless the employee's contract of employment is again renewed, or he is again re-engaged under a new contract of employment, in circumstances such that subsection (1) again applies, he shall be treated as having been dismissed on the date on which his employment under the previous contract or, if there has been more than one trial period, the original contract ended for the reason for which he was then dismissed or would have been dismissed had the offer (or original offer) of renewed, or new, employment not been made, or, as the case may be, for the reason which resulted in that offer being made.

(7) Any reference in this section to re-engagement by the employer shall be construed as including a reference to re-engagement by the employer or by any associated employer, and any reference in this section to an offer made by the employer shall be construed as including a reference to an offer made by an associated employer.

* * *

94 Change of ownership of business

(1) The provisions of this section shall have effect where—

(*a*) a change occurs (whether by virtue of a sale or other disposition or by operation of law) in the ownership of a business for the purposes of which a person is employed, or of a part of such a business, and (*b*) in connection with that change the person by whom the employee is employed immediately before the change occurs (in this section referred to as "the previous owner") terminates the employee's contract of employment, whether by notice or without notice.

(2) If, by agreement with the employee, the person who immediately after the change occurs is the owner of the business, or of the part of the business in question, as the case may be (in this section referred to as "the new owner"), renews the employee's contract of employment (with the substitution of the new owner for the previous owner) or re-engages him under a new contract of employment, sections 84 and 90 shall have effect as if the renewal or re-engagement has been a renewal or re-engagement by the previous owner (without any substitution of the new owner for the previous owner).

(3) If the new owner offers to renew the employee's contract of employment (with the substitution of the new owner for the previous owner) or to re-engage him under a new contract of employment, subsections (3) to (6) of section 82 shall have effect, subject to subsection (4), in relation to that offer as they would have had effect in relation to the like offer made by the previous owner.

(4) For the purposes of the operation, in accordance with subsection (3) of subsections (3) to (6) of section 82 in relation to an offer made by the new owner—

(*a*) the offer shall not be treated as one whereby the provisions of the contract as renewed, or of the new contract, as the case may be, would differ from the corresponding provisions of the contract as in force immediately before the dismissal by reason only that the new owner would be substituted for the previous owner as the employer, and

(*b*) no account shall be taken of that substitution in determining whether the refusal of the offer was unreasonable or, as the case may be, whether the employee acted reasonably in terminating the renewed, or new, employment during the trial period referred to in section 84.

(5) The preceding provisions of this section shall have effect (subject to the necessary modifications) in relation to a case where—

(*a*) the person by whom a business, or part of a business, is owned immediately before a change is one of the persons by whom (whether as partners, trustees or otherwise) it is owned immediately after the change, or

(*b*) the person by whom a business, or part of a business, is owned immediately before a change (whether as partners, trustees or otherwise) include the person by whom, or include one or more of the persons by whom, it is owned immediately after the change, as those provisions have effect where the previous owner and the new owner are wholly different persons.

(6) Sections 82(7) and 84(7) shall not apply in any case to which this section applies.

(7) Nothing in this section shall be construed as requiring any variation of a contract of employment by agreement between the parties to be treated as constituting a termination of the contract.

95 Transfer to Crown employment

(1) Section 94 shall apply to a transfer of functions from a person not acting on behalf of the Crown (in this section referred to as the transferor) to a government department or any other officer or body exercising functions on behalf of the Crown (in this section referred to as the transferee) as that section applies to a transfer of a business, but with the substitution for references to the previous owner and new owner of references to the transferor and transferee respectively.

(2) In so far as the renewal or re-engagement of the employee by the transferee is in employment otherwise than under a contract of employment—

(a) references in section 94 (and in sections 82(4) to (6), 84 and 90 as they apply by virtue of that section) to a contract of employment or to the terms of such a contract shall be construed as references to employment otherwise than under such a contract and to the terms of such employment; and

(b) references in subsection (4) of section 94, as modified by subsection (1) of this section, to the substitution of the transferee for the transferor shall be construed as references to the substitution of employment by the transferee otherwise than under a contract of employment for employment by the transferor under such a contract.

SECTION TWO

Collective provisions relating to redundancies

EMPLOYMENT PROTECTION ACT 1975
(c 71)

Part IV
Procedure for Handling Redundancies

99 Duty of employer to consult trade union representatives on redundancy

(1) An employer proposing to dismiss as redundant an employee of a description in respect of which an independent trade union is recognised by

him shall consult representatives of that trade union about the dismissal in accordance with the following provisions of this section.

(2) In this section and sections 100 and 101 below, "trade union representative" in relation to a trade union means an official or other person authorised to carry on collective bargaining with the employer in question by that trade union.

(3) The consultation required by this section shall begin at the earliest opportunity, and shall in any event begin—

   (a) where the employer is proposing to dismiss as redundant 100 or more employees at one establishment within a period of 90 days or less, at least 90 days before the first of those dismissals takes effect; or

   (b) where the employer is proposing to dismiss as redundant 10 or more employees at one establishment within a period of 30 days or less, [at least 30 days] before the first of those dismissals takes effect.

(4) In determining for the purpose of subsection (3) above whether an employer is proposing to dismiss as redundant 100 or more, or, as the case may be, 10 or more, employees within the periods mentioned in that subsection, no account shall be taken of employees whom he proposes to dismiss as redundant in respect of whose proposed dismissals consultation has already begun.

(5) For the purposes of the consultation required by this section the employer shall disclose in writing to trade union representatives—

   (a) the reasons for his proposals;

   (b) the numbers and descriptions of employees whom it is proposed to dismiss as redundant;

   (c) the total number of employees of any such description employed by the employer at the establishment in question;

   (d) the proposed method of selecting the employees who may be dismissed; and

   (e) the proposed method of carrying out the dismissals, with due regard to any agreed procedure, including the period over which the dismissals are to take effect.

(6) The information which is to be given to trade union representatives under this section shall be delivered to them, or sent by post to an address notified by them to the employer, or sent by post to the union at the address of its head or main office.

(7) In the course of the consultation required by this section the employer shall—

   (a) consider any representations made by the trade union representatives; and

   (b) reply to those representations and, if he rejects any of those representations, state his reasons.

(8) If in any case there are special circumstances which render it not reasonably practicable for the employer to comply with any of the requirements of subsections (3), (5) or (7) above, the employer shall take all such steps towards compliance with that requirement as are reasonably practicable in those circumstances.

(9) This section shall not be construed as conferring any rights on a trade union or an employee except as provided by sections 101 to 103 below.

NOTE
The words in square brackets in sub-s (3)(b) were substituted by the Employment Protection (Handling of Redundancies Variation Order 1979, SI 1979/958.

100 Duty of employer to notify Secretary of State of certain redundancies

(1) An employer proposing to dismiss as redundant—

    (*a*) 100 or more employees at one establishment within a period of 90 days or less; or

    (*b*) 10 or more employees at one establishment within a period of 30 days or less,

shall notify the Secretary of State, in writing, of his proposal—

    (i) in a case falling within paragraph (*a*) above, at least 90 days before the first of those dismissals takes effect; and

    (ii) in a case falling within paragraph (*b*) above, [at least 30 days] before the first of those dismissals takes effect,

and where the notice relates to employees of any description in respect of which an independent trade union is recognised by him, he shall give a copy of the notice to representatives of that union.

(2) In determining for the purpose of subsection (1) above whether an employer is proposing to dismiss as redundant 100 or more, or, as the case may be, 10 or more, employees within the periods mentioned in that subsection, no account shall be taken of employees whom he proposes to dismiss as redundant in respect of whose proposed dismissals notice has already been given to the Secretary of State.

(3) A notice under this section shall—

    (*a*) be given to the Secretary of State by delivery to him or by sending it by post to him, at such address as the Secretary of State may direct in relation to the establishment where the employees proposed to be dismissed are employed;

    (*b*) in a case where consultation with trade union representatives is required by section 90 above, identify the trade union concerned and state the date when consultation began; and

    (*c*) be in such form and contain such particulars, in addition to those required by paragraph (*b*) above, as the Secretary of State may direct.

(4) The copy of the notice under this section which is to be given to trade union representatives shall be delivered to them, or sent by post to an address notified by them to the employer, or sent by post to the union at the address of its head or main office.

(5) At any time after receiving a notice under this section from an employer the Secretary of State may by written notice require the employer to give him such further information as may be specified in the requirement.

(6) If in any case there are special circumstances rendering it not reasonably practicable for the employer to comply with any of the requirements of subsections (1) to (5) above, he shall take all such steps towards compliance with that requirement as are reasonably practicable in those circumstances.

NOTE
The words in square brackets in sub-s (1) were substituted by the Employment Protection (Handling of Redundancies) Variation Order 1979, SI 1979/958.

101 Complaint by trade union and protective award

(1) An appropriate trade union may present a complaint to an industrial tribunal on the ground that an employer has dismissed as redundant or is proposing to dismiss as redundant one or more employees and has not complied with any of the requirements of section 99 above.

(2) If on a complaint under this section a question arises as to the matters referred to in section 99(8) above, it shall be for the employer to show—

    (*a*) that there were special circumstances which rendered it not reasonably practicable for him to comply with any requirement of section 99 above; and

    (*b*) that he took all such steps towards compliance with that requirement as were reasonably practicable in those circumstances.

(3) Where the tribunal finds a complaint under subsection (1) above well-founded it shall make a declaration to that effect and may also make a protective award in accordance with subsection (4) below.

(4) A protective award is an award that in respect of such descriptions of employees as may be specified in the award, being employees who have been dismissed, or whom it is proposed to dismiss, as redundant, and in respect of whose dismissal or proposed dismissal the employer has failed to comply with any requirement of section 99 above, the employer shall pay remuneration for a protected period.

(5) The protected period under an award under subsection (4) above shall be a period beginning with the date on which the first of the dismissals to which the complaint relates takes effect, or the date of the award, whichever is the earlier, of such length as the tribunal shall determine to be just and equitable in all the circumstances having regard to the seriousness of the employer's default in complying with any requirement of section 99 above, not exceeding—

(*a*) in a case falling within section 99(3)(*a*) above, 90 days;

(*b*) in a case falling within section 99(3)(*b*) above, [30 days]; or

(*c*) in any other case, 28 days.

(6) An industrial tribunal shall not consider a complaint under subsection (1) above in respect of an employer's default in relation to a dismissal or proposed dismissal unless it is presented to the tribunal before the proposed dismissal takes effect or before the end of the period of three months beginning with the date on which the dismissal takes effect or within such further period as the tribunal considers reasonable in a case where it is satisfied that it was not reasonably practicable for the complaint to be presented within the period of three months.

(7) "Appropriate trade union", in relation to an employee of any description, means an independent trade union recognised by his employer in respect of that description of employee.

NOTE
The words in square brackets in sub-s (5)(b) were substituted by the Employment Protection (Handling of Redundancies) Variation Order 1979, SI 1979/958.

102 Entitlement under protective award

(1) Where an industrial tribunal has made a protective award under section 101 above, every employee of a description to which the award relates shall be entitled, subject to the following provisions of this section, to be paid remuneration by his employer for the protected period specified in the award.

(2) The rate of remuneration payable under a protective award shall be a week's pay for each week of the protected period, and if remuneration falls to be calculated for a period less than one week the amount of a week's pay shall be reduced proportionately.

(3) Any payment made to an employee by an employer under his contract of employment, or by way of damages for breach of that contract, in respect of a period falling within a protected period, shall go towards discharging the employer's liability to pay remuneration under the protective award in respect of that first mentioned period, and conversely any payment of remuneration under a protective award in respect of any period shall go towards discharging any liability of the employer under, or in respect of breach of, the contract of employment in respect of that period.

(4) In respect of a period during which he is employed by the employer an employee shall not be entitled to remuneration under a protective award unless he would be entitled to be paid by the employer in respect of that period, either by virtue of his contract of employment or by virtue of [Schedule 3 to the Employment Protection (Consolidation) Act 1978] (rights of employee in period of notice), if that period fell within the period of notice required to be given by [section 49(1)] of that Act.

(5) Where the employee is employed by the employer during the protected period and—

(*a*) he is fairly dismissed by his employer for a reason other than redundancy; or

(*b*) he unreasonably terminates the contract of employment,

then, subject to the following provisions of this section, he shall not be entitled to remuneration under the protective award in respect of any period during which but for that dismissal or termination he would have been employed.

(6) If an employer makes an employee an offer (whether in writing or not and whether before or after the ending of his employment under the previous contract) to renew his contract of employment, or to re-engage him under a new contract, so that the renewal or re-engagement would take effect before or during the protected period and either—

(*a*) the provisions of the contract as renewed, or of the new contract, as to the capacity and place in which he would be employed, and as to the other terms and conditions of his employment, would not differ from the corresponding provisions of the previous contract; or

(*b*) the first mentioned provisions would differ from those corresponding provisions, but the offer constitutes an offer of suitable employment in relation to the employee;

the provisions of subsections (7) to (11) below shall take effect.

(7) If, in a case to which subsection (6) above applies, the employee unreasonably refuses that offer, then, he shall not be entitled to any remuneration under a protective award in respect of any period during which but for that refusal he would have been employed.

(8) If an employee's contract of employment is renewed, or he is re-engaged under a new contract of employment, in pursuance of such an offer as is referred to in subsection (6)(*b*) above, there shall be a trial period in relation to the contract as renewed, or the new contract (whether or not there has been a previous trial period under this section).

(9) The trial period shall begin with the ending of the employee's employment under the previous contract and end with the expiration of the period of four weeks beginning with the date on which the employee starts work under the contract as renewed, or the new contract, or such longer period as may be agreed in accordance with subsection (10) below for the purpose of retraining the employee for employment under that contract.

(10) Any such agreement shall—

(*a*) be made between the employer and the employee or his representative before the employee starts work under the contract as renewed or, as the case may be, the new contract;

(*b*) be in writing;

(*c*) specify the date of the end of the trial period; and

(*d*) specify the terms and conditions of employment which will apply in the employee's case after the end of that period.

(11) If during the trial period—

(*a*) the employee, for whatever reason, terminates the contract, or gives notice to terminate it and the contract is thereafter, in consequence, terminated; or

(*b*) the employer, for a reason connected with or arising out of the change to the renewed, or new, employment, terminates the contract, or gives notice to terminate it and the contract is thereafter, in consequence, terminated, then, the employee shall remain entitled under the protective award unless, in a case falling within paragraph (*a*) above, he acted unreasonably in terminating or giving notice to terminate the contract.

NOTE
The words in square brackets in sub-s (4) were substituted by the Employment Protection (Consolidation) Act 1978, s 159(2), Sch 16, para 23(1), (4).

103 Complaint by employee to industrial tribunal

(1) An employee may present a complaint to an industrial tribunal on the ground that he is an employee of a description to which a protective award relates and that his employer has failed, wholly or in part, to pay him remuneration under that award.

(2) An industrial tribunal shall not entertain a complaint under subsection (1) above unless it is presented to the tribunal before the end of the period of three months beginning with the day (or, if the complaint relates to more than one day, the last of the days) in respect of which the complaint is made of failure to pay remuneration, or within such further period as the tribunal considers reasonable in a case where it is satisfied that it was not reasonably practicable for the complaint to be presented within the period of three months.

(3) Where the tribunal finds a complaint under subsection (1) above well-founded it shall order the employer to pay the complainant the amount of remuneration which it finds is due to him.

104 *(Repealed by the Wages Act 1986, s 32(2), Sch 5, Pt I.)*

105 Offence and proceedings

(1) If an employer fails to give notice to the Secretary of State in accordance with section 100 above, he shall be liable on summary conviction to a fine not exceeding [level 5 on the standard scale].

(2) Proceedings in England or Wales for an offence under subsection (1) above shall be instituted only by or with the consent of the Secretary of State or by an officer authorised for that purpose by special or general directions of the Secretary of State.

(3) An officer so authorised may, although not of counsel or a solicitor, prosecute or conduct before a magistrates' court any proceedings for such an offence.

(4), (5) . . .

NOTES
The reference to level 5 on the standard scale in sub-s (1) is substituted by virtue of the Criminal Justice Act 1982, ss 38, 46.
Sub-ss (4), (5) were repealed by the Wages Act 1986, s 32(2), Sch 5, Pt I.

106 Supplementary

(1) . . .

(2) For the purposes of any proceedings under this Part of this Act, the dismissal or proposed dismissal of an employee shall be presumed, unless the contrary is proved, to be by reason of redundancy.

(3) [Schedule 14 to the Employment Protection (Consolidation) Act 1978 shall apply for the calculation of a week's pay for the purposes of section 102 above, and, for the purposes of Part II of the Schedule, the calculation date is—

    (*a*) in the case of an employee who was dismissed before the date on which the protective award was made, the date which by virtue of paragraph 7(1)(*k*) or (*l*) of the said Schedule 14] is the calculation date for the purpose of computing the amount of a redundancy payment in relation to that dismissal (whether or not the employee concerned is entitled to any such payment); and

    (*b*) in any other case, the date on which the protective award was made.

(4) The Secretary of State may by order vary the provisions of sections 99(3) and 100(1) above and the periods referred to in section 101(5)(*a*) to (*c*) above and may vary those provisions or periods either generally or in their application to any description of employees, but no such order shall be made which has the effect of reducing to less than 30 days the periods referred to in sections 99(3) and 100(1) as the periods which must elapse before the first of the dismissals takes effect.

(5) No order shall be made under subsection (4) above unless a draft of the order has been laid before Parliament and approved by a resolution of each House of Parliament.

NOTES
Sub-s (1) was repealed by the Employment Act 1980, s 20(3), Sch 2.
The words in square brackets in sub-s (3) were substituted by the Employment Protection (Consolidation) Act 1978, s 159(2), Sch 16, para 23(1), (6).

107 Powers to adapt foregoing provisions in case of collective agreements on redundancies

(1) If at any time there is in force a collective agreement which establishes—

    (*a*) arrangements for providing alternative employment for employees to whom the agreement relates if they are dismissed as redundant by an employer to whom it relates; or

(b) arrangements for the handling of redundancies;

and on the application of all the parties to the agreement the Secretary of State, having regard to the provisions of the agreement, is satisfied that the arrangements are on the whole at least as favourable to those employees as the foregoing provisions of this Part of this Act, he may make an order under this section adapting, modifying or excluding any of those provisions both in their application to all or any of those employees and in their application to any other employees of any such employer.

(2) The Secretary of State shall not make an order under this section in respect of an agreement unless—

(a) the agreement provides for procedures to be followed (whether by arbitration or otherwise) in cases where an employee to whom the agreement relates claims that any employer or other person to whom it relates has not complied with the provisions of the agreement, and that those procedures include a right to arbitration or adjudication by an independent referee or body in cases where (by reason of an equality of votes or otherwise) a decision cannot otherwise be reached; or

(b) the agreement indicates that any such employee may present a complaint to an industrial tribunal that any such employer or other person has not complied with those provisions.

(3) An order under this section may confer on an industrial tribunal to whom a complaint is presented as mentioned in subsection (2)(b) above such powers and duties as the Secretary of State considers appropriate.

(4) Without prejudice to section 123 below, an order under this section may be varied or revoked by a subsequent order thereunder, whether in pursuance of an application made by all or any of the parties to the agreement in question or without any such application.

NOTE
No orders have yet been made under this section.

SECTION THREE

General provisions relating to unfair dismissal

EMPLOYMENT PROTECTION (CONSOLIDATION) ACT 1978
(c 44)

PART V

UNFAIR DISMISSAL

*　　*　　*

Meaning of unfair dismissal

*   *   *

57 General provisions relating to fairness of dismissal

(1) In determining for the purposes of this Part whether the dismissal of an employee was fair or unfair, it shall be for the employer to show—

> (*a*) what was the reason (or, if there was more than one, the principal reason) for the dismissal, and
>
> (*b*) that it was a reason falling within subsection (2) or some other substantial reason of a kind such as to justify the dismissal of an employee holding the position which that employee held.

(2) In subsection (1)(*b*) the reference to a reason falling within this subsection is a reference to a reason which—

> (*a*) related to the capability or qualifications of the employee for performing work of the kind which he was employed by the employer to do, or
>
> (*b*) related to the conduct of the employee, or
>
> (*c*) was that the employee was redundant, or
>
> (*d*) was that the employee could not continue to work in the position which he held without contravention (either on his part or on that of his employer) of a duty or restriction imposed by or under an enactment.

(3) Where the employer has fulfilled the requirements of subsection (1), then, subject to sections 58 to 62, the determination of the question whether the dismissal was fair or unfair, having regard to the reason shown by the employer, shall depend on whether [in the circumstances (including the size and administrative resources of the employer's undertaking) the employer acted reasonably or unreasonably in treating it as a sufficient reason for dismissing the employee; and that question shall be determined in accordance with equity and the substantial merits of the case].

(4) In this section, in relation to an employee,—

> (*a*) "capability" means capability assessed by reference to skill, aptitude, health or any other physical or mental quality;
>
> (*b*) "qualifications" means any degree, diploma or other academic, technical or professional qualification relevant to the position which the employee held.

NOTE
The words in square brackets in sub-3 (3) were substituted by the Employment Act 1980, s 6.

*   *   *

59 Dismissal on ground of redundancy

Where the reason or principal reason for the dismissal of an employee was
that he was redundant, but it is shown that the circumstances constituting
the redundancy applied equally to one or other employees in the same
undertaking who held positions similar to that held by him and who have
not been dismissed by the employer, and either—

(*a*) that the reason (or, if more than one, the principal reason) for
which he was selected for dismissal was [one of those specified in
section 58(1)] or;

(*b*) that he was selected for dismissal in contravention of a customary
arrangement or agreed procedure relating to redundancy and
there were no special reasons justifying a departure from that
arrangement or procedure in his case,

then, for the purposes of this Part, the dismissal shall be regarded as unfair.

NOTE

The words in square brackets were substituted by the Employment Act 1982, s 21(2),
Sch 3, Pt II, para 17.
Section 58 (dismissals relating to trade union membership) is excluded from this
selection of materials as are other more specialised provisions concerning unfair
dismissal.

SECTION FOUR

The Transfer Regulations

THE TRANSFER OF UNDERTAKINGS (PROTECTION OF EMPLOYMENT) REGULATIONS 1981
(SI 1981 No 1794)

NOTES
Made: 14 December 1981.
Authority: European Communities Act 1972 s 2(2).
Commencement: 1 February 1982 (regs 1–3, 10–13); May 1982 (remainder).
These regulations, which are made under the European Communities Act 1972,
implement the provisions of EEC Directive No 77/189 (see Section Five below). For
the application of these regulations to HM Ordnance Factories and Naval Dockyards, see the Ordnance Factories and Military Services Act 1984 s 4 and Sch 2. For
their application to HM Dockyards see further the Dockyard Services Act 1986
s 1(4).

1 Citation, commencement and extent

(1) These Regulations may be cited as the Transfer of Undertakings (Protection of Employment) Regulations 1981.

(2) These Regulations, except Regulations 4 to 9 and 14, shall come

into operation on 1st February 1982 and Regulations 4 to 9 and 14 shall come into operation on 1st May 1982.

(3) These Regulations, except Regulations 11(10) and 13(3) and (4), extend to Northern Ireland.

2 Interpretation

(1) In these Regulations—

"collective agreement", "employers' association", and "trade union" have the same meanings respectively as in the 1974 Act or, in Northern Ireland, the 1976 Order;

"collective bargaining" has the same meaning as it has in the 1975 Act or, in Northern Ireland, the 1976 Order;

"contract of employment" means any agreement between an employee and his employer determining the terms and conditions of his employment;

"employee" means an individual who works for another person whether under a contract of service or apprenticeship or otherwise but does not include anyone who provides services under a contract for services and references to a person's employer shall be construed accordingly;

"the 1974 Act", "the 1975 Act", "the 1978 Act" and "the 1976 Order" mean, respectively, the Trade Union and Labour Relations Act 1974, the Employment Protection Act 1975, the Employment Protection (Consolidation) Act 1978 and the Industrial Relations (Northern Ireland) Order 1976;

"recognised", in relation to a trade union, means recognised to any extent by an employer, or two or more associated employers (within the meaning of the 1978 Act, or, in Northern Ireland, the 1976 Order), for the purpose of collective bargaining;

"relevant transfer" means a transfer to which these Regulations apply and "transferor" and "transferee" shall be construed accordingly; and

"undertaking" includes any trade or business but does not include any undertaking or part of an undertaking which is not in the nature of a commercial venture.

(2) References in these Regulations to the transfer of part of an undertaking are references to a transfer of a part which is being transferred as a business and, accordingly, do not include references to a transfer of a ship without more.

(3) For the purposes of these Regulations the representative of a trade union recognised by an employer is an official or other person authorised to carry on collective bargaining with that employer by that union.

3 A relevant transfer

(1) Subject to the provisions of these Regulations, these Regulations apply to a transfer from one person to another of an undertaking situated

immediately before the transfer in the United Kingdom or a part of one which is so situated.

(2) Subject as aforesaid, these Regulations so apply whether the transfer is effected by sale or by some other disposition or by operation of law.

(3) Subject as aforesaid, these Regulations so apply notwithstanding—

(*a*) that the transfer is governed or effected by the law of a country or territory outside the United Kingdom;

(*b*) that persons employed in the undertaking or part transferred ordinarily work outside the United Kingdom;

(*c*) that the employment of any of those persons is governed by any such law.

(4) It is hereby declared that a transfer of an undertaking or part of one may be effected by a series of two or more transactions between the same parties, but in determining whether or not such a series constitutes a single transfer regard shall be had to the extent to which the undertaking or part was controlled by the transferor and transferee respectively before the last transaction, to the lapse of time between each of the transactions, to the intention of the parties and to all the other circumstances.

(5) Where, in consequence (whether directly or indirectly) of the transfer of an undertaking or part of one which was situated immediately before the transfer in the United Kingdom, a ship within the meaning of the Merchant Shipping Act 1894 registered in the United Kingdom ceases to be so registered, these Regulations shall not affect the right conferred by section 5 of the Merchant Shipping Act 1970 (right of seamen to be discharged when ship ceases to be registered in the United Kingdom) on a seaman employed in the ship.

4 Transfers by receivers and liquidators

(1) Where the receiver of the property or part of the property of a company [or the administrator of a company appointed under Part II of the Insolvency Act 1986] or, in the case of a creditors' voluntary winding up, the liquidator of a company transfers the company's undertaking, or part of the company's undertaking, (the "relevant undertaking") to a wholly owned subsidiary of the company, the transfer shall for the purposes of these Regulations be deemed not to have been effected until immediately before—

(*a*) the transferee company ceases (otherwise than by reason of its being wound up) to be a wholly owned subsidiary of the transferor company; or

(*b*) the relevant undertaking is transferred by the transferee company to another person;

whichever first occurs, and, for the purposes of these Regulations, the transfer of the relevant undertaking shall be taken to have been effected immediately before that date by one transaction only.

(2) In this Regulation—

"creditors' voluntary winding up" has the same meaning as in the Companies Act 1948 or, in Northern Ireland, the Companies Act (Northern Ireland) 1960; and

"wholly owned subsidiary" has the same meaning as it has for the purposes of section 150 of the Companies Act 1948 and section 144 of the Companies Act (Northern Ireland) 1960.

NOTES
Paragraph 1 was amended by the inclusion of the words in square brackets by the Transfer of Undertakings (Protection of Employment) (Amendment) Regulations 1987, SI 1987/442 (reproduced in full in the first edition of this book) with effect from 24 April 1987.

5 Effect of relevant transfer on contracts of employment, etc.

(1) A relevant transfer shall not operate so as to terminate the contract of employment of any person employed by the transferor in the undertaking or part transferred but any such contract which would otherwise have been terminated by the transfer shall have effect after the transfer as if originally made between the person so employed and the transferee.

(2) Without prejudice to paragraph (1) above, on the completion of a relevant transfer—

(*a*) all the transferor's rights, powers, duties and liabilities under or in connection with any such contract, shall be transferred by virtue of this Regulation to the transferee; and

(*b*) anything done before the transfer is completed by or in relation to the transferor in respect of that contract or a person employed in that undertaking or part shall be deemed to have been done by or in relation to the transferee.

(3) Any reference in paragraph (1) or (2) above to a person employed in an undertaking or part of one transferred by a relevant transfer is a reference to a person so employed immediately before the transfer, including, where the transfer is effected by a series of two or more transactions, a person so employed immediately before any of those transactions.

(4) Paragraph (2) above shall not transfer or otherwise affect the liability of any person to be prosecuted for, convicted of and sentenced for any offence.

(5) Paragraph (1) above is without prejudice to any right of an employee arising apart from these Regulations to terminate his contract of employment without notice if a substantial change is made in his working conditions to his detriment; but no such right shall arise by reason only that, under that paragraph, the identity of his employer changes unless the employee shows that, in all the circumstances, the change is a significant change and is to his detriment.

6 Effect of relevant transfer on collective agreements

(1) Where at the time of a relevant transfer there exists a collective agreement made by or on behalf of the transferor with a trade union recognised by the transferor in respect of any employee whose contract of employment is preserved by Regulation 5(1) above, then,—

(*a*) without prejudice to section 18 of the 1974 Act or Article 63 of the 1976 Order (collective agreements presumed to be unenforceable in specified circumstances) that agreement, in its application in relation to the employee, shall, after the transfer, have effect as if made by or on behalf of the transferee with that trade union, and accordingly anything done under or in connection with it, in its application as aforesaid, by or in relation to the transferor before the transfer, shall, after the transfer, be deemed to have been done by or in relation to the transferee; and

(*b*) any order made in respect of that agreement, in its application in relation to the employee, shall, after the transfer, have effect as if the transferee were a party to the agreement.

7 Exclusion of occupational pensions schemes

Regulations 5 and 6 above shall not apply—

(*a*) to so much of a contract of employment or collective agreement as relates to an occupational pension scheme within the meaning of the Social Security Pensions Act 1975 or the Social Security Pensions (Northern Ireland) Order 1975; or

(*b*) to any rights, powers, duties or liabilities under or in connection with any such contract or subsisting by virtue of any such agreement and relating to such a scheme or otherwise arising in connection with that person's employment and relating to such a scheme.

8 Dismissal of employee because of relevant transfer

(1) Where either before or after a relevant transfer, any employee of the transferor or transferee is dismissed, that employee shall be treated for the purposes of Part V of the 1978 Act and Articles 20 to 41 of the 1976 Order (unfair dismissal) as unfairly dismissed if the transfer or a reason connected with it is the reason or principal reason for his dismissal.

(2) Where an economic, technical or organisational reason entailing changes in the workforce of either the transferor or the transferee before or after a relevant transfer is the reason or principal reason for dismissing an employee—

(*a*) paragraph (1) above shall not apply to his dismissal; but

(*b*) without prejudice to the application of section 57(3) of the 1978 Act or Article 22(10) of the 1976 Order (test of fair dismissal), the dismissal shall for the purposes of section 57(1)(*b*) of that Act and Article 22(1)(*b*) of that Order (substantial reason for dismissal) be regarded as having been for a substantial reason of a kind such as to justify the dismissal of an employee holding the position which that employee held.

(3) The provisions of this Regulation apply whether or not the employee in question is employed in the undertaking or part of the undertaking transferred or to be transferred.

(4) Paragraph (1) above shall not apply in relation to the dismissal of any employee which was required by reason of the application of section 5 of the Aliens Restriction (Amendment) Act 1919 to his employment.

9   Effect of relevant transfer on trade union recognition

(1) This Regulation applies where after a relevant transfer the undertaking or part of the undertaking transferred maintains an identity distinct from the remainder of the transferee's undertaking.

(2) Where before such a transfer an independent trade union is recognised to any extent by the transferor in respect of employees of any description who in consequence of the transfer become employees of the transferee, then, after the transfer—

    (*a*) the union shall be deemed to have been recognised by the transferee to the same extent in respect of employees of that description so employed; and

    (*b*) any agreement for recognition may be varied or rescinded accordingly.

10   Duty to inform and consult trade union representatives

(1) In this Regulation and Regulation 11 below "an affected employee" means, in relation to a relevant transfer, any employee of the transferor or the transferee (whether or not employed in the undertaking or the part of the undertaking to be transferred) who may be affected by the transfer or may be affected by measures taken in connection with it; and references to the employer shall be construed accordingly.

(2) Long enough before a relevant transfer to enable consultations to take place between the employer of any affected employees of a description in respect of which an independent trade union is recognised by him and that union's representatives, the employer shall inform those representatives of—

    (*a*) the fact that the relevant transfer is to take place, when, approximately, it is to take place and the reasons for it; and

    (*b*) the legal, economic and social implications of the transfer for the affected employees; and

    (*c*) the measures which he envisages he will, in connection with the transfer, take in relation to those employees or, if he envisages that no measures will be so taken, that fact; and

    (*d*) if the employer is the transferor, the measures which the transferee envisages he will, in connection with the transfer, take in relation to such of those employees as, by virtue of Regulation 5 above, become employees of the transferee after the transfer or, if he envisages that no measures will be so taken, that fact.

(3) The transferee shall give the transferor such information at such a time as will enable the transferor to perform the duty imposed on him by virtue of paragraph (2)(*d*) above.

(4) The information which is to be given to the representatives of a trade union under this Regulation shall be delivered to them, or sent by post to an address notified by them to the employer, or sent by post to the union at the address of its head or main office.

(5) Where an employer of any affected employees envisages that he will, in connection with the transfer, be taking measures in relation to any such employees of a description in respect of which an independent trade union is recognised by him, he shall enter into consultations with the representatives of that union.

(6) In the course of those consultations the employer shall—

(*a*) consider any representations made by the trade union representatives; and
(*b*) reply to those representations and, if he rejects any of those representations, state his reasons.

(7) If in any case there are special circumstances which render it not reasonably practicable for an employer to perform a duty imposed on him by any of the foregoing paragraphs, he shall take all such steps towards performing that duty as are reasonably practicable in the circumstances.

11 Failure to inform or consult

(1) A complaint that an employer has failed to inform or consult a representative of a trade union in accordance with Regulation 10 above may be presented to an industrial tribunal by that union.

(2) If on a complaint under paragraph (1) above a question arises whether or not it was reasonably practicable for an employer to perform a particular duty or what steps he took towards performing it, it shall be for him to show—

(*a*) that there were special circumstances which rendered it not reasonably practicable for him to perform the duty; and
(*b*) that he took all such steps towards its performance as were reasonably practicable in those circumstances.

(3) On any such complaint against a transferor that he had failed to perform the duty imposed upon him by virtue of paragraph (2)(*d*) or, so far as relating thereto, paragraph (7) of Regulation 10 above, he may not show that it was not reasonably practicable for him to perform the duty in question for the reason that the transferee had failed to give him the requisite information at the requisite time in accordance with Regulation 10(3)

above unless he gives the transferee notice of his intention to show that fact; and the giving of the notice shall make the transferee a party to the proceedings.

(4) Where the tribunal finds a complaint under paragraph (1) above well-founded it shall make a declaration to that effect and may—

    (*a*) order the employer to pay appropriate compensation to such descriptions of affected employees as may be specified in the award; or

    (*b*) if the complaint is that the transferor did not perform the duty mentioned in paragraph (3) above and the transferor (after giving due notice) shows the facts so mentioned, order the transferee to pay appropriate compensation to such descriptions of affected employees as may be specified in the award.

(5) An employee may present a complaint to an industrial tribunal on the ground that he is an employee of a description to which an order under paragraph (4) above relates and that the transferor or the transferee has failed, wholly or in part, to pay him compensation in pursuance of the order.

(6) Where the tribunal finds a complaint under paragraph (5) above well-founded it shall order the employer to pay the complainant the amount of compensation which it finds is due to him.

(7) Where an employer, in failing to perform a duty under Regulation 10 above, also fails to comply with the requirements of section 99 of the 1975 Act or Article 49 of the 1976 Order (duty of employer to consult trade union representatives on redundancy)—

    (*a*) any compensation awarded to an employee under this Regulation shall go to reduce the amount of remuneration payable to him under a protective award subsequently made under Part IV of that Act or Part IV of that Order and shall also go towards discharging any liability of the employer under, or in respect of a breach of, the contract of employment in respect of a period falling within the protected period under that award; and

    (*b*) conversely any remuneration so payable and any payment made to the employee by the employer under, or by way of damages for breach of, that contract in respect of a period falling within the protected period shall go to reduce the amount of any compensation which may be subsequently awarded under this Regulation;

but this paragraph shall be without prejudice to section 102(3) of that Act and Article 52(3) of that Order (avoidance of duplication of contractual payments and remuneration under protective awards).

(8) An industrial tribunal shall not consider a complaint under paragraph (1) or (5) above unless it is presented to the tribunal before the end of the period of three months beginning with—

(*a*) the date on which the relevant transfer is completed, in the case of a complaint under paragraph (1);

(*b*) the date of the tribunal's order under paragraph (4) above, in the case of a complaint under paragraph (5);

or within such further period as the tribunal considers reasonable in a case where it is satisfied that it was not reasonably practicable for the complaint to be presented before the end of the period of three months.

(9) Section 129 of the 1978 Act (complaint to be sole remedy for breach of relevant rights) and section 133 of that Act (functions of conciliation officer) and Articles 58(2) and 62 of the 1976 Order (which make corresponding provision for Northern Ireland) shall apply to the rights conferred by this Regulation and to proceedings under this Regulation as they apply to the rights conferred by that Act or that Order and the industrial tribunal proceedings mentioned therein.

(10) An appeal shall lie and shall lie only to the Employment Appeal Tribunal on a question of law arising from any decision of, or arising in any proceedings before, an industrial tribunal under or by virtue of these Regulations; and section 13(1) of the Tribunals and Inquiries Act 1971 (appeal from certain tribunals to the High Court) shall not apply in relation to any such proceedings.

(11) In this Regulation "appropriate compensation" means such sum not exceeding two weeks' pay for the employee in question as the tribunal considers just and equitable having regard to the seriousness of the failure of the employer to comply with his duty.

(12) Schedule 14 to the 1978 Act or, in Northern Ireland, Schedule 2 to the 1976 Order shall apply for calculating the amount of a week's pay for any employee for the purposes of paragraph (11) above; and, for the purposes of that calculation, the calculation date shall be—

(*a*) in the case of an employee who is dismissed by reason of redundancy (within the meaning of section 81 of the 1978 Act) or, in Northern Ireland, section 11 of the Contracts of Employment and Redundancy Payments Act (Northern Ireland) 1965 the date which is the calculation date for the purposes of any entitlement of his to a redundancy payment (within the meaning of that section) or which would be that calculation date if he were so entitled;

(*b*) in the case of an employee who is dismissed for any other reason, the effective date of termination (within the meaning of section 55 of the 1978 Act, or in Northern Ireland, Article 21 of the 1976 Order) of his contract of employment;

(*c*) in any other case, the date of the transfer in question.

12 Restriction on contracting out

Any provision of any agreement (whether a contract of employment or not) shall be void in so far as it purports to exclude or limit the operation of

Regulation 5, 8 or 10 above or to preclude any person from presenting a complaint to an industrial tribunal under Regulation 11 above.

13 Exclusion of employment abroad or as dock worker

(1) Regulations 8, 10 and 11 of these Regulations do not apply to employment where under his contract of employment the employee ordinarily works outside the United Kingdom.

(2) For the purposes of this Regulation a person employed to work on board a ship registered in the United Kingdom shall, unless—

    (*a*) the employment is wholly outside the United Kingdom, or
    (*b*) he is not ordinarily resident in the United Kingdom,

be regarded as a person who under his contract ordinarily works in the United Kingdom.

(3) *Nothing in these Regulations applies in relation to any person employed as a registered dock worker unless he is wholly or mainly engaged in work which is not dock work.*

(4) *Paragraph (3) above shall be construed as if it were contained in section 145 of the 1978 Act.*

NOTE
Paras (3) and (4), which are italicised, were revoked by the Dock Work Act 1989 s 7(2).

14 Consequential amendments

(1) In section 4(4) of the 1978 Act (written statement to be given to employee on change of his employer), in paragraph (b), the reference to paragraph 17 of Schedule 13 to that Act (continuity of employment where change of employer) shall include a reference to these Regulations.

(2) In section 4(6A) of the Contracts of Employment and Redundancy Payments Act (Northern Ireland) 1965, in paragraph (b), the reference to paragraph 10 of Schedule 1 to that Act shall include a reference to these Regulations.

SECTION FIVE

European materials

General notes

The choice of European materials has, of necessity, to be eclectic. Included are the enabling provisions of the European Communities Act 1972 concerning enactment of European legislation (including some definitions), the so-called 'Mass Redundancies' Directive and the 'Acquired Rights' (or 'Business Transfers') Directive.

(i) Enabling provisions of the European Communities Act 1972

EUROPEAN COMMUNITIES ACT 1972
(c 68)

* * *

2 General Implementation of Treaties

(1) All such rights, powers, liabilities, obligations and restrictions from time to time created or arising by or under the Treaties, and all such remedies and procedures from time to time provided for by or under the Treaties, as in accordance with the Treaties are without further enactment to be given legal effect or used in the United Kingdom shall be recognised and available in law, and be enforced and followed accordingly; and the expression "enforceable Community right" and similar expressions shall be read as referring to one to which this sub-section applies.

(2) Subject to Schedule 2 to this Act, at any time after its passing Her Majesty may by Order in Council, and any designated Minister or department may by regulations, make provision—

(*a*) for the purpose of implementing any Community obligation of the United Kingdom, or enabling any such obligation to be implemented, or of enabling any rights enjoyed or to be enjoyed by the United Kingdom under or by virtue of the Treaties to be exercised; or

(*b*) for the purpose of dealing with matters arising out of or related to any such obligation or rights or the coming into force, or the operation from time to time, of sub-section (1) above;

and in the exercise of any statutory power or duty, including any power to give directions or to legislate by means of orders, rules, regulations or other subordinate instrument, the person entrusted with the power or duty may have regard to the objects of the Communities and to any such obligation or rights as aforesaid.

In this sub-section "designated Minister or department" means such Minister of the Crown or government department as may from time to time be designated by Order in Council in relation to any matter or for any purpose, but subject to such restrictions or conditions (if any) as may be specified by the Order in Council.

(3) There shall be charged on and issued out of the Consolidated Fund or, if so determined by the Treasury, the National Loans Fund the amounts required to meet any Community obligation to make payments to any of the Communities or member States, or any Community obligation in respect of contributions to the capital or reserves of the European Investment Bank or in respect of loans to the Bank, or to redeem any notes or obligations issued or created in respect of any such Community obligation; and, except as otherwise provided by or under any enactment—

(*a*) any other expenses incurred under or by virtue of the Treaties or this Act by any Minister of the Crown or government department may be paid out of moneys provided by Parliament; and

(*b*) any sums received under or by virtue of the Treaties or this Act by any Minister of the Crown or government department, save for such sums as may be required for disbursements permitted by any other enactment, shall be paid into the Consolidated Fund or, if so determined by the Treasury, the National Loans Fund.

(4) The provision that may be made under sub-section (2) above includes, subject to Schedule 2 to this Act, any such provision (of any such extent) as might be made by Act of Parliament, and any enactment passed or to be passed, other than one contained in this Part of this Act, shall be construed and have effect subject to the foregoing provisions of this section; but, except as may be provided by any Act passed after this Act, Schedule 2 shall have effect in connection with the powers conferred by this and the following sections of this Act to make Orders in Council and regulations.

*　　*　　*

NOTES

Sub-ss (5) and (6), which relate to Northern Ireland, the Channel Islands and Isle of Man, are omitted.

The 'Treaties' (s 2(1)) is defined as including those treaties in Pt I of Sch 1 to the Act taken with those referred to in s 1(2) of the Act (s 1(2)).

SCHEDULE 1

Section 1

DEFINITIONS RELATING TO COMMUNITIES

*　　*　　*

PART II

OTHER DEFINITIONS

"Economic Community", "Coal and Steel Community" and "Euratom" mean respectively the European Economic Community, the European Coal and Steel Community and the European Atomic Energy Community.

"Community customs duty" means, in relation to any goods, such duty of customs as may from time to time be fixed for those goods by directly applicable Community provision as the duty chargeable on importation into member States.

"Community institution" means any institution of any of the Communities or common to the Communities; and any reference to an institution of a particular Community shall include one common to the Communities when it acts for that Community, and similarly with references to a committee, officer or servant of a particular Community.

"Community instrument" means any instrument issued by a Community institution.

"Community obligation" means any obligation created or arising by or under the Treaties, whether an enforceable Community obligation or not.

"Enforceable Community right" and similar expressions shall be construed in accordance with section 2(1) of this Act.

"Entry date" means the date on which the United Kingdom becomes a member of the Communities.

"European Court" means the Court of Justice of the European Communities.

"Member", in the expression "member State", refers to membership of the Communities.

SCHEDULE 2

Section 2

PROVISIONS AS TO SUBORDINATE LEGISLATION

1.—(1) The powers conferred by section 2(2) of this Act to make provision for the purposes mentioned in section 2(2)(*a*) and (*b*) shall not include power—

- (*a*) to make any provision imposing or increasing taxation; or
- (*b*) to make any provision taking effect from a date earlier than that of the making of the instrument containing the provision; or
- (*c*) to confer any power to legislate by means of orders, rules, regulations or other subordinate instrument, other than rules of procedure for any court or tribunal; or
- (*d*) to create any new criminal offence punishable with imprisonment for more than two years or punishable on summary conviction with imprisonment for more than three months or with a fine of more than [level 5 on the standard scale] (if not calculated on a daily basis) or with a fine of more than [£100 a day].

(2) Sub-paragraph (1)(*c*) above shall not be taken to preclude the modification of a power to legislate conferred otherwise than under section 2(2), or the extension of any such power to purposes of the like nature as those for which it was conferred; and a power to give directions as to matters of administration is not to be regarded as a power to legislate within the meaning of sub-paragraph (1)(*c*).

2.—(1) Subject to paragraph 3 below, where a provision contained in any section of this Act confers power to make regulations (otherwise than by modification or extension of an existing power), the power shall be exercisable by statutory instrument.

(2) Any statutory instrument containing an Order in Council or regulations made in the exercise of a power so conferred, if made without a draft

having been approved by resolution of each House of Parliament, shall be subject to annulment in pursuance of a resolution of either House.

3. Nothing in paragraph 2 above shall apply to any Order in Council made by the Governor of Northern Ireland or to any regulations made by a Minister or department of the Government of Northern Ireland; but where a provision contained in any section of this Act confers power to make such an Order in Council or regulations, then any Order in Council or regulations made in the exercise of that power, if made without a draft having been approved by resolution of each House of the Parliament of Northern Ireland, shall be subject to negative resolution within the meaning of section 41(6) of the Interpretation Act (Northern Ireland) 1954 as if the Order or regulations were a statutory instrument within the meaning of that Act.

NOTES
Paras 4, 5 omitted.
Para 1(d): Maximum fine increased and converted to a level on the standard scale by the Criminal Justice Act 1982, ss 37, 38. Amendment to maximum daily fine made by the Criminal Law Act 1977, s 32(3).

(ii) *The Mass Redundancies Directive*

EC COUNCIL DIRECTIVE 75/129
(17 February 1975)

On the approximation of the laws of the member states relating to collective redundancies.

THE COUNCIL OF THE EUROPEAN COMMUNITIES,
  Having regard to the Treaty establishing the European Economic Community, and in particular Article 100 thereof;
  Having regard to the proposal from the Commission;
  Having regard to the Opinion of the European Parliament;
  Having regard to the Opinion of the Economic and Social Committee;
  Whereas it is important that greater protection should be afforded to workers in the event of collective redundancies while taking into account the need for balanced economic and social development within the Community;
  Whereas, despite increasing convergence, differences still remain between the provisions in force in the Member States of the Community concerning the practical arrangements and procedures for such redundancies and the measures designed to alleviate the consequences of redundancy for workers;
  Whereas these differences can have a direct effect on the functioning of the common market;
  Whereas the Council resolution of January 21, 1974 concerning a social action programme makes provision for a Directive on the approximation of Member States' legislation on collective redundancies;
  Whereas this approximation must therefore be promoted while the improvement is being maintained within the meaning of Article 117 of the Treaty,
  HAS ADOPTED THIS DIRECTIVE:

Section I—Definitions and scope

Article 1

1. For the purposes of this Directive:

(*a*) "collective redundancies" means dismissals effected by an employer for one or more reasons not related to the individual workers concerned where, according to the choice of the Member States, the number of redundancies is:

—either, over a period of 30 days:

(1) at least 10 in establishments normally employing more than 20 and less than 100 workers;

(2) at least 10 per cent of the number of workers in establishments normally employing at least 100 but less than 300 workers;

(3) at least 30 in establishments normally employing 300 workers or more;

—or, over a period of 90 days, at least 20, whatever the number of workers normally employed in the establishments in question;

(*b*) "workers' representatives" means the workers' representatives provided for by the laws or practices of the Member States.

2. This Directive shall not apply to:

(*a*) collective redundancies effected under contracts of employment concluded for limited periods of time or for specific tasks except where such redundancies take place prior to the date of expiry or the completion of such contracts;

(*b*) workers employed by public administrative bodies or by establishments governed by public law (or, in Member States where this concept is unknown, by equivalent bodies);

(*c*) the crews of sea-going vessels;

(*d*) workers affected by the termination of an establishment's activities where that is the result of a judicial decision.

Section II—Consultation procedure

Article 2

1. Where an employer is contemplating collective redundancies, he shall begin consultations with the workers' representatives with a view to reaching an agreement.

2. These consultations shall, at least, cover ways and means of avoiding collective redundancies or reducing the number of workers affected, and mitigating the consequences.

3. To enable the workers' representatives to make constructive proposals the employer shall supply them with all relevant information and shall

in any event give in writing the reasons for the redundancies, the number of workers to be made redundant, the number of workers normally employed and the period over which the redundancies are to be effected.

The employer shall forward to the competent public authority a copy of all the written communications referred to in the preceding subparagraph.

Section III—Procedure for collective redundancies

Article 3

1. Employers shall notify the competent public authority in writing of any projected redundancies.

This notification shall contain all relevant information concerning the projected collective redundancies and the consultations with workers' representatives provided for in Article 2, and particularly the reasons for the redundancies, the number of workers to be made redundant, the number of workers normally employed and the period over which the redundancies are to be effected.

2. Employers shall forward to the workers' representatives a copy of the notification provided for in paragraph 1.

The workers' representatives may send any comments they may have to the competent public authority.

Article 4

1. Projected collective redundancies notified to the competent public authority shall take effect not earlier than 30 days after the notification referred to in Article 3(1) without prejudice to any provisions governing individual rights with regard to notice of dismissal.

Member States may grant the competent public authority the power to reduce the period provided for in the preceding subparagraph.

2. The period provided for in paragraph 1 shall be used by the competent public authority to seek solutions in the problems raised by the projected collective redundancies.

3. Where the initial period provided for in paragraph 1 is shorter than 60 days, Member States may grant the competent public authority the power to extend the initial period to 60 days following notification where the problems raised by the projected collective redundancies are not likely to be solved within the initial period.

Member States may grant the competent public authority wider powers of extension.

The employer must be informed of the extension and the grounds for it before expiry of the initial period provided for in paragraph 1.

Section IV—Final provisions

Article 5

This Directive shall not affect the right of Member States to apply or to introduce laws, regulations or administrative provisions which are more favourable to workers.

Article 6

1. Member States shall bring into force the laws, regulations and administrative provisions needed in order to comply with this Directive within two years following its notification and shall forthwith inform the Commission thereof.

2. Member States shall communicate to the Commission the texts of the laws, regulations and administrative provisions which they adopt in the field covered by this Directive.

Article 7

Within two years following expiry of the two year period laid down in Article 6, Member States shall forward all relevant information to the Commission to enable it to draw up a report for submission to the Council on the application of this Directive.

Article 8

This Directive is addressed to the Member States.

NOTE

For the domestic implementation of this Directive see the Employment Protection Act 1975 ss 99–107 (see Ch 10 (text) and Section Two (statutory materials).

(iii) The Acquired Rights Directive

This Directive has been considered by the European Court in the following cases: *Wendelboe v L J Music ApS* [1986] 1 CMLR 476; *Abels v Administrative Board of the Bedrijfsvereniging voor de Metaal-industrie en de Electrotechnische Industrie* [1987] 2 CMLR 406; *Botzen v Rotterdamsche Droogdok Maatshappij BV* [1986] 2 CMLR 50; *Mikkelsen v Danmols Inventar A/S* [1986] 1 CMLR 316; *Spijkers v Gebroeders Benedik Abbatoir CV* [1986] 2 CMLR 296; *Foreningen af Arbejdsledere i Danmark v Daddy's Dance Hall A/S* [1988] IRLR 315; *Berg and Busschers v IM Besselsen* [1989] IRLR 447; *Landsorganisationen i Danmark v NY Molle Kro* [1989] IRLR 37; *P Bork International A/S v Foreningen af Arbejdsledere i Danmark* [1989] IRLR 41.

EC COUNCIL DIRECTIVE 77/187
(14 February 1977)

On the approximation of the laws of the Member States relating to the safeguarding of employees' rights in the event of transfers of undertakings, businesses or parts of businesses.

THE COUNCIL OF THE EUROPEAN COMMUNITIES,

Having regard to the Treaty establishing the European Economic Community, and in particular Article 100 thereof,

Having regard to the proposal from the Commission,
Having regard to the opinion of the European Parliament,
Having regard to the opinion of the Economic and Social Committee,
Whereas economic trends are bringing in their wake, at both national and Community level, changes in the structure of undertakings, through transfers of undertakings, businesses or parts of businesses to other employers as a result of legal transfers or mergers;
Whereas it is necessary to provide for the protection of employees in the event of a change of employer, in particular, to ensure that their rights are safeguarded;
Whereas differences still remain in the Member States as regards the extent of the protection of employees in this respect and these differences should be reduced;
Whereas these differences can have a direct effect on the functioning of the common market;
Whereas it is therefore necessary to promote the approximation of laws in this field while maintaining the improvement described in Article 117 of the Treaty,
HAS ADOPTED THIS DIRECTIVE:

Section I—Scope and definitions

Article 1

1. This Directive shall apply to the transfer of an undertaking, business or part of a business to another employer as a result of a legal transfer or merger.

2. This Directive shall apply where and in so far as the undertaking, business or part of the business to be transferred is situated within the territorial scope of the Treaty.

3. This Directive shall not apply to sea-going vessels.

Article 2

For the purposes of this Directive:

(*a*) "transferor" means any natural or legal person who, by reason of a transfer within the meaning of Article 1(1), ceases to be the employer in respect of the undertaking, business or part of the business;

(*b*) "transferee" means any natural or legal person who, by reason of a transfer within the meaning of Article 1(1), becomes the employer in respect of the undertaking, business or part of the business;

(*c*) "representatives of the employees" means the representatives of the employees provided for by the laws or practice of the Member States, with the exception of members of administrative, governing or supervisory bodies of companies who represent employees on such bodies in certain Member States.

Section II—Safeguarding of employees' rights

Article 3

1. The transferor's rights and obligations arising from a contract of employment or from an employment relationship existing on the date of a

transfer within the meaning of Article 1(1) shall, by reason of such transfer, be transferred to the transferee.

Member States may provide that, after the date of transfer within the meaning of Article 1(1) and in addition to the transferee, the transferor shall continue to be liable in respect of obligations which arose from a contract of employment or an employment relationship.

2. Following the transfer within the meaning of Article 1(1), the transferee shall continue to observe the terms and conditions agreed in any collective agreement on the same terms applicable to the transferor under that agreement, until the date of termination or expiry of the collective agreement or the entry into force or application of another collective agreement.

Member States may limit the period for observing such terms and conditions, with the proviso that it shall not be less than one year.

3. Paragraphs (1) and (2) shall not cover employees' rights to old-age, invalidity or survivors' benefits under supplementary company or intercompany pension schemes outside the statutory social security schemes in Member States.

Member States shall adopt the measures necessary to protect the interests of employees and of persons no longer employed in the transferor's business at the time of the transfer within the meaning of Article 1(1) in respect of rights conferred on them, immediate or prospective entitlement to old-age benefits, including survivors' benefits, under supplementary schemes referred to in the first sub-paragraph.

Article 4

1. The transfer of an undertaking, business or part of a business shall not in itself constitute grounds for dismissal by the transferor or the transferee. This provision shall not stand in the way of dismissals that may take place for economic, technical or organisational reasons entailing changes in the workforce.

Member States may provide that the first sub-paragraph shall not apply to certain specific categories of employees who are not covered by the laws or practice of the Member States in respect of protection against dismissal.

2. If the contract of employment or the employment relationship is terminated because the transfer within the meaning of Article 1(1) involves a substantial change in working conditions to the detriment of the employee, the employer shall be regarded as having been responsible for termination of the contract of employment or of the employment relationship.

Article 5

1. If the business preserves its autonomy, the status and function, as laid down by the laws, regulations or administrative provisions of the Member States, of the representatives or of the representation of the employees affected by the transfer within the meaning of Article 1(1) shall be preserved.

The first sub-paragraph shall not apply if, under the laws, regulations, administrative provisions or practice of the Member States, the conditions necessary for the re-appointment of the representatives of the employees or for the reconstitution of the representation of the employees are fulfilled.

2. If the term of office of the representatives of the employees affected by a transfer within the meaning of Article 1(1) expires as a result of the transfer, the representatives shall continue to enjoy the protection provided by the laws, regulations, administrative provisions or practice of the Member States.

Section III—Information and consultation

Article 6

1. The transferor and the transferee shall be required to inform the representatives of their respective employees affected by a transfer within the meaning of Article 1(1) of the following:
  —the reasons for the transfer,
  —the legal, economic and social implications of the transfer for the employees,
  —measures envisaged in relation to the employees.

The transferor must give such information to the representatives of his employees in good time before the transfer is carried out.

The transferee must give such information to the representatives of his employees in good time, and in any event before his employees are directly affected by the transfer as regards their conditions of work and employment.

2. If the transferor or the transferee envisages measures in relation to his employees, he shall consult his representatives of the employees in good time on such measures with a view to seeking agreement.

3. Member States whose laws, regulations or administrative provisions provide that representatives of the employees may have recourse to an arbitration board to obtain a decision on the measures to be taken in relation to employees may limit the obligations laid down in paragraphs (1) and (2) to cases where the transfer carried out gives rise to a change in the business likely to entail serious disadvantages for a considerable number of the employees.

The information and consultations shall cover at least the measures envisaged in relation to the employees.

The information must be provided and consultations take place in good time before the change in the business as referred to in the first subparagraph is effected.

4. Member States may limit the obligations laid down in paragraphs (1), (2) and (3) to undertakings or businesses which, in respect of the number of employees, fulfil the conditions for the election or designation of a collegiate body representing the employees.

5. Member States may provide that where there are no representatives of the employees in an undertaking or business, the employees concerned

must be informed in advance when a transfer within the meaning of Article 1(1) is about to take place.

Section IV—Final provisions

Article 7

This Directive shall not affect the right of Member States to apply or introduce laws, regulations or administrative provisions which are more favourable to employees.

Article 8

1. Member States shall bring into force the laws, regulations and administrative provisions needed to comply with this Directive within two years of its notification and shall forthwith inform the Commission thereof.

2. Member States shall communicate to the Commission the texts of the laws, regulations and administrative provisions which they adopt in the field covered by this Directive.

Article 9

Within two years following expiry of the two-year period laid down in Article 8, Member States shall forward all relevant information to the Commission in order to enable it to draw up a report on the application of this Directive for submission to the Council.

Article 10

This Directive is addressed to the Member States.

NOTE
For the domestic implementation of this Directive see the Transfer of Undertakings (Protection of Employment) Regulations 1981, SI 1981/1794 (see generally, in the text and Section Five (statutory materials)).

Appendix F

Takeovers and Mergers (Employee Protection) Bill 1987

(Note: This Bill was not a government Bill and it lapsed on dissolution of parliament before the 1987 General Election after its second reading in the House of Lords, having been introduced by Baroness Turner of Camden. Although it would have needed considerable refining in the highly unlikely event of its adoption, it none the less makes interesting, if rather dated, reading. The reader is referred to Chapter 1 of this book and to the debates in parliament, namely Hansard H L Deb 9 February 1987 col 427; Hansard H L Deb 25 March 1987 cols 260–282. Extracted in the first edition, it is thought still to be worthy of inclusion in this edition in view of the arguments for reform and extension of the Transfer Regulations' protection.)

1 Consultation rights for trade unions

(1) Any company which:
 (a) is involved in a merger with another company;
 (b) is the initiator, or the subject of a takeover-bid for another company;
 (c) is planning to sell off a subsidiary;
 (d) is planning to buy a subsidiary of another company; or
 (e) intends to effect a transfer of engagement,

shall, as early as possible (and in any case not less than 30 days before any binding agreements are entered into), inform any trade union representing employees in that company.

(2) A company seeking to acquire control of or purchase another company shall disclose in writing the following information to representatives of any independent trade union with members in a company that would be affected:

 (a) the reasons for the proposed takeover, merger or sale;
 (b) the likely legal, social and economic consequences;
 (c) the company's intentions regarding:
  (i) the size and shape of the workforce; and
  (ii) collective agreements covering terms and conditions of employment, pensions and trade union recognition.

(3) On request by the trade union, a company which is subject to the provisions of subsection (2) above shall meet the trade union concerned within 14 days of the request being made.

2 Justification of takeovers, mergers and sales of subsidiaries

(1) When a takeover, merger or sale of a subsidiary is proposed, the company, or companies, involved shall demonstrate to the satisfaction of the Monopolies and Mergers Commission that the change would be in the public interest.

(2) The company shall declare its future plans for output, investment, location of production, integration with existing businesses, and strategic development of the business and employment.

(3) The company shall explain how the change would improve prospects for the enterprise and employees concerned, and a copy of the justification statement shall be provided to the relevant independent trade unions.

3 Definition of the public interest

(1) In determining whether a takeover, merger or sale of a subsidiary is in the public interest, the Office of Fair Trading, the Monopolies and Mergers Commission and the Secretary of State shall consider whether the change would:

(a) maintain and promote effective competition in so far as this is compatible with an international competitive capability and a positive balance of trade;
(b) promote the interests of consumers, purchasers and other users of goods and services;
(c) encourage, through competition, a reduction in costs and the development and use of new techniques and new products, and facilitate the entry of new competitors into existing markets;
(d) be in the interests of the employees of the firm;
(e) maintain production and output in the United Kingdom to the benefit of the economy;
(f) secure national control of strategic industries, or be in the interests of national security.

(2) The Secretary of State shall issue detailed guidelines on the factors listed in subsection (1) above.

4 Procedure for dealing with takeovers, mergers or sales of subsidiaries

(1) An independent trade union shall have the right to refer any takeover, merger or sale of a subsidiary to the Office of Fair Trading if in its opinion:

(a) the proposal is not in the public interest, or
(b) the company involved has failed to meet the requirements of sections 1 and 2 above.

(2) An independent trade union may make representations about any takeover, merger or sale of a subsidiary, to the Office of Fair Trading, of (sic) the Monopolies and Mergers Commission, or the Secretary of State, who shall consider them.

(3) The Secretary of State shall not approve a takeover, merger or sale of a subsidiary if the Office of Fair Trading reports to him that the relevant trade union has not been provided with information, or has been refused a meeting, required by section 1, and any dispute as to the adequacy of the information provided shall be determined by the Office of Fair Trading.

(4) The Secretary of State shall publish any advice given to him under this section by the Office of Fair Trading or the Monopolies and Mergers Commission.

5 Continuity of agreements

(1) All employees affected by a takeover, merger or sale of a subsidiary shall be guaranteed, under a new employer, continuity of employment for the purposes of their contracts of employment as they relate to terms, conditions and pension rights.

(2) A new employer shall recognise any independent trade union that was previously recognised by the former employer or owner, and terms, conditions or pension rights shall not contradict the information given under section 1 above within 12 months of the change of ownership or employer, unless the relevant trade union agrees.

6 Unfair dismissal following takeover, merger or sale of a subsidiary

Where either before or within twelve months of a takeover, merger or sale of a subsidiary any employee is dismissed, that employee shall be treated for the purposes of Part IV (**sic**) of the Employment Protection (Consolidation) Act 1978 as unfairly dismissed if the takeover, merger or sale of a subsidiary or a reason connected with it is the reason or principal reason for his dismissal.

7 Protection of pensions

If a new employer (or a subsequent employer) winds up a pension scheme within 25 years from the end of the 12 month protection period referred to in section 5 above, the pension fund trustees shall deploy the fund surpluses to increase pension benefits up to Inland Revenue limits.

8 Consequential amendments to the Fair Trading Act 1973

The Secretary of State shall by order made by statutory instrument make such amendments to the Fair Trading Act 1973 as are necessary to give effect to the provisions of this Act.

9 Short title

This Act may be cited as the Takeovers and Mergers (Employee Protection) Act 1987.

Select bibliography

(*Note*: on labour material generally, as well as on transfer of employment, the reader is advised also to consult the bibliographical work *Labour Law in Great Britain and Ireland 1978* (Sweet & Maxwell, 1981) by B A Hepple, J Hepple, P O'Higgins and P Stirling. Supplementary lists have subsequently been published in the ILJ. At the time of writing, *Labour Law in Great Britain and Ireland 1979–1990: A Bibliography* by Paul O'Higgins (Mansell, 1992) is forthcoming.)

A BOOKS

Anderman S D *The Law of Unfair Dismissal* (2nd edn, 1985)

Bowers J and Elias P *Transfers of Undertakings: The Legal Pitfalls* (3rd edn, 1989)

The College of Law *Company Takeovers and Business Transfers* (1983)

Davies P L and Freedland M *Transfer of Employment* (1982)

Elias P and others. *Harvey on Industrial Relations and Employment Law* (updated regularly with service and bulletins)

Freedland M R *The Contract of Employment* (1976)

Grunfeld C *The Law of Redundancy* (3rd edn, 1989)

Hepple B A and O'Higgins P *Encyclopaedia of Labour Relations Law* (updated regularly with service)

Incomes Data Services *Employment Law Handbook No 35: Continuity of Employment* (1986)

Incomes Data Services *Employment Law Handbook No 36: Transfer of Undertakings* (1987)

Incomes Data Services *Employment Law Handbook No 47: Transfer of Undertakings* (1990)

Irish Centre for European Law *Acquired Rights of Employees* (Papers from the ICEL Conference, November 1988) (1989)

Kerr on Receivers (17th edn, 1989, ed R Walton)

Knight W J L *The Acquisition of Private Companies* (5th edn, 1989)

Lightman G L and Moss G The Law of Receivers of Companies (1986)

Lingard R *Corporate Rescues and Insolvencies* (2nd edn, 1989)

Longman's *Practical Commercial Precedents* (updated regularly with service)

Pratt J H *Franchising Law and Practice* (1990) (looseleaf with updates: see particularly the section on Transfer of Undertakings at para 7–047)

Sinclair N *Warranties and Indemnities on Share Sales* (2nd edn, 1990)

Smith I T and Wood J C *Industrial Law* (4th edn, 1989)

Tolley's *Employees' Rights in Receivership and Liquidations* (2nd edn) GTE Parsons and WF Ratford

Wine H *Buying and Selling Private Companies and Businesses* (3rd edn, 1986)

Younson F *Business Transfers and Employment Law* (1989)

B ARTICLES, NOTES AND SHORTER PIECES

Bourn C 'Employment Consequences of Business Transfers' (1989) NLJ 1122 (and correspondence to editor from J McMullen (1989) NLJ 1540; C Bourn ibid; R Lowe (1990) NLJ 340)

Bowers J 'Transfer of Undertakings Regulations: The Unresolved Problems' (1984) NLJ 207

Bowers J and Clarke A 'Unfair Dismissal and Managerial Prerogative: A Study of "Other Substantial Reason"' (1981) ILJ 34

Collins H (1985) ILJ 61 (note on *Gorictree Ltd v Jenkinson* [1985] ICR 51, [1984] IRLR 391, EAT; *Apex Leisure Hire v Barratt* [1984] 3 All ER 795, [1984] ICR 452, EAT; *Berriman v Delabole Slate Ltd* [1985] ICR 546, [1985] IRLR 305, CA; *Anderson v Dalkeith Engineering Ltd* [1985] ICR 66, [1984] IRLR 529, EAT)

'Dismissals on Transfers of a Business' (1986) ILJ 244

'Transfer of Undertakings and Insolvency' (1989) ILJ 144

Davies P (1989) ILJ 249 (note on *Wheeler v Patel* [1987] ICR 631, EAT; *Brook Lane Finance v Bradley* [1988] IRLR 283, EAT; *Gateway Hotels Ltd v Stewart* [1988] IRLR 287, EAT; *Forth Estuary Engineering Ltd v Litster* [1988] IRLR 289, Ct Sess)

Davies P and Freedland M 'The Effects of Receivership on Employees of Companies' (1980) ILJ 95

Davies P L 'Acquired Rights, Creditors' Rights, Freedom of Contract, and Industrial Democracy' in (9) Year Book of European Law (1989)

Elias P 'The Transfer of Undertakings: A Reluctantly Acquired Right' (1982) Company Lawyer 147

Freedland M R 'Employment Protection: Redundancy Procedures and the EEC' (1976) ILJ 24

Hepple B A 'Workers' Rights in Mergers and Takeovers: The EEC Proposals' (1976) ILJ 197

(1977) ILJ 106 (note on Acquired Rights Directive)

'The Transfer of Undertakings (Protection of Employment) Regulations' (1982) ILJ 29

Hepple B A and Byre A 'EEC Labour Law in the United Kingdom, A New Approach' (1989) ILJ 129

Howard A 'Buying a business: negotiating the sale agreement' Practical Law for Companies, July 1991, p 23

Incomes Data Services Brief 'Employment Law Problems':
  IDS Brief 399/June 1987 p 7
  IDS Brief 401/July 1989 p 7
  IDS Brief 402/August 1989 p 7
Industrial Relations Legal Information Bulletin 'Guidance Notes on "Transfer of Business"':
  IRLIB 372, 7 March 1989, p 2
  IRLIB 374, 4 April 1989, p 2
  IRLIB 375, 25 April 1989, p 2
The Law Society 'Memorandum on the Transfer of Undertakings (Protection of Employment) Regulations 1981 by The Working Party on Employment Law of the Council's Law Reform Committee' (1986)
McMullen J 'The Transfer of Undertakings (Protection of Employment) Regulations 1981 – Problems and Pitfalls' (1985) LS Gaz 1950
  'Transfer of Undertakings: Recent Judicial Attitudes' (1985) Company Lawyer 254
  'The Transfer of Undertakings (Protection of Employment) Regulations 1981 – Further Problems and Pitfalls' (1985) LS Gaz 3006
  'Management Prerogative, Reorganisation and Employees' Rights on Transfers of Undertakings' (1986) MLR 524
  'The Meaning of Corporate Control of Associated Employers in Statutory Employment Law' (1986) LS Gaz 2923
  'Transfer of Undertakings and the Meaning of "Immediately Before"' (1986) Company Lawyer 251
  'Takeovers, Corporate Restructuring and Trade Union Consultation' (1987) Company Lawyer 225
  'Transfer and Employee Rights: the Regulations' Scope' (1990) LS Gaz, 10 January 1990, p 23
  'Business Transfers: Some European Experiences' (1990) LS Gaz, 17 January 1990, p 25
  'Business Transfers and Employee Rights: the *Litster* case' (1990) LS Gaz, 7 February 1990, p 27
  'Business Transfers and Employee Rights: points for practitioners' (1990) LS Gaz 21 February 1990, p 27
  'Transfer-Connected Dismissals' (1990) LS Gaz, 7 March 1990, p 27
  'A Round-up of Business Transfers and Employee Rights' (1990) LS Gaz, 4 April 1990, p 30
'Business Transfers and Statutory Continuity of Employment' (1991) Solicitors' Journal 720
'Business Transfers and Statutory Continuity of Employment (2)' (1991) Solicitors' Journal 746
Napier B W 'Transfer of Undertakings: A Problem Solved and a Problem Raised' (1987) SLT 166
O'Dair R 'Employees' Rights and Sale of Businesses' (1987) MLR 87
Rideout R W 'The Great Transfer of Employee Rights Hoax' (1982) CLP 233
Ritson J 'Employee Rights on Transfer of the Business' (1985) Insolvency Law & Practice 11

Robertshaw P (1985) ILJ 130 (note on *E Green & Son (Castings) Ltd v ASTMS* [1984] ICR 352, [1984] IRLR 135, EAT and *Angus Jowett & Co Ltd v NUTGW* [1985] ICR 646, [1985] IRLR 326, EAT)

Ryley M D 'Business Transfers after Litster: Dangerous Liaisons?' (1989) 23 LS Gaz 18

Schofield P 'Protection of Employment on Transfer of Undertakings' (1982) JBL 18

Upex R (1984) ILJ 66 (note on *Meikle v McPhail (Charleston Arms)* [1983] IRLR 351, EAT, *Canning v Niaz and McLoughlin* [1983] IRLR 431 and *Premier Motors (Medway) Ltd v Total Oil (GB) Ltd* [1984] ICR 58, [1983] IRLR 471, EAT)

Index